MORE THAN A ROSE

MORE THAN A ROSE

Prime Ministers, Wives and Other Women

HEATHER ROBERTSON

SEAL BOOKS

McClelland-Bantam, Inc.
Toronto

MORE THAN A ROSE
A Seal Book/October 1991

ISBN 0-7704-2460-0

Seal Books are published by McClelland-Bantam, Inc. Its trademark, consisting of the words
"Seal Books" and the portrayal of a seal, is the property of McClelland-Bantam, Inc., 105 Bond
Street, Toronto, Ontario M5B 1Y3, Canada. This trademark has been duly registered in the
Trademark Office of Canada. The trademark consisting of the words "Bantam Books" and the
portrayal of a rooster is the property of and is used with the consent of Bantam Books, 666
Fifth Avenue, New York, New York 10103. This trademark has been duly registered in the
Trademark Office of Canada and elsewhere.

PRINTED IN U.S.A.
JACKET PRINTED IN CANADA

0 9 8 7 6 5 4 3 2 1

"I'm more than just a rose in my husband's lapel!"

Margaret Trudeau, 1976

CONTENTS

· · · · · · · · · ·

ACKNOWLEDGMENTS

. . . .

*T*HIS BOOK could not have been completed or even attempted without the assistance and expertise of the following organizations and individuals:

The National Archives of Canada, particularly Maureen Hoogenraad and the archivists responsible for the prime ministers' papers, enabled me to locate and examine letters and diaries relating to the early prime ministers' wives.

Maureen McTeer and Geills Turner expressed their thoughts and recollections frankly and creatively in lengthy interviews.

Margaret Trudeau cast a searching light on the role of the prime minister's wife in her books, *Beyond Reason* and *Consequences*.

Maxwell Meighen and Mrs. T.R. Meighen assisted me in understanding Isabel Meighen.

Thérèse Lafferty and Madeleine St. Laurent shared their memories of their mother, Jeanne St. Laurent, and Jean Riley helped bring *grandmaman* to life.

Carolyn and Don Weir shared with me stories and photographs relating to Olive Diefenbaker, and Elizabeth Diamond of the Diefenbaker Centre, Saskatoon, guided me through the rewarding collection of Diefenbaker family papers and photographs. Marie Bendas kindly made available personal letters from Olive.

Patricia Pearson Hannah spoke to me at length about Maryon Pearson and gave me access to Maryon's diaries, letters to friends and the letters to Maryon from Ken Kirkwood, as well as to the family history by Herbert Moody. I am also indebted to the late Herbert Moody, Sheila Zimmerman, Christopher Young, Lester Pearson's former executive assistant Mary MacDonald and former Governor-General Roland Michener for their personal recollections.

Louise Reynolds provided me with copies of Agnes Macdonald's articles in *Murray's Magazine*, and Margaret Cohoe made available copies of her private research notes on the life of Mary Macdonald. John Coleman of Bellevue House, Kingston, was a fund of information. Carman Miller of McGill University was a helpful sounding-board on a number of early prime ministers, and Peter B. Waite of Dalhousie University provided invaluable assistance on both Annie Thompson and R.B. Bennett.

Lucie Brunet of Ottawa superbly researched the chapter on Zoé Laurier and Émilie Lavergne and assisted me with summarizing and translating the Laurier letters; Charles Fisher generously discussed his own research into the Laurier-Lavergne relationship, and Paul Stevens of York University offered guidance based on his own research on Laurier.

Christopher Plummer and John Kimble Abbott responded to my queries about Lady Abbott and Kate Oxley made some inquiries on my behalf.

I found *Wives of the Canadian Prime Ministers* by Carol McLeod a very useful basic reference and Susan Riley's *Political Wives* a provocative analysis. Carla Wittes provided background on the living wives.

Ken Rubin assisted me in dealing with the intricacies of the Access to Information Act.

Curtis Fahey edited my manuscript with an unsentimental and professional historian's eye; all speculation and interpretation are my own.

Andrew and Aaron Marshall cheerfully survived this wife's and mother's eighteen months of computer confinement.

INTRODUCTION
· · · · · · · · · ·

*O*F ALL THE castes in Canadian society, wives are probably the most ignored, denigrated, exploited, ridiculed and abused. The dumb, dippy wife is a staple of television comedy, newspaper columnists depict their wives as fools or shrews, and until recently "Take my wife, *please*" jokes were standard dinner-party entertainment. In shows such as *The Honeymooners* and *All in the Family*, the plight of women married to violent, stupid and vulgar husbands was considered hilariously funny until wife beating came out of the closet, and in some quarters it is still common for men to refer to "the wife," allowing her as much individuality as the car or the house.

Yet until the 1960s, to be some man's wife was the only respectable career open to a woman. Women who failed to catch husbands went to work at menial or low-paying jobs, married women stayed home. Wives cooked and cleaned and raised children, and their society was restricted to other wives. Wives were financially and intellectually dependent; they were expected to share their husbands' interests and opinions and a good wife sublimated herself entirely into her husband's identity. Wives were both possessions and projections of their husbands, who showed off their importance by dressing their wives in diamonds and fur – the little mink stole was *de rigeur* in the 1950s – and who measured the value of their labour by their wives' idleness.

In return for giving up her independence and identity, a wife acquired authority in domestic and moral affairs: she was the "angel of the home," and her husband's ethics, however sleazy, were judged by the behaviour of his "better half." In a puritanical society like Canada, a wife's behaviour was highly circumscribed and subject to intense scrutiny, but because spinsterhood was such an unpleasant alternative, and divorce degrading, she accommodated herself to her role and attempted to fulfil it in a way that would please her husband and suit herself. By the 1960s, a wife was such

1
·

an integral part of her husband's persona that corporations promoted their executives only after screening the suitability of their wives.

Then wives bailed out. Of all the social and political upheavals of the twentieth century, the liberation of women may be, in retrospect, the most significant. By the 1970s, wives had their own names, their own property and their own jobs; marriage was a contract between equals and divorce an acceptable termination. A wife's work in the home was of no social or monetary value, and her role as arbiter of morality had vanished with morality. Wives had become not only obsolete, but objects of scorn, sneered at as parasites and prostitutes; a woman could no longer identify with her husband, she had to be a person in her own right and accountable for her life.

The story of the revolt of the wives is played out with the clarity of a morality play in the lives of our prime ministers' wives, and the drama is not a contest between the prime minister and his wife, but a struggle for power between The Wife and the Other Woman, the independent woman who demands an equal place in political life, on her own merits. Ordinary wives live in obscurity, but prime ministers' wives are dragged into the public spotlight, whether they like it or not, and are ideal targets for observation, speculation and criticism. As public figures, they represent women as a whole, and their attitudes and behaviour can be taken as a reflection of our society's accepted values, but, like movie stars, prime ministers' wives are also objects of fantasy, worship or loathing, depending on the popular mood, and the public's response to The Wife tells us a great deal about our secret fears and assumptions.

In 1867 the prime minister's wife, Agnes Macdonald, was a figure of formidable social and moral authority. Lady Macdonald knew that her power derived exclusively from her husband, Sir John A. Macdonald, and she devoted herself entirely to his career. Not only did Agnes set a model of puritan deportment – in striking contrast to her husband – she established herself as an energetic hostess and dispenser of patronage, a role successfully adopted later by Zoé Laurier. Banned from the political bearpit, both wives established fiefdoms in the dining-room and parlour, and wielded power as informers, guardians and gossips.

When Canadian prime ministers were knighted in the years before the First World War, their Ladies had the highest social rank, second only to that of the wife of the governor-general, and they were treated with obsequious flattery by the press, however glaring their deficiencies or peculiar their behaviour. Despite, or because of, this attitude, very little is known about many of the early wives. Harriet Bowell died before her husband, Mackenzie Bowell, became prime minister and Lady Abbott has vanished into almost complete obscurity. Few prime ministers bothered to save their wives' letters, and gave their wives only a brief, obligatory mention in their memoirs. With rare exceptions biographers have ignored the prime ministers' domestic relationships entirely, or have romanticized their marriages out of all recognition. Early wives were not expected to attend political meetings, and if they did they never made speeches; as long as women had no right to vote they had no right to political opinions. Women who were interested in politics had to express their views and use their influence obliquely, through a man; Émilie Lavergne, a married woman who delighted in political intrigue, was Wilfrid Laurier's "dear friend" and *éminence grise* for twenty years.

A more formidable rival to The Wife arrived in 1921, the first federal election in which women had the right to vote, when a single woman, Agnes Macphail, was elected to the House of Commons. Macphail, young, charming and feminist, raised the possibility that a woman could have power without a man, and although it took forty years for Agnes's example to sink in, the prestige of The Wife began to wane. It waned also because between 1921 and 1948 both prime ministers, Mackenzie King and R.B. Bennett, were bachelors. King managed socially perfectly well with the ghost of his mother and another man's wife, Mrs. Patteson; Bennett didn't manage well at all, partly because his younger sister, Mildred, married and left Ottawa soon after his election.

Until 1957, the wives enjoyed a high degree of privacy: as models of the wifely virtues, they were admired for staying at home out of the public eye. Television destroyed that. Prime ministers' wives were still models of the wifely virtues, but they had to play *I Love Lucy* without a script in the glare of the kleig lights. Television exposed The Wife to the mob, and diminished the social distance that had been the source of her status and respect. Now she was judged not only by her husband's colleagues and enemies, but by millions of people she had never met. She had no political role to play, and her role as hostess and fixer disappeared once the prime minister could establish instant contact with the voters. Seated primly on a chair with nothing to say or do, The Wife began to look foolish, especially when the Other Woman made it into the Cabinet.

As her status slipped, the prime minister's wife became vulnerable to malicious public criticism. Her husband's power no longer protected her; instead, she became a lightning rod for political attacks directed at him, yet she had no control over his personal conduct or political policies. In 1965 Maryon Pearson was not treated with the sycophantic deference shown her predecessor, Olive Diefenbaker. Sarcastic and abrasive, Maryon broke all the rules of decorum, a signal that The Wife's plaster face was cracking, and ten years later Margaret Trudeau smashed The Wife to pieces. No subsequent wife has succeeded in putting her back together again, and only one has tried. As women have been elected to the House of Commons in increasing numbers and been appointed to the Cabinet, the Senate and the Supreme Court, chosen party leader, women have been Speaker of the Senate and governor-general, the prime minister's wife has become irrelevant, a rather pathetic vestige of another era.

Fifteen women have filled this onerous and thankless role in 125 years, and this book profiles every one of them except the shadowy Lady Abbott. I have also included Isabella Macdonald and Edna Diefenbaker, who died before their husbands became prime minister, as well as the famous "mistresses," Émilie Lavergne and Joan Patteson. In addition, since The Wife's role cannot be understood without the prime minister's Mother, particularly Isabel Grace Mackenzie King and Mary Bannerman Diefenbaker, or without the Spinster, Agnes Macphail, these women are included too.

Four of the wives are still living, and one or more might have the distinction of being a prime mninister's wife and a prime minister's mother. Most are Canadian-born; Agnes Macdonald was born in Jamaica, Isabella Macdonald and Helen Mackenzie in Scotland, Mila Mulroney in Yugoslavia. Four of the wives grew up in Manitoba, three each in Quebec and Nova Scotia, two in Ontario and one each in Saskatchewan and British Columbia (Harriet Bowell's origins are unknown). None of the wives is American, and not one was born in Toronto. Only two, Zoé Laurier and Jeanne St. Laurent, are French-Canadian.

Like their husbands, the wives are middle class, although some come from straightened financial circumstances. The most socially prominent is one of the most obscure, Mary Bethune, Lady Abbott. Mary was the daughter of John Bethune, the Anglican archbishop of Montreal in the mid-nineteenth century, a position that placed him in the very centre of Montreal's "Square Mile" of wealthy Scots bankers and merchant princes, and Mary's lawyer husband, John Abbott, joined their privileged ranks.

Olive Diefenbaker was also the daughter of a clergyman, but she was raised on the prairies in plainer Baptist circumstances. Respectable poverty has never been a handicap to a future Wife. Zoé Lafontaine was a homeless waif sheltered by friends when she met Wilfrid Laurier; Agnes Macdonald's father went bankrupt. Nonetheless, both were young women of impeccable morals and behaviour, and Zoé's guardian, a doctor, was higher in social rank than Laurier, the son of a farmer. Three of the wives – Jane Mackenzie, Isabel Meighen and Maureen McTeer – were raised on farms; one, Annie Thompson, was the daughter of a Halifax ship's captain.

On the whole, the wives knew what they were getting into. Agnes Macdonald and Margaret Trudeau married prime ministers; Olive Diefenbaker, Maureen McTeer and Geills Turner married MPs. Except for Jane Mackenzie, Harriet Bowell, Frances Tupper and Maryon Pearson, they married ambitious young lawyers with their feet on the ladder and their eye on the main chance, and five of them married lawyers named John.

They also married father figures. Agnes Macdonald and Margaret Trudeau were young enough to be their husbands' daughters – Pierre Trudeau was two years older than Margaret's mother – and both wives were keenly aware of the chasm the generation gap created: "I'll win in the end," Margaret told Pierre during one bitter quarrel, "because I'm going to live longer." Mila Mulroney and Maureen McTeer married men thirteen years older; Isabel Meighen was nine years younger than her husband, Arthur, Geills is nine years younger than John Turner. Olive was seven years younger than John Diefenbaker, Maryon four years younger than Lester Pearson. The wives share a more unusual characteristic: absent fathers. Four of the wives' fathers died when they were children or teenagers, leaving them impoverished and emotionally bereft. Zoé Laurier's father deserted her mother, Annie Thompson's father was away at sea, Edna Diefenbaker's father drifted around Saskatchewan and Maryon Pearson's father worked such long hours that she rarely saw him. Mila Mulroney's father immigrated to Canada when she was four, leaving Mila and her mother to follow the next year. It's not unusual that these women would marry men who would also be away a great deal of time, and would not expect their own emotional or intellectual needs to take precedence over their husband's pursuit of his private white whale. They were accustomed to being self-reliant, and knew how to find companionship within their families or in the society of other women: the tea party, the bridge club and the telephone provided the wives with a female support network that saved them from isolation and depression, and at least one, it seems, had a longstanding love affair.

Each of the fatherless girls bonded emotionally with the one parent she could trust, her mother, and the mothers seem to have been women of exceptional strength of character. They had to be to survive, and by doing so they became matriarchs of formidable influence. So were the mothers of the prime ministers: Sir John A. Macdonald, Mackenzie King, R.B. Bennett, Louis St. Laurent, John Diefenbaker, Pierre Trudeau and John Turner all had mothers of legendary reputation to whom they were exceptionally devoted. In The Wife, they found another Mother hidden in a girl's dress, although King stuck with Mother to the end, and Bennett loved his sister Mildred best of all.

Some of the wives feared their mothers, some resented them, but they all obeyed. "Oh dear, what a fix I was in tonight," Annie Affleck confided to her diary when she and Thompson were courting. "He had kissed me and held me in his arms. When he had gone, Mama was in the room when I came back. She never spoke. How I trembled! Still I thought I would keep quiet and if there was nothing to say she would have to begin. After a while she spoke quite pleasantly. Perhaps if I had spoken first and asked her what the matter was she might have said 'You know very well' and then dear knows I might have told on myself. I will never forget the agony of those few moments."

Although the contemporary wives like to give their fathers credit for their achievements, in fact they have chosen to follow their mothers' example: they are all good cooks, accomplished hostesses, devoted mothers and careful housekeepers, well-dressed, well-mannered women to whom it is still terribly important *to do the right thing*. They are over-achievers, women who have been trained to fulfill the expectations of others and to take responsibility not only for their own lives but for the world. The cost for all the wives has been high: drug addiction and emotional breakdown are recurrent themes in their stories.

With a few exceptions, the wives have left little in the way of diaries, memoirs or personal correspondence, or what they have left has been lost or discarded. The Wife's voice has been silenced, and she has been so severely edited out of history that she has become the Invisible Lady of Canadian politics.

This book is not an attempt to look at the prime ministers from the perspective of their wives, although seen through a private eye, with their pants down, so to speak, the men reveal themselves to be remarkably neurotic, insecure, physically inept and irresponsible about money. In some cases the husband's letters, lovingly saved, offer the only insights we have into his wife's life and character, but I have tried as much as possible to tell each wife's story in her own words, from her own point of view, concentrating on the things that interested her. Politics was often a peripheral concern, important only insofar as election campaigns and controversy affected her husband's health or temper, and many of the issues that seemed so crucial at the time have faded from memory, while the wives' concerns remain contemporary.

The fragmentary archival resources and lack of documentation make it impossible to present a complete portrait of every wife, and Margaret Trudeau's autobiographies illustrate how dramatic the gap can be between public myth and private reality. I have tried to focus on the experience of each wife which I found most significant in order to present a composite portrait of the archetypal figure who has had such a powerful grip on our imaginations.

CHAPTER 1

The Invisible Lady: Isabella Macdonald

ISABELLA CLARK rearranged the lace collar on her new blue silk dress for the hundredth time that morning. She felt embarrassed, all decked out in her Sunday best in the middle of the week, but her sister Margaret had persuaded her, saying that the blue exactly matched her eyes, and besides, how often did they have company? Almost never, to tell the truth. The sisters' stone farmhouse, Ballafreer, was three miles from the village of Douglas on the Isle of Man in middle of the Irish Sea, and the three sisters, Margaret, Isabella and Jane, lived there alone. Their only regular callers were the local tradesmen, but in the spring of 1842 a letter from Canada disrupted the quiet routine of their lives: their cousin, John Alexander Macdonald, would be arriving at the end of June.

The Macdonalds had left Scotland for Kingston, Ontario, in 1820 when John was five and Isabella was eleven. Had they met? It was unlikely. Their mothers were half-sisters, but the families were not close. Isabella's mother had married a captain in the British army, but Helen Macdonald had married badly, and beneath her. Hugh Macdonald was in trade, a rough Highlander with a weakness for whiskey and no head for business. Hugh's successive bankruptcies had reduced the family to penury, and John, the Macdonald's only son, was apprenticed as a clerk at the age of fifteen to support the family. He was a lawyer now, but from what Isabella had heard, lazy and something of a roustabout.

Isabella pressed her forehead against the cool glass of the window. An hour until ship time. The ticking of the grandfather clock reverberated in the silent parlour. She held her icy hands over her heart and took a deep breath. Maybe John wouldn't come. Maybe he would miss the boat. No no, the disappointment of not seeing him would be worse. After all, he wasn't a suitor. She had given up on that. She was over thirty, a penniless orphan without a dowry. Isabella didn't blame eligible young men for turning their attention elsewhere, but she felt guilty about being so totally dependent on Margaret's charity.

She was too proud to go into service as a governess, and she was terrified of strangers. If only she wasn't so painfully shy! Isabella found it agony to meet people. She was struck dumb; her tongue stuck to the roof of her mouth, her throat constricted, her heart pounded in her ears, her vision blurred, her head whirled and her stomach cramped until she was certain she would faint or be sick. Overcome by panic, she would run away and lock herself in her room for days, unable to sleep or eat, paralyzed by splitting headaches, her entire body wracked by spasms. The doctor said that her nerves were too highly strung, the slightest strain stretched them to the breaking-point.

She had been sent to the Isle of Man to rest and get plenty of fresh air, and the doctor gave her medicine to strengthen her nerves. Should she take some now? The trouble was that the medicine made her so drowsy she might sleep through John's whole visit. That would never do! Isabella tried hard to be obedient, but sometimes she felt so sad, so restless and irritable she wanted to scream.

She was relieved when Margaret bustled in with a cloth-covered tray holding a decanter of whiskey, a single glass and a box of cigars. Margaret knew about men. Margaret was twelve years older than Isabella, and a widow. She had married a wealthy American, John Ward Greene, but three months later Greene died, leaving Margaret a small pension and an estate entangled in debt. Margaret never remarried, and for nearly twenty years she had been more of a mother than a sister to Isabella. Isabella could not remember her mother; she had died when Isabella was four, and Isa and Jane had been living with a crofter family when Margaret rescued them.

Margaret Greene cast a critical eye over the room. The floors were scrubbed and the rugs beaten, the lace curtains were freshly starched and their few precious pieces of family silver shone on the mantlepiece. Whatever young John A. Macdonald might report back to his mother, he would not be able to say that his future wife was a poor housekeeper.

Margaret knew that John's visit to the Isle of Man was not entirely fortuitous: she had helped to arrange it, with the aid of another sister, Maria Macpherson, the Macdonalds' neighbour in Kingston. The Macdonalds, Macphersons and Clarks were all members of a large and relatively incestuous Highland clan. In the Victorian era, marriage between cousins was accepted, even encouraged – the queen set the example, as she did in everything else for sixty years – and Helen Macdonald naturally turned to her kinsfolk to find an acceptable wife for her son. John was twenty-seven, well established in a law practice in Kingston, but he showed no interest in female companionship except of the coarsest kind and spent his evenings carousing with his cronies. Even if John had been interested in a respectable match, prospects in Kingston were poor for a struggling young man without social connections obliged to support a widowed mother and two unmarried sisters. Helen was fearful that her beloved son would run off with a common tramp, or sink into sodden drunkenness like his late father, Hugh. Isabella was older, accomplished and without prospects; she would be a steadying influence on John, and a help around the house.

John had a reputation as a clever, cocky young man and Margaret assumed that he must have guessed the real motive for his trip to Great Britain, paid for, it was said, by a big win a cards, but in fact by his father's insurance policy. She prayed he would not be boorish or insulting, or ruin their reputation in the village, or break Isa's heart. Isabella's cheeks

Helen Macdonald, John's strong-willed mother, was illiterate but said to be intelligent and lively.

were flushed, and she had crumpled her handkerchief into a small, wet ball.

Margaret needn't have worried. John's visit was a great success. His charming, sunny ways put the sisters at ease immediately and he soon had them in fits of laughter over his escapades. The days passed in a whirlwind of picnics and drives by the seashore, shopping excursions to the village and gossipy evenings by the fire. All Douglas was enchanted by this tall, slim, lively young man with the shock of curly black hair who was instantly on terms of the most intimate friendship with everyone. John A. Macdonald dressed like a dandy and walked with a swagger and the homeliness of his rough, pockmarked face with its big, bulbous nose was relieved by wide-set, luminous dark eyes that gazed thoughtfully on everything he encountered.

With John at her side, Isabella felt fearless. She laughed and chattered away like a girl. She felt truly happy, free, for the first time in her life. John seemed magical, an angel who suddenly suffused her world with light, and as she listened to his strangely accented voice, Canada seemed as romantic as Xanadu. When John left, after only three days, it seemed as if the sun had gone behind a cloud.

As he was leaving, John said in his joking way, "Why don't you come to Canada?" As the miserable days passed, Isabella turned his question over and over in her mind. Why not? She was feeling well–she hadn't been ill since John's visit–and the climate in Canada was said to be invigorating. She could make herself useful to Maria, who had four young children to raise, and cease to be a burden to Margaret. Margaret urged her to go: if she felt unhappy or unwelcome, she could always come back. Isabella Clark sailed for Canada alone in the spring of 1843. She arrived in Kingston in June, the guest of Maria and James Macpherson.

The whole family was pleased with Isabella's quiet, gentle ways, and no one was more smitten than John Macdonald. Isa, as he began to call her, was totally unlike the practical, down-to-earth, strong-willed Macdonald women. John was enchanted by Isa's refinement and delicacy of temperament, her feminine frivolities, her self-effacing, rather childlike eagerness to please. She shared his love of books, his delight in children. Why, he and Isa even looked alike! They had the same long, fleshy nose and wide mouth, although Isa's skin was pale and her curly hair golden brown.

The only known picture of Isabella Clark. She was seven years older than John.

Their courtship was quick and intense; on September 1, 1843, only weeks after she had arrived, Isabella and John were married in St. Andrew's Church, Kingston. No one was happier than John's mother. Isabella was a lady, she would be a credit to John, and as a kinswoman she would know that John's first loyalty would always be to his mother.

John took Isa home to the stone house on Brock St. he shared with his mother and sisters, Margaret and Louisa. The house was not large, and apart from their bedroom, the young couple had no rooms of their own. John took the situation for granted, but Isa found it traumatic. Her privacy was gone, and she was living among strangers, three proud, prickly, sharp-tongued women who saw her as a rival for John's love. Isabella had nothing but ancestry in common with the Macdonald women and she found their Canadian manners crude, even vulgar. Why, they did all their own housework, and Aunt Helen couldn't even read or write! However, ignorance did not prevent Aunt Helen from expressing critical opinions on every topic and issuing orders she expected to be obeyed.

If only John had been there! But John was almost never home. During the day he was at his office or in court, and almost every evening was taken up with political meetings. Isa hadn't expected to marry a politician,

John Alexander Macdonald.

but John had been elected to the city council in March, just before she arrived, and now there was talk of making him the Conservative candidate for Kingston. Isabella had always thought politics a rather gentlemanly pursuit, and she was unprepared for the roughness of political life in Kingston, a rowdy, noisy frontier town full of immigrants, speculators and drunks.

She had thought Kingston a pretty place, like Bath, when she first saw it from the lake. Its limestone buildings glowed pearl grey in the morning sun, but the harbour was noisome with the reek of tanneries and fishmongers, and the streets were rutted roads through deep mud. Most of Kingston was built of brick, and the houses were both small and squalid. Brock St. was a main thoroughfare, and even at home Isabella was nearly deafened by the steady racket of wagons and the yelling of deliverymen. She was shocked that she was expected to go out unaccompanied to the shops, to make pleasant conversation with tradespeople so as not to appear "hoity-toity," and to get John elected. Getting John elected was the obsession of the Macdonald women, and of John himself. Politics brought out a wild, harsh side to John she had never seen before; it was almost as if she didn't know him. Sometimes he came home very late reeking of whiskey; at least then he would fall asleep and not press his desires on her. Lonely and frightened, Isabella lay awake in the dark, her head splitting, her body stiff with the effort not to run away.

Where could she go? This was her home now. Oh, how she missed the quiet cottage on the Isle of Man! It was gone too. Margaret had inherited the Greene family estate in Georgia, and she and Jane were now in Savannah. Savannah! The soft name bore the scent of magnolia blossoms and sea breezes; closing her eyes, Isabella saw lovely women in white dresses reclining against cushions, loose strands of their hair lifting slightly in the slow movement of their fans. Isabella dreamed of Savannah, and slept.

Outwardly Isabella seemed happy and content; she never complained or nagged or lost her temper and John always found her sympathetic to his difficulties. She tired easily and often spent the afternoons lying down, but that was understandable under the circumstances, and her shyness only made John more tender towards her. His attentiveness increased during the winter when Isa developed crippling pains in her face and legs. The doctors diagnosed neuralgia and blamed Kingston's damp cold. In the spring John took Isa south to Savannah.

The vacation with her sisters seemed to do Isabella good, but her health deteriorated seriously during the following year in Kingston. On June 11, 1845 Isabella wrote a teasing letter to her sister Margaret Greene about lavender bonnets, yellow stockings and the Macdonalds' still uncertain plans to visit Margaret in New Haven, Connecticut, for the summer. "I am thank God, *much* better," Isa wrote, "but my head is very confused & I am not sure what I say, only I know I grumble about lavender satin & blonde." For all its cheerfulness the letter has a distraught, almost hysterical tone; the first half is taken up with Isa's efforts to find a nurse to attend her for the summer. A subsequent letter from John's sister Margaret confirms Isabella's "inability to take care of herself" and reveals that, as a nurse, John, however willing, was "nearly as useless as a child."

Isabella's illness was much more serious than she let on. John Macdonald wrote to Margaret Greene on July 11, 1845:

"Isabella has been ill – very ill – with one of her severest attacks. She is now just recovering and I hope has thrown off for the time her terrible disease. Still this is not certain, and at all events it has left her in the usual state of prostration that follows every attack. It may be days – nay weeks – before she has rallied sufficiently to attempt any journey. What to say or do, I know not."

The next day Isabella appeared close to death:

"Her pain has in a great measure left her, but her debility is in the greatest possible degree alarming. She is weaker than she has ever yet been, and there are symptoms, such as an apparent numbness of one limb, and an irregularity in the action of the heart, that made me send for Dr. Sampson, altho against Isabella's wish. He saw her this morning and says he cannot relieve her, and I ought not, my beloved sister, to disguise from you that he thinks her in the most precarious state. I do not hesitate to tell you that unless God in his infinite mercy works an immediate change for the better, it is impossible for her to remain in her exhausted state for many days. God bless and protect both of you my beloved sisters and enable you to meet the impending anguish with fortitude and resignation."

However, six days later Isabella was well enough to begin her journey to New Haven. John wrote from Oswego, New York, on July 18: "We arrived here this morning at about one o'clock. The exhaustion produced by carrying Isabella down to the boat was dreadful to witness. We thought she would die on the deck. The weather was so stormy that all our party were sick, Isabella dreadfully so, and yet strange to say her health and strength seemed to return to her and we are now safely landed and lodged at Welland House. Isa is of course much fatigued with the journey, but is stronger in appearance and pulse than the moment before we left my house at Kingston."

What was Isabella's illness? "It has a frankly bizarre character and does not fit any recognizable single medical syndrome," says Dr. James McSherry of Queen's University. McSherry diagnoses her illness as psychosomatic in origin, "representing a form of cultural and social maladjustment reminiscent of the shock experienced by war brides." According to McSherry, Isabella's "sickness behavior" allowed her to flee the oppressive Macdonald household and to take refuge with her sister Margaret in Savannah, where she immediately felt better. In October 1845 John described Isa's harrowing journey south in a letter to Margaret Greene from Philadelphia:

"Her fatigues were very great and she was obliged to subdue pain by opium, but still she kept up her spirits. Only think what a journey she had. First to be carried down a narrow stair at Jersey and over to the cars; a journey in the cars for about 70 miles to Bristol; to be carried in a chair from the cars to the steamboat; a voyage of 22 miles to this city & lastly and worst of all a quarter mile's drive in a hack over the rough streets here. It was enough to fatigue a convalescent & was fearful for a confirmed invalid. I am delighted to see her bear it so well, for she from fatigue and opium combined, slept from 10 o'clock last night until the morning and is now easy and in good spirits. She never speaks of it, but I am perfectly conscious of how much she suffers from being away from you & without the aid of your untiring and judicious attentions, which were always at hand by night & by day when needed.''

Baffled as to the cause of her mysterious illness and helpless to cure it, Isabella's doctors attempted to relieve her agony by administering the most accessible and effective pain-killer of the period: opium. On November 3, 1845 John wrote to Margaret Greene: ''Isabella was very tired all Friday, as you may imagine, but hoped everything from her night's rest. Unfortunately her rest was disturbed. On Saturday morning she was visited by your friend Mrs. Biddle, and exerted herself too much, so that in the evening she was a good deal exhausted and was threatened with tic so that she had recourse to opium. It rained all night and all Sunday and she felt out of sorts and uncomfortable all day. She slept a good deal during the afternoon but not much during the night. This morning was unsettled and damp and Madame Isa still felt uncomfortable so we have stayed over. She has had a good day today, has walked a good deal & eaten pretty well, and if she only has a good night will be bright as need be tomorrow.''

In Baltimore Isabella suffered a relapse. The Macdonalds had trouble finding hotel rooms, and the consequence, Macdonald wrote, ''was great exhaustion & great suffering by Isabella. She was in great agony all night & the two following days and was obliged to have recourse to opium, externally and internally, in large quantities.''

Opium gave Isabella temporary relief, but her symptoms returned once the opium wore off. ''Isabella has been very miserable,'' John wrote to Margaret Greene on November 20. ''The tic encouraged by her weakness from fatigue has made a furious attack upon her, which she is *manfully* resisting with the assistance of the blister and pill box. I trust that as her fatigue leaves her, so will her persevering enemy.''

Isabella may have suffered from migraine headaches and possibly from *tic doloureux*, a form of neuralgia that attacks the face. However, neuralgia, while unpleasant, is intermittent. It is not fatal and does not produce the permanently crippling effect that made Isabella unable to walk. Nor does it account for her extreme chronic fatigue. Almost everything wearied Isabella. Fatigue brought on insomnia, and insomnia triggered agonizing spasms that required opium.

"Several acute episodes were terminated by heavy opium consumption over a number of days, and were then followed by a return of symptoms at a time interval, suggesting a withdrawal syndrome," observes Dr. McSherry. Withdrawal of a drug can recreate psychosomatically the pain that the drug originally relieved, even though the original cause no longer exists.

By the winter of 1845 Isabella was taking opium in such large doses, and was obviously so familiar with its effects, that she may have been addicted for years. Opium was almost the only effective pain-killer in the early nineteenth century; ether, chloroform and cocaine had not yet come into general use, and opium had the added benefit of inducing delightful dreams. Opium's addictive effects were well known – a number of famous Englishmen, among them the poet Coleridge, were opium addicts – yet its benefits were generally seen to outweigh the risks. Women were particularly vulnerable to addiction since opium was used in childbirth and as a remedy for headaches and menstrual cramps; opium formed the basic ingredient in dozens of popular cordials believed to have miraculous powers to cure female complaints. If Isabella had originally been prescribed opium for migraines or cramps, the symptoms would reappear, in greater intensity, as soon as she stopped taking the drug. At this point her illness would be psychosomatic, a form of neuralgia later called neurosis.

Isabella's dependency on Margaret Greene may have been related to her dependency on opium; her sister may have innocently given her opium in the first place, or found a doctor who did. A shy, romantic, emotional girl would be particularly susceptible to the magic of the opium dream, and opium would be Isa's perfect, irresistible escape.

John apparently did not know of Isa's illness when they married: his letters document his appalled discovery, shattered hopes and ultimate resignation. Isabella's spasms and headaches may have been the result of her attempts to give up opium after her marriage, believing that marriage and motherhood would cure her. Sex was a universal panacea for "the vapours" in Victorian virgins, and in December 1846 Isabella became pregnant.

Isabella was then living in a rooming-house in New York City in the care of a Dr. Washington, a specialist who had a large, profitable practice among genteel women. Isa was too ill to live in Kingston, and so frail that John's sister Margaret Macdonald stayed with her as a nurse. Her condition is reflected in a letter from John to Margaret Greene on January 20, 1847:

"I hear regularly twice a week from New York, and on the 11th, my birthday, poor Isabella sent me a few lines of congratulation in her own trembling handwriting. Altho' very slowly she is still strengthening and I have yet hopes that skillful treatment directed specifically to the first cause of her illness may restore her to some degree of health. She, poor dear girl, will not allow herself to hope, so perhaps it is only my sanguine temperament that allows me to do so.''

It is astonishing that an invalid who was scarcely capable of writing a letter would be well enough to have sexual intercourse and conceive a child. It appears that both John and Isa felt that pregnancy would be her last hope – a child would give Isa a compelling reason to live a normal life – but Isa's pregnancy was a nightmare for the whole Macdonald family. By the fourth month she was suffering such excruciating abdominal pain that Margaret summoned both John and Isabella's sister, Maria Macpherson, to her bedside.

"We found Isa considerably beter than our fears led us to anticipate," John wrote on April 5. "Dr. Washington says she is in a very critical situation arising from the continued attacks of uterine neuralgia. These attacks, he apprehends, may bring on a premature confinement, and if so, God alone knows what may be the consequence. Still he is not without hopes of being able to prevent an abortion, and in such case her health will probably be completely restored. She is quite calm & resolute, and is much encouraged by Maria's presence. Margaret became quite frightened and nervous from her not knowing what to do, and lost her usual presence of mind. Isa saw that, and felt a corresponding depression, but Maria's skill, cheerfulness and confidence of a happy issue has done much to set her at ease.''

Isa spent the next four months sedated and confined to bed; she went into labour on August 1, 1847. "She suffered for some hours tremendously,'' John wrote to his mother, "when we called in Doctor Rogers, a physician celebrated for the use and application of the *Lethean* or somnific gas [ether]. She was too weak and her nerves in too disordered a state to give her enough to set her asleep. She suffered dreadfully all night and about 8 this morning was so weak that the Doctors determined to use the forceps, as she was quite unable to deliver herself. They succeeded to a miracle, and I am delighted to tell you that she was delivered of a healthy and strong boy. The first word the poor thing said, after being informed that the child was alive and not deformed, was to tell me to write you, and to ask you to give it a name, which in her name and my own, I now do.''

Helen Macdonald named the baby John Alexander, and little John was immediately spirited north to Kingston in the care of his aunt Maria. He was a big baby, with fair hair and blue eyes, *"very large & nose to match"* his proud father said, but terribly thin. No wonder, said Maria, since he had been living on pills for so long.

Childbirth did not cure Isabella. Her old tics and pains returned; Dr. Washington's leeching and blistering treatments did nothing to help her. John remained with her until mid-September, but his departure precipitated another crisis: "Unfortunately the doctor advised her to try & walk across the room," John reported to Margaret Greene. "She did so, and in consequence was attacked with severest pain – not neuralgic – and has since been obliged to take a great deal of opium. She is again better and struggling for strength enough to join me in Canada this winter."

Isabella had exhausted the resources, and probably the patience, of both the Macdonalds and her sister Margaret. She was no longer the only invalid: Jane was dying of tuberculosis and John's mother had suffered a series of strokes. There was no one left to nurse Isa. Deprived of her son and abandoned by her family, Isa made a desperate effort to recover, and in June 1848 she returned to Kingston.

"Next Tuesday Isabella will have been at home for a fortnight," John wrote to Margaret Greene on July 9. "She bore the journey wonderfully well, the desire to see her child keeping her up, & not in any way prejudiced by the fatigue with the exception of a cold which she caught on the way. For some time after her arrival and after the excitement was over there was a considerable reaction, and she was much exhausted. Her cough too shook her grievously but some prescription given by Doctor Hayward has relieved her and she is now nearly free of it.

"She daily continues her exertions to sit up a little and contrives to do so for about ten minutes. She has now one source of interest which was denied her, the society of her boy. At first he was shy & uncomfortable in her room, which is in some degree darkened and as she could not dandle him, or toss him about, a ceremony which the young gentleman insists upon from all who approach him. He is now however great friends with her, and sits most contentedly in the bed with her surrounded by his toys, which he throws about, much to her inconvenience I am sure. He is very healthy, and observant & altogether an interesting child and poor Isa, as well as your humble servant, are as you may suppose very proud of him."

A clue to Isa's mental state is given by a letter she wrote at this time to Margaret Greene, who had apparently just left Philadelphia:

"My own most precious & most darling Sister,

"I sincerely sympathize in your leaving dear, dear Mrs. Biddle & most precious Husband. Full well I know how your spirit *must* be borne down by the hourly *yearning* for her society. For that unfailing *true-hearted* friendship and communion—earth alas! so *very* seldom affords. My dear, *dear* Mrs. Biddle, how I *reverence* her worth, her *true-heartedness*, her *never* to-be-doubted *truth* of feeling *under all* circumstances. My darling sister it is perfectly holy & my very soul bows before her as only God's Holy Spirit has given us for an example, but to which alas! *I* may not hope to attain. My dear, dear Mrs. Biddle. How I reverence her! How my weary, *weary* spirit bows before her. May God's holiest, richest mercies *rest, now & ever, abidingly* on her and hers.

I rejoice you are with Mrs. Field. Dear, beautiful, *Porcelain* Mrs. Field. So different from the *gilt delf* of everyday life. I really would dread seeing her often, my own darling precious sister, *you* know how *headlong* I ever go & I much fear I would love her but too fondly. I really *yearn* to *look* on her again, to hear *her voice* & look at those beautiful eyes. To me her bright, *sparkling* society would be a rich blessing. I so *long* to see her sit by my bed again & her beautiful daughter sitting on it. I really now wonder how I ever had the courage—the *self-denial*—to obey the doctors in New York and sometimes refuse her. I know they need not ask it now. But I must finish darling sister. It is very late and John is receiving company downstairs & Baby is asleep beside me. He is not well & oh darling darling sister my very soul is bound up in him. God pardon me if I sin in this. But did I not purchase him dearly?"

Isabella's almost incoherent letter, with its heavy underlinings and overwrought language, suggests that for all her outward calm, Isa was irrational and depressed.

She was also tubercular. She did not recover from her cold; her hacking cough got worse and she spat up blood. The noises from the street grated on her nerves, she suffered constantly from tic and took opium daily. Frantically searching for the quiet Isabella demanded, John rented an elaborate Italianate villa on the outskirts of town. The "Pekoe Pagoda" as the Macdonalds called it – it is now a Macdonald museum, Bellevue House – cost a good deal more than John could afford, but it was bright and comfortable and the tall windows overlooked the lake. The Macdonalds moved in at the end of August, a month after little John's first birthday.

"He is in good health," John wrote to Margaret Greene. "He sits by the hour now with his Mother, as contentedly as possible, and smiles &

crows away from one end of the day to the other." Three weeks later, little John Alexander was dead.

He might have died of typhoid or cholera, measles, scarlet fever, meningitis, polio, smallpox or any of the virulent contagious diseases that killed so many children before vaccines. As Isa's letter suggests, he may have been more sickly than his father wanted to believe, or he may have had an accident. The cause of death was never mentioned, but Isabella became obsessed with the idea of "replacing" little John, and a year later she was pregnant again.

Isabella's second and last pregnancy marked the end of her feeble attempts to live a normal life. At John's urging she had attempted to get out of bed for a few moments a day, lying on a sofa or sitting up in chair, and sometimes she joined him for dinner in the dining-room or at a small table by her bedside. She knitted and sewed a little and directed the servants from her room, taking obsessive pains about John's meals with, he said gratefully, "the most laudable attention to economy & horror of waste." John jokingly called her the "Invisible Lady":

"The Invisible Lady's voice, orders & behests are heard & obeyed all over the house & are carried out as to cupboards which she never sees and pots & pans that have no acquaintance with her. Not a glass is broken or a set of dishes diminished but she knows of and calls the criminal to account for."

But Isabella was now forty; when her sister Jane died in November 1849, during Isabella's fifth month of pregnancy, Isa reached the end of her emotional resources. "During the last week Isabella has been struggling with her feelings," John wrote to Margaret Greene on December 9. "Her duty to others, especially to her unborn offspring, compelled her to subdue all agitation & she was apparently calm & resigned for most of the time, but the struggle has been too much for her. Her anguish of mind banished sleep, and this brought on exhaustion, bleeding from the throat, and a terrible attack of neuralgia. Last night she was fearfully ill, so ill I was alarmed about her. I attribute this attack altogether to the attempted suppression of her emotions, but now that sorrow has had its way, I trust she will not tonight have a recurrance of her sufferings."

Isabella took to her bed, made her will, arranged the portraits of her sisters around her and prepared for death. For the next three months she suffered such terrible pain the doctors expected the baby to be delivered prematurely; however, on March 13, 1850 Isa gave birth to a second healthy, robust son. She wanted to name him John, after his dead brother, but the superstitious Macdonalds prevailed and the boy was called Hugh after his grandfather Macdonald.

Isa never really knew her son; Hugh was raised by nurses and, after the age of seven, by John's sisters Louisa and Margaret. Tubercular, totally bedridden, confined to a silent room where the shades were always drawn, Isabella slipped away to Lotusland. Her only visitor was the doctor, with his needle. John took her with him to Toronto in 1855 but it made no difference: the "Invisible Lady" was a hopeless addict. Isabella Macdonald died in Kingston on December 28, 1857 at the age of forty-eight.

In *John A. Macdonald: The Young Chieftan*, Donald Creighton gives a poignant portrait of the grieving Macdonald: "It was all over now – the agony of worry, the aching feeling of incompleteness, the patched habit of cheerful resignation. But for twelve years it had twisted his whole life. He had become a family man whose home was a hotel or a lodging-house; a bachelor husband who had to go for companionship to bars and lounges and smoking rooms; a frustrated host who drank too much on occasion, partly because it was the only way he could entertain, and because it passed the empty time, and because it was an easy way to forget."

Yet as Isabella's health deteriorated, John A. Macdonald's political fortunes steadily rose. In October 1844, a year after his marriage, he was elected to the Legislative Assembly as a Conservative member for Kingston; three years later he was appointed to the Cabinet as receiver-general and in 1854, when Isabella's illness was terminal, he became attorney-general for Canada West. Macdonald did not let Isabella's invalidism interfere with his political career; he was away from home attending sessions of parliament up to six months out of every year, and when the House was not in session he went off campaigning. Isa's illness freed him from the constraints of conventional family life and from the tedium of polite society, which he loathed. It gave him long hours to read, work and think, and with his wife safely tucked away in Savannah, New York or Kingston, Macdonald was at liberty to devote himself body and soul to his mistress: politics. It was in those grubby bars and lounges, the legendary smoke-filled rooms of politics, that Macdonald came to know intimately his fellow politicians and learned the subtle moves of political intrigue, a game at which he became an incomparable master.

Isabella's illness perversely worked to her own advantage as well. "There is an overtly manipulative appearance to much of her conduct," observes Dr. McSherry. "This illness was a chronic condition with periodic exacerbation which often coincided with John's absences on business and settled rapidly on his return." In other words, Isabella used her illness to capture John's attention and to keep him with her; in the first three years of their marriage, Macdonald spent months at her bedside, to the serious detriment of his income, practice and political prospects. For an energetic, intelligent young man of affairs like Macdonald, the boredom and frustration of idle weeks cooped up in sickrooms in strange cities must have been unbearable. His letters suggest him to be a kind, empathetic, devoted husband, but a hard edge is glimpsed in the sarcastic phrase "Madame Isa," and there must certainly have been times when John became angry and rebelled.

"Had Isabella been a more assertive person or the Macdonald family circle less matriarchal the outcome might have been entirely different," says McSherry. "She would scarcely have been human had she not entertained some doubts and concerns about her marriage. However, it was by then manifestly impossible to have expressed them in that environment for the die was already cast and her predicament insoluable. Her illness gained attention and an opportunity for self-assertion which became its own positive reinforcement, a learned behavior which permitted her to exert a degree of control in a situation where she was otherwise powerless."

By being ill rather than angry or rebellious, Isabella gained sympathy, and within a year of her marriage she dominated the entire Macdonald household. By becoming bedridden, she acquired a bed and a room of her own, and eventually her own house. She freed herself from bossy old Helen Macdonald and John's cantankerous sister Louisa; his gentle sister Margaret became her nurse. Waited on hand and foot by doctors, relatives and servants, the "Invisible Lady" was a queen in her own kingdom, autocratic, capricious and feared. Illness freed Isabella from all social conventions; she went nowhere and saw no one she chose not to see. It freed her from domestic drudgery and the responsibility of child-rearing, and it gave her the power to inflict pain on others, especially her husband, who suffered agonies of anxiety and guilt. Ultimately it enabled her to escape the world entirely.

Isabella's illness worked for her because invalidism was an acceptable, even enviable, form of behaviour in the Victorian era. The pale, languorous figure *en déshabillé*, hair loose, reclining on a couch, expressed both moral and physical rebellion against the buttoned-up puritanism of muscular

Christianity, but the provocative eroticism of the invalid's behaviour was chilled by the shadow of death. Elizabeth Barrett Browning was the quintessential invalid among women, Chopin among men, and they were both romantic cult figures. Invalidism allowed Isabella to express herself sensually and emotionally, but only in a way that was ultimately suicidal.

Fourteen years of marriage to his *cara spousa*, his "dear wife" as he called her, taught John A. Macdonald some hard truths about power and the dark secrets of the human heart. If it ever occurred to him to quit politics to enable Isabella to get well, he rejected the idea. Perhaps her condition was, as he believed, hopeless. Instead, he withdrew so completely into politics he rarely saw his wife, and had to be summoned from Toronto to her deathbed. Isabella staked her life against John's ambition. John won.

CHAPTER 2

"That Mole-Catcher of a Wife of His": Agnes Macdonald

$\mathcal{S}$USAN AGNES BERNARD first caught John A. Macdonald's eye in a Toronto hotel dining-room in 1856; she was twenty, he was forty-one. Macdonald, attorney-general for Canada West, was in Toronto for the session of the Legislative Assembly, which alternated between Toronto and Quebec City after the parliament building in Montreal had been burned by a mob in 1849, and Susy, as she was called, had come in from Barrie with her brothers for a little political excitement. The Bernards were an old Jamaican plantation family, and they brought to Canada the traditions of public service they had practised as magistrates and militia officers in the West Indies. Hewitt and Richard Bernard were lawyers, their religion was Church of England and their politics were Conservative; Susy, the youngest in the family and the only girl, was plain, pious and proud.

From his vantage-point at his favourite table, Macdonald watched the girl cross the room. She was tall and thin, angular and rather raw-boned. Her straight brown hair was pulled severely back in a braid and her skin was sallow, almost swarthy. She was no beauty; her jaw was heavy, her chest flat and her hands large, but John was taken by her long, slightly crooked nose, so much like his own, her deep-set dark eyes and the ironic smile that played around the corners of her determined mouth. He liked her erect carriage, her smart hat and the way the shimmering silk of her dress changed colour as she walked, like a parrot's plumage. There was something unconventional, exotic, about this girl, something that made him think of Georgia, warmth and oranges.

Who was she? Macdonald leaned across the table to his dinner companion. He didn't know; he knew only that the family was English and lived near Lake Simcoe. Macdonald did not pursue the matter; he was still, in name at least, a married man.

Susy Bernard had been in Barrie less than two years. Hewitt had established a law practice there in 1851; Richard joined him the following year and Susy and her mother in 1854. A backwoods town in northern Ontario was an odd place for people of the Bernards' social pretensions, but the family had fallen on hard times. Like all Jamaican plantation owners, the Bernards had used slaves to plant and harvest their crops of coffee and sugar cane, and the abolition of slavery in 1834 caused the Jamaican economy to collapse. Freed slaves looted and burned the plantations, and the Bernards, like hundreds of others, were driven into bankruptcy. Their father, Thomas Bernard, sold the ancestral family estate in 1840 and eked out a living as an attorney in Spanish Town; in 1850 he died of cholera, leaving his children virtually penniless.

Dependent on her mother's small inheritance and the charity of English relatives, Susy spent the next four years with cousins in England where she studied her catechism and was taught singing, drawing and French. She likely would have preferred to remain in England, but poor relations are as welcome as mice, and marriage prospects for a girl in her circumstances were better in Canada.

Susy did not notice John A. Macdonald until two years later at a concert in Toronto, when Hewitt pointed him out sitting with a group of ladies in the front row of the balcony. Macdonald was now co-premier of the Province of Canada, and Hewitt was his private secretary. Susy too had come up in the world: after toying with "Susannah Agnes" and "Agnes Susanna," she had decided to call herself Agnes. Contemplating Hewitt's "Chief" with a critical eye, Agnes was struck by Macdonald's "forcible, yet changeful face, with such a mixture of strength and vivacity, and his bushy, dark, peculiar hair as he leaned on his elbows and looked down."

Agnes and her mother now lived with Hewitt in Toronto, but Hewitt was in no hurry to introduce his sister to his new boss. Agnes was very young and Macdonald was a recent widower, a middle-aged man-about-town with a taste for loose women and strong drink. Hewitt, or Colonel Bernard as he was called, was one of those slightly down-at-heel gentlemen-of-all-work who populated British colonies during the salad days of the Empire and attempted, without success, to raise the moral tone of the natives. Hewitt likely disapproved of Macdonald's personal habits, especially his drinking, and it wasn't until the winter of 1860 that Macdonald, on his own initiative, paid a call on Agnes and her mother.

It was no whirlwind romance. Ardently pursued by eager widows and matrons with marriageable daughters in tow, Macdonald was enjoying his freedom, and Agnes, caught up in the gay life of official society, was likely angling for a handsome officer – the Irish Guards were particularly in vogue – or, if the fates smiled, an English lord. Agnes was a healthy, adventurous young woman, and her passion for dancing and tobogganing was heightened by her acute sense of sin.

"A pleasant flavour of mischief was added to the sliding attractions of the day," Agnes wrote later in *Murray's Magazine*, "for Mamma often said 'No' and then came the excitement of being caught some bright moonlit night a mile or so from home, packed with one's bosom friend on a 'coaster,' as the sled was called, tearing down a steep forest roadway, and

Agnes, destined to become Lady Macdonald: plain, pious and proud.

then scudding away, breathless, dishevelled and nearly shaken to death, over the frozen surface of some lonely, pine-fringed lake.''

In Quebec City with Hewitt for the alternate sessions, Agnes delighted in the regimental balls and fast winter sleighrides to Montmorency Falls. Snuggled into a light sleigh next to a Guards officer in a fur cap, fur robes tucked up to her chin, her head wrapped in a white wool scarf or ''cloud,'' Agnes shrieked with pleasure as the sleigh flew across the ice, the horses kicking up a cloud of ice and snow. Winter picnics at Montmorency were *the* social events of the season: the wild race to the

Sir John A., destined to become Agnes' "good old boy."

falls was followed by an afternoon of tobogganing, a sumptuous feast served in the fairy-tale ice cave beneath the falls, a romantic ride home by starlight and dancing in the Music Hall until dawn. Many young women "got" their guardsmen at Montmorency Falls, but Agnes did not.

In 1865, when the government began to move bag and baggage to Ottawa, Agnes was twenty-nine and a spinster. Macdonald was then engaged in a different kind of matrimonial adventure, trying to unite Canada East and Canada West with New Brunswick, Nova Scotia and Prince Edward Island to form the Dominion of Canada. Perhaps Hewitt had discouraged Macdonald's interest in Agnes, or John was too wrapped up in politics to have time for courtship. At any rate there was no incentive to persuade Agnes to follow Hewitt to the raw new capital: Agnes and her mother sailed for England.

A year later in London, Agnes bumped into John A. Macdonald on Bond St. Macdonald had come to England to shepherd Canada's new constitution through the British parliament; Agnes was Christmas shopping. John proposed two weeks later, and on February 16, 1867, after an engagement of less than six weeks, Agnes Bernard and John A. Macdonald were married in St. George's Church, London.

Was it impulse, inspiration or delayed reaction? Both John and Agnes loved a show, especially if they were at the centre of it, but they were also hard-headed and opportunistic. John needed a wife. He had never had one in the complete sense of the word, and it wouldn't do for a prime minister to be holed up in seedy bachelor digs with his male secretary. He wanted a hostess, and he needed someone to look after him. All his life Macdonald had been waited on by his mother and sisters; they had cooked his meals and mended his clothes, raised his son and cared for Isabella. As the only son, and breadwinner, John had taken their services for granted, but just before Isabella died, Margaret, his favourite sister, up and married a professor, James Williamson, and after Helen Macdonald died, the Williamsons took both Louisa and young Hugh into their home. Now, at fifty-two, Macdonald was alone. Agnes had youth, energy and, for a woman of her time, education: she had been to Paris; she could speak French, paint in watercolours and she loved to read, although, as Macdonald would discover, her taste ran to romantic novels. She was not giddy or frivolous, and independent enough to be interesting. According to E.M. Biggar, Macdonald's first biographer, John was attracted to Agnes because she had "a keen wit, a quick perception, a liberal mind and a certain unselfishness of heart which would well become the wife of a public man."

And Agnes would be marrying a "lord" after all. John A. Macdonald became the first prime minister of Canada on July 1, 1867, and in honour of the occasion, Queen Victoria made him Knight Commander of the Most Honourable Order of the Bath. He was now Sir John, and plain Agnes, a bride of less than five months, was Lady Macdonald. To celebrate her splendid new status Agnes bought a splendid new diary; her first entry, dated July 5, 1867, is suffused with the pride and excitement she felt at this dazzling reversal in her fortunes:

"My beautiful new Diary Book! I am ever so pleased with it and have been examining and admiring it for a full ten minutes! The lock too! My diaries as Miss Bernard did not need such precautions, but then I was an insignificant young spinster and what I might write didn't matter, now I am a great premier's wife & Lady Macdonald and 'cabinet secrets & mysteries' might drop or slip off unwittingly from the nib of my pen.

"That is, they might do so, if my pen had any nib or if I knew any cabinet secrets, which I certainly don't – but then a locked diary looks consequential and just now I am rather in that line myself – I mean the consequential line of course – My Husband's new title is just five days old, so, for a short time longer, I may be excused for some little bumptiousness . . .

"Here, in this house, the atmosphere is so awfully political that sometimes I think the very flies hold Parliaments on the kitchen tableclothes! In theory I regard my husband with much awe – in practice I tease the life out of him by talking of dress & compliments when he comes home to rest! Today he rebelled, poor man, & ordered me out of the room. I went at once, but he relented, the good old boy, and after he called me back – he got the worst of it!"

The newlyweds rented a large house near Parliament Hill that they shared with Agnes's mother, Theodora, and her brother Hewitt, who had been promoted to deputy minister of justice. Unlike Isabella, Agnes apparently enjoyed a crowd, and her home was always full of Bernard and Macdonald relations. Living conditions in Ottawa were primitive: there was no running water or sewage, the streets were mud and the city a giant construction site. Saws at the lumber mills screeched all day and the river was choked with floating timber; workmen's shanties straggled along the riverbanks, washing fluttered in the breeze and cows and pigs wandered at will through the main streets. Hewitt described it as the "Ultima Thule of ennui and wretchedness."

Agnes and her mother threw themselves into the business of housekeeping. Agnes couldn't even boil water, and while she had a hired cook and a manservant, she was helpless about planning menus or giving instructions. John was a plain but picky eater, and judging from Agnes's grocery lists, they lived on a diet of mutton chops, steak and vegetables. Agnes made an attempt to copy out recipes but soon abandoned the effort, and John's insistence on frugality prompted her to keep detailed daily records of every penny spent. Agnes's first dinner party was a flop – she cooked the meal an hour too soon – and she would always consider the housewife's role a burden.

Agnes was in an awkward position. She was too young to fit in with John's contemporaries, and many women deeply resented the fact that this homely, foreign, unknown woman had snatched the prime minister from under their noses–much was made of her dark complexion and her Creole background. Young Agnes was serious, reserved and intimidating. She did not flirt, or enjoy cards. She disliked needlework, and she abhorred gossip. She had little small talk and no talent for flattery. In spite of Agnes's proper upbringing. Macdonald could hardly have found a bluestocking less suited to be an Ottawa hostess.

John would also not have appreciated being called a "good old boy," or, in Agnes's next diary entry, "my blessed old Husband." Agnes was very aware of her husband's age and treated him with a daughterly combination of respect and condescension. She was the first prime minister's wife to marry a father figure. Thomas Bernard died when Agnes was an impressionable thirteen: Agnes lost not only her father, but her home, her country, her financial security, her independence and her social position. By marrying John, she gained them back, and more, but the experience left her insecure and fearful about money, status and illness.

She had good reason to fear. Macdonald was deeply, hopelessly in debt and forced to borrow just to meet the monthly bills. His position as prime minister was secure only until the next election, and Agnes worried constantly about his "weakness." Macdonald had apparently promised to quit, or at least control, his drinking when he married, and it was Agnes's unhappy role to be his conscience. In the early months of their marriage his behaviour seems to have been exemplary, and Agnes fretted more about the epidemics of cholera, typhoid and smallpox that swept through Ottawa. At one point the stench of sewage in John's study was so strong he had to move to the third floor.

Isolated socially in a rough frontier town where she knew almost no one, Agnes was often tense and depressed.

"I gave a little party for Hughie, tea & games & supper," she wrote in January 1868, "but it was very stupid and I could do nothing to promote gaiety myself – somehow, hard as I battled it, I felt lowspirited and dull. Sir John was charming, however, & we could not have done without him." Macdonald was the life of any party, and his easy ways seem to have made Agnes feel even more maladroit. Rather than bend to her husband's mold, Agnes resisted. She would not be the only prime minister's wife to complain about the mail: "How ungrateful I am to hate the sight of the long, delicate envelope addressed in various styles of pointed feminine hands. I don't think I could ever make a friend of a woman who wrote a pointed hand – answering these effusions takes up so much time.

Agnes made few friends. She became prickly, defensive and hypercritical of others. "I feared Mrs. Rose's cosy, yet cutting smile," she confided to her diary. "She is really good, I know, but somehow seems wordly . . . I feel she is dangerous." Mrs. Rose was the wife of one of Macdonald's oldest friends, John Rose, who went on to a brilliant career in England: Agnes was already sending out signals that Sir John and Lady Macdonald were going to rule the roost in Canada. Ladies of higher rank, like Lady Young, wife of the governor-general, received short shrift:

"Mama & I drove to Rideau Hall & found her ladyship reclining on a padded chintz sofa in a room heavy with the scent of hyacinths, arrayed in a rich robe of violet satin, thickly quilted and trimmed with swansdown. She was close to a blazing wood fire & the double-windowed room was very hot. I think too much luxury, tho' wonderfully pretty to look at, is not healthy or wise."

Agnes concluded that "a gay, unthinking life is not only wrong and perverted, but most unsatisfactory . . . the reaction, sure sooner or later to come, is something dreadful to endure, & a humble, thriving, self-recollecting, self-denying life is not only the *safest* & *best* but the happiest beyond all compare."

Agnes's sanctimonious puritanism was a shock to Ottawa, and to her husband. She joined St. Alban's Anglican Church and began going to services daily: her patronage secured the primacy of St. Alban's in Ottawa for decades to come, although Macdonald himself was Presbyterian. Agnes seemed to understand something about John others did not: politics was play, and he was essentially a solitary man, happiest alone with a cosy fire and a good book. Agnes was building them both a private world:

"John came home early & Mama went out walking after dinner so we had *such* a jolly *resting* evening – no visitors or telegrams or letters or fuss. My Husband devoted himself for a time to 'Patience,' his well-beloved game. I shall ever think of him sitting absorbed in the cards, leaning on a large green table in my dressing-room. He says it rests his mind & changes the current of his thoughts more than anything else." Agnes persuaded John to observe Sunday as a day of rest – no Sunday politics! – and to accompany her, reluctantly, to morning services at St. Alban's Church. Home became a haven where Macdonald could shake off political worries. Agnes observed: "Oftentimes he comes in with a very moody brow, tired and oppressed, his voice weak, his step slow, & ten minutes after he is making clever jokes & laughing like any schoolboy, with his hands in the pockets and his head thrown back."

As a politician, Macdonald was canny, manipulative and weak-willed. Agnes soon had the old boy figured out: "It is extremely painful being asked to beg John to interfere in getting places for my friends," Agnes wrote in December 1867. "He is so just that I know it is distressing to him to be asked for what he does not think it right to give, & yet I cannot refuse to do all in my power for my good old friends." Agnes could be a pest. Macdonald responded to her coaxing and wheedling the way he responded to all political importunities, by telling her to go away, and when she didn't, he gave in. "He is a powerful and popular man," Agnes wrote gratefully, "& withal the humblest, least assuming, most gently judging of all mankind."

What did John think of Agnes? His letters to her have been lost or destroyed, and he was not a confiding sort. It was a fractious, difficult time in Canadian politics, and Macdonald was chronically worried that Confederation would come apart at the seams at any time; he must have been grateful for Agnes's enthusiasm and loyalty. Agnes spent hours in the gallery of the House during debate, and they worked out a private code of hand signals which allowed her to pass messages to him. She often walked to his office in the East Block to accompany him home, and waited patiently on the steps immersed in a book. John tried to persuade her to read educational biographies and political tomes, but they bored her; she preferred sentimental poetry and the religious tracts that were popular at the time.

While on the surface Agnes appeared nervous and submissive – even in her diary she liked to call her husband "Sir John" – she had a strong sense of her own importance. Agnes seems to have seen her marriage as a bargain, and while she would faithfully perform her wifely duties, John would have to pay a price, and it would not be cheap. Agnes loved flashy, fashionable clothes and John indulged her taste for the latest London styles, although he could not afford it; he was too poor even to keep a horse and carriage. He bowed to her will in the case of "Sunday politics," strong drink and religion, but he had no intention of allowing his wife to boss him around, and appears to have met Agnes's coaxing and cajoling with a stubborn resistance that caused her to lose her temper.

"I know my love of power is strong," she confessed to her diary in a guilty moment, "so strong that sometimes I dread it influences me when I imagine I am influenced by a sense of right. John generally explains it all to me – he is so wise. Sometimes I am sure my wilfulness must try his patience – but he is habitually the most self-controlled person one can imagine. I never met anyone, except my mother, whose self-restraint was so perfect."

John won the power struggle, at least temporarily. He shared no political secrets with his wife and solicited no advice. When not at the House, he spent most evenings alone in his study or with his colleagues. Agnes got the message: "I am not very anxious to become too political in style," she wrote. "So few women are clever, consistent & intriguing enough to make any useful use of political knowledge & bias, & when they are too amateur in it they are bores, or make mischief."

Like many thwarted, ambitious women, Agnes decided to live vicariously through her husband: she would become the most devoted, the most loving, the most perfect wife in the world for "my darling":

"I do like to identify myself with all my Husband's pursuits & occupations. He is so busy and so much older that I would soon fall out of his life if I went on my own way – as I might do, disregarding him. On the whole I think he likes me near him . . . I have found something worth living for, living in, my Husband's heart & love."

On John's fifty-third birthday, January 11, 1868, she wrote: "At home till 3, then to the Department with my Husband & then the drive with him across the ice – such smooth sleighing! The whole country is a sheet of unbroken snow – dazzling to look upon – the air is *rare* with cold. It is most invigorating. My House is warm and cosy – when we go in, my dressing room looks so snug, with the blazing fire & bright gaslights as we bundled in after our cold drive and John said 'How comfortable this is.' It pleased me much – to make his house cheery & pleasant & to know that he is happy & at ease is indeed sweet to me. All my strong Heart's devotion is so entirely given up to him that my only fear is such affection is sinful and too all engrossing.''

Yet tragedy once more struck Macdonald's household, and during the next two years Agnes's Job-like sense of sin would grow to dominate her life.

John was bankrupt. He kept the frightening details from her, but he had gone deeply into debt to the Commercial Bank of Kingston, and in January 1868 the bank failed, leaving Macdonald, a director, owing $80,000. Always lazy and careless about money, Macdonald had frittered away his law practice and lost heavily on real-estate speculation. Now he had nothing; he didn't even own the house they lived in. Their only income was John's small, precarious salary as prime minister.

Bankruptcy brought on one of Macdonald's famous ''attacks,'' the first since his marriage. Macdonald was a binge drinker; after months of self-discipline and hard intellectual labour, he would ''break out'' on a bender that lasted for weeks or months. Holed up in bed in a nightshirt, a bottle of French claret in one hand, a popular novel in the other, Macdonald refused to see anyone. Sometimes he quite literally disappeared, turning up days later in some seedy hotel: one summer, a rumour circulated that he had drowned. Eventually, rested, bored and full of beans, he emerged fresh as a daisy and ready for the fray. Macdonald's drinking did not impair his ability to accomplish an immense amount of work or undertake arduous election campaigns while apparently ''under the influence,'' and it added enormously to his popular legend. Drink seems to have been Macdonald's escape from stress and, literally, an ''attack'' on colleagues he felt had let him down.

Agnes responded with an attack of self-righteous renunciation. ''I have given up wine,'' she wrote sternly in February 1868. ''This is for example's sake, & because I think it is unnecessary – therefore wasteful. Cards I would fain eschew – for I dislike all games of cards but the one of 'Patience' which we read 'Albert the Good' [the late Prince Consort] was fond of. I hope to be able to take a right stand about balls and to set my face against theatricals.'' Agnes also gave up novels.

Her attempts to make John guilty apparently made the situation worse. ''I feel distressed about his health,'' she lamented on February 22. ''Dr. Grant spoke to me about it again today and I felt fidgety & nervous in consequence. I know too that I troubled my own darling – my over-anxiety was the cause of it." Overwhelmed by feelings of responsibility, Agnes became restless and nervous, even after John's bout with the bottle ended and he was restored to his usual happy self.

"I only pray & hope life's sunshine may never dazzle me," Agnes wrote fearfully on March 25, 1868. "The shadow that for so long dimmed its brightness has passed away. I trust its memory may never so fade, but keep us ever watchful and humble – gossiping today – and very much time wasted – this must not be."

On April 6 she again referred to the "heavy shadow which at one time, & for so long, darkened my life" and once more on April 26: "I know that whenever I am called away from Ottawa & from my round of duty (poor as it is) here, that I shall need great watchfulness & much prayer to keep alive the flame of the Holy Spirit lighting up my heart & showing me the good way. And I know furthermore that if my feeble faith were to fail and my eyes to fall from looking upward, that the Shadow which once darkened my life would assuredly lower again!"

The "Shadow" may have been John's drinking, but it appears to refer to something within Agnes herself; she seems destructively compelled to snuff out the slightest ray of joy. She took refuge in religion, and nagged mercilessly if John claimed to be too tired or too busy to go to church. She wrote sarcastically: "The very men who consider an hour & a half on Sundays as a most lavish expenditure of time at church do not think a four hour conversation after bedtime as anything at all."

Agnes developed neuralgia. The pains, confined largely to her face, were minor and intermittent, but how John must have felt the cold ghost of Isabella at his side! Did he marry neurotic women, or did he drive them mad? He must have felt too Agnes's anger: "It is so much easier to bear the discomforts one imposes on oneself than to bear the trials others make you endure," she snapped at her diary. "I think it would be far less difficult to give up all reading except of religious tendency, to go to church in the cold grey of morning & to wear an unbecoming habit than to bend one's will to another's, or to bear patiently a hidden *home cross*."

Only a year after her marriage, Susy Bernard, the girl who loved tobogganing and dancing, had become a self-righteous prude: Agnes refused to receive a Cabinet minister's wife who had previously been divorced, and she later disapproved of Macdonald's clever young justice minister, John Thompson, because he was a "pervert" – he had converted from Methodism to Catholicism. The feeling was mutual – Thompson called Agnes "that mole-catcher of a wife of his."

Agnes's rigour was tempered, however, by a lively curiosity and a taste for sensation. She waited up for John until 2:30 a.m. on the morning of April 7, 1868, and was just falling asleep "when I was roused by a low, rapid knocking at the front door. In an instant, a great fear came upon me. Springing up, I threw on a wrapper & ran into my dressing-room just in time to see John throw up the window & hear him call out 'Is there anything the matter? The answer came up fearfully clear & hard thro' the cold moonlight morning – 'McGee is murdered – lying in the street – shot thro' the head.' The words fell like the blow of a bar of iron across my heart – it was too dreadful."

Thomas D'Arcy McGee was a popular minister in Macdonald's Cabinet and a good friend; John and Hewitt rushed out and didn't return until 5 a.m. Agnes was awake, praying for their safety and eager for the gory details: "When John came home he was much agitated, for him, whose self-command is so wonderful. He had found our poor friend's body lying in his blood – dead at the door of his lodging – shot from behind by a cowardly assassin hand as he was in the act of turning his latch key to let himself into his house! The bullet had passed into the lower part of the back of his head and had come thro' his mouth, carrying away two or three of his teeth. As the shot was fired the landlady was in the act of opening the door from the inside & she heard the shot & saw the pistol flash. Her life was saved by a miracle – the ball lodged in the door she was holding."

In September, Agnes was an excited spectator at the trial of the tailor accused of the murder, James Patrick Whelan. "It was deeply, fearfully interesting," she confessed to her diary. "We had seats close by the Chief Justice. The court was always thronged tho' everyone was admitted by ticket & hundreds sent away. The dingy court-room – shall any of us forget the scene – the shabby, anxious gazing crowd, the rugged home-spun line of attentive jurors, the large deliberate, complacent Prisoner's counsel . . . his lean-faced assistant who put the questions . . . the stout, sturdy handsome looking Irishman, counsel for the Crown, with a keen blue eye & heavy sensual mouth, the ponderous judge with his ponderous notebook . . . and *The Prisoner* right opposite, sitting with folded arms within the wooden dock, listening silently hour after hour to the deliberate unfolding of his *doom*! A small, mean-looking yet determined Irish man of some eight & twenty with a longish head and brownish hair brushed back, a low, wrinkled forehead, blue, intent, cunning eyes, coarse Irish features & a long reddish beard, dressed in black with a small black tie, but on the last day but one of the trial, a bright green cravat.''

Although Whelan vehemently protested his innocence, Agnes, like John and most of the spectators, was firmly convinced that Whelan was an Irish revolutionary, ''a ruffian, a low, foul-mouthed, whiskey-drinking idler,'' and McGee's assassin. Whelan was convicted and sentenced to death, but the verdict gave Agnes pangs of conscience. ''They tell me he *cannot feel*!!'' she wrote. ''If men then do not feel, then capital punishment is useless murder. It cannot do any good as an example.''

Agnes did not attend Whelan's public hanging on February 11, 1869; she was near death herself. On February 8 she gave birth to a seriously deformed, hydrocephalic daughter.

Agnes's pregnancy had been joyful. ''Again a happy, tranquil day,'' she wrote on September 24, 1868. ''And my 'New Hope,' so bright while so strange! Can it be that some day I shall have the sweet happiness of being a Mother? It seems so wonderful & yet so beautiful – I can hardly express what a new life it has given me.''

She went into labour on the morning of February 7, writing, with her customary conscientiousness, at 7:30 a.m.: ''I am ill now and suffering. O God my Father and ever Constant Blessed Comforter, help me patiently to bear my pains & to be prepared for all things. I read this morning in my chapter & prayer, & then my darling held me in his arms until just now, when I feared to disturb his precious sleep & I got up, softly turning out the gas, & left him.''

Her next entry, dated April 1, tells the story of a very difficult birth:

''She is lying asleep in her blankets, my very own darling Baby – my little daughter, the sweet gift from Heaven, my Mary, a dark-eyed, soft thing, my child.

''What words can tell how my heart swells with love & pride as I look at her. God gave her to me to cherish & she *is* truly dear. How little I thought when last I wrote on these pages that before another sun rose I should have been face to face with death, and yet so it was – not only my life but my Baby's was in great, great danger, & yet a marvellous power was with me & seemed to overshadow me . . . it almost seemed as if a *presence* stood by my bed & cheered me.

''My Baby was born on the morning after I last wrote, at 15 past 3.

Her first cry seemed to bring me to life. The effect of it was truly surprising – a rush of life seemed to come to me, and a kind of wild exultant joy, tho' I had felt before fast sinking – I had been ill for so many hours – 24."

Mary, with her shrivelled limbs and grotesquely misshapen head, was not expected to live, and as long she did she would be mentally and physically handicapped, yet it was nearly three months before the doctors could persuade Agnes to accept the truth. "The day has been stamped with the world's great seal, it is graven, I think, with the word 'disappointment,' " Agnes wrote on May 1. "Perhaps yesterday was one of the saddest times in my life – let it pass – let it die – only teach me, Heavenly Father, to see the lesson it was destined to teach, and while I learn it, to do so cheerfully."

That Agnes and Mary both survived is a testament to Dr. Grant's medical skill, although it was eight weeks before Agnes was strong enough to walk to church and she may have been permanently damaged. Caesarians were still experimental, and one woman in one hundred and fifty died in childbirth, usually of infection. Sex was such a taboo in the Victorian era that doctors were trained to examine their female patients by touch, without looking at their sexual organs, while the women were clothed. As a result, female sexuality was largely a matter of folk wisdom and superstition. Pregnancy and menstruation were never named, or even mentioned in medical encyclopedias; women were chronically "ailing," or suffering from "sick headache." Not only was sex sinful, but it was fraught with fear and danger.

The Macdonalds had no more children. Mary's delivery may have made it impossible; perhaps doctors advised against taking the risk. Contraception was primitive – abstinence was the most reliable method – but condoms were in widespread use, primarily, as now, as protection against venereal disease, which was both epidemic and incurable. Possibly Macdonald was concerned about genetic defects as well as his advancing age and dire financial straits. His son, Hugh, was now nineteen, an unprepossessing youth with pale, pop eyes and a receding chin. John had taken great pains with Hugh's education, but the boy had been raised by his aunts in Kingston and hardly knew his father. Macdonald insisted that Hugh study law, but Hugh preferred the army and a row broke out between them in 1870 when John refused him permission to go west with the militia to put down a rebellion led by the fiery Métis visionary, Louis Riel.

In 1869 the Hudson's Bay Company offered to sell to Canada its rights to the entire North-West for 200,000 pounds sterling. The deal would link Ontario and British Columbia north of the 49th parallel, and Macdonald jumped at the opportunity to more than double the size of the country. However, no one consulted the inhabitants of the territories, a community of Scottish settlers at Fort Garry on the Red River and a nomadic population of Indian and Métis buffalo hunters. When surveyors arrived to stake out farms, the Métis rebelled, captured Fort Garry and set up a provisional government. One man was executed and several killed in skirmishes before British regulars and Canadian militia arrived at Red River; Riel fled to the United States and a new province, Manitoba, joined Confederation.

Macdonald made a botch of Red River – Riel would return to haunt him – and the rebellion took a toll on his health. In June 1870 he collapsed in his office with an attack of gallstones so severe he was not expected to live. He lay on his couch for a week, unable to move, and spent six weeks recuperating in the Speaker's apartments before he could go home. Agnes rushed to his side, and won Ottawa's grudging respect with her devoted nursing. She also found a new role for herself: martyr. She had her photograph taken kneeling in a tragic pose by Mary's tiny, twisted form, neither looking at, nor touching, her child.

John began drinking steadily. Everything went wrong with his scheme to build a railway to the Pacific Ocean, and in the summer of 1873 he became embroiled in a scandal that blighted his personal reputation and nearly ruined his political career.

Macdonald had entrusted his beloved railway project to a consortium of financiers headed by Montreal steamship magnate Sir Hugh Allan; strapped for cash during a bitter election campaign in 1872, Macdonald asked Allan to finance the Conservative cause; Allan's Conservative interest was obvious – the Liberals were threatening to veto his railway. Macdonald won the election, but a few months later the Liberals revealed in the House that Sir Hugh Allan's company had contributed more than $100,000 to the Conservative campaign and Macdonald had sent a self-incriminating telegram to Allan: "I must have another ten thousand. Will be the last time of calling. Do not fail me. Answer today."

Humiliated, Macdonald retreated into depression and drink. On November 3, 1873 he rose in the House, pale and shaking, to defend himself in a brilliant five-hour speech, but it was too late. Defeat was certain, and two days later Macdonald resigned. Macdonald's secretary and biographer, Sir Joseph Pope, gives an account of Agnes's reaction that indicates the distance that had grown between them. Hearing John come

Agnes the martyr with "my crippled, helpless child, Mary."

home early and go directly to his room, Agnes went to ask if anything was wrong.

" 'Well, that's got along with,' John said.

" 'What do you mean?' said she. 'Why, the Government has resigned,' and arraying himself in his dressing-gown and slippers, and picking up two or three books from a table close by, 'It's a relief to be out of it,' he added as he stretched himself on the bed, opened a volume and began to read, intimating that he did not wish to be disturbed."

CHAPTER 3

· · · · · · · · · ·

Plain

Jane

Mackenzie

☙

$\mathcal{J}$ANE SYM MACKENZIE was forty-eight when her husband, Alexander, became Canada's first Liberal prime minister in 1873. It was a sudden and somewhat sordid victory: the Liberals produced stolen documents to prove Sir John A. Macdonald guilty of taking bribes from railway contractors, and while Jane knew her husband to be a man of scrupulous honesty, she knew also that muck stuck to the hands of those who threw it, and the mire of Canadian politics was virtually bottomless.

Jane had already spent a lifetime in politics. Her father, Robert Sym, was an ardent Reformer; the Sym homestead in the black swamps and hardwood forests of Lambton County was a community gathering place and a hotbed of radical debate when young Alexander Mackenzie arrived in the little Lake Huron boom town of Port Sarnia in the summer of 1847.

The Syms, like the Macdonalds and Mackenzies, were Highland Scots who had made the bitter choice of immigration, but unlike the Macdonalds, the Syms seem to have had no influential relatives or pretensions to gentry; in 1821 Robert and Agnes Sym settled in the remote wilderness of Lanark County, Ontario, where Jane was born on March 22, 1825. Agnes Sym died while Jane was still a child and in 1837 her father moved his children to a farm near Port Sarnia where Lake Huron empties into the St. Clair River. That was the year William Lyon Mackenzie marched his rebel band of farmers down Yonge St. in an abortive revolt against British colonial rule, and in the rebellion's aftermath of hangings and deportations Robert Sym would find the frontier of western Canada fertile soil for a man of his liberal views.

The Syms were Baptists, a small and somewhat subversive sect in a British colony where the Church of England claimed to be the official or "established" church. Like other religious minorities, the tight-knit little community of Baptists in Port Sarnia also functioned as a social club, self-help group, board of trade, poetry society and political organization. Sunday mornings after church the argumentative Scotch congregation gathered at the Sym farmhouse to criticize the sermon and castigate the Conservatives. Little Jane would serve an enormous lunch, wash the dishes and quietly listen to the talk.

A God-fearing Baptist and strict teetotaller, Alex Mackenzie found a warm welcome in this little community on the American border. At first sight Mackenzie was unprepossessing, a wiry, almost gaunt young man of medium height with a shock of reddish hair, unruly whiskers and a craggy face that looked as if it had been hewn out of the granite of his native Scotland. He wore a working man's rough, baggy clothes and his callused hands revealed his trade as a stonemason. Mackenzie's education was limited – he had left school at thirteen to help support his widowed mother and six brothers – but he read voraciously, spoke frankly and had strong views.

Mackenzie's plain appearance concealed a sharp mind and keen ambition. Only twenty-five when he arrived in Port Sarnia, Mackenzie had already worked as a contractor building military installations at Kingston, Ontario, and canals along the St. Lawrence. Soon he was hard at work building one of Port Sarnia's first public buildings, the jail.

For five years Alex Mackenzie was nothing more to Jane than a friend of the family. Mackenzie had a family of his own, his wife, Helen, and an infant daughter, Mary, as well as his mother and six brothers recently arrived from Scotland. Mackenzie had fallen in love with seventeen-year-old Helen Neil in Scotland and when the Neils decided to immigrate in 1842, Alex came along. The Neils were prosperous enough to afford cabin passage to Montreal and Mackenzie was spared the horrors of the pestilent immigrant ships. In 1845, when Alex was well established as a stonemason in Kingston, he and Helen were married. Only a few streets away from the Mackenzies, the up-and-coming Conservative lawyer, John A. Macdonald, was settling down with his wife, Isabella.

Like Isabella Macdonald, Helen Neil Mackenzie became an invalid. On holiday near Morrisburg in the summer of 1845, she came down with a severe fever and ague attributed to the low-lying marshes near the riverbank. The fever returned the next summer when Helen was pregnant. A drunken doctor overdosed her with calomel, a deadly mercury-based potion believed to cure cholera. The baby was safely delivered but Helen never fully recovered.

Family tragedy dogged Mackenzie as relentlessly as it did Macdonald. The Mackenzie's first-born child died in the summer of 1847 and Helen slowly wasted away. Chronic illness did not prevent her becoming pregnant: Mary was born in 1848 and a son in 1850. Only Mary survived. Helen Neil Mackenzie died on January 4, 1852. She was twenty-five.

Alexander Mackenzie married Jane Sym the following June. She was twenty-eight, he was thirty-one. It was to a certain extent a marriage of convenience: Mackenzie needed a housekeeper, Mary needed a mother and Jane, having taken her mother's place for nearly twenty years, was superbly qualified. Dale Thomson in *Alexander Mackenzie: Clear Grit* describes her as a "dutiful young girl" whose "appearance and demeanour already bore evidence of the hard labour that seemed her lot in life." Yet Jane was no drudge. She could read and write – a later photograph shows her with a book, a pince-nez perched on the end of her nose – and she corresponded regularly with her husband during the many months they were apart. She was small, with a graceful carriage, fine hands and long, straight blond hair. Jane's features were plain and her round head seemed too big for her body, but her face always had a pleasant expression. The first prime minister's wife to be born on a farm, Jane Mackenzie was the first, but not the last, to suffer the opprobrium of being "country." She is the only one who seems never to have made an enemy.

Marriage brought Jane a comfortable home in Port Sarnia and a five-year-old daughter whom she raised as her own. Jane never had children. For twenty years she lived a conventional life as the wife of a prosperous businessman and influential politician. While to the sophisticates of Toronto and Montreal Port Sarnia seemed as far away as Tuktoyaktuk seems today, it was just across the river from the United States and closer to the modern American cities of Chicago and Cleveland than the backwater of Upper Canada. No wonder one of the main planks of the Reform platform, along with universal suffrage, was free trade.

The years were often lonely for Jane. In 1861 Mackenzie was elected as a Reform member for Lambton. When he wasn't campaigning or away at the sessions of the House, he was chasing around the countryside trying to organize a party notorious for its factions, misfits, rebels and prima donnas. Mackenzie was one of those responsible for bringing into politics the hot-tempered, imperious and opinionated publisher of the Toronto *Globe*, George Brown; later as party leader Mackenzie was driven to despair by the tantrums of his neurasthenic justice minister, Edward Blake.

Jane often didn't see Alex for months at a time; even then he would frequently stop off for only a few hours before disappearing once more in a cloud of dust. Sometimes she was glad to see him alive.

"His meeting in Fisher's schoolhouse nearly ended in disaster," Dale Thomson writes of Mackenzie's 1867 election campaign. "The building was so packed with rowdies that he had to abandon any attempt to outline his programme. When he and his travelling companion tried to leave, strong arms blocked their path. Some held the nervous horses' heads; some tried to upset the carriage; others tried to pull the two men down into the crowd. Mackenzie succeeded in getting aboard the vehicle but his friend was badly pummelled before he managed to clamber up behind. The rearing and plunging horses broke loose from their tormentors and dashed off at full gallop down the country lane with other carriages laden with opponents – 'yelling and howling like savages' according to the *Observor* – in hot pursuit. A mile down the road a barricade of rails had been erected over a culvert. The horses skidded to a stop, the rails were heaved aside and the flight continued down the dusty trail. The horses were well suited to such a western campaign; in a few miles they had outdistanced their pursuers. Mackenzie continued on his schedule through the 'swamps of Lambton.' "

Mackenzie could give as good as he got. Accused of disloyalty to the queen at a meeting a few days later, Mackenzie retorted: "Loyalty to the Queen is a noble sentiment in which all true Liberals share, but loyalty to the Queen does not require a man to bow down to her manservant, her maidservant or . . . her ass!" In the resulting uproar the chairman of the meeting punched a Mackenzie supporter in the face; the Mackenzie man knocked the chairman to the floor. A riot was prevented by a fortuitous thunderstorm that sent the combatants running for shelter.

Jane Mackenzie did not campaign with her husband – it was apparently too dangerous – and she did not live in Ottawa during the sessions of parliament. Few wives did. The sessions lasted only three or four months, and out-of-town MPs rented rooms by the week or month in local boarding-houses or hotels. Cheap, shabby and dirty, the rooming-houses were not considered decent accommodation for ladies, and hotels attracted single women of dubious reputation respectable ladies were wise to avoid. Moral distinctions were more rigid than class ones in Victorian Ottawa, and although an MP's wife might be of very humble social standing, she could not be seen to associate with "common" or "loose" women without being shunned by polite society. This did not apply, of course, to her husband, and married MPs often acquired pretty "nieces" who kept them company during the session.

With the House sitting twelve to eighteen hours a day, there was nothing for visiting wives to do except drink tea, gossip or listen to the debate. Unaccustomed to being idle, women such as Jane were quickly bored. MPs received no living allowance, and the Mackenzies, like most of the others, were frugal with both time and money. Jane had better things to do at home in Sarnia, and she didn't move to Ottawa until Alex became Liberal leader in 1873.

They rented a house on Kent St. near the House of Commons. They were alone – Mary had married the year before – and Jane practised the open-house kind of entertaining she had known in Sarnia. By inviting Conservatives as well as Liberals to her parties, Jane cleverly silenced the malice of Tory guests too well mannered to insult her hospitality and she always had a plentiful supply of champagne, wine and hard liquor on hand for her guests, even though the Mackenzies were abstainers. She had the misfortune, however, to be cast in the shade by the young wife of the new governor-general, the dazzling, daring Hariot, Lady Dufferin.

Spectacularly rich Anglo-Irish aristocrats, Lord and Lady Dufferin whirled into Ottawa just as the austere, unpretentious Mackenzies were settling in. A strikingly handsome, Byronic figure who liked to dress up in Elizabethan costume to show off his legs, Dufferin was mad for dancing, tobogganing and figure skating; Hariot loved theatricals and salmon fishing. The gaiety at Rideau Hall never stopped: Dufferin would dance until dawn, then be off hunting or skating; Hariot received guests at a garden party in her last days of pregnancy, leaning against a padded post to take the weight off her feet. The Dufferins built an indoor tennis court, now the Tent Room, and a toboggan slide that was the sensation of the Ottawa winter season. Although one of their aides-de-camp broke his leg on the slide and died soon after, the accident only briefly interrupted the fun.

The Dufferins' extravagant entertainments and sporting style created a new "society" in Ottawa that was young, rich and *insouciant*. It was not a crowd in which Jane Mackenzie felt at home, and she wisely did not compete. She learned the fashionable dances, and she was vain enough about her appearance to wear an elaborate hairpiece coiled around the crown of her head, but she dressed simply and kept away from the limelight. The wife of a man who refuses to kiss the queen's ass is unlikely to

Jane Sym Mackenzie,
"the best of wives."

Her "ever affectionate
husband," Alexander
Mackenzie.

truckle to a Lady, and Mackenzie himself was leery of the Dufferins'
imperial pretensions. However, he made a hit with Lady Dufferin:

"I sat between Mr. Mackenzie and Mr. Cartwright," she wrote in
her journal in December 1873. "I like them both. Mr. Mackenzie is very
straight-forward, and very Scotch, in accent and looks." Lady Dufferin
never mentions Mrs. Mackenzie, and Jane remained plain Jane until the
end of her life: Alexander Mackenzie twice refused a title.

In the spring of 1874 fire destroyed the Mackenzies' Kent St. house
and all their belongings, including the letters they had written to each
other over twenty years. None of Jane's letters has survived, but there are
a handful of letters from Alex to her written during the years after the
fire. The first was sent that August when Jane was vacationing in Quebec,

likely the guest of a wealthy Liberal family at Rivière du Loup or Murray Bay. Mackenzie's letters have the rather arch, literary quality of the self-taught man and his spelling is not always perfect, but they reveal a teasing sense of humour and youthful gallantry that belie his public reputation as a stiff-necked old stick.

Ottawa, August 9, 1874

My loved Wife

Pardon me for writing you again after writing you yesterday. I will try not to sin again for some time. This day is so hot that when I came home from church I could not sit in an easy chair and read and could not lie on a bed or sofa, so I got a hard chair and set to work to bring up all arrears of domestic correspondence, and now the last and best is for you.

The question is, where are you? I presume you are vindicating your title to the Baptist profession by immersing well and thus at once sticking to your principles and laying in a stock of health for the winter. A horrible thought just strikes me, however: What if you should now suddenly grow fat and become the "gross feme" of the family!! No doubt the compensating laws of nature are very admirable and it may be satisfactory to know that we keep up the weight between us, but I would rather carry my own share of it. Allan Cunningham in one of his songs says

> "Her white arm would be a pillow for me
> Fa' softer than the down
> I wad lap her up rich i' the faulds of love
> Heavens armfu' o my Jean."

This is all very fine but the "armful" might become too serious though I don't object to the pillow.

Alex knows he can't fool his Jeannie – he is wretchedly lonely and his feelings have been hurt:

I see some Tory papers say I am eaten up with ambition. I think I know myself, and can honestly say that I am not. I am ambitious to succeed in governing the country well and without any reproach but beyond that my ambition is of a very humble kind. I am ambitious, or anxious rather, to have it in my power to spend a little time with you when and where the anxieties of public life will not harrass existence. I think I have ambition enough, however, to strengthen me to fight in, I hope, a manly way, the base herd of hireling scribes who would for political gain write away a man's character, and courage to back up that ambition.

Going on to praise himself at some length, Mackenzie realizes he is being a bit of a bore:

I am afraid I am writing far too long a letter. I suppose I need hardly write you at all as these letters may not reach you, but when you are away and I at home I always feel uneasy and like to write. Do you mind Dr. Duncan's beautiful lines to his wife?

"The miser hands firmer and firmer his gold,
The ivy sticks close to the tree when its old,
And still thou growest dearer to me, Mary Hay
As a' else turns eerie and life wears away."

I am afraid that in avowing these as my own sentiments that you may come to the conclusion that I cannot get on alone. Now don't flatter yourself with such a notion. You see there is such a luxury in doing what I please and just as I please. Not being able to read in bed for want of good eyes is one trouble no doubt but I mean to make up for it by an excursion among my shirts, clothes *and things* and sew on all the buttons and fix the button holes.

Good night my dear Jane. From your ever affectionate husband,

A. Mackenzie

When a letter from Jane arrives the next day Mackenzie's spirits perk up:

I received your letter today dated from Quebec. If your letter had not come I thought of advertising for you – as "A disconsolate husband would be glad to hear tidings of his wife who left Ottawa on the morning of the 4th and has not since been heard of. Her age about ———, skin fair, hair mixed, teeth good and nearly new, small, fat docile disposition and had $30 in her pocket." Do you think this would find you? I saw the Sergeant last night. He told me he was going down today and I asked him if he saw you not to mention that I was crying. Mr. Buckingham [Mackenzie's secretary] and I use up a handkerchief daily. I think of using a towel after this for economical reasons. If you stay away much longer it may come to a sheet.

Informing Jane that he has fired their manservant for sleeping in the spare bedroom, Alex ends on a note of very contemporary apology:

> We had a small shower this evening, just enough to wet me to the skin as I was coming home. That accomplished it stopped. Mr. Macdonald is well and so is your leige Lord (if it be not presumptuous for any man nowadays to call himself a woman's lord). I am at least dear Jane your ever affectionate husband,
>
> A Mackenzie

After the fire, the Mackenzies found themselves another house, Cliffside, on Wellington St. overlooking the Ottawa River with a magnificent view of the Gatineau Hills (the site of the present Supreme Court). In 1875 they travelled to Paris and London, where they had an audience with Queen Victoria, then spent several weeks in Alex's beloved Scotland. "The truth is that the Queen is an ill-tempered, exacting woman slightly tinged with the mental weakness which affected her uncle and grandfather," Mackenzie wrote acidly to his daughter, Mary. Jane spent most summers in Sarnia, fleeing the heat and flies and what Alex called "the press and ceremony" of the capital. For Mackenzie the summer months were taken up with political expeditions to other provinces to keep the party faithful loyal and true. He writes of a banquet in Montreal:

"One very pretty French lady paid me such marked attentions that if you were within reach you would have been somewhat concerned as to the result. I was sure my little lady had some special object in view. An hour or two before I left she managed a tête-à-tête so well she was able to solicit a Senatorship for her Papa! a Judgeship for her sister's husband! and a cabinet office for her husband!!

"All my love dreams were dissipated in an instant. Till then I imagined I had more personal attractions than you or I supposed, and I feared the danger of being among appreciative ladies in your absence. On sober reflection I conclude I am safe."

The French lady was certainly wasting her charms. Mackenzie hated the hordes of office-seekers, party hacks and incompetent fools who swarmed around him eager for favour or position. His abhorrence of corruption led him to introduce examinations for candidates seeking government positions, a reform that probably contributed to his early defeat.

The Mackenzies' five years in Ottawa were turbulent. The transcontinental railway scheme collapsed, and British Columbia threatened to join the United States or become a separate colony. Mackenzie's cautious, piecemeal solution to the railway crisis, short rail lines linked by wagon roads and shipping routes, was violently condemned, and the economy slipped into a severe depression that Liberal frugality did nothing to relieve. Mackenzie's moral righteousness did not eliminate patronage, and his reforming zeal made him countless enemies.

Jane's worst moment came on June 17, 1878. It was the middle of the election campaign, and the Mackenzies had returned to Ottawa from a exhausting speaking tour to celebrate their twenty-fifth wedding anniversary. Inviting a few friends in for a quiet party, they were stunned when a crowd of jubilant well-wishers rushed into the house and showered them with gifts. Alex was furious. "My evening's enjoyment is utterly destroyed by the sending of presents," he admonished one guest. "I never felt so mortified in my life. It looks as if we had got the little evening party up on purpose."

The guests were insulted, the party was ruined and the next morning Jane had the humiliating task of rewrapping all the presents and returning them to their owners. Exactly three months later, on September 17, 1878, the Mackenzie government was defeated. Old Tomorrow, Sir John A. Macdonald, was back.

The Mackenzies sold Cliffside to the new minister of public works, Dr. Charles Tupper, and moved to Toronto where Alex had a partnership in a small insurance business. Like Agnes Macdonald, Jane found herself more and more in the role of nurse. Thin to the point of emaciation, Mackenzie had suffered for years from bouts of debilitating intestinal pain he called dysentry but which was probalby colitis. Now he lost his ability to speak, although his mind remained clear, and in 1882 he suffered a stroke that left him partially paralyzed. He had reluctantly resigned the leadership of the Liberal Party in 1880, but he retained his seat on the Opposition benches as the member for York East, a silent, shattered figure who looked much older than his sixty-odd years.

When Alex was in Ottawa in the spring of 1880 he wrote Jane a rather egotistical but touching tribute:

Ottawa, March 2, 1880

My dearest Jeannie,

It is pleasant to count the days, now few, until I see you again. I think I am just as keen and enthusiastic as I was 27 years ago to see you and be with you. Then I liked you for what I believed you was, now I love you for what I know you are. Then I had no doubt you would make my life happy or at least would do your best to do so. Now I can say you have more than realized all my hopes and expectations and I look back on 27 years of happiest married life and I look forward with cheerfulness to what remains to us of life on this earth. In trying circumstances you nobly did your share in maintaining my position. My warmest love you had before, but that commanded my admiration and I daily receive the strongest evidence that no one ever had a stronger hold on all hearts than you have here. I am very proud of all this. I always feel backward in language of a demonstrative character and will only say now what I always think, that I have the best of wives. God bless her.

Mackenzie's investments and a Liberal Party trust fund of $10,000 enabled them to live in relative comfort on Wellesley St. near Queen's Park. Alex became the first president of the North American Life Assurance Company in 1881, a position he held for eleven years, and he and Jane travelled frequently to Italy, Switzerland and Scotland. Alex's health deteriorated rapidly after 1890, and he died on April 17, 1892. Jane lived less than a year; she died of a bowel inflammation on March 30, 1893.

CHAPTER 4

*The Barefoot
Baroness:
The Return
of Agnes
Macdonald*

$\mathcal{I}$T APPEARED THAT the Pacific Scandal of 1873 had ended Sir John A. Macdonald's political career. He came close to being disqualified from holding public office, and while he halfheartedly continued as leader of the Opposition in the House of Commons, he resumed the practice of law, commuting between Ottawa and his office in Toronto. Agnes often accompanied him, and she was in Toronto when her mother Theodora died suddenly on February 26, 1875.

"Ah! My mother! My mother!" Agnes wept to her diary on March 11. "Gone from me, gone to your sainted rest. Can you see your desolate child now? Can you hear me mother, and do you forgive? So much that might have been different, that is what makes my pain so very, very keen, that fearful thing regret! So [to] say I miss her is to say nothing. Every moment of every hour, waking & sleeping, speaking or silent the beloved face ever near me for more than 30 years smiles at me still, but in the silence & with the crushing knowledge she is gone my heart seems near bursting."

Theodora had been Agnes's closest friend and confidante, and she was never replaced in her daughter's affections. The following year John's sister Margaret died, and Hewitt became a recluse, crippled by what seems to have been arthritis. Agnes's little family was falling apart. Hugh and his father became irrevocably estranged when John violently objected to Hugh's engagement to a Roman Catholic widow; Hugh married her anyway and moved to Winnipeg, Manitoba, where he enjoyed a long and prominent career as a magistrate, an alcoholic and his father's son. Only Daisy, the child of that marriage, carried on the Macdonald line.

In 1875 Agnes and John moved to Toronto and the following year bought a house at 63 St. George St. that bore a striking resemblance to the "Pekoe Pagoda" in Kingston where John and Isabella had lived, and their first son had died, nearly thirty years before. Macdonald was more sentimental than he let on. Years later Agnes came across a box of the dead baby's toys John had never been able to discard, and at the end Macdonald was buried in Kingston, with Isabella and his mother.

Agnes had very little time for her Toronto house; during the next two years she was on the road campaigning with John in the biggest political comeback in Canadian history. Macdonald was a witty and effective platform speaker, and in the laughter that followed his sly jokes his skullduggery was forgiven. "We were feted everywhere," Agnes wrote. "Such constant dissipation as it was, flattering too, but so unsatisfactory and fatiguing, yet I know I liked it all, the prominent part I had to play, the pretty dresses to wear, the compliments to listen to . . . I feel how frivolous it makes me." For all her disapproval, Agnes was susceptible to being "petted" or flattered, and she must have been jubilant when Macdonald returned to power in September 1878.

Agnes was only forty-two, a little stouter and much wiser. "I was over-confident, vain & presumptuous in my sense of power," she confessed to her diary. "I fancied I could do too much & I failed – signally. I am more humble now." Humility is not a word Agnes's contemporaries would have used to describe her, and she and John divided their spheres of influence into public and private: John would be boss in the House, Agnes in the house.

"My lord and master who in his private capacity simply lives to please and gratify me to the utmost extent of his power, is *absolutely* tyrannical in his public life so far as I am concerned," she told a friend. "If I interfere in any sort of way he will be annoyed, and more, he will be 'disinclined.' I know him *so* well!"

Agnes loved to play "lady" to Macdonald's "lord," and as Lady Macdonald she defined the powerful, yet subservient role of prime minister's wife with a force that kept it intact, like a piece of Victorian crockery, for a hundred years. Agnes never uttered a political opinion in public, although she had plenty in private, but for the next thirteen years she was the acknowledged arbiter of taste and morals in the "sub-Arctic lumber village" that was Canada's capital.

Agnes's dominion was her home, Earnscliffe, a lovely stone house (now the residence of the British high commissioner) overlooking the Ottawa River that Macdonald bought in 1882. Earnscliffe cost more than Macdonald could afford, but Agnes "*coaxed hard*" and John gave in; Agnes then spent $7,000 renovating, starting a trend that would later get out of control at public expense. John didn't give a fig where he lived as long as he had a quiet room, a desk and a pile of books, and Agnes furnished Earnscliffe simply, at least by late-Victorian Gothic Revival standards. The Macdonalds were no longer poor; Conservative supporters had raised a testimonial fund of $68,000 to care for Agnes and Mary in the event of John's death, and Agnes's future was secure.

Earnscliffe was Agnes's fortress; she learned to entertain with energy and efficiency, if not imagination: the Macdonalds hosted a dinner for Conservative MPs every Saturday night, preceded by an open-house buffet, and Agnes was "at home" to the ladies Wednesday afternoons. Macdonald's colleagues, secretaries and cronies were constantly coming and going and his aging, eccentric sister Louisa often came to stay. The Macdonalds tried to live frugally – they kept chickens and a cow – but during the sessions Agnes spent from $700 to $1000 a month, according to her records, a huge amount for a small family, indicating that the money went on wine and liquor and the cost of serving elaborate five-course meals to hundreds of guests. Agnes was always in debt to the butcher and sometimes had to borrow a dollar or two from her servants, Oswald and Julia; she had a part-time cleaning woman and sent her laundry out to be washed. Her account books note $25 loans from Sir Leonard Tilley, a close friend of Macdonald; the prime minister of Canada was apparently obliged to hustle enough money to get him through the month, and Agnes scrupulously paid the money back.

At home, Agnes was free to express whatever opinions she had. "I was never an extremely strong party spirit," she said, "never one of those truly admirable women who believe one side can never be right & the other never be wrong." Agnes's judgments were strictly personal: "I have a horribly weak spot for Laurier!" she confessed. "I wish with all my heart he were in our camp, soul and body, as he might be – he is millions too good for the others." Wilfrid Laurier, alas, was a Liberal. As for her husband's friend Mackenzie Bowell: "I never liked him and he never liked me." Protective of John's status and defensive about his "weakness," Agnes tended to isolate Macdonald from the younger, more bohemian members of the Conservative Party, often bright and capable men, and to surround him instead with teetotalling old warhorses from Confederation days. Did Macdonald, who had once spent so many happy hours in the drunken democracy of saloons, find Agnes's social conventions claustrophobic, or was he secretly jealous of the younger men? Macdonald never groomed a successor, and he did not object to becoming the "Old Chief," the hero of a personality cult, encouraged by Agnes, that made him a legend long before his death.

The centre of Agnes's sphere of influence, the hub around which her family revolved, was Mary. Mary was now in her teens, a big girl, but severely hunched and confined to a wheelchair. Mary would never walk, although she made agonizing attempts with iron leg braces, and her arms were so severely twisted she was unable to feed or dress herself. Mary's head was enlarged, but she was not as intellectually handicapped as it had at first been assumed. Like her father, whose curly hair she inherited, Mary was a sociable personality who loved stories, simple games and picnics. She spoke with great difficulty, but she could comprehend what was said and respond to questions or express her feelings in other ways. She learned to spell, and could eventually peck out short notes on a tiny typewriter.

Mary's surprising progress was due to her parents' acceptance of her as she was, and their determination to make her life as complete and happy as possible. Mary was nicely, even elaborately, dressed and liked to have her picture taken; she was introduced to the Macdonalds' visitors and invited to all the childrens' parties, where she easily made friends. The Macdonalds spared no expense to make sure Mary had the best of care; she was constantly accompanied by a nurse, a servant, her mother, or all three. Accustomed to anxious attention, Mary, like any spoiled child, became something of a tyrant; when she felt bored or neglected she caught cold and had to be fussed over. Mary's strong-willed, demanding personality must have reminded John of his mother, her invalidism of Isabella.

John hid his memories and disappointment under a mask of teasing; he treated Mary almost as a pet – his nickname for her was "Baboo" – writing her funny notes, telling her stories, showing her off. Agnes was the opposite: Agnes suffered Mary. She displayed her "crippled, helpless child" as a beggar would wave a crutch. Mary was Agnes's penance, her burden, another *home cross* to bear. Agnes's *Pieta* performance would be an onerous burden for future wives, yet Agnes's charity began, and ended, at home. After Mary's birth, Agnes dropped the one charity she reluctantly patronized, the Protestant Orphans' Home. It was years before Agnes would leave Mary for more than a day at a time; many more years before determined little Mary finally freed herself from her mother's suffocating grasp.

Agnes found her own freedom the summer she turned fifty. She loved travelling by train in the prime minister's luxurious private car, *Jamaica*, and in 1885 Agnes was one of the first tourists to ride the new Canadian Pacific Railway to Banff. The following summer she persuaded John, now rather indifferent to the great railway he had brought into being, to make an inaugural trip to Vancouver. The CPR provided every attention, including the company of an obsequious superintendent, a man Agnes calls only "Mr. E."

Agnes spent most of the trip on a folding chair on the rear platform of *Jamaica*, soaking up the retreating scenery with enthusiasm, but by the time the train entered the Rockies she was tired of seeing everything disappearing down a telescope. When the train stopped at Luggan Station, just below the Great Divide, she got out and walked up to the front to stretch her legs. A huge, snorting black engine was getting up steam to pull the train through the Rockies. Mr. E. invited Agnes to inspect the monster; Agnes was delighted:

"From the instant my eyes rested on the broad shining surface of its buffer-beam and cowcatcher, over which a bright little flag waved from a glossy brass pole, I decided to travel there and nowhere else for the remaining 600 miles of my journey!"

Her enthusiasm was not shared: "When I announced my desire to travel on the cowcatcher," Agnes wrote, "Mr. E seemed to think that a very bad job indeed. He used many ineffectual persuasions to induce me to abandon the idea, and almost said that I should not run so great a risk; but at last he so far relented as to ask what I proposed using as a seat. Glancing around the station platform, I beheld a small, empty candle-box lying near, and at once declared that was 'just the thing.' Before Mr. E could expostulate further, I had asked the brakeman to place the candlebox on the buffer-beam and was on my way to *Jamaica* to ask the Chief's permission. The Chief, seated on a low chair on the rear platform of the car, with a rug over his knees and a magazine in his hand, looked very comfortable and content. Hearing my request, after a moment's thought he pronounced the idea 'rather ridiculous' then remembered it was dangerous as well, and finally asked if I was sure I could hold on. Before the words were well out of his lips, and taking permission for granted by the question, I was again standing by the cowcatcher, admiring the position of the candle-box and anxiously asking to be helped on."

Macdonald was obviously resigned to giving Agnes her own way as long as it got her out of his hair, and the prospect of his wife falling into the Fraser canyon apparently did not alarm him.

"Behold me now," she crowed, "enthroned on the candlebox, with a soft felt hat well over my eyes, and a linen carriage cover tucked around me from waist to foot. Mr. E has seated himself on the other side of the headlight. I turn to him, peeping around the headlight, with my best smile. 'This is *lovely*,' I triumphantly announce, see that a word of comfort is necessary, '*quite lovely*; I shall travel on this cowcatcher from summit to sea!'

"Mr. Superintendent, in his turn, peeps around the headlight and surveys me with solemn and resigned surprise. 'I suppose – you – will,' he says slowly, and I see that he is hoping, at any rate, that I shall live to do it!"

The engine hurtled down the side of the canyon, Agnes and Mr. E. suspended in mid-air above the rapids of the Kicking Horse River. Agnes was exhilarated: "The river, widening, grows white with dashing foam, and rushes downwards with tremendous force. Sunlight flashes on glaciers, into gorges and athwart huge, towering masses of rock crowned with magnificent tree crests. Breathless – almost awe-stricken – but with a wild triumph in my heart, I look from the farthest mountain peak, lifted high before me, to the shining pebbles at my feet! Warm wind rushes past; a thousand sunshine colours dance in the air. With a firm right hand grasping the iron stanchion, and my feet planted on the bufferbeam, there was not a yard of that descent in which I faltered for a moment."

When the train stopped at Palliser, "the Chief and his friends all walked up to the cowcatcher to make a morning call. I felt a little 'superior' and was rather condescending. Somewhat flushed with excitement, but still anxious to be polite, I asked 'would the Chief step up and take a drive?' To the horror of the bystanders he carelessly consented, and in another moment had taken the place of Mr. E, the latter seating himself at our feet on the buffer-beam. There was a general consternation – the Chief rushing through the flats of the Columbia on a cowcatcher! Everyone is horrified. It is a comfort to the other occupant of the buffer to find someone else wilful, and as we steamed away towards Donald, at the eastern base of the Selkirks, I felt not so bad after all!"

Macdonald alighted at the next station, relieved to return to his chair on the rear platform, but Agnes rode on, heart pounding, cheeks flushed, as the train rocketed over the precarious trestle bridges of the Roger's Pass:

"Over Surprise Creek the trestle is 180 feet high, but I peeped down into it quite unconcernedly, not without a certain satisfaction to find I had such a 'good head.' At Stoney Creek the trestle is 286 feet above a most glorious ravine. The effect was here much heightened by huge, vapoury smoke-clouds hanging in fantastic shapes about the immense valley, and a certain vagueness of distant, misty outline which, in the warm, tender evening light, was inexpressibly beautiful."

The danger of flying debris and the train crew's stories of men killed along the tracks only excited Agnes, and she rode the cowcatcher from 8 a.m. to 8 p.m. every day, insisting that the train stop at night so she wouldn't miss a thing. She refused to come down when they encountered a forest fire, "and a very new and very hot sensation it certainly was to fly through a bush fire on a cowcatcher, as we did, with bent heads and closely-gathered skirts, to avoid breathing the heated air or catching fire." Nor was she deterred by dark tunnels:

"During a halt I am told that one of the tunnels is 'wet.' This means that the arching rock is full of springs which pour on the train as it passes. An umbrella and waterproof are therefore necessary for me – now sole occupant of the cowcatcher – and with praiseworthy economy I take off my hat, tuck it safely under my wraps, and prepare to encounter the 'wet' tunnel thus equipped! We plunge into a few moments' darkness – water splashing and dripping on every side – and as we emerge into sunlight again, and stop just beyond the tunnel, I see a party of young English sportsmen standing near the roadside . . . Just imagine the feelings with which these well-regulated young men beheld a lady, bareheaded and with an umbrella, seated in front of an engine, at the mouth of a tunnel in the Gold Range of British Columbia! I am sorely afraid I laughed outright at the blank amazement of their rosy faces and longed to tell them what fun it was; but not being 'introduced, you know,' I contented myself with acknowledging their presence by a solemn little bow – which was quite irresistible under the circumstances!"

Since the prime minister did nothing to restrain his wife, Agnes was left, no doubt with some satisfaction, to her fate, and while she had some dizzy moments when she was afraid she would lose her grip, she survived the trip unscatched. As far as Macdonald was concerned, Agnes could do her thing and be damned, and he was equally indifferent to the jeopardy in which he placed the train crew, who risked their jobs and faced criminal prosecution had the prime minister or his wife been injured. Both John and Agnes loved a good caper, preferably at someone else's expense, and Agnes's wild ride – the eroticism would have thrilled Freud – symbolized a subtle power shift: Agnes was prepared to use her clout as the prime minister's wife to indulge a personal whim, and the prime minister would allow her to do it.

Macdonald was now over seventy, weary, worn out, plagued by chronic illness variously diagnosed as "gout," "liver" or "catarrh of the stomach." It was now John's turn to become the invalid while Agnes played the nurse, a role that admirably suited her and gave her formidable influence over John's political activities. Jealously guarded by Agnes, Macdonald refused to retire; he had been an MP for nearly fifty years, prime minister for more than twenty, and he seemed invincible. However, he collapsed with bronchitis during an exhausting election in the winter of 1891, and he had hardly recovered when he suffered a stroke. A second, massive stroke at the end of May left him paralyzed and at 10 p.m. on June 6, 1891, with Agnes holding his hand, he quietly slipped away.

Macdonald's death precipitated another summersault in Agnes's fortunes: she was elevated to the peerage as Baroness Macdonald of Earnscliffe, then she ran away.

John was hardly cold in his grave when Agnes packed up Mary and hopped on a train for the Banff Springs Hotel. There, swathed in yards of black crêpe, Baroness Macdonald worked on her new role as the grieving widow. Stout, strong and imperious, Agnes made a formidable widow. Even her appearance was intimidating: her hair was now snow white, a striking contrast to her dark skin, and her big, bulldog jaw was stubbornly set. Baroness Macdonald demanded, and got, respect. She also got cheap rates and other "attentions" because Baroness Macdonald was always broke.

Macdonald left Agnes well provided for. In addition to the Conservative trust fund, there was a marriage settlement and an insurance policy. Agnes also had an inheritance from her mother, and after Hewitt's death in 1893, the remnants of the Bernard estate. The press pegged Agnes's fortune at $200,000; she denied it, but it was enough to provide her with about $9,000 a year, a very comfortable income in an age when respectable men raised large families on $1,500. John also left Agnes Earnscliffe,

The Baroness, a white-haired old witch with reactionary opinions, would
eventually abandon Canada for England, Switzerland and the Riviera.

expecting, no doubt, that she would continue to live there quietly with
Mary.

Agnes had other ideas. Baroness Macdonald preferred hotels, *de luxe*
hotels where the food was delicious, the service sycophantic and the guest
list impeccable; in a hotel Agnes could escape the drudgery of housekeeping, which she found laborious, and the anxiety of entertaining, at which
she was awkward. In a hotel she could be entertained in the congenial
company of people of her social class, to whom she could feel oh so slightly
superior.

Agnes soon discovered that there *were* no people of her social class in
North America; Agnes was the only peeress on the continent, not to
mention the only widow of a prime minister. She also discovered that
being a baroness was a very expensive privilege; most peers were rich –
titles were sold to vulgar men who made it big in thread, coal or, in
Canada, railways – and Agnes's moderate inheritance left her feeling like a
country cousin, a feeling she knew, and resented. She threatened to get rid
of the title – ''How the very *word* Baroness annoys me!'' she wrote to
Joseph Pope – but she delighted too much in signing herself ''Macdonald

of Earnscliffe'' in letters to friends to give it up. Instead, Macdonald of Earnscliffe came to the conclusion that she was poor; the widow would not only grieve, she would use her widowhood to extort every possible advantage from her situation.

Agnes's first victim was Eliza Kirkup, who, with Agnes's permission, had preserved one of Macdonald's funeral wreaths and exhibited it in her shop window. A $150 bill from Miss Kirkup for preserving the wreath provoked a barrage of furious letters from Agnes to Joe Pope: ''I should like Miss Kirkup to know that her conduct in writing to ask for an order when she intended to ask such a ridiculous price, as well as exposing the wreath without permission was simply disgraceful . . . I should like you in any future correspondence you have with this woman to tell her how much annoyed I was at this vulgar and impertinent advertisement.'' Poor Miss Kirkup got $75.

These are not the words of a woman prostrated by grief; Agnes was angry. Her sudden flight from Ottawa seems to have been provoked by blind, destructive rage: Earnscliffe was rented out, first to the new prime minister, Sir John Abbott – Agnes soon complained that he hadn't paid in full for the wine and coal he used – and then to strangers, although all of the Macdonalds' furniture and personal possessions remained in the house, prey to damage, loss and theft. Agnes also walked away from their summer home at Rivière du Loup, leaving it full of furniture, books and papers; she left valuable silver everywhere – a small log cabin she had built in Banff was abandoned to the porcupines complete with a sterling tea service. Fortunately Joe Pope grabbed Macdonald's papers, but Agnes took not the slightest interest in Pope's memoir of Sir John and politely refused to read his manuscript.

Agnes was gone for good. She spent the winter in a New Jersey sanitorium where Hewitt was dying, and most of the next year at the Hotel Dallas in Victoria, British Columbia, where she quarrelled with her old friends, snubbed new ones and sank into a blue funk of neuralgia, insomnia and self-pity. ''I lead a very regular life, almost that of an invalid, as I am almost,'' she wrote to Pope. ''I feel very homesick here – it is very far away. We keep so entirely to ourselves that I have ample leisure for thinking over the past and dwelling on all that had best be forgotten but which can never be forgotten by me as long as life lasts . . . as usual I say very little about it but try in my own poor way to do what I think Sir J. would like until we meet again.''

Agnes, as usual, was doing what *she* would like: in June 1893, two years after John's death, Agnes sailed for England, where she finally found her peers. Taken up out of obligation or curiosity by Macdonald's old friends among the Lords, Agnes, her mendicant widow's role well rehearsed, settled into a trivial, *fin de siècle* round of Mayfair dinners and country weekends, none of which she could afford to reciprocate, and camped out in an endless succession of hotels, boarding-houses, villas and spas, none of which was satisfactory. Agnes always travelled first class, with a companion for Mary, a courier and a maid, and she always complained about the cost:

"I shall not go out at all this season," she wrote self-righteously to Pope, the youngest and most patient of the trustees of Macdonald's estate. "The late hours bore me horribly . . . I want to keep in and not waste money."

In England, Agnes reverted to her role of "insignificant spinster," although she was no longer young or insignificant. At heart she was still Susy Bernard, the girl who forty years before had shared the rootless sisterhood of boarding-houses with her widowed mother. Agnes was the widowed mother now, and, like Isabella, she would choose to spend the rest of her life in the society of women. Many of them were servants: Agnes always judged people by their attentiveness to her. It was as if Agnes had married to become a widow: her widow's weeds, like a nun's habit, protected her from ever having to bow again to a man's will.

Why was Agnes so hostile? Did she feel that John, by dying, had destroyed her life? Or did his death release her repressed anger at his drinking, his power, his age? Did it revive the betrayal and abandonment she had felt when her father died? Why, except for her title – it was *hers* after all – did Agnes eventually sever every association with her dead husband?

Agnes, for all her confessional writing, was seldom frank about her motives, and very narcissistic. She strikes poses in her photographs, and in her diary she writes about herself as if she were a character in a play, Agnes observing Agnes. This dissociation is also evident in her observations of John: "How many times a day, think you, when the sun is warm & bright in summer days, do I see the grey suited man's figure in a slouched grey hat, standing on the wide veranda at Rivière du Loup?" she wrote to Pope after Macdonald's death. "It has its hands in its pockets and its kind cheerful face is turned to the blue sea and the blue mountains and all the rest is a green, still picture & we are *so* happy!'' There is a peculiar distance about this little cameo: it is a view from across the room, the view of a secretary or visitor, and although Agnes is talking about a vision, the use of ''it'' rather than ''he'' is chilling. For all her protestations of happiness, whatever bargain Agnes made with John seems not to have engaged her heart.

In 1900 Agnes sold Earnscliffe for a song – she claimed her memories were too painful to live there – and instructed the caretaker to remove only her own personal belongings: Bernard family silver and memorabilia, Mary's childhood toys and an odd assortment of blankets, snowshoes, crutches and a case of stuffed birds. These things were squirrelled away in various parts of Ottawa, including Joseph Pope's attic: Pope's inventory lists only one item, a dressing case, belonging to John. Macdonald's huge library was dismantled and sold – Agnes had so little interest in reading she begged Pope *not* to send her magazines – and everything else in the house was put up for sale at public auction: hordes of scavenging souvenir hunters descended on Earnscliffe and carried off Macdonald's most intimate personal possessions, including the bed in which he died.

Agnes made only $18,000 from the sale of the house and contents, but she could hardly have found a more effective way of insulting her beloved husband's memory, wounding his friends and snubbing his family: Hugh received only a few fragments of his father's possessions. Agnes's *auto-da-fé* at Earnscliffe effectively ended her association with Canada. Baroness Macdonald now spent the social season in London, the spring in Switzerland and wintered in Italy or the south of France.

''One can live more cheaply on the continent, although it is an exile,'' she wrote smugly to Pope from the *de luxe* Le Grand Hotel in Cannes. ''No one feels it more than we do.''

Truthfully, Agnes loved the Riviera. For years she rented villas in Alassio or San Remo where the ''old, broken-down invalid'' – actually a woman in her sixties who walked five miles a day – entertained a constant stream of friends and relatives with picnics, sight-seeing trips and long hikes through the hills. Agnes used black-edged notepaper for ten years after Macdonald's death, but she was too restless and easily bored to be the recluse she claimed. The hypocrisy of Agnes's poor wandering widow pose is revealed in a letter to Pope from Cannes in March 1901, two months after Queen Victoria's death:

"I find myself repaid for the great expense & trouble & anxiety of leaving England by the renewal of my health. The warmer drier air & sunshine & the congenial outdoor life have worked wonders & my cough is gone & Mary is doing remarkably well. My health was, of course, my first consideration for Mary's dear sake, & I *had* to leave England, but in any case I found as a Peeress & with my husband's great name I could not live there on my income. Cannes, you will say is a very expensive place. So it is, but I know no one and intend to know no one here. We live the quietest possible life and *very* carefully, only enjoying the place & its lovely surroundings . . .

"I spent a day with Lady Derby at Beaulieu last month. I have also been to Monte Carlo with the Morrows & Swinyards – all old friends. Please don't imagine *I play*. I am never tempted but think Monte Carlo a horrid place and the Casino a great bore . . . I do all I can to keep out of the way of prominence & expense – the Coronation will, however, be an immense temptation. Fancy I should have a Peeress' seat!"

The coronation of King Edward VII was a temptation Agnes had no intention of resisting. "I had made up my mind to turn my back on all the fuss, which for me has *no* attraction," she wrote to Pope in May, "but so many, in fact all my friends seemed to think I ought to go. The 1st 'Canadian Peeress' – they rang the changes on it – so I am going, if I am summoned, which no doubt I shall be. Summons for Peers and Peeresses come last of all, being signed by *the King's own hand*.

"My costume is in hand – crimson velvet, boddice & train, petticoat of frilled chiffon & Irish lace, train & robe trimmed with miniver fur – all *most* costly – alas! I fitted on a coronet Friday. How the wheel goes round! A small Creole child without a shilling brought to this mighty island, quite unknown & unnoticed, and here I am among the first at the Coronation of Kings! It seems so strange & undeserved a revolution, where others who were brought over as I was & at the same time are, so to speak, nowhere still! But of course every phase of life is ordered and willed and I owe *all* to the great man who made me his wife."

Agnes closes her gleeful letter with a familiar plaint: "Meantime the expenses of being here [in London] at this season are very great and I write to know if I may have a little more money? Our rooms are more expensive, and tho' I decline *all* evening invitations & never leave cards, go near the opera or any such extravagant place, I still find I am too well known now to get on absolutely without a little more cash."

Agnes was stingy and selfish; it didn't occur to her that her niece Dora, an impoverished widow with a young family, might have used some of the furnishings from Earnscliffe – everything that wasn't sold rotted away in storage until it was eventually thrown out. Yet she spent lavishly on Mary and herself. Accustomed to John digging into the bottomless pockets of the Conservative Party to silence her "coaxing," Agnes viewed her bank account as a pocket that mysteriously filled up as soon as she took money out. After a while the pocket stopped filling up – Agnes's monthly cheques were late, she received no statements and her trust fund seemed to be shrinking. Panicky, Agnes decided to transfer her estate to the Royal Trust Company in Montreal, a reasonable move since none of her trustees was a banker, but her request precipitated an acrimonious fourteen-year squabble that estranged Agnes from her last friend, Joe Pope.

Unhappily Agnes was right: her trustees had been negligent and her affairs were in a mess – valuable CPR stock had been sold at a serious loss, the revenue from the sale of Earnscliffe earned less in interest than the rent the house had paid, and her lawyer had embezzled $4,000. Typically, Agnes vented her fury on the man who did his best to sort it out, Pope: when Pope told Agnes that he had sold Macdonald's papers to the archives for $5,000, thinking she would be grateful, she exploded: How dare he *sell* John's papers! He should *give* them to the nation! Fortunately the sale went through, but Agnes cut Pope dead with a cruel letter, ending an association that went back thirty years. She also upbraided Hugh when he drank heavily after his only son died: the violence of Agnes's reaction to Hugh's "dreadful sin" hints at the repugnance she must have felt for John's "sin."

Agnes always placed responsibility for her actions on someone else; now Mary was the excuse for Agnes's self-indulgence. Agnes could never leave her "crippled, helpless child," and Mary required amusement, fresh air, a warm climate, sunny rooms and "the best of everything." In fact, while Agnes was entertaining in the drawing-room upstairs, Mary was usually with the servants downstairs. Mary, now over thirty, an odd, doll-like figure in her wheelchair, was not the kind of daughter Agnes could take into fashionable society, and Mary was perfectly happy to be with simple people who talked frankly to her. Mary hated being carried around the continent like a steamer trunk, surrounded by gawking strangers who spoke a language she couldn't understand; she loved the English seaside resorts of Ramsgate and Brighton where she could sit on the boardwalk

Baroness Macdonald of Earnscliffe, with Mary. Never again would she bow to a man's will.

in her chair and watch crowds of people who were just as freakish as she was. Agnes *loathed* Ramsgate and Brighton.

Mary rebelled; she developed such "very *fixed* ways and wishes" that Agnes left her more and more with her paid companion, Sarah Coward, who understood Mary with a subtlety Agnes, with her own rigid ideas and conventional attitudes, could not. With Coward's help Mary's speech improved and she developed independence; Mary knew she would always be a child, but she was no longer a baby, or "Baboo."

As the lights went out on the British Empire, aging Baroness Macdonald became an anachronism of London society, a monument to be visited, like the Sphinx, a fat, white-haired old witch with beady black eyes and reactionary opinions, especially on the vote for women, which she strenuously opposed. Caught in Switzerland when war broke out in 1914, Agnes, with her customary idiosyncrasy, fled to her villa in Italy. She and Mary did not return to England until the spring of 1920, when they took rooms in a boarding-house in the seaside resort of Eastbourne. Eighty-four, Agnes was failing; her friends and friendships were all dead, and Canadians thought *she* was dead.

In late summer Agnes suffered a stroke that left her paralyzed; she slipped into a coma and died on September 5, 1920. Agnes was buried in Eastbourne, half a world away from John, her "strong Heart's devotion." She left almost nothing: her small Bernard inheritance went to two great-nieces and everything else to Mary.

Mary was fifty-one, resourceful and bright enough to write a wistful little letter to Joseph Pope: "I should like to have news of some of the people whom I knew when we were all at Earnscliffe . . . what has become of Sarah who was my nurse when I was a little girl?" Leaving Ottawa had not been Mary's idea – being uprooted from her familiar surroundings so soon after her father's death must have been terrifying – but she would never return. In 1933 Mary Macdonald died in Hove, near Brighton, cared for her by her devoted friend and companion of twenty-eight years, Sarah Coward.

CHAPTER 5

The Love Affair of Annie and John Thompson

A COLD WIND off Bedford Basin whips spray against Annie's face. She pulls her hood back and lifts her head to its salty sting, laughing with the pleasure of it. Annie Affleck would run away to sea if she were a boy, but the best she can do is to walk out on the winter nights when the wind billows her cape like the sail of a pirate ship scudding before a storm. How far has she walked tonight? Miles and miles, and not another soul to be seen in Halifax on such a night! Annie's cheeks feel numb and the rain is running in icy rivulets through her hair. Never mind, she is calmer now and the walk has warmed her up. At home she will have her tea and dry her hair by the fire. Home is more *bearable* when she has been out for a while.

As Annie turns up Gottingen St. she hears footsteps behind her, light steps, shoes, not sailors' boots. Sailors go about together and make a lot of noise. Annie quickens her stride.

"A harsh night, Miss Affleck," a man's voice says beside her. "May I see you to your door?"

Annie shrugs and sticks her nose in the air. Out of the corner of her eye she catches a glimpse of a boy about her own height with a thin, white face and deep-set dark eyes. How did he know her name? She turns and looks at him. The boy smiles shyly and tips his hat. Water trickles off the brim and runs up his coat sleeve. He pretends not to notice.

"John Thompson," he blurts out, making a little bow. "I, I mean we, my family, I live just up the street, number 95. I pass your house every day."

Uninvited, Thompson falls into step beside her. Annie pulls her hood up. She feels resentful. She has seen Thompson on the street. She has paid him no mind. She pays him no mind now.

"What brings you out in such a storm?" he asks.

And what business is it of yours? Annie wants to retort, but she bites her tongue. The Sisters of Charity tell her she has to restrain her saucy ways now that she is twenty-one and a *lady*, but who says being a lady means suffering impertinence?

"I may ask the same of you," she says tartly.

The boy blushes and looks at his shoes. Annie is embarrassed. She didn't mean to suggest anything *improper*.

"It was a rude question, I'm sorry," Thompson says. "Asking rude questions is my profession, poor as I am at it. Sometimes I forget that not everyone is a criminal."

A criminal! Annie's ears perk up. Maybe this Thompson is more interesting than he looks, although he is the most unlikely looking little excuse for a policeman she could ever imagine. He is an even more unlikely looking lawyer, although that is what he claims to be and Annie, to tell the truth, has never met a lawyer before. By the time they arrive at Annie's door it is clear to her that Thompson is a gentleman at least, and well spoken, so when he asks if he may call the following evening she tosses her head and says yes, he may, if he has nothing better to do, and flounces in, feeling in much better spirits than she had when she left.

If anyone had told Annie Affleck on that cold November night in 1866 that she was falling in love with a future prime minister, she would have laughed until she cried. John Sparrow David Thompson, for all the sonority of his name, was an impoverished twenty-one-year-old Halifax lawyer who supplemented his meagre income by taking shorthand. A short, silent young man with a low, broad forehead and a thick-lipped sensual mouth, Thompson looked, in the words of one contemporary, "like a country butcher dressed for a wedding." Yet Thompson's stolid appearance concealed a quick, disciplined mind, biting wit and an inferno of anxious energy that would make him prime minister at the age of forty-seven, and kill him two years later.

Had anyone told Annie that she would one day be Lady Thompson, she would have laughed even harder. Annie was a ship captain's daughter, the eldest of the eight children of James and Catherine Affleck. The Afflecks were decent, respectable Roman Catholics who valued education enough to send their daughters to a convent school, and like other Maritimers of their class, they were proud, blunt-spoken and contemptuous of pretence or affectation. At twenty-one, Annie's future was clear – she would marry another poor, proud, decent Catholic and raise a lot of poor, proud, decent children. And she did, in her own way, as Lady Thompson, the wife of Canada's first Catholic prime minister.

Annie was exceptional: intelligent, ambitious, self-confident and beautiful. She had languorous hooded eyes, a classic profile, a Cupid's bow mouth and a small, round chin; her skin was alabaster and her thick, wavy hair shone like burnished gold. No matter that Annie Affleck talked like a fishwife, John Sparrow David Thompson fell hopelessly in love.

Annie knew her worth, and she wasn't going to be bowled over by some sprig in a dark suit. Thompson's siege lasted three years. Six months, from June to December 1867, are chronicled in Annie's diary. By coincidence, Annie's diary parallels Agnes Macdonald's: in the Confederation summer of 1867, Annie was nine years younger than Agnes, single and living in Nova Scotia, a province that did not embrace a united Canada without violent opposition. Annie's cynical attitude is a dramatic contrast to Agnes's enthusiasm:

"Monday 1st July. Our first day as Canada. The Union of the Colonies was celebrated in a very lame manner although I suppose the Confederationists will trumpet it in the most graphic manner. The bells rang or tolled just as you please and a few weak guns were fired. I staid in the house and sewed all day. The day was very warm and dusty. Thompson came in the evening around about 7 o'clock. I put on my hat and we strolled out on the common. The programme said there would be fireworks. We looked and I saw about a 1/2 dozen fire rockets and there was about one dozen spectators. The archbishop had his residence illuminated in quite a grand way and a band playing on top of the house – quite a crowd were collected there – the Asylum looked very well – the Province Building had a few candles half on in a few of the windows and a tar barrel burning on the Parade – a smoky procession of the fire brigade – home about 1/2 past 10 feeling very tired."

Annie's laconic tone reflects her unromantic attitude to life: nobody was going to put one over on Annie Affleck. Thompson, an innocent intellectual, must have found Annie's street-smart sarcasm both shocking and stimulating, and no doubt he perceived very quickly that it was a pose; Annie's cool, careless manner concealed a sensitive, sensual woman whose emotions were deep and explosive. In the privacy of her diary, Annie's suppressed desires often expressed themselves as the "blues": "Felt wretched, sick and blue," she wrote the day before her twenty-second birthday. "Got home about 1 o'clock, laid down and cried myself to sleep." No Shadow oppressed Annie; she just had a good bawl.

The main reason for Annie's blues in the summer of 1867 was the persistent attentions of John Thompson and his arch rival, O'Flaherty. O'Flaherty – Annie never uses his first name – seems to have been first on the scene and his name suggests he had the advantage of being Catholic; Thompson had the almost fatal flaw of being a Methodist. Protestant-Catholic courtships were scandalous in the 1860s, and it's a tribute to the Afflecks' tolerance, and Thompson's charm, that he got in the door at all. A lawyer, however, was not to be sneezed at, and Thompson cleverly disarmed suspicion by pretending to be Annie's tutor: "Thompson in and we had our french and shorthand," Annie writes on June 22. "So ends the day."

Annie worked seriously at her lessons and was eventually able to read and write both French and shorthand with considerable proficiency; the Afflecks never suspected that shorthand was the Trojan horse Thompson would use to carry off their daughter. First he pitched his tent in the Afflecks' front parlour; he came in almost every evening, Saturdays, and Sundays after mass. The presence of the ubiquitous young tutor caused trouble with O'Flaherty: "Thompson in for a short time," Annie writes on Thursday, July 4. "O'F came in the evening and we made up friends, for how long I do not know."

Annie became almost paralyzed with anxiety: "Energy, life, resolution, ambition, strength, I am without any of them now. I seem to live one day after another neither useful in this world nor preparing for the next." On Tuesday she returned from an evening walk to find O'Flaherty waiting in the parlour.

"I felt strangely weak, a powerless feeling as if – well it is no use talking. He talks in riddles. And then where was my tongue? What did he mean I cannot understand. Was it a test of will? Speak I could not if my life depended on it. Surprise took away all power of acting. I went to the door with him and said good night as usual – after he had gone I would have given worlds for ten minutes talk with him."

Did she reject his clumsy proposal? O'Flaherty was angry enough to want to make Annie jealous by walking out with another woman. The next night, when Annie was out with Thompson: "About 9 o'clock we met O'F with ———. Well I came home and said or tried to say my french. Well how my face burns when I think and I will never forget what's more. He said he would be in tomorrow night. I doubt it very much.

Will it be always the same? Will I always be getting into ———. Well never mind, you cannot help it now.''

Annie's jealousy of O'Flaherty wasn't lost on Thompson. The next day, when he should have been at work, he seems to have lingered outside her house. When Annie started out for a walk at four o'clock, she ''met Thompson on the way and he came with me, the air lovely, everything looked so green and fresh. Home again about 1/2 past 6 – on our way we met O'F and he bowed. Well that bow said a great deal. I thought that perhaps he would have been in this evening but no – the triumph is his now sure enough.

''Thompson came in about 9 o'clock. We had our french lesson. So ends this day. And now not another word about O'F. He has had the best of it. He acted his part well and now I suppose is enjoying his revenge. But let him rest now out of my mind altogether, he that I would of once dared anything for. So much for friendship.''

Annie blames O'Flaherty for causing the breach, but she went walking with Thompson. Annie had instinctively made up her mind, and her relationship with her young Pygmalion now became an understanding: ''Friday, July 12th, 1867 – a quiet, hazy sort of day and evening. Thompson came in about 1/2 past 7. I felt weak and dull. Put on my hat and we walked out to the cemetery up on the hill and stood and talked until nearly dark. Talked quietly and gravely. Home about 9 o'clock. Said our french and he was very kind.''

Like most suitors, Thompson probably talked about himself. He was in no position to propose marriage, and Annie was in no hurry to exchange the sewing, sweeping and scrubbing of her life at home for more of the same. ''We had rather an argument – about wifely submission,'' Annie writes on August 2. It's not hard to guess who won that one. Then, on August 28, ''we talked about work and a woman's position.'' Thompson had awakened Annie's mind; she began to brood about her position in life and how she could better herself. Annie was by no means reconciled to a life of dutiful obedience – she will run the Thompson household like a sergeant-major – and she was asking astute questions about her limited options before making her choice: years later a snobbish rumour would circulate that Lady Thompson had once worked in a shop, and she probably did. She spent more time reading and writing; her punctuation and penmanship improved and she devoured the latest books by Macauley,

Dickens, George Eliot and Washington Irving. Thompson had excellent taste in literature; he read all the great Victorian novels hot off the press.

Annie and Thompson spent the hot summer nights talking by the open window or going for long, moonlight walks around the Common; on weekends they took the streetcar out to Bedford or rowed on the Northwest Arm. "I never spent a pleasanter afternoon," Annie confesses after one excursion. The lovers spent every spare hour together but officially they were still "friends," and Annie wasn't above hedging her bets: "Thompson came in and soon after O'F. We played whist. Thompson went about 1/2 past ten. O'F staid a few minutes longer. I felt queer and excited. I could not say what I wanted to. He asked me if we were not as good friends as usual. I said yes, although the word almost choaked me. I would have given almost anything if I could of said what I wanted to but pride would not let me and now in spite of myself I must go on acting but it cannot last much longer."

O'Flaherty laid a counter-siege, but Thompson was invariably on the scene when he called and neither would budge. What was Annie to do? "Thompson and O'Flaherty in and we played whist" becomes an almost nightly refrain in Annie's diary. What a wonderful scene: a tiny, dark parlour, a coal-oil lamp casting a pool of light on the card table, Annie's sister Johanna acting as chaperone and fourth hand and Annie, her golden ringlets fresh from the curling iron, trying to make conversation while her two angry young suitors glare at each other across the table. The strain began to tell: "Thompson in about 1/4 to 8 and we were just going to have a quiet chat when O'F arrived," she writes on August 24. "Played whist and we were beaten. Felt tired and cross, my head ached and everything went wrong." Annie and Thompson had a fight and Annie fell into a blue funk: "Went into chapel and said a few prayers and had a good cry –felt better after that."

Unassuming little Thompson now showed the bold tactical skill that separates prime ministers from O'Flahertys: "Thompson in and we talked until 9 o'clock," Annie writes on September 5. "Then he went–it is the first time that he has kissed me a good night." The word "kissed" is in shorthand: Annie got Thompson's message–shorthand will be their secret code for love. Books were all well and good, but Annie really wanted kisses; so did Thompson, and their relationship immediately became passionate.

"I felt quite weak, he was kind – how could I live without it now, I wonder?" Annie confides three nights later, and in shorthand the following Friday: "I kissed Thompson tonight. Heaven help me if I am doing wrong. I can't live without some kindness." O'Flaherty departed in a huff – "O'F sent back the book he borrowed with his compliments, so ends that friendship" – and Johanna made herself scarce; Annie and Thompson spent every stolen moment locked in each other's arms. "Ring or no ring," Annie admitted, "it was pleasant, pleasant to be petted – lonesome I would be without him now." Writing in shorthand, Annie makes it clear that petting doesn't mean flirting, as it did to Agnes Macdonald – "I sat on his knee, put my arms around him and kissed him this evening." Annie and Thompson were a respectable, religious pair of mid-Victorian virgins who were frank and guiltless about physical love. "Is it me or

John "Grunty" Thompson, an uxorious husband who depended upon his wife.

merely passion that makes me so lonesome for him?'' Annie wonders, ''I shudder to think of having to get over liking him if ever I should have to.''

By New Year's Eve Annie and Thompson were promised to each other: ''When he kisses me and tells me that I am all to him I feel happy, and when he goes I think only that tomorrow evening I will see him again for now I live for him . . . Who would have thought this night last year that he was to make me contented with life and that I would look up to anybody.'' The courtship was long and perilous; Thompson was often away at county court sessions and Annie's mother kept an eagle eye on his letters, but Thompson easily circumvented Mrs. Affleck's censorship by writing a polite ''Dear Annie'' note, followed by a long letter in shorthand to ''My own baby dear.'' After receiving four of Annie's letters in one

Annie Thompson, "my own baby dear."

mail he wrote in shorthand: "My own pet, there never were such darling notes written before. They made me so happy I laughed over them and kissed them and prayed for Annie when I went to bed–and thought about her in the long black dress with that pretty frill for her shoulders . . . I hope dear pet they did not make a fuss at home about my writing–I wish I could give you a kiss now and get a box on my ears and then a hug and a kiss and be called your darling."

The perseverance that won Annie finally won over the Catholic church; by episcopal dispensation, John Sparrow David Thompson and Annie Affleck were married in the bishop's palace Portland, Maine, on July 5, 1870. Less than a year later he converted to Catholicism; fourteen months later Annie gave birth to their first child.

The baby lived only a few minutes. It was one of many sorrows Annie would suffer: her father was lost at sea, one of her young brothers drowned, another was killed in a mining accident and three more of her babies died in infancy. Annie bore nine children in twelve years and raised five to adulthood – two sons, John and Joe, and three daughters, Mary Aloysia or "Babe," Helena, and Frances or "Frankie." Constantly pregnant, Annie soon discovered that she had another baby on her hands – Thompson. In court Thompson was noted for his thoroughness and *sang froid*, but domestically he was helpless. He paid $12,000, an exorbitant price, for Willow Park, a ramshackle white elephant of a country house on the outskirts of town without central heat or indoor plumbing: the maintenance drove Annie nearly mad and the mortgage crippled them financially. Thompson never knew, and cared less, how much money was coming in or where it was going; he was constantly gouged by trades-people and exploited by panhandlers. Annie had to take over the household accounts and pay the bills; she lived in a panic of chronic insolvency. She also had to make sure that Thompson was clothed: he wandered off into snowstorms without his overcoat, lost his gloves and left town without his suitcase. Annie fretted constantly about his health. She soon began calling him "Child" and "Baby": he was five months younger than she.

Thompson's biographer, P.B. Waite, describes Thompson as "an uxorious husband who depended upon his wife, leaned on her, listened to her, vegetated without her, who was, as Thompson said, like Charles II of Spain without his queen–disagreeable, restless and dangerous . . . Thompson had a look of controlled sensuality . . . a lively temper, an acute sensibility, a natural modesty, a powerful intelligence; this parallelogram of forces was held in balance under high tension. He was an intensely nervous man, though you would have had a hard time to find it out. He did not reveal himself easily; he detested the shallow arts by which men made themselves popular.''

Self-taught, self-disciplined and strong-willed, Thompson hid his ambition under a mantle of shyness that fooled people who did not know him. His public manner was cold and aloof. He had little time for friends or relatives and none at all for his widowed mother: after his marriage she disappears from his life so completely she may as well have been dead. Perhaps his religious conversion caused an estrangement, but it was Annie who played the role of the bossy, scolding Mama who pushes her brilliant, sensitive little boy to the front.

''My dear Baby,'' she wrote to Thompson in Ottawa, where he was lobbying for a judgeship, ''You remember the wisdom of the little newsboy 'Sing out or you'll never sell Bill.' You must insist even if you give it up in a month. Mind, I don't care a snap about it and I don't think at your age I would want you to go on the shelf but still when it was once asked for it would only seem as if a person were a kind of a child to be put off with fair words.'' Annie also gives a glimpse of her own ambitions: ''I can't see why we can't find a gold mine when we want it so much. I would dearly like to see you a minister with a big home, plenty of servants and the best table that money could set for a while, then settle down afterwards, but as we won't find the mine you would only feel miserable wanting to do lots of things and not being able to afford them.''

Thompson got the judgeship, and Annie later took credit for pushing him into politics before he became ''mildewed'' on the bench. Lady Aberdeen, the wife of the governor-general, commented: ''He was averse to it & he only finally went when Lady T. packed his portmanteau & put it on the cab and practically turned him out of the house to catch the train.'' Once Thompson was in Ottawa Annie showered him with advice: ''My poor Kitten – Could you step out of your shell a bit and be a little friendly with some of the men? You must not mope. It would never do.'' But moping was what Thompson did away from home – Kitten quite literally lost his mittens and didn't know where to find them: ''Everything is so lonesome that Ottawa seems more than hateful & I am blue about everything and want a judgeship again.''

Thompson feared that his conversion to Catholicism would permanently blight his career, but in fact it won him the support of the powerful

Catholic hierarchy, and his legal skills attracted the attention of Sir Charles Tupper, a father of Confederation and the *éminence grise* of the Nova Scotia Conservative Party. Tupper's son, Charles Hibbert, was one of Halifax's leading lawyers, and it wasn't long before the young Tupper was pressuring Thompson to join the Conservative cause.

Politics offered almost the only opportunity for advancement in the conservative, class-conscious society of Halifax. A small, grey city of weatherbeaten frame houses marching up the steep streets from Bedford Basin, Halifax was a tight-knit colonial community where patronage, nepotism and family pedigree determined social status and financial success. Like the Afflecks, most of the population were sailors, traders and fishermen; the wealthy merchant class was closed to a poor man like Thompson, and the Admiralty was a world unto itself. Thompson needed powerful patrons like the Tuppers, and although he professed to despise the flagrant corruption of Nova Scotia politics, he never said no.

Only a year after his marriage, Thompson was elected to the Halifax city council; in 1877 he was elected to the Nova Scotia legislature as the Conservative member for Antigonish and provincial attorney-general, and served briefly as premier before the government fell in 1882. Judgeships were also political plums, as Annie well knew, and after three years on the Supreme Court of Nova Scotia, Thompson was summoned to Ottawa as minister of justice and attorney-general in the government of Sir John A. Macdonald. Seven years later he was prime minister.

Although she was left alone with a young family, Annie identified completely with Thompson's political ambitions – she knew he would never forgive her for standing in his way–and she soon became his Halifax agent, fixer and confidante. She was a much more combative personality. "My poor old tired Tory," she wrote during the Nova Scotia election of 1882, when Thompson thought he was going down to defeat, "I know that you are feeling badly but surely child you cannot be sick that you are so dull or you would tell me. I wish that I could be with you for one ten minutes to talk square to you. You want to know how I'll feel if you are beaten, well child, except for you being disappointed and tired to death not one row of pins. You know I never thought it worth the journey down [to Antigonish] that all the honor to be had out of it was yours already and except that we never gave up a fight yet I wouldn't mind if you put on your hat and left them tomorrow. It is better to fight as long as you started and be beaten than not to fight at all. So keep up your courage and I'll go part of the way to meet you coming home. Win or lose they can't keep you from me much longer. So now my old baby, you must not be such an awful, awful baby until you get home again and then I'll see how far you can be indulged. So goodnight and lots of kisses. Annie." Thompson won his seat.

Annie exacted one price from Thompson for his frequent lengthy absences: he must write to her every day, even if it was only a few lines, and God help him if he missed. Annie wrote daily in reply; her letters are full of gossip about family and friends, problems with the house, the cow and the hired man, her futile attempts to sell Charley, the horse, and tender stories about the children: "They all wanted to get in bed with me last night and they were awake long before daybreak throwing boots at one another and sitting on my head. So now pet good night with ever so much love and kisses without number from me and the children, your own Annie."

Annie dashed off her letters in spare moments, often writing two or three consecutive notes in one letter and two or three letters a day: her youngest sister, Fanny, described her as "an immense sheet of paper, bottle of ink, and bad pen." Her hasty scrawls reflected her immediate thoughts and emotions. Annie always said what was on her mind, and if she was feeling angry, sad or sexy, Tory soon knew about it. Letters were Annie's way of dealing with the blues his absences brought on, and she made no attempt to pretend a cheerfulness she didn't feel: "Brownie dear, the children are all asleep and everything is very quiet and I am very lonely. I can keep my courage up and listen to the frogs singing until one in the morning if I know that you are on your way home but when you are away it seems as if we are all orphans and as if we didn't belong to anybody. Good night my pet and I hope that you will take care of yourself, Annie."

Thompson wasn't about to let guilt or homesickness interfere with his schedule; his letters were intended to keep his "dear Pet" mollified while he went about his business: "I would like to have a lot of hugs from my own poor little dolly that I am so very, very fond of," he wrote early in their marriage. "I will have a lot of them to get from her when I get home again. Baby dear, the Quinn business will keep me till late tomorrow evening and I do not think I can get through so as to come home on Saturday. Take good care of yourself and please goodness I will be with you on Monday night. My own little baby goodnight and God bless you for a darling. I send a lot of kisses for you and the little fellow, your own Grunty."

In order to keep their spirits up and their lines of communication open, "Baby" and "Grunty" played a literary game that lasted all their married lives, the ritual of courtly love. Thompson was the knight errant, alone and palely loitering in some dingy rented room or defying the Liberal dragon in Antigonish; Annie was his distant queen, a tyrannical, whimsical mistress who granted or withheld her favours depending on his prowess: "I cannot advise you about coming home," she wrote haughtily, "at the same time it won't do for you to stay until doomsday. How in the world are you getting on for clean shirts? I only put in four so you must have on your last clean one now."

Thompson pretended that all other women were repulsive. "Last night I dined at Sir John's," he wrote on his arrival in Ottawa. "Lady Macdonald was very pleasant but as ugly as sin. Lady Tilley was there. She tried to be pleasant and did not need to try to be ugly." Thompson's acid comments about various women's warts and beards reassured Annie that he had not succumbed to the Ottawa "sirens" and the game gave their separation erotic intensity. Grunty indulged his sexual fantasies. He signs off several letters with a teasing promise to give Annie a good "whipping" or "warming" if he finds she hasn't behaved herself when he gets home. Whipping and spanking were staples of Victorian pornography: by pretending to be children, sophisticated adults could indulge in all kinds of forbidden erotic conduct. The Thompsons had a very enthusiastic sex life: Thompson was once bold enough to ask his wife if her "monthly sickness" would be over when he came home; she coyly evaded his "pert" question. Grunty and Baby's literary game likely reflected a real playworld; "I am so fond of you that I want to give you a licking," Thompson wrote gleefully. "Licking" could mean spanking; it probably means cunnilingus.

The game began to lose its savour for Annie when Thompson went to Ottawa in 1885. He would now be away from Halifax for most of the year, and there was no question that Annie and the children might join him. They could not afford to maintain two houses, and the uncertainties of politics made it impossible to abandon their home in Halifax. So Annie stayed behind. She was forty, fat and frumpy, a "country wife" with four children still at home – Frankie was only four – condemned to semi-widowhood as a cook, nurse and charwoman. Back home at draughty Willow

Park, putting up storm windows, cleaning the cellar and poisoning rats, Annie would have no share in Thompson's glittering success, the success she had given her life to create.

"Of course I felt very badly after leaving you at Bedford and have been in a daze ever since," Thompson writes apologetically from Ottawa. However, he makes Annie responsible for their separation – "I could not have stood the depression so long as this but for feeling all the time that you wished me to do what I have done" – and for his peace of mind. "One thing I enjoin on you as a most sacred duty to the children and to me: to take the most scrupulous care of your health and comfort, keep the house warm, keep all necessary repairs made and let me feel easy when I think of home." Well, la-de-da! The self-important tone of this first Ottawa letter must have shocked Annie, and even worse, it is signed formally with Thompson's initials, J.S.D.T. The distance between Ottawa and Halifax was an emotional chasm.

Annie did not hide her hurt. She was not about to be tossed away like an old shoe, and if Grunty thought he could feel easy thinking of home, he had another thing coming. Annie's urgent daily accounts of Babe's cough, Joe's sore arm, Charley's sprained foreleg, the perilous state of their finances and her own physical "weakness" soon had Thompson back in his customary state of nervous apprehension. In truth, as the "baby minister" and a total stranger to his colleagues, some of whom cordially disliked his "monkish" manner, Thompson was none too sure about how to find his way in official Ottawa.

"Two hours after I arrived on Wednesday I was at the department," he writes to Annie in October. "I walked through four of the offices and found them as deserted as the enchanted Palace. At last in my own room I found the electric bell and rang the knob called 'messenger.' A boy appeared and I made him bring my letters but none of the clerks appeared that day excepting the Deputy who called in on his way to some other work and explained his surprise at seeing me by saying that they saw I had been tendered a banquet in Halifax and took for granted I would not be in Ottawa for another week."

Thompson had discovered that it would not *do* to appear to work too hard in Ottawa, where business was transacted over leisurely luncheons and late-night dinners and men were judged more by their claret, cigars and the cut of their waistcoats than by the contents of their dispatch boxes. In his Antigonish boots and homemade suit, short, porcine Mr. Thompson was very much a bumpkin. He made the mistake, for economy, of taking rooms at a shabby, unfashionable boarding-house and it wasn't until he was elected to the Rideau Club that he gave his first successful formal dinner. The menu – oysters on the half shell, soup, fish, oyster patties, forced meat, roast beef or turkey, plum pudding, fruit, claret, coffee and cigars–explain why so many members of parliament, like Thompson, were "giants" weighing in at two or three hundred pounds and more. Thompson could eat a five-course lunch followed by a seven-course dinner, wine and cigars and go to bed hungry after a snack. Men who didn't smoke took snuff or chewed plug tobacco – every public building, including the House of Commons, was lined with spitoons – and liquor was so much a part of political life that a saloon was located directly beneath the Commons chamber so the honourable members, using a staircase behind the Speaker's chair, could refresh themselves constantly in the heat of debate.

Annie understandably worried about Thompson's health. In Ottawa he got no exercise, no fresh air and no rest except for Sundays, which he hated because idleness made him feel lonely for home. He also had the worst job in Macdonald's Cabinet – the responsibility for prosecuting the instigators of the second Riel rebellion, including Louis Riel himself. The rebellion had broken out in the North-West in the spring of 1885 when several white settlers had been massacred by Indians. Following a series of skirmishes between Riel's Indian and Métis guerillas and British troops, the rebellion was suppressed and Riel captured.

Riel was found guilty of treason and sentenced to hang, but as the date of his execution neared a public outcry was raised for clemency. A French-speaking, Catholic mystic, Riel had become a political martyr in Quebec, a folk hero who represented minority rights against the brute force of English Protestant authority. Annie's political judgment turned out to be more astute in the long run than Thompson's:

"They said Riel's hanging depends on you," she writes on November 5, two weeks before the execution date. "It does not, does it? But of course however they decide you will be to blame. I don't think that I'd hang the poor wretch, he can do no more harm. Of course if he was anything but a fool I'd hang him for then he would be dangerous. At any rate, mind that he is not to hang on 10 November, your birthday!" During the night Riel preys on Annie's conscience: "Let Riel go to prison. If you hang him you make a patriot of him. If you send him to prison he is only an insane man. Lots might like to be patriots, but not one a crazy man."

Riel was hanged November 16, 1885. "There has been a good deal of excitement here today," Thompson writes to Annie the next afternoon. "And there is a great deal in the province of Quebec – more than there need be about such a paltry hero who struggled so long and so hard for the privilege of hanging . . . The French members of cabinet are feeling pretty uneasy. It is too absurd for anything. A Frenchman thinks a French Riel is the noblest work of God, and he may be a thief and a murderer but there is not rope enough made to hang him. Riel was a vulgar, cowardly thief – too mean to commit murder – he got the Indians to do that for him . . . The Governor, Sir John and the French members have all been threatened but do not feel at all disturbed. Sir John says he has had in the course of his political life at least a hundred letters threatening him with instant death. I fancy the truth is that a politician finds life so unpleasant that a threat of death is the last thing to terrify him."

Thompson's black wit is not lack of emotion; in fact the excitement of the execution aroused him: at midnight he writes Annie a note – "I feel this evening I should like to have a game of bezique with you for the old stakes! Do you remember? Now you cannot accuse me of writing polite letters . . . now my saucy old girl I should like to be near you to give you a good shake and [in shorthand] a good spanking."

Thompson was trying to coax his Pet out of a snit his own stupidity and insecurity had caused. On the previous Sunday, in the middle of the Riel crisis, Thompson suffered an attack of kidney stones that left him prostrated with pain and stupefied by morphine. On Tuesday morning Annie received the following telegram: "I am ill but not seriously so. Do not be disquieted. J.S.D.T." Annie knew immediately that something was wrong; she packed her suitcase and prepared to hop on the next train to Ottawa. The next day Thompson telegraphed again: "Do not think of coming. Am quite recovered and will be very much distressed if you leave Halifax."

"No woman would leave Halifax after that!" Annie wrote to him in a fury. Annie unpacked her suitcase, lit candles in front of her statue of St. Anthony, and cried. Didn't Tory want her any more? Was he shacked up with some floozie? Why did the newspapers say he was too sick to read his mail if he was quite recovered, and what was wrong with him? Ottawa was in the grip of a smallpox epidemic. Was Thompson going to die alone without her? Thompson's excuse didn't make things any better: "My complaint was one that a woman is supposed to know nothing about and I did not want you to make your first appearance at Ottawa under these circumstances.'' Annie, the mother of nine children, was not supposed to know that her husband had a penis.

"I promise to be very careful about offering my services again," she writes sarcastically, "as not for the world would I make things awkward for you. [Do you have] a Code Ottawa where it would be strange for a man's wife to be with him under those circumstances? Send it to me at once that I may study up."

"Your letter is very cruel and unfair," Thompson replies on November 15. "I thought I deserved some credit for being plucky and cheerful in the midst of suffering and for avoiding placing you in an awkward and trying position. It seems not. For some reason a new trial is threatened to be added to all the others – the greatest one of all – that of my little pet being out of sympathy for me! Is it so? If not, tell me in shorthand what you think you deserve for so unkind a letter. Your own much aggrieved Tory. J.S.D.T."

Now that she had Tory on the defensive, Annie once more established her dominant position in their relationship: "I think I was right," she tartly replies to her "poor Child." "You tell me how weak you are and how much you have suffered and all the time you were trying to deceive me with your airy telegrams and breezy notes. Of course I was not blindfolded a bit. All the time you were suffering not knowing what moment inflamation might set in and I was left to suffer at home without being able to do anything for you. As to that trash about women not knowing anything about that complaint I did not suppose you would make such a childish excuse. And you can leave the case to Sir John or any right-minded lawyer and if they don't say I was right I'll give in. And if you want to test the case in another way, put it to yourself and think of my being as sick as you were and not letting you come to see me. You could not say a crueller thing to a woman than to tell her that she could be done without . . . Now dear do tell me the truth and never try your dodging again because what is the good of bogus news? You know how fond I am of you and if I were able how I would do to push you to the front and mind remember I never at any time pretended to have wings." Annie closes with a demand that Thompson write her a "very, very nice letter, one of your nicest."

Thompson writes dozens, none of them quite satisfactory: "My own little darling," he pleads on December 9. "What a goose you are to doubt that I love you dearly when the greatest sacrifice a man can make is being made by me in living here without you. Night and day I am thinking: 'Is it possible I have left her and cannot see her for a moment?' My own sweet little girl keep on loving me–I get very cross with you only when I believe that you have ceased to love me. If I was near you I could convince you of all I say. Now be bright and happy because I am just counting the hours until I can get back to the nest with my little nestling–not for the holidays but for life. Lots of kisses from Grunty."

Annie had made her point, and it would be only a matter of time before Annie visited Ottawa, whether he liked it or not. Annie suspected the real motive behind Thompson's telegrams: he was afraid she would embarrass him. Ottawa wasn't any bigger than Halifax, but it had acquired a gloss of pretension, and few politicians were more in the public eye than the controversial minister of justice. Thompson had not yet made his maiden speech in the House of Commons, and not a few people, including his Cabinet rivals, hoped he would fall flat on his face. What would they think about his bluenose wife with her waterfront language, her homemade clothes and her total contempt for "genteel airs"?

Annie and Thompson both shunned fashionable society in Halifax; Annie visited friends to collect gossip but she loathed pompous parties where she had to play the "wife of" the justice minister and she usually went, when she went at all, to poke fun at the affectations of her hosts for Thompson's amusement. They were both essentially anti-social, two people who found in each other a world sufficient for themselves; they were both touchy, nervous and easily hurt, but while Thompson hid his thoughts under a mask, Annie spoke, as she wrote, straight from the heart. The fact that she was usually right didn't mend people's hurt feelings, but Annie wasn't going to change. She had the confidence that comes from self-knowledge: Annie needed to climb no social ladders because she was already there.

"If I could only go just to be a comfort to you and not to have to go out and get dresses that would be expensive and useless after," she writes about coming to Ottawa for the 1886 spring session. "I would not like to go up until the day after the House meets as I would have to go to the opening which might be awkward without any person to go with me." Annie was really saying that she didn't have any clothes and she didn't have any jewels and the opening of a new session of parliament was the most intimidating thing she could think of. The ladies were forced to attend in formal gowns, although the ceremony took place in the morning, and the fashion parade was always led by the aristocratic wife of the governor-general whose diamonds, *hauteur* and flashy London style always knocked the socks off her Canadian competition. Annie knew a no-win situation when she saw one, but Thompson was horrified at the prospect of his ragged wife lurking in a broom closet.

"You *must* come at least a week before the opening," he replies frantically. "You are to make sure too to get yourself nice dresses for the opening, for evenings and for the hotel. You may use them or not as you like but you know there is nothing so embarrassing as to feel that one is shabby and there will be enough to embarrass even with all in one's favour. Now pet remember these are commands, not mere advice."

Commands didn't cut much ice with Annie. She buried herself in the household accounts, knowing that Thompson hated getting long letters about unpaid bills. She didn't tell him when she would arrive, or if she would arrive at all. "You must come up and come as soon as you can," Thompson pleads. "Be sure to leave no later than [February] 16th. Get a very nice dress for the opening. It will do for all other occasions and I will pay for it out of my Ottawa estimate. Now my darling do not go back on me again." Annie doesn't even look for fabric for her dresses until February 2: she finds some grey velvet in the house and buys fourteen yards of black silk velvet for $4.50 a yard. She can't resist a bargain: "They had at Smith's a cream silk flecked with crimson, very pretty but so old-fashioned that it might be quite fashionable again. There was 14 1/2 yards and the price had been $4.00 a yard but I got the dress for $20.00. So now are you satisfied even if we are broke. I spent $83.40 just for those two. It will take $150.00 at the very least to get the things I'll need if not more."

To hurry her up Thompson offered to send a government railway car to bring her to Ottawa. This was a mistake. "Now mind this and no nonsense I won't have the *car*," she writes on February 5. "You must let me go up my own way and I'll be very comfortable but if you insist on the car I'll stay at home as all the nasty envious people in town would say far more annoying things than if you stole several thousands. Now don't be a growler nor a baby and I'll soon be with you."

February 16 came and went with the dressmaker still hard at work and Annie dithering about closing the house and boarding out the children. She arrived in Ottawa the day after the House opened.

On March 22, with Annie in the gallery, Thompson made a brilliant four-hour speech defending the execution of Riel; he was immediately singled out as the coming man in the Conservative Party, the only rival to the eloquent Liberal, Wilfrid Laurier. Thompson's weakness was his hatred of campaigning, and Macdonald saw to it that his baby minister got his baptism of fire in an Ontario election the following November.

"The reception on our arrival was simply wonderful," Thompson writes to Annie from Owen Sound. "All the houses were covered with flags and bunting. There were arches everywhere and brass bands at every corner. There were fully 10,000 people in the streets – all cheering and shaking hands. The working men were on top of one arch and dropped a wreath of flowers over Sir John's head. We had lunch and then went to the skating rink which was packed to suffocation. I spoke first for an hour and a half – after that Sir John and then we adjourned for dinner where there was a great company. Then at 7:30 we returned to the rink which was packed again. Meredith spoke an hour and a half, White about as long then Sir John half an hour and then we closed up and returned to the car. The streets were illuminated. In the daytime we were escorted by carriages and men on horseback and at night by a torchlight procession."

This experience in Owen Sound was repeated throughout Ontario every day and night for weeks. Canada was still a rural country with less than five million people scattered in small villages and isolated homesteads; an election campaign was by far the most exciting thing in most people's lives, and they demanded their money's worth. With as many as six or seven speakers sharing the platform and speeches of three hours not uncommon, it wasn't surprising that meetings lasted all day and far into the night. In Cobourg Thompson found the Opera House "crowded to suffocation, so much so that 4 men fainted. Very few could hear us as in the centre of the hall they were trampling on each other and struggling for life."

For politicians it was an ordeal: "We have to go from the car to meetings dirty and often in ragged clothes and in spite of fatigue and the exhaustion of one's brains of anything to say we are supposed to be up to the boiling point of excitement which prevails among the audiences." Thompson was amazed at Macdonald's stamina: "He goes through all these hardships quite gaily while his daily life at home is of itself tormenting enough." After addressing forty-three meetings, Thompson lost his fear of the hustings but not his sense of humour: "At Listowel we had a mounted escort of Canadians and *ladies* and after the meeting a torchlight procession. The meeting was another hopeless mob. A bell rung on the platform could not have been heard at the door but the cheering was deafening. A light gallery ran all around the hall and was crowded with ladies. Just as we got to the platform a large section of this gallery gracefully descended and pitched all the ladies in a beautiful disorder on the heads of the people below. Strange to say no one was hurt except a doctor whose back was injured and, as Sir John said, 'He could mend his own back.' We all shouted for three or four hours except Sir John who gave it up.''

Before long Thompson was feeling cocky enough to challenge the Old Chief himself: ''He is showing some of the failings of age in being very suspicious,'' Thompson confides in Annie. ''He has had something in his nose against me for a little while past – but instead of submitting like the others do I showed fight and treated him with considerable impudence. I ignored his opinion on a legal question and talked to the other members of council over his head. I think he has got over it. I said I did not care and that he might go to ———. I kept up the game by not speaking to that mole catcher of a wife of his at the dinner at Gov't House. Of course the poor old fellow is worried to death that I do not care for him and I am so determined to let him see it that I could insult him at every turn. This is unheard of heresy here because the practice is to worship him from afar even when he is ugly.''

Thompson's impudence won Macdonald's respect: in November 1887 Thompson was sent to Washington as legal adviser to a British-Canadian delegation negotiating sensitive issues of trade and territory with the Americans. The treaty was thrown out by the United States Senate, but in August 1888, to his total surprise, Thompson was knighted. ''I am very nervous about the title,'' he wrote to Annie, now Lady Thompson. ''It is all the talk.'' Thompson was only forty-two and his knighthood insulted many of Macdonald's more senior colleagues. ''All the more satisfaction at getting it,'' Sir John Thompson said smugly. Lady Thompson's feelings are not known, but can probably be summed up by her seven-year-old daughter, Frankie, who said to her mother: ''If you had a friend who was used to calling you Mrs. Thompson and she had to call you Lady Thompson, wouldn't it make her throat tickle!''

Annie would rather have had Thompson than the title. He had been away so much in the past two years that he had seen Frankie once in nine months. Thompson's relationship with his children, as with Annie, was by correspondence. He sent the two boys away to boarding-school in

England although they, and Annie, fought the move bitterly, and the oldest girls went to convents in Quebec. Annie felt isolated at Willow Park, nearly two miles from town, and she often walked in twice a day to look for mail, but letters weren't enough. Annie sank into profound, paralyzing depressions, barely able to get out of bed. Her "weakness" no longer brought Thompson to her side with hugs and kisses; she felt lonely, rejected and resentful. She huffily rejected Thompson's invitations to join him in Washington and all his protestations of love and loneliness did not heal the hurt of his absence. Thompson wasn't in love with another woman, but he was in love with himself, and his increasing self-esteem made Annie feel inferior.

"I know that often I have been a great trouble to you," she wrote, "but don't you see you'll have to put up with me because now I am like Charley, no one would want to give one-tenth of what I cost you." Annie is only half-joking; she felt more and more like a broken-down old horse. A fight with Thompson about selling Charley provoked her to stand up for herself: "I have been suffering from nervous prostration ever since you left. It is just as much as I can stand and I've fought bravely to stand it. I know that I have often been a great trial to you but some fools won't learn by experience and I am one of them. I've always been taking heart and no matter how bitter you'be been to me I've coaxed you and made up when to say the least I was not always wrong, as if time and time again I had not been put down, you always looking like the aggrieved party. Once for all I think I know my place. I'll take as good care of the children as I can, lay out your money to as good advantage as possible but I must neither ask nor suggest about business outside of that. I was always too fond of you not to wish that you had a better wife than I have been to you, but with all my shortcomings until fortune favours so that you are able to make a wiser choice, I remain your faithful wife, A.E. Thompson."

Annie could be disagreeable and dangerous too. Thompson was both exasperated and distressed by her letters. The fun had gone out of their game. Annie was no longer pregnant, her children were growing up, she wasn't content with love letters, she wanted love. Annie seemed to sense, in a way Thompson did not, that they didn't have much time left together. She often thought about the past, sometimes with regret for the hard choice made, but she never planned for their future.

Annie's unhappiness prompted Thompson to relocate his family in Ottawa. It would be expensive. They couldn't afford to buy a house, yet

Thompson had become something of a snob. "We must live in a way that is in keeping with the position we hold, " he wrote to Annie, "not merely for the sake of self-respect but in order to make the position of any value to us." Thompson clearly had his eye on the prime minister's job; to get it he needed to cut a bit of a swath. He estimated that the costs of running the house, entertaining and raising the children would come to $6,900 of his $8,600 salary, an estimate that proved to be disastrously low. He rented a brick house at the corner of Metcalfe and Cooper streets and in March 1888 Annie arrived bag and baggage from Halifax with her daughter Frankie, her sister Fanny, cousin Minnie, cook, dog, canary, clocks and all the furniture from Willow Park.

Annie was probably glad to get out of the old, cold house where she had spent so many wakeful nights alone listening to the wind whistle through the cracks in the walls, but Thompson could not bear to part with it, and Willow Park was neither sold nor rented. In Ottawa, the newly christened Lady Thompson gave dinner parties for Conservative members every Monday and Tuesday night, and on Wednesday afternoon she received. The rest of the week she called at other wives' teas and sat in the gallery of the House when Sir John was speaking. Annie did not develop any airs: while Sir John was wining and dining his colleagues upstairs, Annie was downstairs cooking the meals – in one year she estimated that she cooked for two hundred and fifty people. Her motto was simple: "Feed 'em, feed 'em, feed 'em!"

Annie's title gave her the freedom to be herself. For all her outspoken originality, she wasn't particularly eccentric by Ottawa standards. She was better educated and less "countrified" than many of the Cabinet wives, and as for the Opposition, Madame Laurier was just as simple in her tastes and the Lauriers were even poorer. Men must have found Annie attractive; she was still relatively young, witty and sexy – Thompson's frequent trips to Halifax had made him the butt of some of Macdonald's more salacious quips – yet both her manners and her morals were impeccable. She had raised five bright, handsome children and little Frankie, with her mother's bold ways and her father's fair curls, was everybody's favourite.

Within three years Frankie was crippled and apparently dying. She developed abscesses on her hip – apparently tuberculosis of the bone – which did not heal. A year in bed in traction didn't help, and with Annie at her side she was in Montreal undergoing surgery when Sir John A. Macdonald suffered his paralyzing stroke on May 31, 1891. Thompson was the last minister to speak to Macdonald that afternoon.

*John and Annie Thompson with family and friends in Muskoka, August
1894. Their sons, Joe and John, are seated in front. Helena is seated
beside John, Babe stands behind Annie and Frankie (in the dark dress)
stands behind her father. To the left is Thompson's friend and successor,
Mackenzie Bowell.*

"He may live for part of the night," Thompson wrote to Annie in
Montreal. "The Grits can hardly keep their feet on the ground for joy. I
am trying to bring about an arrangement by which Abbott will be the
new Premier. The opposition will come principally from the French, who
do not like him. There is a great deal of talk about me but my intention is
that if I should have the offer I shall refuse it peremptorily."

Macdonald's approaching death unleashed a frenzy of conspiratorial
activity amongst his possible successors that came down to a fight between
a Montreal senator, John Abbott, and Sir Charles Tupper. Tupper was
Thompson's mentor; however, "the old tramp" had a reputation for
corruption that made Thompson balk: "There is a heavy attempt to boom
Tupper got up by the boodlers. It is a sickly boom however and people
laugh when the names of those who are helping are mentioned as they are

all men who have escaped trial for felony. Quite a number are determined to change the party from gov't to opposition rather than be destroyed by Tupper. When all this fuss is over how sick we shall be of it!''

Thompson's house was crammed with people day and night during a convivial six-day death watch. "The guests are getting on well and having a pretty good time though of course all entertaining is suspended," Thompson joked to Annie. Thompson's Catholicism made him attractive to the French Canadians, and unattractive to the Orangemen, a very powerful Protestant force in the Conservative Party. Annie advised him to bide his time. He did. A week after Macdonald died, John Joseph Caldwell Abbott was sworn in as Canada's third prime minister.

Did Thompson cleverly back a man he knew would soon fade? Abbott was seventy, a sour-faced corporation lawyer who had funnelled illegal money to Macdonald during the Pacific Scandal. "I hate politics," Abbott said bluntly. "I hate notoriety, public meetings, public speeches, caucuses and everything that I know of that is apparently the necessary incident of politics."

His wife, Mary Bethune Abbott, apparently shared his views; she seems to have taken no part in politics during Abbott's eighteen months as prime minister. It's doubtful that she even came to Ottawa. The daughter of John Bethune, the Anglican dean of Montreal, Lady Abbott was old, she may have been ill; she was certainly a woman of immense wealth and such exquisite discretion that she left virtually no trace of her life.

Abbott's job was to clean up the chaos and corruption Macdonald had left, and he did it so efficiently that the Conservatives increased their majority in the House by thirteen seats in a series of by-elections. However, Abbott had neither stamina nor stomach for the job. Suffering from "exhaustion of the brain and nervous system," he sailed for England in October, leaving Thompson an undated letter of resignation to use at his discretion. Thompson used it: on December 4, 1892 Sir John Thompson became prime minister of Canada. Grunty had made it.

The price was too high. In 1894, the government became embroiled in a constitutional crisis over the right of Manitoba's French Catholics to have publicly funded separate schools, and after a bitter session, Thompson apparently suffered an attack of angina. He was exhausted, his feet and legs swelled ominously and he was ordered to rest. He and Annie spent August at a cottage in Muskoka with their children: a snapshot shows a forty-eight-year-old Thompson with the sagging, shapeless body of a man of seventy-eight. A Toronto doctor discovered evidence of Bright's and heart disease, but Thompson's own doctor, the venerable James Grant, was more diplomatic. "My dear Duckey," Thompson wrote to Annie in Muskoka, "I saw Dr. Grant. He took a very cheerful view of the case, gave me a prescription and a diet. The diet is about what I have been living on. The prescription is to reduce my size moderately. He says the heart is very sound and that the nights in the House have been too hard on me. I am to take no spirits."

Annie wasn't fooled. She could read between the lines of Dr. Grant's prescription: arteriosclerosis and kidney disease. The doctors advised Thompson to take a year's rest – there was nothing else they could suggest – and Annie begged him to resign. Resign! How ridiculous! How would he support his family! Thompson had few investments and no savings; his only assets were some vacant lots in Halifax and Willow Park. He had been scrupulous about refusing political gifts; there was no testimonial fund for Annie as there had been for Agnes Macdonald and Thompson had even refused a party offer to buy them a house. He had two sons studying law in Toronto, two daughters at a convent in Paris and Frankie at home; Frankie was recovering but she would always be lame and her medical bills were enormous. His prime minister's salary of $9,000 barely covered their expenses; without it they would starve. Thompson carried on. He promised Annie that he would resign after the next election, if they won.

In November 1894 Thompson sailed for England to be sworn in as a member of Her Majesty's Privy Council, an honour previously extended only to Macdonald. He boarded the train for Windsor Castle on the morning of December 12. The best witness to the subsequent events is the lord steward of Windsor, the Marquis of Breadalbane:

"I saw Sir John on the platform at Paddington today and travelled to Windsor in the same saloon with him. He appeared all right then and at the meeting. After being sworn in, he retired to the luncheon room and while we were sitting there he suddenly fainted. One of the servants and I each took an arm and we got him to the next room and placed him beside the window. I got some water for him and sent a servant for a little brandy and in a short time he recovered somewhat and seemed much distressed at having made what he regarded as a scene, remarking 'It seems too weak and foolish to faint like this.' I replied 'One does not faint on purpose, pray don't disturb yourself about the matter.' He then begged me to return to my luncheon but of course I would not hear of this and remained with him until he seemed to have completely recovered and rose to accompany me. I offered him my arm but he walked unaided, cheerfully remarking 'I'm all right now, thank you.'

"In the meantime, Dr. Reid, the Queen's physician, arrived. Within two or three minutes of Sir John's return to the luncheon room, and, I believe, before he had tasted what had been placed before him, I saw him suddenly lurch over and fall almost into Dr. Reid's arms. At the request of the doctor the ladies at the table went out and the doctor and I and some servants alone remained. We did all that was possible, but I felt his pulse and was confident that no aid could prevail. The doctor had the same view and it unhappily proved all too correct."

The Marquis went to some pains to quell suspicions that Thompson may have been poisoned – he died of a massive cerebral hemorrhage – but the death of the prime minister of Canada at the queen's table in Windsor Castle created an international scandal and a royal problem in etiquette. What was to be done with the body? Thompson couldn't be buried in England, and he couldn't be simply shipped home in a box. The aged queen rose to the crisis. Nobody loved a funeral more than Victoria, and to Annie's profound anguish, she saw to it that Thompson's funeral was one of the most morbid of her reign.

In Ottawa, Annie learned of her husband's death from a newspaper reporter; the church bells were tolling before Thompson's friends summoned up the courage to tell her. Poor Annie. All those years of solitude and sacrifice, for *nothing*! "Never to hear his voice again," she cried out, "never to hear him come in the door, never to hear him come up the stairs again – never, never – oh! I am afraid of the nights & I am afraid of the days & I am afraid of the years & if it were not for the children I should long to creep away in some corner and *die*."

Annie's best friend in her grief was Ishbel Aberdeen, the wife of the governor-general, a brisk, compassionate young woman who remained steadfastly at Annie's side during the next awful weeks. "I found her very brave & strong & quite natural & like herself but utterly overwhelmed at the thought of being *alone*," Lady Aberdeen wrote in her diary December 13. "She spoke of how he had been her all in all – there was nothing else she cared for in life, & that all the rest of the world were indifferent to her besides him & this ever since she first knew him."

Thompson did not repay Annie's devotion. He died without a will; his estate amounted to $5,500 in life insurance, $2,500 in the bank, $1,000 in household goods – an indication of their poverty – and about $11,000 in Halifax property and mortgages. Debts consumed the savings and insurance policies, and Willow Park, for which Thompson had paid $12,000, was sold for $2,000. As Annie feared, Thompson left his family penniless.

Annie now had to endure the humiliation of public charity. The Cabinet started a national subscription to raise money for Annie and the children: the name of each donor was entered in a ledger along with the amount contributed. Annie, who hated owing a cent to *anyone*, at first refused to have anything to do with it, but cruel reality forced her to back down. The subscription, plus a grudging $25,000 from the House of Commons, raised $62,500, enough to give her a decent income of $2,800 a year. Lord Aberdeen offered to pay for the boys' education until they had finished school. Annie accepted. The Aberdeens were aristocrats cut from democratic cloth; they had children close in age to the Thompsons' and with exceptional grace welcomed the late prime minister's brood into Rideau Hall as members of their own family.

Ishbel Aberdeen, an educated feminist and social radical who abhorred Ottawa's genteel airs, gives an acute assessment of Annie's public persona: "She is a woman by herself at Ottawa & has naturally not made many *friends* there, being so taken up with her husband & her children & not being of the kidney of the society people there. But people are very much mistaken who think her merely a domestic woman, knowing nothing of politics or the world outside. She is unfortunately a bit cynical & looks on politics as a game of chess, but she has a clear head & good judgement & has been of infinite use to Sir John, I am sure, for he was perhaps too much disposed to believe everyone as good as himself . . . He was a gentleman, so courteous & kindly to everyone & to all alike – never bored & ruffled as far as anyone could see, though Lady T. says he felt anything going wrong even in small things acutely."

Thompson's body was laid out in Windsor Castle; the queen was wheeled in to view the remains and ordered a requiem mass at midnight. The following day the body was taken to London in a plumed hearse where it was embalmed and displayed in the Chapel of St. James. Another requiem mass was attended by a motley crowd that included South African industrialist Cecil Rhodes, poet laureate Lord Tennyson and the old tramp, now angling for Thompson's job, Sir Charles Tupper. A British warship, the *Blenheim*, steamed up from Gibraltar to take the body back to Canada. It was December 22 before the *Blenheim*, painted black, left Portsmouth with Thompson lying in state in the captain's cabin. The funeral would be in Halifax on January 3, 1895, three weeks after Thompson's death.

Annie was excluded from the funeral arrangements. Over her violent objections, Sir Charles Tupper stuck to the entourage like a barnacle, wringing every possible ounce of personal advantage out of the publicity. When Annie and the children arrived in Halifax on December 30, she found that her request for a simple open funeral car had been deliberately disobeyed. Ishbel Aberdeen, who gave Annie refuge from the mob of mourners in her private railway car, describes the scene in the provincial legislature where Thompson's casket was to lie:

"The whole interior of the room is draped in purple & black & silver. The windows are closed & draped with flowers standing in front of them & the roof is also hung with black. Electric light has been introduced & the whole effect is good, relieved by the masses of flowers & the purple carpet. We all went on to see the funeral car. Lady Thompson made a special request that there might be no plumes & no roof with heavy black coverings & hangings, for Sir John had a horror of those things. Unfortunately the car is nearly finished & there is a roof & there are hangings & there are plumes . . . she was persuaded by the Archbishop to let the car remain unchanged on account of the work though she dislikes it very much."

The *Blenheim* docked at Halifax in the pouring rain at noon on New Year's Day. "The landing was very simply done," wrote Ishbel Aberdeen, who was standing there in the rain with her husband. "The coffin was borne from the landing place to the gun carriage by eight soldiers, covered with the Canadian flag. Very soon all was made & the gun carriage drawn by four artillery horses & preceded by the King's Band playing the Dead March & afterwards Beethoven's Funeral March & the escort marching with arms reversed – the whole scene was solemn & touching in the extreme." Annie's pride must have seen her through – Lady Aberdeen reported that Annie was "bearing up bravely."

Annie had her Tory to herself for the last time that night. The coffin was taken to the house where she was staying, but the lid was screwed shut: Thompson's face had been so disfigured by the hemorrhage that it was thought best not to allow her to see him. He was buried two days later after a high mass in the Halifax cathedral. "It took an hour and a half for the procession to reach the cemetery, though it was only a mile," said Lady Aberdeen. "The funeral car was the only blot to my mind for it looked like a great four post bed on wheels, quite apart from the horrid black plumes & the six draped horses. The crowds behaved admirably, & evinced real feeling & reverence, no jostling or pushing, no loud talking & not a cigar or pipe to be seen. Lady Thompson was much prostrated after the service. She went to the cemetery about 5:30, but there were still hundreds of people there, so she went the last thing before coming to the car about 11:30 . . . we started from Halifax at 6:50 this morning, Lady Thompson having slept on our car overnight as we did ourselves. She was very exhausted & was able to get some sleep though breaking down from time to time.''

Annie fled Ottawa, but not before she had packed up all Thompson's papers, including their love letters, into thirty trunks. Annie's ''accumulations,'' as Ishbel Aberdeen called them, were her only possessions; Annie carried Grunty's past, and his future, with her until she died. ''Lady Thompson is feeling the reaction now badly,'' Ishbel noted in February 1895. ''She scarcely knows what to do with herself & by way of relief has begun tearing the house to pieces & packing up everything which make her surroundings look very desolate, seeing she is not to make her move to Toronto for three months yet. She is finding it difficult to find a suitable house there.''

Ishbel and Annie went house hunting, and after Lady Aberdeen put the arm on a Conservative financier, a house was quickly found for Lady Thompson in fashionable Rosedale. Annie was able to rent the house for three years for $600, but the suburban location, far from downtown and the boys' law school, must have reminded her unhappily of Willow Park. She moved to 18 1/2 St. Joseph St., near St. Michael's College. Annie lived there with Frankie until April 10, 1913, when she died in hospital of inoperable cancer.

CHAPTER 6

. . . .

The

Dutiful

Wife:

Frances

Tupper

$\mathcal{A}$FTER JOHN THOMPSON'S shocking death in 1894, Ishbel Aberdeen promised Annie Thompson that Lord Aberdeen would never call on the "old wretch," Sir Charles Tupper, to form a government. The Aberdeens kept their word – Aberdeen called on Mackenzie Bowell – but Tupper was too clever for them: eighteen months later he achieved his life's ambition at last.

Mackenzie Bowell was over seventy, a widower with extreme Protestant views, a suspicious temperament and rudimentary education. Bowell's selection is testimony to the confusion and decay of a rudderless government that had held power for seventeen years, and Bowell, an indecisive politician, never had the full support of his caucus. As Thompson had feared, Tupper would scheme for power even if he destroyed the party in the process, and he did. In the spring of 1896, Tupper staged a cabinet coup that pushed Bowell aside, and on May 1 the old wretch, still hearty at seventy-five, was sworn in as the fifth prime minister of Canada.

It is an irony of politics that Frances Tupper, whose tenure as prime minister's wife is the briefest – sixty-eight days – was perfectly groomed for the role. In a marriage that lasted sixty-five years, Frances devoted herself entirely to her husband's career, discharging, in the words of her obituary in 1912, "many arduous and responsible social duties in a manner always creditable to herself, her husband and the Dominion." It was a convention of the time for the press to lavish fulsome praise on the wives of prominent men, usually in proportion to the opprobrium heaped on their husbands, and Lady Tupper owed her saintly public stature at least in part to the fact that her husband was generally regarded as a scoundrel.

One of the most egocentric and ambitious men ever to occupy public office, Sir Charles Tupper was also one of the most successful: he was a premier of Nova Scotia, a father of Confederation, a member of Sir John A. Macdonald's Cabinet, and, from 1884 to 1896, Canadian high commissioner in London. He had been knighted in 1879 and made a baronet in 1888; he had also acquired a substantial personal fortune that he considered a just reward for his services to the nation.

Frances Tupper had just turned seventy in the spring of 1896. She was a big, vigorous woman with a lantern jaw – it is hard to imagine her being called "Fanny" or "Frankie" – an air of refinement and an apprehensive expression. No wonder, she was married to the biggest boor in the country.

Frances Morse had married beneath her. She was born in Amherst, Nova Scotia, into a British colonial family of judges, lawyers and civil servants – her father was protonotary for Cumberland County – with close connections to the Admiralty. Her father's obituary in 1884 describes him as being "at one time quite wealthy, but his kind disposition led him to assist many people with loans, by whom he met with considerable loss." Frances was sent to a finishing-school in Massachusetts rather than to England and she was only twenty when she married a local boy, Dr. Tupper.

Marriage to a country sawbones was not particularly desirable for a girl of Frances's class. Medicine was a rough and brutal trade in an age when whiskey was the standard anesthetic and most diseases were incurable; doctors' lives were unpredictable and their bills often unpaid. Charles Tupper was a rough and brutal man who had already developed a shady past: rumours circulated that Tupper had jilted a young widow who had paid for his medical education in Edinburgh. However, Tupper was handsome, energetic, a good Baptist and not likely to question the size of Frances's dowry. Indeed, for impecunious and ambitious young Tupper, Miss Morse's social prestige and family connections were all he needed to launch himself on a political career.

"I made an offer of marriage to Miss Frances Morse of Amherst," Tupper records in his memoirs. "Having obtained the consent of her parents, she accepted my proposal and we were married on the 8th of October, 1846." In a personal memoir of more than five hundred pages, this is Tupper's 'affectionate' reference to his wife.

The Tuppers' daughter Emma was born nine months later and nine years later, when Frances was pregnant with her fourth child, Tupper went into politics. "One of my strongest opponents was my dear wife, who expressed the earnest hope that I would be defeated," Tupper said after he had won his seat. Frances's wishes clearly counted for nothing, in fact her antagonism probably egged him on, and Tupper later liked to attribute his political success to his wife.

"He never wanted for language," wrote a political colleague, George Ross. "His vocabulary was copious but not varied and was more torrential than judicial. He was always serious; I never knew him to perpetrate a joke, not even to interpolate a humorous remark. He was equally impervious to the sallies of an opponent. He always spoke from a full chest and with a splendid volume of voice and wrestled with his subject as a strong man could wrestle in the amphitheatre with an antagonist. To him opposition was as objectionable on one side of the House as on the other, and he laboured as hard to demolish the humblest member who opposed him as he did when himself in opposition to demolish the strongest member of the Cabinet."

Tupper's bullying and bellowing enabled him to score a great coup in Nova Scotia politics – he outshouted the brilliant Reformer Joseph Howe, and won Cumberland for the Conservatives. Rewarded with a Cabinet appointment, Tupper moved his medical practice to Halifax and left his wife and children in Amherst. The Ram of Cumberland County, as Tupper came to be known, found the political pastures very green indeed; by 1864 he was premier of Nova Scotia and in 1867 he joined the first Confederation Cabinet of Sir John A. Macdonald. Tupper lived in Ottawa for the parliamentary sessions and established a medical practice at the corner of Gerrard and Jarvis streets in Toronto, where, according to the Toronto *Globe*, he "practiced his profession at times when he was not stumping the country with Sir John." Where was Frances? She does not appear to have been in Ottawa or Toronto, and she may have been left with the children on a farm in New Brunswick.

Tupper's gallivanting around suggests that he likely kept a mistress, or several mistresses. Certainly his bachelor behaviour raised eyebrows. Hector Charlesworth, a contemporary journalist, slyly observed that Tupper's "gallantry made him very popular with the ladies in private conversation." Tupper lost no opportunity to bring about those intimate tête-à-têtes: "Tupper insisted on my going to Vespers with him yesterday," John Thompson wrote to Annie in 1887 from Washington where he and Tupper were involved in negotiations with the Americans. "I suspected he had a trick in it and sure enough he called for a young lady. I was intended to be a 'gooseberry' but I paid him off by taking her entirely under my charge. She is a Catholic and very nice and sensible. He had met her travelling in England with her father who is since dead."

Frances, Lady Tupper, and her husband, Sir Charles Tupper, "the biggest boor in the country."

Thompson was no prude but he found the "old tramp's" conduct disgusting; sixty-eight-year-old Tupper was making a fool of himself and threatening the whole delegation with scandal; moreover, Frances would soon be coming to Washington for the winter season. In spite of Thompson's intervention, Tupper was irrepressible: the next night at dinner he ogled a pretty woman across the table. Thompson pointed out a handsome young man who was also interested in her: did Sir Charles wish to challenge his rival to a duel? Tupper blanched and backed off. Thompson told Annie that he did not think Tupper would discuss such subjects with him again.

The ram's flirtations were never innocent of intent and frequently successful. In Washington Tupper regularly visited a secretary, Josephine Bailey, who did confidential typing for the Canadian delegation. According to a lawsuit she filed in 1891, Miss Bailey became pregnant by Tupper and, on his advice, had an abortion. She later came to Ottawa and asked him for a job in the civil service. Tupper turned her down. It may have been blackmail – the suit was dropped or settled out of court – but Tupper's vulnerability to a lawsuit or a divorce action did not improve his status in the Conservative Party. Macdonald tried shipping him off to London as high commissioner, but the position only fattened his monumental ego and enlarged his scope of action.

Tupper's virility did him no harm back home in Cumberland County where he won election after election; the voters were men after all, and Tupper's predecessor, Joseph Howe, had survived rumours that he had populated Nova Scotia with illegitimate children. Tupper's profession gave him intimate access to all ages and classes of women, many of whom were eager to be seduced by a famous man who could promise there would be no embarrassing consequences. Tupper, like most doctors, would have been adept at abortion, a simple, relatively safe procedure in expert hands, necessary when women's lives were at risk, convenient when their reputations were in danger. Tupper was popular with women: Agnes Macdonald liked him so much that she lobbied hard for him to succeed Sir John, possibly one reason why Tupper failed.

Frances stuck it out. What else could she do? She did what most women in her circumstances did, devoted herself to her children and her social obligations. As a mother Frances was considered an outstanding success: none of her children inherited their father's coarseness. Emma married an English officer and the three boys became prominent lawyers;

Charles Hibbert, the second son, was knighted for his services to the Conservative cause and William, the youngest, became lieutenant-governor of Manitoba. Given their father's abusive personality it may have been a blessing that he was rarely home.

Frances always went to Ottawa for the opening of the parliamentary sessions; the fancy dress balls and state dinners were a perfect opportunity for her to show the flag, and if Lady Tupper heard whispers and saw pitying glances, a swish of her jewelled satin train put the backbiters in their place. The Tuppers were rich – Sir Charles's reputation for lechery was far exceeded by his reputation for greed – and Frances loved to dress up. A letter from Frances to her son Charles Hibbert reveals how a knighthood could compensate for her humiliation: "You know that your father does not care for these honours, and I am sure for his own sake would have preferred to remain plain Mr. Tupper, but there are other things to be taken into consideration. I am sure he deserves the honour – he has merited any distinction Her Majesty could confer by his lifelong devotion to his country – his self-sacrifice. Of course his wife and children may express this to each other."

Frances's few existing letters suggest that she completely accepted the Great Man myth her husband created for himself. Frances probably believed as implicitly in Sir Charles's fidelity as she did in his humility. Convention was her shield and security; as Devoted Wife, Loving Mother and Gracious Hostess her life had meaning; if she denied the myth she would be forced to confront the stark reality of rejection, anger and despair.

"Lady Tupper is going the rounds every day, calling, calling, calling," John Thompson wrote Annie from Washington. "The wives of the judges all receive one day, the wives of the Cabinet ministers another and so on the whole week with great parade in the newspapers about what each one wore and which young ladies assisted in pouring out the tea. They feel simply insulted if you do not call and Tupper is quite indignant because I do not go." Frances did what Sir Charles told her to do. In 1901, when she was seventy-five, she wrote to a friend: "It caused me a pang when my husband told me that he had offered our house for sale, not that I cared so much for Ottawa but it was our home – and I had settled in it hoping never to move again." Tupper also never thought to ask his wife where she might like to live: she preferred Montreal, he chose Victoria.

In Ottawa as the prime minister's wife, Lady Tupper's social position was precarious; her husband's reputation and innumerable enemies meant there were places, like Rideau Hall, where she might be snubbed. It didn't matter. Tupper was forced to call an immediate election, and on June 23, 1896, six weeks after he became prime minister, Sir Charles Tupper led the Conservative Party to crushing defeat at the hands of Wilfrid Laurier's Liberals. It was a humiliating campaign – everywhere Tupper went he was booed and shouted down – and Frances, for once, must have been thankful she had been excluded. Tupper still clung to power. On July 2 he went to persuade the governor-general, Lord Aberdeen, to let him carry on.

"It was his birthday," Ishbel Aberdeen wrote in her diary. "The plucky old thing came down blooming in a white waistcoat & seemingly as pleased with himself as ever – he did not at all appear as the defeated Premier come to render an account of his defeat to the representative of the Sovereign. Not he! Down he sat & for an hour & a half harangued His Excellency." It didn't work: Aberdeen sent for Laurier.

The Tuppers celebrated their fiftieth wedding anniversary in Opposition. They were showered with gifts, all gold, but Tupper could not resist one more rudeness – he returned the Aberdeens' engraved box with an insulting letter. Defeat destroyed his reputation for invincibility and effectively ended his political career: four years later, when he was nearly eighty, Tupper was beaten in Cumberland, and the next year he resigned as Conservative leader.

Old, adrift and discredited, Tupper had to depend for emotional support on his wife and children. Frances stuck it out for another sixteen years, putting up with the restlessness and selfishness of the man she submissively and slightly sarcastically called "my husband":

"My husband only decided to go to England a few days ago," she wrote to a friend on March 1, 1905. "We are sailing from Halifax on the *Bavarian* on the 7th . . ." Frances Tupper may not have wanted to go to England, but she died there on May 11, 1912 at the age of eighty-six. Her husband lived another three years, haunted by Frances's ghost:

"Dreamed I saw my Darling," Tupper wrote in his diary on January 8, 1915, and on September 14: "Dreamt I saw my Darling. 63rd time." Alone and forgotten, Tupper died of a heart attack on October 30, 1915. He was ninety-four.

CHAPTER 7

The Good Wife and the Other Woman: Zoé Laurier and Émilie Lavergne

$\mathcal{T}$HE SUMMER OF 1867 was the most miserable of Zoé Lafontaine's life. Confederation, pfft! Who gave a fig for Canada except the rich anglais up on the mountain? Now she would have to speak English and become a Protestant. Never! Zoé would never speak English, no matter how much Laurier persisted, she would not renounce her religion, let Laurier do as he pleased. But what did it matter? Laurier was gone.

Wilfrid Laurier was practising law in Arthabaska, a village in the Eastern Townships a hundred miles from the city of Montreal where Zoé Lafontaine waited anxiously, almost desperately, for his letters. Was he dying, or getting better? His letters made it impossible to know. "Yesterday morning, around five o'clock, I had a sudden hemorrhage," he wrote on July 6, 1867. "Fortunately, I had drugs on hand. I took several heavy doses, one after the other, and the blood stopped flowing almost immediately. At nine o'clock I was able to get up and go to court. I got back quite tired in the evening, too tired to write to you. I went to bed early and only got up this morning. I felt quite well all day, except for a feeling of weakness, but my chest is completely clear.

"I am anxious to write to you, my beloved, because I know that you will be disappointed in not receiving any letters today. Please do not worry. My illness is not very serious this time. I can walk, go out and my face has not changed at all, whereas on previous occasions I was forced to stay in my room, and sometimes in bed. I do not know what caused this sudden attack. I am not tired, and did not do anything excessive.

"Chère bonne Zoé, ever since I left Montreal I have only thought of you. The last few days which I spent with you will never leave my memory. I never get weary of thinking how kind you are, how much you love me. Yes, dear Zoé, I do sincerely believe that there exists no one under the sun who is as kind, as devoted, as compassionate as you are. I am happy to think I will have the best wife in the world.

Believe me forever, ton ami, Wilfrid.''

Laurier's letters always left Zoé in a state of exultation and despair. Her heart leapt at the reassurance that he wished to marry her, and sank at the news of his illness. Wilfrid offered her hope, but it seemed to be a vain hope.

Eight months had passed since Laurier left Montreal, eight tearful, lonely months while Zoé waited for Wilfrid to die, or set their wedding date. He had done neither, and Zoé was becoming uneasy. Had he found another woman in Arthabaska? In his letters Laurier said he loved her, and only her, but then why didn't he marry her? If he was dying, they would have a few happy months together, if not, then why endure this agony of separation? Wouldn't they be better off together? Zoé would nurse Laurier back to health in no time at all, and if it came to the worst, she would rather die a widow than an old maid.

Zoé Lafontaine was twenty-six and she had been waiting for Wilfrid Laurier for seven years, ever since the wet September night she opened the door of the house on St. Louis Street to find a tall, pale young man shivering on the steps. At first she laughed, he looked so much like a lost puppy, then she noticed how his dark curls clung like rose petals to his forehead, and fell in love.

At first they were just friends, shy and stiff together, two homeless waifs sharing a common lodging. Wilfrid Laurier was an official boarder at the Gauthiers', not because they needed the money, far from it, but because their families had known each other in the village of St. Lin, and Madame Gauthier promised to keep a motherly eye on Wilfrid while he was at McGill University. Zoé's position was much more ambiguous. She was described as a ''piano teacher,'' which she was, but she was also a baby-sitter, governess, housemaid, cook and dependant.

Zoé's father, Godefroi-Napoleon Lafontaine, a bailiff, deserted his wife and only child while Zoé was still a girl. Madame Lafontaine eked out a living giving piano lessons to the children of the French-speaking *bourgeoisie* of Montreal, one of the very few occupations open to a respectable single woman in the middle of the nineteenth century, and saw to it that Zoé received a basic education at the Sacred Heart Convent, probably as a charity pupil. Zoé was a devout Catholic but apparently had no religious vocation, or perhaps loyalty to her mother and a love of music prompted her to reject the convent for the poverty, humiliation and uncertainty of life as an itinerant piano teacher.

Among Madame Lafontaine's pupils were Emma and Hannah, the two eldest daughters of Phoebe and Séréphin Gauthier. The Gauthiers were a romantic ménage. Phoebe, the daughter of a Jewish merchant from Manchester, England, had originally eloped with Séréphin Gauthier's uncle, also named Séréphin, a doctor in St. Lin. When her husband died of tuberculosis, leaving her a young widow with infant children, Phoebe married Séréphin the nephew, a doctor in Montreal. The Gauthiers were relatively affuent, cultivated and exceptionally generous: when Madame Lafontaine became too ill to teach, they offered her and Zoé refuge in their own home.

Zoé had a roof over her head, and that was all. She certainly had nothing but love to offer a handsome, clever, ambitious young lawyer like Wilfrid Laurier. Laurier himself had little enough. The family farm in St. Lin provided a bare living; his father earned extra income as a surveyor. When Laurier arrived at McGill he still wore homespun and stayed away from social functions because of his peasant clothes. Over six feet tall, slender and erect, Wilfrid Laurier was blessed with the head of a Caesar, an aristocrat's insouciant air and a cavalier's romantic name – his mother knew English well enough to read *Ivanhoe* – but his big feet and huge, ham hands would always betray his farm-boy origins. Zoé, at eighteen, was the urbane sophisticate, slim and petite, her thick, dark hair parted in the middle to frame her perfect oval face and gentle dark eyes.

Superficially they had little in common except poverty. Wilfrid was the student, the intellectual, his nose always buried in a book; Zoé cared nothing for books. Her interests were people, *affaires*, marriages, deaths, scandals, cooking, children, charity. Wilfrid was radical, liberal, anti-clerical, Zoé conventional and religious; Wilfrid was moody, passionate, temperamental, Zoé straightforward and self-disciplined. Yet beneath all these differences they shared a profound private bond: like Zoé, Wilfrid had been abandoned.

Laurier's mother died of tuberculosis when he was seven. He barely remembered her, only that she liked books and music and beautiful paintings. His father immediately married their housekeeper, a pleasant but uneducated woman, and started a second family. At the age of ten Laurier was sent away to school, first to New Glasgow to learn English – Laurier always spoke English with a slight Scots burr – then to the French Catholic college of L'Assomption, then to McGill to study law. When Zoé met him, still a teenager, Wilfrid was alone, unloved, insecure; only Zoé knew the cold, deep well in his soul, the grief and rage that turned all joy to pain, all love to fear.

Wilfrid was in love with death, that much was clear. Why else did he run around all winter in only a thin shirt, and stay up all night reading, and shout himself hoarse at political meetings and work himself into such a state of nervous exhaustion that he had to spend weeks in bed, burning with fever and coughing blood, so that even Zoé, with all her candles to the Virgin, expected any day to hear that Wilfrid was dead. Phoebe Gauthier warned Zoé against falling in love with a dying man, but that's precisely why Zoé did love him – Laurier needed her – and in spite of Phoebe's misgivings, their intimacy grew deeper in the domestic comfort of the Gauthiers' house.

They secretly agreed that they would marry as soon as Wilfrid was able to support a family, but his first practice was a failure – the partners spent all their time arguing politics – and Laurier's cough grew worse. In October 1866 he collapsed at his desk, blood from his lungs staining the papers beneath him. He appeared to have only months to live, and a token job was found for him editing a radical *rouge* newspaper in the Eastern Townships. The paper immediately went bankrupt, leaving Laurier in debt, unemployed but alive. Now, at twenty-five, he was starting over in Arthabaska, and playing politics.

Illness did not prevent Laurier from jumping enthusiastically into the 1867 federal election campaign. He toyed with the idea of offering himself as a Liberal candidate in Arthabaska but rejected it as presumptuous; instead he made a name for himself speaking at all the *assemblées contradictoires* in the villages. Since the meetings were usually held in the churchyard after Sunday mass, it was an ideal opportunity for an anti-clerical Liberal to challenge the authority of the church on its own ground and, with luck, cause a row.

Laurier was an instant success. In a crowd his height, his pallor, his flowing chestnut hair and his haughty, handsome face commanded immediate attention, and he held the crowd enraptured with his voice, a strong, melodious voice that rose over the babble like the sweet, clear song of an oboe. Laurier's appearance was so romantic, his manner so passionate, his voice so beautiful, that nobody cared if his speech was dull and pedantic: they weren't listening. Laurier was a charismatic performer who commanded attention, devotion, adoration simply because he was enchanting.

His political success brought a miraculous improvement in Laurier's health and spirits; he was no longer a pathetic invalid but a charming, ambitious, self-confident young man who obviously enjoyed the sudden attention of the Arthabaska establishment.

"I have just been invited to a *grand soirée* which will take place at M. George Pacaud's home on Tuesday evening," he wrote to Zoé on September 6. "I have always had, as you know, little liking for these things, but since one must not behave like a bear I have decided to go. The entire Pacaud family is very kind to me and I do wish to maintain their friendship. Peoples' opinions are sometimes strange: for instance, there isn't an insult which I have not heard said about the Pacaud family in general. I have found them to be kind, courteous and particularly devoted to their friends. They are the best friends I have here."

Did Zoé sense that the powerful Pacaud family was her great rival for Laurier? All Zoé's letters to Wilfrid have been lost or destroyed, but we know from his reply on September 12 that she dashed off an angry note. "I got the impression from your last letter that you thought I was neglecting you," Laurier writes contritely. "This thought pains me, but I hope to think I am mistaken, isn't that so dear? You know that I love you." Laurier quickly backtracks on the social front: "All kinds of parties rain down around here. On Monday, it was at Dr. Poisson's, the next day at M. George Pacaud. I didn't attend either of them. I was too tired."

Whatever Laurier might tell Zoé, he had no intention of living like a bear. Laurier needed to surround himself with friends who would constantly reassure him he was loved, and not alone. In Arthabaska he found this circle in the Pacauds, a legendary clan of prosperous farmers and merchants whose radical politics were rooted in the unsuccessful 1837 rebellion against British colonial rule. The Pacauds were now Liberals, fighting for Quebec's rightful place in a new Canada, and in the educated, bilingual Laurier they found their ideal ambassador to Ottawa. The Pacauds were much more than Laurier's friends, they were his mentors, patrons and the Liberal "bosses" of the Eastern Townships. Over the next thirty years the Pacauds would run Laurier's election campaigns, staff his office, influence his policies, choose his candidates in Quebec, raise his money, pay his bills and nearly ruin him.

Although Wilfrid was promised to Zoé, in Arthabaska he played the field as a bachelor. "Last Sunday there was a *grande soirée* at Edouard Pacaud's," he wrote her in October. "A week ago Saturday there descended on the village a veritable swarm of people from Quebec City, composed of the daughters of M. Pacaud, their boyfriends and girlfriends and husbands. I was invited; you have known for a long time that I have always been lukewarm towards these things, and of my solitary nature. However, it is necessary to take heart against fate, and I went. To tell the truth, I didn't regret it. I had a good time. Meanwhile, and this will not surprise you dear, the women of Quebec City are not the equals of the belles of Montreal. There was a young lady there whom I think – without vanity – was making eyes at me, however I can boast of irreproachable fidelity. I love only you, no one but you.''

Laurier was fatally attractive to women, knew it and used it. This little vignette could only have caused Zoé a sleepless night. It was plain to her, and to Wilfrid, that the Pacauds were matchmaking, and he was going along with it. Apparently he thought she should do the same: "You said in your last letter that you do not enjoy yourself and don't go out at all," he wrote. "Why is this? For everyone it's a time for parties and fun. Why don't you take advantage of it? You know that I am not jealous, on the contrary, it hurts me to see you always alone in your room with your sad thoughts.''

As usual Laurier's thoughts were on himself: "I only make heartsick and sad those who love me. And meanwhile you love me always. Oh, bonne Zoé, there is no one in the world as wonderful as you. Chère bonne Zoé, I love you, yes, I love you and I love you dearly, but my dear, it is bitter to me to cause you so much wretchedness. I know that I do you wrongs, involuntary wrongs, but true nonetheless. I know, my beloved, that you do not reproach me, but I reproach myself. Au revoir, bien chère, a bientôt. Ton ami, Wilfrid.''

Zoé would not be allowed the luxury of suffering more than Wilfrid. Suffering was essential to Laurier's romantic self-image. An avid reader of poetry and fiction, young Wilfrid found in the Romantic poets of the early nineteenth century masculine models who legitimized his frail, consumptive, feverish persona. Playing the Byronic hero, the tortured genius doomed to an early grave, Laurier made virtues out of his cough, his fatigue, his *souffrances*. He wore his hair long and affected a bohemian indifference to dress, society, authority. He spent weeks in bed, *en déshabille*, and his favourite words, repeated obsessively in his letters, were *ennui* and *hélas*!

Having cast himself as the Romantic Hero, Laurier gave Zoé the role of Fair Maiden, the pure, beautiful, inaccessible virgin for whom the hero dies of love. He opens every letter with "Chère bonne Zoé" and praises her virtue, her love, her patience. "My dear kind Zoé," he writes in September, "I love you so much. You have no idea. My love is not flashy or noisy, but it is deep. My mouth says little, but my heart feels greatly. I do not know how to define the effect you have on me. When I am close to you, I feel happy, serene, calm. I often enjoy trying to analyze my feelings, being aware of what has happened to me since I have known you. I always come to the same conclusion: you have been my good angel, indeed, you have made me do all that you wanted me to do, you have led me & it goes without saying, you have always led me in the right path."

For practical, down-to-earth Zoé the role of "good angel" was highly unsatisfactory; she wanted a husband and babies. She was not convinced by Laurier's flowery, repetitive protestations of love; she accused him of coldness, a fault he admitted but excused: "Yes, perhaps I am cold on the outside, but my heart conceals strong emotions which no one can guess. I love you so much I could never express it."

If lust was one of those emotions, it was very carefully concealed. In sharp contrast to John Thompson's priapic shorthand notes to Annie, Laurier's love letters to Zoé during this critical separation are devoid of erotic phrases or suggestive words. He offers no praise for her physical beauty, no hugs or kisses, no pet terms of endearment or secret codes. He expresses no fear of losing her, no wild desire to take her in his arms or even hold her hand. It was a private, even clandestine, correspondence so there was no need to be discreet. Was Laurier shy, puritanical? Or did the ambiguity of his letters reflect a deeper ambiguity about his sexuality?

The exact nature of Laurier's illness has always been a subject of controversy. His symptoms appeared to be tubercular, yet his illness was cyclical, bouts of prostration followed by long periods of good health, and unlike most consumptives, Laurier lived to a ripe old age, dying, at seventy-eight, of a stroke. His illness also seemed to be related to his personal fortunes: when things were on the up he was full of vitality; in times of anxiety or unhappiness his hacking cough returned and with it lassitude, exhaustion and *ennui*. His illness first became serious just when his law practice was starting to flourish and marriage to Zoé was imminent; it allowed him to flee Montreal to a remote village where he was unknown,

myself to have hopes, even high hopes, as long as God grants me health,"
he wrote her a year later. "Unfortunately I am afraid I carry in my chest
the seed of death, that no power in the world can remove."

Laurier's visits to Montreal became less and less frequent, often he
cancelled at the last minute. More worldly women would have read the
warning signs; they would have been alienated by Laurier's morbidity and
histrionics, his love letters that read as if he had copied them out of a book,
his refusal to commit himself to an engagement, yet his unwillingness to
break off the *affaire* if that's what he desired. Zoé had strong misgivings.
She must often have wondered if Wilfrid didn't see her simply as a sister,
a nurse, a saint, a friend or a housemaid. He loved her, yes, but was he in
love with her?

The priest warned Zoé against Wilfrid – Laurier was an apostate, a
revolutionary, an agent of the devil – and the Gauthiers did their best to
discourage the relationship. "They will try in vain to separate us, the
whole world can't prevent it," Wilfrid wrote defiantly, but Zoé had her
own secrets: she had another suitor, Pierre Valois, a country doctor and a
friend of the Gauthiers. Zoé faced a terrible dilemma: Emma Gauthier was
to be married in May 1868 and Hannah was grown up; Zoé's usefulness
to the Gauthiers had come to an end. Her mother was dead, Zoé was now
on her own. Valois offered her love, security, respectability; Laurier . . .?
Zoé could wait no longer; if Laurier didn't formally ask for her hand by
New Year's Day, she would marry Valois.

The presence of a rival seemed to stiffen Laurier's spine. He embarked
on a drastic regime of drug therapy "in the hope that I will get back on
my feet at last, for our happiness together." As with Isabella Macdonald,
Laurier's "cure" involved heavy doses of opiates, a treatment that possibly
explains his "laziness." He promised to work hard "to hasten the moment
that will unite us forever," and he painted a rosy picture of their life
together in Arthabaska: "I don't know why I find myself so well off here,
I think it is a foretaste of the happiness I will savour later when you will
be here, my love, in this paradise on earth. Never have I enjoyed such
calm, such tranquility, such peace of mind. Often it happens in the happiest
circumstances that one's mind is agitated, restless, feverish, one doesn't
really know why, it doesn't require anything more to poison all the happiness within my grasp. In Montreal I found myself exactly in that situation. Here, on the contrary, there is none of that. I am sure it will be the

same for you when you are here in Arthabaska. My God, I will do everything in my power that it will be as soon as possible."

But *when*? Laurier had been in Arthabaska a year; he had never once invited Zoé to visit, and she had never received as much as a polite note from his landlady, Madame Poisson, or from any of the Pacauds. Did they even know she existed?

"I am very sad, my love, to see you so sad too," Laurier wrote in December. "For more than a month all your letters breathe suffering. You seem to be in the grip of a constant depression every hour of every day. And the worst of it is, I am the cause. Alas, when I see everyone, even your confessor, in league against me, and you resisting everyone, I feel unworthy of all this love. Oh Zoé, I do not merit that you should deny your own happiness for me. Everyone else in your position would long ago have broken the bonds which until now and for so long have brought you nothing but trouble. When I think of all this, and I think of it often, I don't know what to do, and I feel regret and great pain."

This is an invitation, almost a plea, for Zoé to put them both out of their misery. Laurier drops a broad hint that other women have caught his eye: "Since I have been here I have had the opportunity to see and get to know lots of young ladies. They are all obsessed with two things, clothes and good times. Apart from clothes, apart from parties, there is nothing else for them in the world. Oh Zoé, there is no one in the world as good as you! Pray for me, pray for me often." As always Laurier is being equivocal: he disapproves of the frivolous young ladies, but their frivolity attracts him; he asks Zoé to reject him, then to pray for him.

Trapped in this emotional bind, Zoé fell into despair. She made no secret of her emotions. "For several weeks your letters betrayed so much bitter resignation that I too was totally griefstricken," Laurier wrote on December 26. "Oh my beloved, you don't know how I love you! My life is attached to your life, I am happy if you are happy, and I suffer when you suffer." Wilfrid wrote that Dr. Poisson had diagnosed his illness as bronchitis, not tuberculosis: "I am almost cured and will be completely by summer. Like you I hope the new year that is beginning will be happier than the last. I am confident it will be perfectly happy."

However, New Year's Eve came and went without a marriage proposal. Laurier spent several days with Zoé in Montreal, and his next letter seems to be an elegy to their love affair: "Oh Zoé, the day I see you happy, even though I am dying, will be the best day of my life. Alas, why have the heavens refused me wealth and health? I would be so happy to use them for your benefit . . . think about your old friend from time to time. Like you, he regrets not being still in Montreal but for him it is always a great joy to remember the wonderful days of the past."

As gently and tactfully as possible, Zoé tried to bring her relationship with Wilfrid to an end.

"Yesterday and the day before I had two long, anxious days," Laurier wrote frantically on February 26. "Your letter which usually arrived Tuesday morning did not arrive until today. Tuesday I was not totally upset. I thought there must be a delay in the mail, but the next day there was still nothing. Alas, the tone of your letters during the last three weeks has made me terribly anxious. In all other circumstances this delay would not have alarmed me but your preceding letters filled my head with dark thoughts and I fear everything without yet admitting my fears. Dear Zoé, I felt more acutely than ever because I feared how hard it would be for me to lose you. Beloved, I will never be able to love anyone else, and if I lost you I would never get over it."

This is Wilfrid's last letter before their marriage ten weeks later. Zoé likely wrote Laurier to say that she had accepted Pierre Valois, and their correspondence ceased. Zoé had been frank about Valois, but her warning had failed to dent the impervious shell of Laurier's egoism: "I know that M. Valois is in love with you and it wouldn't surprise me if your cousin loved you too," Laurier replied. "You cannot prevent men being taken with you, but love only me and I will be happy."

Zoé was to marry Valois at the end of May 1868 in a double wedding with Emma Gauthier and her fiancé, François-Xavier Coutu, but on May 13, 1868 Zoé eloped with Wilfrid Laurier. The astonishing details of what has become one of the great romantic legends of Canadian history are given by Joseph Schull in his biography of Laurier. According to Schull, Laurier was quietly at work in Arthabaska on the afternoon of May 12 when a telegram arrived from Dr. Gauthier in Montreal: "Come at once, a matter of urgent importance." Laurier took the night train, arriving in Montreal the next morning hungry and dishevelled. Dr. Gauthier ordered him to strip and tapped his chest. Laurier had chronic bronchitis, he pronounced, nothing more, and what did he plan to do about Zoé Lafontaine? For two months Zoé had been in tears; she didn't want to marry Valois, it would be Laurier or no one. Emma's wedding was ruined, everyone was upset. Laurier had promised Zoé marriage; was he a man of honour or a cad?

125
•

Laurier was shown into the library to make up his mind; a startled Zoé was brought downstairs to meet him. Moments later Hannah Gauthier peeked in to find the tearful lovers in each other's arms. The household exploded with happiness. A dispensation was obtained from the bishop for their wedding to take place that evening. Godefroi-Napoleon Lafontaine was located and his permission secured. A marriage contract was drawn up: Laurier provided Zoé with an annuity of $300, Zoé's dowry was sixteen shares in a building society and her piano. At 8 p.m. in a small brick chapel on Dorchester St., with only the Gauthiers as witnesses, Zoé Lafontaine and Henri-Charles Wilfrid Laurier were married in a double ceremony with Emma Gauthier and François-Xavier Coutu.

"The first sight that greeted Laurier as he came back to the house with Zoé on his arm was the face of Pierre Valois," writes Schull. "Zoé gasped and ran forward contritely. It was unforgivable – she had sent no message – her head had been in a whirl all day. The forgotten suitor took her hand and then the hand of the bridegroom, forcing a smile that pained a happy man to see. There must always be winners, there must always be losers, said Valois; he had never quite believed in his luck. He raised his glass with the others when the toasts came."

An hour later Wilfrid was on the train back to Arthabaska, alone: he had an important case in court the next morning. Wilfrid and Zoé Laurier spent a chaste wedding night one hundred miles apart.

Unfortunately Schull offers not a shred of evidence to authenticate this story. He appears to have spun it out of hearsay or based it on anecdotes recalled decades later. Like any legend it is distorted: it was Dr. Poisson in Arthabaska, not Dr. Gauthier, who diagnosed Laurier as having bronchitis, and Laurier's letters to Zoé suggest that the Gauthiers opposed his suit because they feared for his health. Pierre Valois's behaviour is even less credible. What jilted lover toasts the rival who humiliates him? Valois's *sangfroid*, if his encounter with the newlyweds occurred at all, suggests that he was a "gooseberry" and his engagement to Zoé may have been a hoax cooked up, with his acquiescence, to force Laurier's hand.

Who cooked it up? The finger points to Hannah Gauthier, a mischievous teenager and Zoé's confidante. "Annette" was also a favourite of Wilfrid and a go-between. Hannah may have sent the telegram herself when it appeared that Laurier wasn't going to rise to the bait. Schull's version of the marriage portrays Laurier as a weak buffoon railroaded into a loveless match by a manipulative woman and her scheming friends, yet Wilfrid's last panicky letter to Zoé shows him almost beside himself with fear that he has lost her. Laurier was young, naive, egotistical and inhibited, but when Zoé was gone he may have realized the depth of his emotional dependency on her and he may have orchestrated his own elopement.

In his political life Laurier was certainly capable of courageous, even Quixotic, acts. The speed of the "shotgun" wedding suggests a planned conspiracy, and the complications of the plot the kind of melodrama that would have appealed to Laurier. An elopement, even a chaste elopement, is always instigated by the lover, and it could be that the whole thing was cooked up by Hannah and Wilfrid, with Zoé's tacit acceptance, to circumvent the Gauthiers' objections. There is no doubt about Laurier's happiness:

"Ma Zoé!" Wilfrid writes ecstatically from Arthabaska the next morning. "In spite of all the anxiety I feel at finding myself far away from you, you have no idea how happy I am, you cannot possibly have any idea. Oh my darling, how I love you! How I love you! And when I think I was in danger of losing you . . . but enough of these evil thoughts.

"My marriage has thrown the village into a state of shock. A revolution could not have been more overwhelming. I have received countless handshakes. At breakfast this morning I announced my marriage to the Poissons. Madame P was so happy she had tears in her eyes. She asked me to tell you she offers you her house with pleasure. I thanked her warmly for you, darling. Everyone here already loves you, my beloved.

"I worked all day like a slave and there is plenty more work waiting for me. However I am full of courage. How sweet it is to feel beloved.

"Au revoir, mon cher ange, I hold you close; love me, think of me, pray for me, for your husband, Wilfrid."

However Laurier managed to get married, he was relieved, relaxed and overjoyed. As always he was very self-conscious about the part he was playing:

"I am taking my new role as married man very seriously," he writes to Zoé on May 15. "Everyone is very anxious to see you here, darling, the women particularly. How anxious I am to see my darling again! I want to see her dear face, with those beautiful eyes that shed so many tears for me. Oh, my angel, how sweet it is to feel myself loved by you, and how sweet to say to myself: I am the one she loves, I am the one she chose among all. I feel my heart full of joy in spite of all the anxiety of being separated from you, darling. I am calm, my life seems infinitely happy. Au revoir, I kiss you like the good husband I will always be, ton ami, Wilfrid."

Zoé arrived in Arthabaska a few days later with her suitcase and piano. The jealous village *belles* must have been astonished to find that the mysterious Montreal *femme fatale* who had made off with Laurier was a demure little thing in a plain, high-necked dress who went to mass every morning and lived for gossip and cards. Zoé fit into Arthabaska like a hand into a glove. As she had known all along, domesticity dramatically improved Wilfrid's health; his law practice grew and, more important, he won the local seat for the Liberals in the Quebec provincial election of 1871. In 1874 Laurier went to Ottawa as MP for Drummondville-Arthabaska and took his place as a backbencher in the Liberal government of Alexander Mackenzie; three years later he was appointed to the Cabinet as minister of inland revenue, already the most influential federal Liberal in Quebec.

Zoé and Wilfrid always recalled their years in Arthabaska as the happiest of their lives. People of very simple tastes – they ended their lives as they began, dependent on charity – they were content to live in three rented rooms *chez* Poisson until Laurier built a simple brick house on the outskirts on town in 1876. Zoé busied herself with bazaars, cooking and the church; she grew plump and double-chinned, happiest digging in her vegetable garden or feeding her pets. She went back and forth to Montreal to visit Hannah and took a keen interest in the affairs of everyone associated with Arthabaska, Laurier and the Liberal Party. Laurier's portrait of Zoé as Madonna is misleading: her later letters and brief contemporary accounts suggest that while she was modest, she was also friendly, talkative and cheerful, a *bonne femme* who bossed her husband around and felt happy in her own domestic world. She had no intellectual pretensions, but she played the piano well, which Laurier enjoyed, and they both fancied birds. The Laurier household included an aviary as well as tropical fish and a menagerie of cats and dogs they called their "children."

The absence of children lay like a darkening shadow over the Lauriers' lives as the years passed and Zoé gave no evidence of becoming pregnant. Childlessness is always a source of gossip and speculation, but in Catholic Quebec in the 1870s it was evidence of sin and the Lauriers' private tragedy became both a religious and political issue: to his Conservative Catholic enemies, Laurier was either a devil or a pervert.

Laurier's sexuality was a potent component of his political charm – women mobbed him at public meetings, grabbing at his clothing in a frenzy – and he exploited his attractiveness with subtlety and skill. In an era when most Canadian politicians were content to wear one shapeless black homemade suit year in, year out, regardless of food stains, tobacco juice or mud around the pant cuffs, Laurier adopted an elegant costume – cut-away coat, striped trousers, vest, cravat and a high, starched collar – that made him look older, wealthier and, since he always wore his hair long, effete. He was one of the first politicians to wear a pale grey suit with matching grey silk topper; his suits were always well tailored, his hair immaculately barbered. He shunned hunting, fishing and sports; he did not smoke and drank only wine.

Laurier's fastidious dress was matched by his Pre-Raphaelite manners. "He holds his hands as if holding a flower between thumb and finger," observed an admiring acolyte, Mackenzie King, who described his prime minister as "artistic" and "gentle as a child." Men were fascinated by Laurier's languor, his slightly contemptuous, world-weary air of *ennui*. What was this delicate faun doing in the bearpit of politics?

Laurier's sexuality was as ambiguous as everything else about him, and, like Mackenzie King, speculation about his sexuality would haunt his political career. Laurier's imaginary flower suggests Oscar Wilde, who appeared on stage holding a lily, and by the end of the century the romantic pose of the suffering aesthete was almost exclusively homosexual. Many homosexuals, like Wilde, were married, and although homosexuality was a crime as well as a sin, even aggressive homosexual behaviour did not prevent men having successful public careers. Homosexuality was the love that dared not speak its name, and nobody else did either. Women were not supposed to know about sex at all, and a man who revealed that he knew about homosexuality was suspect himself. A man's private life was his business; it was only when sex became public that it became an issue.

All his life Laurier formed strong emotional bonds with men and before his marriage he lived in an almost communal society of young men who suffered from the same symptoms of hysteria, fever and nervous depression that he did; some of them remained intimate friends long after. Marriage, of course, was the sure "cure" for homosexuality. Did Dr. Poisson diagnose the real nature of Laurier's "illness" and urge him to marry? And did Laurier, sick and miserable, grasp at this straw?

The only public witness on the question of Laurier's sexuality was his good friend Judge Marc-Aurèle Plamondon, who declared emphatically that Laurier was impotent. How would he know? Was he covering for Laurier? Laurier may simply have been sterile. Laurier's recurrent fever, coupled with his love for fur coats, layers of clothing, warm fires and heavy quilts could have reduced his fertility almost to nil. Laurier was also away from home for weeks at a time, worked late into the night and was often in a sweat of anxiety.

If Wilfrid and Zoé had any secrets, they took them to their graves. Speculation about their private lives would likely have died away except for a sensational rumour that swept through Quebec in 1887 after Laurier became Liberal leader, and was widely believed after he became prime minister in 1896: Laurier had fathered an illegitimate son. The boy's mother, and Laurier's alleged mistress, was the wife of his law partner Joseph Lavergne, and Zoé's closest friend, the witty, clever, *trés chic* Émilie Lavergne.

Laurier seems to have met Émilie Barthe at one of the Pacaud's *grandes soirées* shortly after he arrived in Arthabaska – she may have been the girl making eyes at him in 1867. Émilie's mother, Louise, was a Pacaud, a sister of the seven powerful Pacaud brothers, and Émilie's cousin Ernest Pacaud was Laurier's campaign manager and good friend. If Laurier paid attention to Émilie at all, he would have seen a small, homely young woman with crooked teeth and bulging, hooded eyes who made up for her lack of physical charms by dressing extravagantly and being especially vivacious: Émilie was certainly one of those girls obsessed with clothes and entertainment Laurier so primly disapproved of.

Émilie's name would have caught Laurier's ear: her father, Joseph-Guillaume Barthe, was something of a celebrity in Laurier's radical *rouge* circle. In 1838 Barthe was imprisoned for publishing a poem praising the exiled rebels of 1837, and he later caused a sensation by publishing an article called "Canada Reconquered by France." In spite of its inflammatory title, the article merely advocated increased French immigration to Quebec, a cause Barthe promoted, without success, for the rest of his life.

A dilettante who dabbled in law, medicine, politics and diplomacy, Barthe managed to fritter away the family fortune – his father had been a ship's captain with a successful trade, probably in rum, between the Baie de Chaleurs and the French Antilles – and Émilie's prospects for marriage diminished with the size of her dowry. In 1876, when Émilie was twenty-

(Above left) Zoé Lafontaine.

(Above right) Zoé Laurier, wife of a simple avocat *in Arthabaska.*

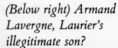

(Centre) Wilfrid Laurier was fatally attractive to women, knew it and used it.

(Below left) Wilfrid's "dear friend" Émilie Lavergne at the height of her influence.

(Below right) Armand Lavergne, Laurier's illegitimate son?

131

eight, a marriage was arranged with a family connection, Joseph Lavergne – her sister had married Lavergne's brother Louis – and Émilie arrived in Arthabaska just as Wilfrid and Zoé were moving into their new house. The Lavergnes established themselves nearby, close to the Laurier-Lavergne law office, and the two couples became inseparable friends. In 1878 Émilie gave birth to a daughter, Gabrielle, and in 1880 to a son, Armand.

Was Armand Laurier's child? Photographs of Armand taken at various times in his life offer few clues; some show a vague resemblance to Laurier, others none at all. If Armand looked like anyone, it was his mother. It seems incredible that Laurier, who prized loyalty highly, would have an affair with his partner's wife, especially so soon after their marriage, and would risk personal and political disaster on the threshhold of fame. Laurier, for all his Baudelaire mannerisms, was conservative, even prudish, when it came to morality, and unlike Sir Charles Tupper, developed no reputation as a seducer. The village life of Arthabaska would have made an illicit liaison almost impossible – the Lauriers' house was always crowded with servants, relatives, friends and neighbours, as was the Lavergnes' – and in fact the one eye-witness to leave an account of the relationship between Laurier and Émilie was her sharp-eyed young nephew, Renaud Lavergne.

Renaud Lavergne was two years older than Armand and as a child he was in and out of his aunt's house a great deal. He frequently encountered Wilfrid and Émilie together, and years later described their relationship, as he saw it, in a brief typewritten memoir. Renaud Lavergne's memoir is almost the sole source of information about Émilie, and since many of the stories in it seem to have been told to him by her, Émilie plays a much larger and more significant role in the story than may have been the case:

"When I bound myself in friendship to Laurier," she told Renaud, "I saw very quickly that this young deputy of the future was still in certain ways only the little greenhorn of St. Lin. His wife was not the person who could teach him even those elements of etiquette which a man of the world should know, above all a political man destined by his talents to enter the highest circles. He did not even know the correct way to eat an orange at table. I made him understand that this lack of etiquette would hamper him among the English elite with whom he would be called to mingle in Ottawa. I taught him then to eat, to dress with taste, in a word, all that a gentleman should know. As he was a man of wit, he understood it."

This portrait of Laurier as a slob reflects Émilie's image of herself as a sophisticated socialite, a woman of the world who would show Arthabaska a thing of two: Émilie was fond of repeating that she had lived in Paris, where she had known Victor Hugo and the poet-politician Lamartine, and that she had been to London, where she had learned English and how to serve afternoon tea.

"For Gabrielle, Armand and me, five o'clock in the afternoon was a delightful time, for my aunt, a *fête: le thé à l'anglais!*" recalled Renaud Lavergne. "For the beauty of the event she lit a few logs in the fireplace, but our attention was quickly drawn to the maid who came in with the tea things on a big silver tray. As soon as it was placed on a small, low table, my aunt lit the alcohol lamp under a silver kettle with a handle inlaid with ivory. Waiting for the water to boil, she passed us small cakes to calm our impatience. Then she brewed the tea in the matching teapot. Before serving the tea very hot in a pretty china cup, she poured us a big bowl of chocolate."

This portrait of Émilie serving tea to children in an obscure Quebec village reveals a woman living a rather pathetic fantasy. Émilie had lived in Paris, yes, or rather in Passy, near Paris, but she had lived there from 1853 to 1856 as a small child. Her Paris fashions were almost certainly imitations run up by a clever little dressmaker in Quebec City and her social graces, like her English, were probably picked up in Montreal where the Pacauds had many friends among the anglophone elite. Any suggestion that Émilie taught Laurier etiquette, or chose his clothes, is absurd. By 1880 Laurier was nearly forty; he had been a Cabinet minister for three years, an MP for six, he had dined frequently with the governor-general, without criticism of his table manners, and had long since caused a sensation in the House with his elegant clothes.

Was Laurier there for tea? Renaud doesn't say. He does say that Laurier visited Émilie every morning at eleven o'clock, rising from his office desk with the words, "Joseph, if you will permit, I will go talk with your wife." Renaud and Armand were often bearers of letters between Laurier and Émilie:

"On our return from college, we would find the two of them seated in the parlour, often with a book in hand, which they were reading or discussing. My aunt would call us to say hello to M. Laurier and to tell him about our scholastic achievements."

It was the most compromising position in which Renaud ever found Wilfrid Laurier and Émilie Lavergne.

Scandalous rumours of Armand's parentage would not have arisen, or been believed, had there not been a special friendship between Laurier and Émilie that was known and accepted. Émilie told Renaud that her relationship with Laurier had always been "proper"; her husband Joseph accepted it as a platonic bond between two unusually intelligent, inquisitive people who needed stimulating companionship. Émilie read voraciously; she was opinionated, articulate, a clever conversationalist who like to be *au courant* with all the latest trends in fashion, ideas, politics. In Arthabaska Émilie was stagnating; Laurier was her lifeline to the world. He spoke with her in English and shared her passion for British history, he brought her books from the parliamentary library and discussed them with her, he told her the latest news and explained the issues that were absorbing his attention in Ottawa.

"She admires Laurier as I do," Joseph told his worried brother Louis. "I have a good wife, why humiliate her unjustly? To lose her love at one blow? To destroy the peace of the family? I have a wonderful home, wonderful children. Altogether, I prefer to live in peace and let people talk."

Zoé, for whom Émilie secretly had such contempt, accepted the friendship. She had no choice, and if Laurier were impotent she had little fear that Madame Lavergne would seduce him. Laurier too let people talk: gossip about Émilie and Armand would not prevent him from becoming prime minister; in fact it may have helped, scotching rumours that he was "queer."

In Ottawa, far from Zoé and Émilie, Laurier loathed the tedium of the sessions and often spent days cooped up in his room reading. "The best thing about being a member of parliament is the indemnity," he wrote to Zoé a month after his election in 1874. Like most rising politicians, Laurier was preoccupied with money; he was always in debt and always anticipating windfalls which never materialized. Like Annie Thompson, Zoé kept the accounts and paid the bills. Although he was now quite robust, Laurier clung to his role as neurasthenic invalid. He complained about the weather – Ottawa was either too damp or too dusty – and fretted over finding hairs in his boarding-house food. He suffered frequently from bouts of fever coupled with a hacking cough, cold sweats, insomnia and delirium brought on by morphine.

After the defeat of the Mackenzie government in 1878, Laurier stayed on as an MP but was increasingly restless, unhappy and bored. He was the logical successor to Mackenzie when the latter stepped down in 1880, but he was only forty and a French-Canadian, and was passed over in favour of Edward Blake, who couldn't bring himself to lead the party and couldn't bear to quit. Then, in 1885, Laurier's moment came. That summer Laurier accused the Macdonald government of instigating the North-West rebellion by indifference and contempt for the native people: "I say give these men justice, give them freedom, give them their rights . . . and you will have contentment, peace and harmony where today discord, hatred and war are ruining the land." Laurier's passionate defence of civil liberties established him firmly as the leading spokesman for Liberalism in Canada, and his speech created the groundswell of popular sympathy for Louis Riel that caused much trouble for Sir John Thompson, Riel's executioner. The riots that broke out in Quebec after Riel was hanged were a tribute to Laurier's eloquence and power. In Quebec, Riel was a martyr not only to minority rights but to French Catholicism, and when Laurier condemned Riel's execution as an act of vengeance he won the grudging support of both French nationalists and the Catholic Church. His election as Liberal leader in 1887 revealed how far he had come since his days as a humble lawyer in Arthabaska.

But real power was not to be his until the election of 1896, when he trounced Tupper's Conservatives in an election fought largely over the Manitoba schools question. For Zoé, the move to Ottawa was difficult. The city was not a hospitable place for French-Canadian politicians, and Zoé had reason to be apprehensive as the wife of the first French-Canadian prime minister. British imperialism was at its chauvinist apotheosis, and as far as Ottawa's insular anglophone aristocracy was concerned, the Québécois, like the Chinese, the Zulus and the aborigines, were little more than superstitious savages. The racist theory of Anglo-Saxon superiority was accepted so completely that it was believed to be self-evident: wasn't the Empire itself conclusive proof? Laurier succeeded in the House of Commons only because he spoke in English: men who spoke in French, however eloquently, never achieved recognition outside Quebec. Zoé's imperfect, halting English would brand her as a *habitant*, yet few of the English-speaking wives could speak French, and saw no reason why they should. Zoé would have to speak English to the English, or not speak at all, and either way she would be patronized as an uneducated, simple-minded woman interested only in her kitchen, her husband and her *ménagerie*.

"Madame Laurier is shy and prefers talking French," observed Ishbel Aberdeen, "but is very pleasant when one comes to talk to her. She looks sad – feels having no children." Ishbel Aberdeen no sooner got Annie Thompson settled in Toronto than she took Zoé under her formidable wing. The Aberdeens were radical Liberals and sympathetic to Laurier, and Zoé was the kind of natural, sensitive woman without "side" who appealed to Lady Aberdeen. In the next two years the Aberdeens and the Lauriers would develop a personal friendship that went beyond politics: the Aberdeens dined *chez* Laurier in Ottawa, a favour they bestowed on no one else, and visited Arthabaska before returning to England. The formalities were strictly observed, but this obvious preference made the Aberdeens bitterly unpopular with the Conservatives and raised questions about the governor-general's impartiality.

Zoé's other great friend was Émilie Lavergne. Joseph Lavergne had been elected to parliament in 1887, and during the sessions Émilie stuck to Zoé like a burr: "Dinner party for 30 tonight, very bright," Lady Aberdeen wrote in her diary. "M. Laurier took me in, and His Excellency Mme. Laurier and Mme Lavergne." This is a peculiar *tableau-à-trois*. Where was Joseph? That was a question others were asking too.

"Madame Lavergne and Mlle. Lavergne have arrived in town and taken apartments at the Russell," the society columnist Amaryllis wrote in *Saturday Night* on September 15, 1897. "Judge Lavergne is also staying at the Russell." Amaryllis then described Émilie as "a brilliant woman called by many the Canadian Lady Chesterfield." Lady Chesterfield was well known as a close "friend" of the former British prime minister, Benjamin Disraeli, and Amaryllis was clearly implying that Émilie Lavergne was Laurier's mistress.

Neither Laurier nor Émilie attempted to stifle this speculation, although Amaryllis's innuendo was blatant, malicious and damaging. Gushing over one of Émilie's glittering receptions at which *le tout Ottawa* seemed to be present, Amaryllis remarked: "Madame Lavergne, like the capable hostess she is, managed to collect any quantity of men, so that very few ladies were left without cavaliers." Zoé Laurier, on the other hand, "gives a card party nearly every afternoon and loves best to entertain her intimate friends, all of whom are of the feminine gender. She is, of course, always charming to men, especially men on the right side of politics, but she infinitely prefers women's society." In case anyone missed her point, Amaryllis made it perfectly clear in her account of a fashionable *tableau vivant* Émilie presented at the Russell Theatre, starring her daughter Gabrielle as Our Lady of the Snows: "One found one's gaze straying over to the balcony to see how the Premier was taking it all."

Laurier couldn't have been taking it very well. No politician could afford to be publicly embarrassed, and Émilie appeared to be flaunting her intimate relationship with the prime minister. The Lavergnes lived only a few doors from the Lauriers on Theodore St. in Ottawa – the same proximity they enjoyed in Arthabaska – and as Amaryllis slyly noticed, they were a permanent fixture at the Laurier dinner table. Émilie went everywhere with Zoé, although she regarded Zoé as a fool: "Madame Laurier did not have the intellectual capacity to interest a man of the calibre of her husband," sneered Renaud Lavergne.

Émilie was now nearly fifty, still slender and beautifully dressed. She was noted for her wit, lively conversation and the extravagance of her entertainments. She was also known to be Laurier's *éminence grise*: "Mr. Erskine away for the day in Arthabaskaville to see the Lavergnes – & perhaps the Lauriers," Lady Aberdeen wrote in her journal on December 15, 1894 when it appeared the Liberals might be asked to form a government. Mr. Erskine was the governor-general's aide-de-camp and confidential go-between, and his first stop was Émilie.

What was the relationship between Laurier and Émilie Lavergne? In 1963 Renaud Lavergne gave a packet of forty-one letters to Quebec historian Marc La Terreur saying they were letters from Laurier to Émilie she had given to Renaud shortly before her death. The letters, all but two of them in English, appear to be part of a lovers' illicit conspiracy: they have no salutation and no date, Émilie is never mentioned by name and the signature is only "W.L." Friends and relatives are referred to by initials and Zoé is never mentioned. English was a code language in nineteenth-century rural Quebec, and the letters contain several expressions of warm, rather guilty affection: "Proud I am of your friendship, nay of your affections," Laurier writes in May 1891, "& could I yell it on the top of the houses, prouder yet would I be. Goodby to you, friend so dear & every day dearer. I must close & still my heart clings to this paper. Again goodbye for only a few days I hope, & until then & forever God bless you."

This letter, written when Laurier was fifty, suggests that his relationship with Émilie was intimate and emotional, yet the language of the letters is peculiarly stilted and ambiguous. Laurier addresses Émilie only as his "friend," his "dear friend" or "my dearest friend," describing himself "of all your friends the truest." Did "friend" mean "lover" or "beloved" in their private code? Was it necessary to reassure Émilie that she was his "friend" over and over again in the same letter, or was Laurier reminding her that she was nothing more than a friend? He never once says "I love you" or "I embrace you," although he sends love to her children, and for all their secretiveness, the letters contain none of the little jokes and endearments characteristic of love letters. Laurier's tone is arch, literary and pompous.

In their egoism and repetition of stock phrases, the letters resemble Laurier's courtship letters to Zoé, but they have none of the emotional warmth of the earlier letters. If Laurier is in love with Émilie, his passion is well under control. The letters reveal that Laurier and Émilie did not share a love of good books and intellectual discourse, but a delight in gossip and political intrigue: Laurier comments smugly on the troubles of mutual friends and drops broad hints that Émilie should cultivate certain powerful people he admires. Laurier was no more an intellectual than Émilie: apart from best-seller biographies of the French courtesan Madame de Staël, Empress Josephine and Mary Shelly, his taste ran to soppy poetry and the biographies of famous British politicians which he mined for appropriate quotes to give his English speeches an aura of erudition. In both French and English Laurier's vocabulary was extremely narrow: he used "ennui" to mean everything from boredom to anxiety, impatience, nervousness, loneliness and chronic depression, and "love" could be interpreted as respect, regard, affection, admiration, friendship or flattery. Laurier seems to have had no interest in art and his idea of music was a singsong around Zoé's piano; far from being an anglophile, Laurier wrote English as if it were French and misspelled Shakespeare as "Sheakpeare." Reading seems to have been simply a way of filling up empty time; anxious and insecure like Émilie, Laurier needed to be constantly active, *engagé* and amused.

When they first met, Émilie's bold sensuality may have ignited a *grande passion* that swept away all common sense and discretion, and in the throes of erotic fantasy, Laurier possibly held out to her the promise of a new life together once he left politics. His letters contain a number of ambiguous passages expressing his desire to flee "to some remote corner with the books and all those I love." The remote corner was usually the sunny hills of Arthabaska, "our silent commonplace abode," where Émilie was waiting, but so was Zoé. He sends Émilie a book and repeatedly urges her to read the chapter on "St. Ann's Hill": "Put the book aside; keep it in readiness that I may point out to you what has most struck me, what would be my dream, what picture now haunts me. I would fondly dream of the rest of St. Ann's Hill, after the toils in which I am engaged." If, as Charles Fisher states in *Dearest Émilie, The Love Letters of Sir Wilfrid Laurier to Madame Émilie Lavergne*, the book was a recently published biography of the British politician Charles James Fox by Henry Wakeman, the chapter on St. Anne's Hill refers to the country retreat Fox shared in retirement with his mistress, Mrs. Armistead.

Did Laurier and Émilie plan to run off together, and did Laurier, as he had with Zoé, prevaricate until the crucial moment had passed? The idea seems insanely self-destructive. Where would they go? How would Laurier support them? Was gregarious, devout Émilie prepared to endure social ostracism, humiliation and eternal damnation? Was Wilfrid prepared to ruin his political future and abandon Zoé without a penny?

By 1891 any such fantasy had become, for Laurier at least, a fading dream. Power was within his grasp, and in the chaos that followed Macdonald's death Laurier had more interesting things to do than write sentimental notes to his "dear friend."

Émilie sensed the change in her fortunes; her letters became so bitter and unhappy that Laurier was constantly cajoling her out of a bad mood: Émilie complained she was lonely and bored, she was getting wrinkled and fat, Laurier was sarcastic, her friends were mean to her, she hated politics. Émilie was pushing her relationship with Laurier to a crisis, but Laurier smoothly evaded a confrontation. Wilfrid and Émilie were now a middle-aged couple who had known each other well for at least fourteen years. Émilie accuses him of being cold, and Laurier's letters give the impression that he was conducting an elaborate but tedious flirtation, trapped in a game he would just as soon get out of. But how? Émilie was his partner's wife, Zoé's friend and his nextdoor neighbour; Émilie was also a very dangerous enemy.

"She was merciless towards an adversary," wrote Renaud Lavergne. "She knew where to find his weak spot in order to ridicule it." Émilie certainly knew Laurier's weak spot. Was Laurier afraid of blackmail? The cryptic, equivocal style of his letters seems to have been a calculated defence against the possibility of someone using them to incriminate him, and the most likely person, in the event of a quarrel, would be Émilie herself.

Laurier may have been protecting himself from a woman he loved, but did not trust, or he may have been using Émilie, as he used everyone else.

Émilie was a woman of very substantial political influence in Arthabaska: "My aunt entertained a great deal," recalled Renaud Lavergne. "She took the place of Édouard Pacaud, whose house, until his death, was the centre of the Pacaud–Laurier–Lavergne–Cannon clan, which included people passing through Arthabaskaville especially when the court was sitting. My aunt's salon therefore became neutral ground."

With her huge, interlocking family and vast network of political contacts, both English and French, Émilie Lavergne became the matriarch of the powerful Pacaud empire. Laurier was totally dependent on her friendship and support: Edouard Pacaud had made Laurier, Émilie could break him. She was Laurier's confidante, messenger and spy; she was his contact with his campaign manager Ernest Pacaud in Quebec City, his organizer, assistant, publicist and, most important of all, Émilie was his banker.

Laurier had no money. He had long since relinquished his law practice to Joseph Lavergne; until 1896 he and Zoé lived on his meagre stipend as an MP. In the years before he became prime minister, who paid for Laurier's expensive clothes, the ceaseless round of parties in Arthabaska and receptions in Ottawa, his private secretary, Ulric Barthe, a cousin of Émilie, the delicious dinners and French wines that made him respected in political circles? Who paid for Laurier's election campaigns, his advertising, the bribes that were a necessity of Quebec politics? Who enticed supporters with promises of railway contracts, and handed out patronage after the Liberals won?

It appears that Laurier's money came from the Pacauds' *bourgeois* friends in Montreal and Quebec City, the same unscrupulous promotors and financiers who bankrolled Sir John A. Macdonald, and the money likely came to Ernest Pacaud, via the gracious Madame Lavergne, in a way that would arouse no suspicion. Laurier may have had only the vaguest idea where the money had been obtained, and would not have asked; he would have sent his bills to Pacaud, and they would have been paid.

Ernest Pacaud was partisan, reckless and impulsive, and Laurier's surviving letters to Émilie were written at a time when Pacaud's affairs were exploding in public scandal, a scandal that could have tainted Laurier with corruption. Ernest Pacaud had been the go-between in a $1-million payoff by the Liberal premier of Quebec to a crooked railway promoter, and $100,000 of that money had stuck to Pacaud's fingers. The Conservatives were asking: had it gone to Laurier?

In anxious, almost panicky letters written to Émilie while the Pacaud scandal was at its height, Laurier dwells on his sense of foreboding and impending doom; he fears he may have to resign and "commence my career anew"; he suffers from painful coughing spells, fever, insomnia, fatigue and morphine-induced delirium; he broods on old wounds and "miseries"; he paces fretfully around his room waiting impatiently for letters from Émilie and sends off telegrams if they are late; he worries about his mail being opened and complains about "uncertainties": "How much they weigh on me! How they rack both mind & heart! How miserable is life!"

Laurier's *angst* could be interpreted as lover's jitters, except his letters contain repeated references to Ernest Pacaud, as well as to his powerful Quebec mentor, Laurent-Olivier David, and to Edward Blake, the former Liberal leader. Laurier seems to be almost pleading with Émilie – he refers to her as Pacaud's "private secretary" – to keep him informed of developments. Since Laurier cannot contact Pacaud himself for fear of being implicated, he uses Émilie as a courier: "You will give him comfort & advice . . . I cannot give up the poor, imprudent, erring boy. I love him, & above all I owe him so much. You speak of what you owe him, it is I who am his debtor. Though I have always been his friend, my affection for him would not be half what it is, if he had not had such a part in the molding of my heart for life." What did Laurier mean? "The molding of my heart for life" could be interpreted by Émilie as an oblique declaration of love, and a reminder of her duty to assist and protect her lover. Laurier never hesitated to use "love" in a purely political context.

Émilie didn't fail: Ernest Pacaud was prosecuted, convicted and fined (he was later acquitted on appeal) but not a shred of evidence was uncovered linking Laurier to Pacaud's $100,000. Once the crisis blew over, Laurier's letters to Émilie became more formal and infrequent and a year later he adopted the familiar elegiac tone: "Alas! how time flies! the flight of time would be nothing if before it goes away, it had brought to us the share which seems due to us of those blessings which are in sight & yet unattainable." He urged Émilie to find other interests: "Why do you not employ your activity in litterary [*sic*] work, for all your letters show me what latent powers you have of litterary [*sic*] production & litterary [*sic*] excellence."

Laurier flattered Émilie shamelessly, absurdly comparing her to Madame de Staël. The role of *courtesan* was one Émilie fancied, and Laurier's letters are sexually suggestive: as he did with Zoé, Laurier entices

Émilie to fall in love with him, while reminding her that it is hopeless. Did Émilie realize she was being manipulated? Did she care? Émilie got her pound of flesh. Laurier was her ticket out of town.

In Ottawa, Émilie quickly set the town on its ear, and if it occurred to Madame Lavergne that Paris gowns and *grandes soirées* were inappropriate for the wife of a humble backbencher, or that her regard for Laurier appeared to be a little too warm, she didn't care: Émilie had her day in the sun.

But Ottawa was not Paris, and Émilie was not Madame de Staël; Émilie's attempts to estalish a brilliant *salon* only aroused the jealousy of the dowdy, unsophisticated Ottawa *anglais*, and the greater her success, the more virulent their malice. According to Sandra Gwyn in *The Private Capital*, Amaryllis was a poor, plain young spinster, Agnes Scott, who, by virtue of her old Ottawa family, hung around the fringes of Rideau Hall society and was automatically invited everywhere. If Madame Lavergne noticed Miss Scott at all, she probably snubbed her. This was a mistake. Amaryllis could make or break reputations, and she broke Émilie's.

Ishbel Aberdeen now had Ottawa firmly under her thumb, and she was not about to be challenged by a *parvenue* from Arthabaska. The Aberdeens were Presbyterians, and Ishbel, for all her radicalism – as a young woman she had patrolled the London slums dragging prostitutes off the streets–enforced puritanical standards of conduct in both public and private life. After the *tableau-à-trois* at Rideau Hall, Madame Lavergne is conspicuously absent from Lady Aberdeen's diary, although Ishbel cultivated the wives of the French-Canadian judges and senators, and made Zoé Laurier vice-president of her pet organization, the National Council of Women. Gabrielle Lavergne's name is also missing from the small group of eligible girls Ishbel welcomes to Rideau Hall as friends for her daughter Marjorie; nor was Gabrielle, a willowy, attractive young woman, noticed among the débutantes who formed the fashionable May Court club.

Lady Aberdeen may have had a frank talk with her new prime minister about Madame Lavergne, but Émilie's days were numbered when, on the evening of June 21, 1897, Queen Victoria conferred on Laurier the Grand Cross of St. Michael and St. George. Sir Wilfrid's knighthood immediately catapulted humble Lady Laurier over the head of smart Madame Lavergne: Zoé, with her country ways, would be welcome at Windsor, and Émilie, for all her witty repartee, would not.

For the queen's Diamond Jubilee celebration at Westminster Abbey, Lady Laurier wore pearl grey silk and diamonds in her hair. Zoé had become very fat, but she was no longer dowdy. Her favourite ornament had once been a crucifix, but now she blossomed out in plumes and ruffles, embroidered flounces and beaded lace rosettes. The youthful style was not becoming—with her white hair and double chin Zoé looked like a sagging, top-heavy wedding cake—but she was letting it be known that she could now afford to dress as expensively, if as badly, as everyone else.

Zoé owed her new status to the queen, but her new money came from Toronto. The Liberals had prospered since the homespun days of Alexander Mackenzie, and one who had prospered most was Laurier's new post-master-general, the hard-drinking millionaire William Mulock. Shocked to discover that Laurier could not afford to buy a house in Ottawa, Mulock immediately raised $100,000 to ensure that the prime minister and his wife would be able to live in appropriate style. Mulock justified this handsome gift on the peculiar ground that the prime minister should be free from the temptations of bribery, and Laurier accepted the money as nimbly as he had accepted a title. The influence of the Pacauds was at an end: Laurier was now in the pocket of the Toronto financial establishment, a power shift of profound political significance.

Thanks to Mulock's money, Zoé had a large, homely yellow brick house at 335 Theodore St. furnished in the gilt and brocade Louis XVI style Zoé seems to have favoured in her Pompadour incarnation. Amaryllis reported that Zoé's companions were "three cages of birds, two cats and two tiny Pomeranians who sit on the most luxurious chairs and sofas and to whom she feeds chocolates." Amaryllis seems to have been intent on making Lady Laurier as eccentric as Madame Lavergne was vulgar; she neglected to say that Zoé also had a companion, Yvonne Coutu, daughter of her old friend, Emma Gauthier, and an Irish manservant, Tilley.

Wilfrid and Zoé lived in the house for the rest of their lives. Their domestic routine differed little from that during their years in Arthabaska. Laurier had breakfast at 9 a.m. with the Ottawa *Citizen*, then disappeared into his library with his secretary and the mail. If the House was in session he would leave for his office at 11 a.m., come home for dinner at 6:30 p.m. and return to the House for the evening session at 8 p.m. When the House was not sitting Wilfrid spent most of the day and the evening in his library writing letters, working on speeches or reading in his armchair by the fire.

Wilfrid, like Zoé, was a homebody. He always treasured the "monk-ish" quiet of his office or study, a fire crackling in the grate, a cat purring on his lap. (Could Laurier's illnesses have been allergies?) It is hard to imagine Wilfrid putting up with Émilie's incessant chatter for more than an hour, and he didn't. He abhorred fresh air and exercise; he never rode a horse or drove a buggy or car, he simply hopped on the streetcar that ran past his front door. He hated travel: his trip to the Jubilee at the age of

Sir Laurier, the grand seigneur.

fifty-five was his first trip abroad; he showed not the slightest interest in visiting Paris or Rome and he went to the United States, reluctantly, for the hot springs. It is doubtful that Laurier ventured as far west as Toronto before becoming prime minister.

Lady Laurier, more cultivated than the women who condescended to criticize her.

Caring for this conservative, often cranky man must have been a chore for Zoé, and as Laurier grew older he became more and more the *grand seigneur* who liked to gather his followers around him in an admiring throng. Zoé was one of the busiest hostesses in Ottawa: on Wednesdays and Saturdays she held formal dinners for the Cabinet ministers and their wives, including judges, local dignitaries and, in turn, all the Liberal members; every Sunday, after mass, a formal luncheon for twelve to fourteen guests was followed by a general open house, where the curious might risk a brief word with the prime minister, then dinner *en famille* with relatives or out-of-town visitors and finally an evening of cards with friends. During the week Laurier liked to invite odds and sods of party faithful home for dinner on a moment's notice. When Zoé wasn't overseeing the loaves and fishes in the kitchen, she was drawing up guest lists, planning menus, ordering groceries, washing dishes, cleaning house and making polite conversation with total strangers in English and French. Forced to converse with unilingual anglophones from Nova Scotia and Ontario, Zoé was the first prime minister's wife to become fluently bilingual, although her written English, like her written French, was always idiosyncratic and ungrammatical. "I belong to everyone and to no one in particular," she lamented. "I would rather be the wife of a simple *avocat* in Arthabaska."

Zoé was the first prime minister's wife to take a genuine interest in the arts. Her musical training had been only at her mother's knee and her talent as a pianist was undeveloped, but her appreciation of music went far beyond the popular songs and music-hall jingles that passed for entertainment in a country where classical music was rarely, if ever, played. Zoé's interest in classical music was serious: people who came to her recitals were expected to sit quietly on straight chairs and listen, the way civilized people did in Europe, and not gossip, and shuffle their feet and yawn in the performer's face.

Culture of any kind was new to Ottawa, and the idea that to curry favour with the prime minister's wife one should have to sit through an hour of noise by some unspeakable German caused a great deal of resentment. Zoé persevered. While Émilie Lavergne was holding euchre parties to aid St. Luke's hospital, Zoé was organizing benefit *musicales* featuring young Canadian performers she wanted to send to Paris. In addition to raising money, Lady Laurier's concerts gave the young musicians the prestige of her patronage as well as a rare opportunity to be noticed, and one of her protégés, Eva Gauthier, became a famous concert soprano. Zoé

Laurier was considerably more cultivated than the women who condescended to criticize her.

Zoé was more influential with Laurier too than most people guessed.
"She had a great deal of common sense, good judgment and prudence,"
wrote her close friend, L.-O. David. "She knew when to keep silent and
speak out at the proper times. She did not try to puff herself up and make
herself important by indiscreet talk." Zoé knew that there was room in
the limelight for only one Laurier, and any attempt to share it would
embarrass Wilfrid and herself, but through her enormous network of card-
playing friends – it may have been bridge in the evenings, but it would
have been poker in the afternoons – she was a valuable source of information for Laurier. Zoé was also judgmental and fiercely partisan: politics, to
Zoé, was people, and power was doing what you could to help the
deserving.

Laurier jokingly called Zoé his "Minister of Public Charity." Every
beggar, office-seeker, opportunist, widow, orphan and aggrieved Liberal
who banged on the prime minister's door soon learned that Lady Laurier
had her foot in. Zoé read all their pleas, investigated them, sorted them
out and every day presented Laurier with the favoured few in a wicker
basket: he was said never to turn her down. Zoé also banged on the doors
of the ministers in the interests of a particular cause or client, and seldom
went away disappointed. When Laurier brought in the civil service commission to make appointments according to ability and seniority, he said
to Zoé: "My poor dear, you have lost your job!"

For Laurier, she was always his *chère bonne Zoé*: "My wife is a real
Madeleine," he told his friend L.-O. David, "a dead bird, a dog with a
crushed paw will make her burst into tears." Laurier's portrait is typically
romanticized and condescending, but everyone praised Zoé's concern for
the poor and the unfortunate. Zoé had known poverty, and she would
never be ashamed of it.

Poverty was considered a vice at the end of the nineteenth century, a
consequence of ignorance, sloth and sin, and the poor were avoided as a
source of both moral and physical contamination. When Ishbel Aberdeen
arrived in Ottawa she was shocked by the slums of Lower Town, the
squalid streets, the acres of workers' shacks surrounding the lumber mills
and the large number of foundlings' homes and orphanages where unwant-
ed babies were left to die. Open sewage, contaminated water and unpas-
teurized milk were the sources of most of the virulent diseases that swept

through Ottawa, affecting rich as well as poor, and women like Lady Aberdeen were among the first to see that filth was the root of disease: the early feminist movement in which she played a prominent part grew out of women's concern about the high rate of child mortality. Ishbel Aberdeen organized the Victorian Order of Nurses to provide care to those who could not afford it, and made compassion for the sick and impoverished a respectable emotion. Her efforts created violent controversy, but she found an ally in Lady Laurier, and Zoé established the prime minister's wife in her role as Lady Bountiful.

"Ma chère amie," Laurier wrote to Zoé on his thirty-fourth birthday in 1875. "I wish I were home so I could embrace you. I embrace you with all my heart . . . au revoir, ma bonne amie, yet once more I embrace you." Twenty-four years later, in 1899, Laurier wrote his "chère bonne amie" an affectionate letter from Washington enclosing a cheque for $300 at Zoé's request. Joking that she has more money than he does, he closes: "I embrace you like the wonderful wife that you are." Their letters are missing for the years of Laurier's relationship with Émilie, but nothing before or after suggests that Wilfrid and Zoé were ever estranged. Laurier's letters to Zoé are the easy, intimate letters of a husband to a wive he loves, and he is more frank about his kidney stone than John Thompson was with Annie.

Laurier ended his relationship with Émilie Lavergne in 1900. He appointed Joseph to the Supreme Court of Quebec in Montreal and returned all Émilie's letters to her by a messenger known to them both, Rodolphe Boudreau, clerk of the Privy Council. It was a cruel and cowardly thing to do, and if he hoped Émilie would reciprocate, he was disappointed. Émilie kept his letters, and nursed a bitter grievance for the rest of her life. The Lavergnes' departure was maliciously noted in the Ottawa press. After praising Joseph as a member of the "old guard" who was "always a gentleman and one who reflected credit on his race and province," the article said: "Of his charming wife, who now leaves Ottawa for good, a volume might be written. She was not popular, we have reason to believe, among some of the 'unknown wives of well-known men,' mostly on account of her nationality, her attractive graces and gifts, but she could be courteous to such people. She impressed observing people of other races as a superior woman, who could shine at any court, even at Tuileries, or who with her accomplishments might have consoled and brightened Napoleon in his last hours at St. Helena."

Laurier continued to profess himself Émilie's "true, warm and sincere friend," and on his sixtieth birthday in 1901 he wrote to her: "I do not for one single moment forget you. The friendship of the past has been too close to be followed by absolute separation. I cannot help regretting the good old times." However, when Émilie wrote two years later requesting an increase in judges' salaries, Laurier declined, and in 1909 Laurier passed over Joseph Lavergne for the post of chief justice of Quebec. Émilie never forgave him. Following Joseph's death in 1922 she entered the Grey Nun's convent in Montreal as a paying guest, and died there in 1930 at the age of eighty-two.

Zoé can't have regretted the departure of the woman who had cast a dark shadow over her life for so many years. Wilfrid's open friendship with Émilie, however platonic, was insulting to Zoé, and by allowing it to be dragged through the press Laurier gave credibility to venomous gossip that irretrievably damaged Zoé's reputation. In 1900 Zoé's spirits were also lifted by the Liberals' great election victory, and her political passions shine fourth in a letter to Lady Aberdeen in Scotland:

"I thank you from my heart for your kind congratulations & let me tell you how flattered I am by your warm appreciation of the last election results in favour of my husband. I know you have always taken such a great interest in the success of the good cause that I was not surprised to see the satisfaction you expressed in your letter.

"If our friends are rejoicing with us, our adversaries are *devastated* – they were so confident about winning. We did not understand where all this assurance came from. They were counting, I presume, on this cry of race and religion which they used so much against my husband. Our side was also certain of victory. As for myself, I did not worry a moment.

"The poor *Bleu* party is completely disorganized. Sir Charles [Tupper] should have ended his political career more gloriously. He and his party were beaten: this is more than enough to destroy a man."

Zoé doesn't forget to give Ishbel the gossip:

"Sir Adolphe Caron is seriously ill in the Victoria Hospital. I believe that the fight was not solely responsible for his serious illness, he had been indulging in all sorts of excesses for a long time. He will not leave the political scene blessing his friends, who treated him shabbily.

"Lord and Lady Minto [the Aberdeens' successors] have shown themselves to be fairly sympathetic to my husband's cause. Lady Minto is generally well-considered but her greatest successes are in the world of 'sport': skating, bicycling, all outdoor amusements. That is where she excels. As far as Lord Minto is concerned, no good and no harm are said of him. I often hear people say 'What a difference from Lord and Lady Aberdeen.' Yes indeed, and we will never know others like them.''

Zoé knew how to lay on flattery with a double-edged trowel. Zoé's capacity for wit and malice must have equalled Émilie's, and she too was an opponent to be reckoned with. Was that the root of their friendship? Did they both laugh at Laurier?

Laurier had a great many "chères amies": as an old man he was writing ardent letters to Marie-Louise Pacaud, the elderly widow of his friend Ernest. "Laurier enjoyed the company of clever women," observed his confidant, L.-O. David. "and towards them he showed a particular tenderness, an exquisite *politesse*." In his letters Laurier taunted Émilie with stories of trysts with old flames who were, he implied, younger, prettier, more amusing and more affectionate than she. Émilie suffered paroxysms of jealousy, as Laurier no doubt intended. He appears to have been a parlour *roué*, a seductive man who loved the chase, but feared the conquest. Impotent or not – impotence didn't stop George Bernard Shaw from pursuing women relentlessly – Laurier was a flirt. Marriage gave him the freedom to play at seduction, with no commitments: *hélas*, there was always Zoé.

Zoé did her best to make Wilfrid's life safe and comfortable and she probably viewed his *amours* as part of his compulsive need to boost his fragile ego. Earthy, no-nonsense Zoé must have tired early of Wilfrid's *ennui*, his hypochrondria, his narcissistic posturing: if he wanted to write coy little *billets doux* to his *amies*, well at least she didn't have to read them. Zoé's life had been hard; she was used to putting up with things. She may have adored Laurier, she may have secretly despised him. She put up with him.

Between 1900 and 1911 Laurier enjoyed fame that eclipsed the memory of Macdonald. Millions of immigrants from eastern Europe and Great Britain poured into the new western provinces, bringing an unprecedent boom in manufacturing, railways and real estate. Cities sprang up, vast fortunes were made, and the *rapprochement* between English and French Canadians seemed to be solid, although there were recurrent controversies about Canada's involvement in British imperial adventures. Laurier was admired as a great orator and great statesman, the Sun King who prophesied that the twentieth century belonged to Canada.

Zoé was eclipsed. She began to suffer from severe headaches and blurred vision and her eyesight gradually failed; she struggled on bravely, leaning on Laurier's arm, but became increasingly sensitive about her infirmity, embarrassed at not being able to recognize old friends, unable to perform all the myriad little household tasks that had been her pride and strength. She lost confidence; for the first time she felt she was a liability to Laurier. How could Laurier appear in public with an ugly, doddering old woman on his arm? Zoé kept to the house and Laurier travelled alone.

In 1911 Laurier went into an election on a popular platform of free trade with the United States, but in the last days of the campaign the

Zoé, now blind, with Wilfrid on their 50th wedding anniversary, May 13, 1918.

151

Conservative cry went up "No truck nor trade with the Yankees!" and the Liberals went down to stunning, unexpected defeat. Laurier was devastated. Now Zoé, not he, was an invalid, and at seventy, he was too old to return to law or start a new career, too old, in truth, to carry on as Liberal leader. But Laurier carried on. After years of pining for "those hills where my heart is," Laurier never seriously considered retiring to Arthabaska; his passion for the countryside seems to have been as artificial as his passion for women.

The outbreak of the First World War in 1914 caught Laurier in a dilemma: his immediate, uncritical support for Great Britain shocked his supporters in Quebec, yet because of their lack of enthusiasm for what they saw as a foreign war, the French-Canadians appeared to the rest of Canada as slackers and traitors. As a French-Canadian prime minister, Laurier had surrounded himself with conservative anglophones and had picked fights with Quebec nationalists, but in 1917 he aligned himself with Quebec in opposing conscription for military service. Laurier's senior anglophone members, his most trusted colleagues and closest friends, defected *en masse* to form a pro-conscription Union government with the Conservatives. Laurier was left to lead a ragtag Liberal rump to certain disaster. After fifty years of dedication, inspiration and glory, Wilfrid Laurier was back where he started.

There was no one influential or respected enough to replace him as Liberal leader. Erect, elegant, alert at seventy-seven, Laurier continued to go to his office every morning at 11 a.m., lunch at the Rideau Club and have dinner at home. Zoé was now quite deaf and completely blind. When people told her Laurier was not looking well, she lamented: "How can I tell? *I cannot see him!*"

Laurier suffered a stroke in his office on the afternoon of February 15, 1919. He died peacefully at home the next night, his hand in Zoé's. One of the first mourners to appear at the door of 335 Theodore St. was Sir Wilfrid's bright-eyed, self-appointed son, Mackenzie King. King found Laurier lying in a bronze casket in his court uniform, surrounded by children from the convent kneeling in prayer. Leaning over the body, King observed: "My first feeling was one of desire that he had been dressed in his black coat, the one he was accustomed to wear in Parliament. I thought his face looked very worn & there was a mark on the forehead where he had struck himself when he fell in his office on Saturday afternoon. The face was drawn. I felt the man had gone, with him the spirit. The body was a mere shell. I scanned the features carefully. There was evidence of pain & suffering, little of repose. I could not but wish Sir Wilfrid had had more faith in his life. He was an agnostic.''

King turned to Zoé and observed that love was stronger than death. *"But he is not here!"* cried Zoé.

L.-O. David said Laurier had only one regret: "It is too bad that I will not leave a son."

Zoé lived for nearly three more years, bedridden but with her wits about her. The cause of her blindness was never specified: it may have been cataracts, glaucoma or diabetes. In August 1919 Zoé was the guest of honour at the Liberal convention that chose Mackenzie King as leader. Zoé had tried to marry King off to no avail; perhaps in hope she left King 335 Theodore St. in her will.

Zoé developed pneumonia in the fall of 1921. "I think I am dying," she said to her nephew, Robert Laurier, on Hallowe'en. "I feel so tired, so tired that I would like to have a long, long rest, but I cannot sleep.' Zoé closed her eyes, and a few moments later she said: "I think I will meet him soon." When Robert asked "Who?" Zoé did not reply. She slept, and died quietly in the early hours of November 1, All Souls' Day.

CHAPTER 8

City Mouse, Country Mouse: Laura Borden and Isabel Meighen

*W*HEN THE HOUSE OF COMMONS went up in flames on the frosty night of February 3, 1916, Laura Borden sat at home with the curtains drawn, refusing even to glance at the lurid glow in the western sky. She knew the House was sitting late, and Rob would be there. Was he safe or badly burned, alive or dead? Laura hovered by the telephone, trying to shut the noise of the alarm bells out of her ears. Finally, the phone rang. It was Rob. He had escaped in his shirt-sleeves, his hair and eyebrows badly singed. Could she send an overcoat?

Laura's reaction to one of the most spectacular and tragic fires in Canadian history was characteristic of her attitude to life: she turned away. Annie Thompson would have been up on the Hill beating out the flames with her bare hands, but Laura Borden, who grew up only a few streets from Annie's old home in Halifax, was a colder fish, a bundle of nerves who froze her fears into a shell as brittle as the mantle of ice that formed that night on the gutted shell of the House of Commons.

Laura's heart was as empty as that blackened building where her husband had spent the past twenty years of their marriage, twenty years out of twenty-six, and she had spent ten of those years alone in Halifax while Rob was in Ottawa. Laura was now fifty-four, childless and depressed. She had suffered a breakdown that winter, the result of exhaustion, pneumonia and the war. She had tried so hard to *do something*, but the harder she tried, the worse things seemed to get, so she stopped trying.

Laura Borden had not been prepared for war. Who had? At the end of July 1914 she and Rob were golfing in Muskoka when word came that Austria had declared war on Serbia. They prolonged their vacation three more days, hoping that the crisis in eastern Europe would blow over, then Rob left for Ottawa, leaving Laura behind in case he could return. On August 4, 1914 Britain declared war on Austria and Germany; since

Canada was part of the British Empire, its participation was immediate and unquestioned.

Canada had no army, only a motley, ill-equipped militia. Canada's army would be civilian, and as patriotic fervour fanned across the country, men threw down their tools, left their farms and offices and schools and rushed to enlist. Weeks later, resplendent in khaki uniforms, they were sailing to England; months later they were butchered in Belgium. The war's appetite for flesh was insatiable: thousands and thousands and thousands of men disappeared across the ocean, only the crippled came back. The rest were buried in Flanders' fields, or fought on.

The women remained at home, abandoned, impoverished and terrified. They were alone, without money or jobs, many trying to raise families on soldiers' pay of $1 a day. Horror stories of German rape and butchery in Belgium created widespread panic, and anyone opposed to the war was persecuted or jailed. With the sudden break-up of their families, women lost their security; they were thrown back on their own economic and psychological resources. The more adventurous went to the front as nurses or found jobs in munitions factories, discovering for the first time the freedom a paycheck could bring, but working for wages was still a shocking, degrading concept for most women, reeking of spinsterhood and the sweatshop, a life of poverty on the fringes of society. Conditioned for generations to be dependent, women now turned to churches and charities for support: What could they do? The churches and charities replied: Win the war! How? Knit!

So the women knitted. They knitted scarves, sweaters, undershirts, tuques, balaclavas and socks, millions and millions of socks, and when they weren't knitting they rolled bandages, millions of bandages. It was laborious, time-consuming work – a factory in Toronto could turn out more socks in an hour than most women could knit in a year – but it made women feel useful and took their minds off their worries. All of these socks and bandages had to be collected and sent overseas, and the logical agency to do this was the Red Cross.

Charity work had not been particularly fashionable before the war; it was associated with disease, dirt, vice, and, in Ottawa, the bossy liberalism of Lady Aberdeen, all things conservative women were trying to avoid. However, the war made charity a holy crusade, and its High Church was the Red Cross. The rich preferred cheques to socks, and the wives of wealthy distillers fought tooth and nail to see who could make the biggest financial splash: all contributions were reported to the last penny in the press, along with the name and social pedigree of the donor. The money poured in before there was any idea what to do with it and unseemly wrangles broke out over how it should be spent, and by whom.

Laura Borden was one of the first to volunteer for the Red Cross. It was expected of her as the prime minister's wife, and Laura always did what was expected. She had experience. In Halifax she had been active in the Victorian Order of Nurses and the Aberdeen Association; in Ottawa she had been elected vice-president of the National Council of Women and regent of the Daughters of the Empire. Her interest in charity was largely social: a generation of gentility had turned Lady Aberdeen's feminist, activist organizations into empty shells of snobbery, valued chiefly for their association with aristocracy: Laura Borden's charitable activities in 1898 had primarily involved a lavish farewell banquet for Lady Aberdeen.

Accustomed to quietly hemming sheets for the VON, Laura was unprepared for the public spotlight and power politics of the Red Cross, where she was caught between aggressive heiresses angling for knighthoods for their husbands and the disapproving *doyenne* of Ottawa society, the wicked Hun herself, Princess Louise, Duchess of Connaught, wife of Queen Victoria's third son, Prince Arthur, Duke of Connaught and governor-general of Canada.

The Duchess of Connaught was Prussian. The minister of militia, Sam Hughes, wanted to have her interned as an enemy alien. This did not amuse the duchess, who was hard to amuse. The duchess decided to prove her patriotism by giving more time and money to the Canadian Red Cross than anyone else, and she did. This did not amuse the distillers' wives, who were hopelessly out-classed by an enemy alien.

Laura Borden was the first prime minister's wife to be pushed into a public role, on her own, in a no-win situation. It became painfully obvious that women's efforts were not going to win the war, and Laura could tell from Rob's face that the war was not being won. Laura knew the truth, but she could not speak it, and in public she had to wear a brave face. It was hard, and harder still as the casualties mounted and everywhere women appeared in mourning, devastated by grief, fury and despair. Laura Borden provided the perfect role model: she broke down.

The Great War smashed the crystal palace of Victorian society; a hundred years of myths and dreams and certainties came crashing down into

*"Old girl," Laura
Borden in corsetted
chins-up fashion.*

*Robert Borden, a
hopeless hypochondriac.*

muck and rubble. Everything Laura believed in and bargained for no longer mattered; in a revolutionary age, Lady Borden was an anachronism, and she had developed a startling resemblance to another anachronism, Queen Mary, the wife of King George V of England. Laura and the queen were only five years apart in age, two tiny, plain women with the same frizzy brown hair, high cheek-bones, straight noses, long upper lips and small, close-set eyes. Laura must have been aware of the similarity because she imitated the queen's taste for fussy clothes with high, very tight collars, a corsetted, chins-up fashion that made them both look censorious. Laura, however, was the Canadian. She didn't have the queen's dressmaker or the royal jewels – she wore almost no jewellery at all, not even earrings, although she could easily have afforded it – and her weathered face was devoid of make-up. The effect was peculiar: an athletic, outdoorsy woman decked out in frills and feathered hats.

The schizophrenia of Laura's appearance is a key to her personality. She was a self-made "lady," carefully stitched together like a piece of delicate embroidery, but liable to unravel under pressure.

Laura Bond was the youngest daughter of a Halifax hardware merchant, Thomas Bond, who died when she was a girl. Thomas Bond left his family a comfortable house, but not much else, and Laura's mother took in boarders to make ends meet. It was a respectable occupation for a widow, but not a blue-ribbon pedigree for a future Lady, and Laura's starchiness may have been an attempt to hide her humble background. She did have a musical education, and played the organ at St. Paul's Anglican church on Sundays as well as for weddings and special festivals.

Laura seems to have met the up-and-coming Halifax lawyer, Robert Laird Borden, in 1886 when he was thirty-two and she was twenty-four. They likely met in connection with her father's estate–Borden handled the insurance on the Bond house–and when Laura went to Antigonish for the summer they began exchanging "My dear Miss Laura" and "My dear Mr. Borden" letters which were both formal and flirtatious. "I had such an unpleasant dream about you on Tuesday night that I can't shake off the effects of it even yet," Laura writes to Mr. Borden in June. "I hope you are all right and a *very good boy*–I suppose I may give up all idea of seeing you this summer–do you know I am afraid I am getting very selfish."

Borden was staying in a primitive cottage on the Northwest Arm, rowing back and forth to Halifax morning and evening. He was already developing a belief in the restorative powers of fresh air that would become an obsession over the years, and he was a serious insomniac: "Sleeplessness still claims me for its own," he writes to Laura. "Sometimes I feel very weary of myself and of life."

Laura's and Rob's greatest bond was a mutual concern about their health. "I think I told you I gained 6 lbs after I came," she writes in September, "well, it is a sad fact to relate but nevertheless it is true, I have lost 4 of the said 6 lbs–I don't know whether to attribute it to tennis or sleeplessness." Laura was thin to the point of anorexia, yet she was energetic and athletic: "August has been very wet, too wet even for tennis, although it might as well rain for all the interest the girls take in the game; I can't understand them, they don't seem to take any interest in any outdoor game. Perhaps they are not strong, but still they don't tire of dancing. Out of a club of 21 members it is a difficult matter to get four for a set – yesterday afternoon after a great deal of persuasion we managed to have a game. I think it was very well put by a lady the other day – she was in Antigonish trying to sell a new method for fitting dresses and she said: 'I was never in a place where all the young ladies were so helpless.'"

Laura's restless impatience shows in her letters; by the end of August she is "wild to get home" although she still has six weeks to go. "Are you ill or what is the matter?" she writes frantically to Borden after three weeks pass without a note from him. "I just felt today that if I did not write and see what was the matter that I would do something desperate. I am invited out this evening but feel so 'down on my luck' that I don't think I will go." Borden replies and Laura's tone becomes more intimate: she calls him "little boy" and teases him about having his thick, curly hair cut too short.

Laura could hardly make her feelings clearer; Borden is more circumspect – he sends her books and sheet music. Laura dutifully plays the music and reads the books; Borden was a passionate reader who could recite long passages of poetry from memory and Laura was anxious to please. "I am committing *In Memoriam* to memory," she tells him proudly. "Do you think I will ever get through it? I know 109 verses perfectly – can repeat them without a mistake – but you see that is only a seventh. I am going to conquer it if I can." She does: three months later she reports that "it takes me just 2 hours and 5 minutes to repeat it." Was anybody listening?

"I can hardly realize that I will probably see you sometime next week," Laura writes on September 21. "Oh dear me, I must not dwell upon it or I will want to start in the train with my letter."

Laura's ardent feelings were not reciprocated, or if they were, other considerations intervened: it would be three years before Laura and Rob were married. Borden was a slow-spoken, slow-moving man – some thought him slow-witted as well – with a lugubrious bass voice and a nervous, introspective temperament. A farm boy from Grand Pré, Nova Scotia, Borden had clambered up the ladder to a partnership in the prestigious law firm founded by Charles Hibbert Tupper and John Thompson; he was a business lawyer and a careerist, a self-made man who repressed his own impulses and emotions in order to conform to the expectations of others. Perhaps he felt that he could do better than little Miss Bond; perhaps he was indifferent to women, yet pressured to marry, at the awkward age of thirty-five, because bachelorhood would limit his social connections and harm his reputation. "Little boy's" pet name for his young wife was "old girl," a negative, asexual, spinsterish epithet for an active, eager woman eight years younger than he. "Little boy" suggests that Borden, like Thompson, played an infantile role, but while Thompson was "Baby" sucking happily at Annie's breast, Borden was an insecure six-year-old sucking up to his governess. Rob was determined to be looked after, but Laura would be more nanny than mummy, and their childlessness may have been a matter of choice.

Photographs show Borden to be a stocky, rough-hewn man's man fond of a good cigar and a glass of whiskey, and until he became prime minister, when he began to dress like a Mississippi gambler, he looked like an unmade bed. His passions were golf, fishing and gardening, his obsession was the precarious state of his health. Borden didn't look neurotic, but he was a hopeless hypochondriac; as well as chronic insomnia, he suffered from bouts of "nervous exhaustion," indigestion and flatulence, a particularly embarrassing affliction for a politician. The cause was stress, and doctors prescribed a plain, low-fat diet, but until he succumbed to old age at eighty-four, Robert Borden believed himself to be hovering on the verge of madness and death.

Laura lived in fear that she would inadvertently cause Rob to become ill or depressed, and when "little boy" was under stress he threw tantrums. Shortly after he went to Ottawa as a Conservative MP in 1896, Rob wrote Laura berating her savagely for sending his tennis shoes instead of his cycling shoes. Laura replied smartly that if his handwritting were better she might be able to understand his directions, but her spunkiness soon disappeared. "You must do what you think is right, dearie," became her constant apologetic refrain. And he did. Although casual about his own appearance, Borden was fastidious about his home; he had to approve every purchase and everything had to be top quality. He also had to approve the people Laura associated with, and he clearly didn't approve of her family; in letters to her husband spanning thirty years, Laura never once mentions her mother. In 1916 Rob writes to Laura in Antigonish offering his sympathy on the death of "your brother": his brother-in-law doesn't even have a name. He was equally curmudgeonly about his own family.

Borden did approve of people who would advance his interests. In 1894 he bought Pinehurst, a pretentious frame house on the Northwest Arm near Armdale, the residence of Sir Charles and Lady Tupper; not surprisingly, Borden was nominated as a Conservative candidate two years later. While the Thompsons had avoided the Tuppers like the plague, Lady Tupper was Laura's constant companion, although it was not necessarily

Laura's idea of a good time – she made excuses to put Lady Tupper off so she could work in her garden, coming in reluctantly to dress for dinner with the lieutenant-governor or the admiral of the fleet. "How sick I will feel if you aren't here and I have to go alone," she wrote to Rob. She went alone.

Laura's garden was her refuge and her solace. She could happily spend a whole day on her knees digging dandelions in the rain; she planted the flower-beds and ordered fresh gravel for the driveway. Laura was a shy, simple person who spun a bright cocoon of busyness to please her husband and hide her solitude; she loved roses and birds, her St. Bernard dog Taffy and her cat, Lady Jane; she loved Rob too but he didn't seem to care.

Rob left Laura at Pinehurst, in the company of her pets and two servants, until she nearly went mad from loneliness. Why? They had no children in school; Borden was making more than enough money to afford two establishments; Laura was young and vivacious, an asset to a middle-aged politician anxious to make an impression, yet Robert Borden spent the rest of his life putting as much distance as possible between himself and his wife, while still professing affection and maintaining appearances.

The distance was more emotional and psychological than physical. Borden's letters to Laura are frightening in their frigidity, flat, banal, repetitive little notes about the weather, his dinner companions and his health. He is lonely, he misses her, but his letters are always the same length and the phrases are repeated, year after year, with no variation of feeling. Laura could have written them herself, and his salutations and sign-offs might have come from an etiquette book: "My dearest Laura, all my love, your devoted husband, Rob." In honour of their wedding anniversary in 1918 he writes from his fishing camp: "The twenty-eight years have been very happy years, have they not, and crowded with much incident." This is not an anniversary sentiment that asks or deserves a reply, although it is possible to speculate what Annie Thompson might have said.

Borden had a dry wit and as a wartime prime minister he hobnobbed easily with some of the most brilliant and powerful people in the world, yet his letters to Laura are devoid of humour, anecdote or insight. He reveals nothing of his thoughts, his impressions or his feelings, if he has any. He writes to Laura after visiting wounded soldiers during the war: "It is pathetic and trying to one's composure to see them and speak to them." Borden was more concerned with the effect of the soldiers' suffering on himself than he was with their pain. For years Laura waited in vain for an exclamation mark, a scribbled note in the margin, an intimate message that could not have been written by Borden's male secretary. Rob only became passionate about fish – in a box of twenty-five dead bass Laura would find an ecstatic note about "this delightful, secluded spot," Echo Beach. Laura never went to Echo Beach, and Borden's fishing companions were all male.

"Oh, how forlorn I felt when you turned away and went back to the train," Laura writes to Rob early in her marriage. "I was so glad it was raining because that accounted for the big raindrops that would get in my eyes." She bought herself a bicycle and a pair of bloomers, played tennis and golf, entertained at tea and plunged into renovating the house, fearful

Sir Robert and Lady Borden, they did things together that allowed them to keep the maximum amount of distance between them.

that Rob wouldn't like the results – sure enough he grumbled about the lack of a study – yet all her activities didn't begin to fill the long, empty hours.

"My dearest Husband, it is so lonely here without you I do not know what to do," she writes in May 1896. "I have not had any sleep worth speaking about since you left." The enthusiasm and playfulness of the young Laura disappeared after her marriage; she took no further interest in books or music. She certainly wasn't interested in politics. Tucked away in Borden's official papers was the following formal note from Laura, dated February 7, 1906: "I hereby give my consent in your getting out of politics and – quick." Borden didn't, of course; although believing himself on the verge of nervous collapse, he was always promising.

Laura's letters are also of uniform length and style. She always opens with "My dearest Husband" or "My dearest Rob," and signs off "Your loving wife" or "Your devoted wife, Laura." She tries to keep up a brave front, but her heart is heavy and her feelings hurt: "Only a letter over four days since you left and I am homesick for you, dearie. Will you be back on Saturday week, do you think? Goodnight, sweetheart, with all my love."

As the years passed and Rob became more immersed in politics as party leader – he succeeded Sir Charles Tupper in 1901 – Laura's plaintive-ness turned to impatience and finally to anger. "Dearie, I am so disap-pointed about your delay," she writes in July 1904. "I had been expecting to see you no later than Monday and now must wait another week." Four days later she scrawls: "Your two letters arrived today and your return is put off still later; surely those men might let you leave on Friday so you could reach home on Saturday. There is nothing to write about and I am feeling disgusted with politics. It means we have no summer now at home. I feel perfectly certain the House could have prorogued last week if you had all made up your minds to do it but the trouble is you all go on and talk, talk. I have a feeling you will not get home until the end of August so will not be surprised if I get a note to that effect."

Was Laura's repressed anger incendiary, or was it simply fortuitous that Pinehurst caught fire in 1905? There was no attempt to rebuild the gutted house, but Rob dithered so long over buying a house in Ottawa that Laura finally took matters into her own hands: she found a run-down mansion on the Rideau River and insisted on buying it. Rob gave in. Glensmere, as they called the house, became a showplace, and after Rob became Sir Robert and prime minister in 1911, Lady Borden was the Old Girl of Ottawa, a faintly ludicrous figure in a vast plumed hat who tootled around the city in an electric car that inevitably slowed to a stately stop in inappropriate places.

By the time war broke out Laura had fabricated a life as fragile as one of her Dresden teacups; once shattered, it could be mended, but the cracks would always show. She never fully recovered from her breakdown. When the war ended in November 1918, Laura did not accompany Rob to the Paris peace conference, and he was away more than six months. He returned so exhausted that his doctors advised him to take a year off; in January 1920 Borden sailed for England via Florida and Cuba, alone. Pleading illness and shyness, Laura stayed behind, more interested in the problems of veterans and refugees than in dining with Lord This and Lady That in London.

With Rob away Laura no longer had to pretend. She could hide in her rose garden, an aging figure from a vanished era. Yet by staying home, Laura showed more compassion and political sense than her husband, who abandoned his post as prime minister when Canada was suffering the severe aftershocks of war and revolution. Leaving the country to drift during a period of social and economic crisis, Borden quickly lost the confidence of the voters.

Half of those unhappy voters were women. In 1917, hoping to win support for conscription, Borden had extended the vote to the female relatives of servicemen; women, enraged at being so arbitrarily and cynically excluded, demanded and got universal suffrage in 1919, and, not surprisingly, many of them intended to vote Liberal. Laura must have been pleased with the extension of the vote to women: years before she had written to Rob a delighted account of a debate between a leading American suffragette, Mrs. May Wright Sewall, and the attorney-general of Nova Scotia: "It was the best thing that has been in Halifax for years. The hall was packed with all the 'elite' of the city. She is a wonderfully ready speaker and I thought quite 'floored' the attorney-general."

Sir Robert Borden finally retired in July 1920 on grounds of ill health; he was sixty-six and many observers didn't expect him to last the year. However, retirement proved a miraculous cure and Borden enjoyed the role of avuncular elder statesman, a granite monument to be visited by foreign dignitaries in the gardens of Glensmere or wheeled out from time to time for political banquets. He and Laura did things together that allowed them to keep the maximum amount of distance between them: they golfed and they gardened. Rob had his own rock garden at the rear of the house, a little glen of indigenous shrubs and wildflowers sloping down to the river with wooden bridges crossing a natural stream. Neither of them mucked about with their hands; a gardener did the digging and a housemaid cut the roses. In June and July, Laura's rose garden yielded more than one hundred fresh blooms a day; Rob counted every one.

The Bordens made golf, gardening and fishing fashionable in Ottawa, and Rob was such a fetishist about fresh air that he slept outdoors on his veranda under a crude canvas cover from the time the snow began to melt until the first blizzard, snug as a bug in woollen socks and a knitted cap. As they grew older and more eccentric, Sir Robert and Lady Borden turned into fairy-tale figures in a gingerbread house, mysterious relics of an Empire that now existed only in memory.

By 1938 Sir Robert's death had been anticipated for so long that it was greeted almost with relief, as if the burden of the war had finally been lifted from the nation's shoulders. Laura, the last prime minister's wife to be a Lady, lived two years longer; she died at seventy-eight in 1940, in the first year of her second war.

As the most able and energetic member of Sir Robert Borden's Cabinet from 1911 to 1920, Arthur Meighen had the unenviable task of doing all the nasty and unpleasant jobs his prime minister had no stomach for. Arthur Meighen antagonized Quebec by championing conscription, enraged women by extending the franchise only to the female relatives of servicemen, infuriated labour by crushing the Winnipeg General Strike in 1919 and alienated the western farmers by advocating a high tariff. By the time Meighen succeeded Sir Robert Borden as prime minister in July 1920 he was the most unpopular man in Canada.

"An arresting, alarming, almost melodramatic figure," in the words of journalist Bruce Hutchison, Meighen was a caricature of the icy intellectual, a classic "egghead" with a high, domed forehead, cold eyes and a tall, skeletal body. Meighen's Ichabod Crane appearance, coupled with his rigid views and talent for making enemies, made him an inviting target for satire. It didn't help that he was the first prime minister to come from the prairies, and that his constituency, Portage la Prairie, Manitoba, was dismissed by Ottawa sophisticates as the last word in hicksville. Meighen's

Arthur Meighen, an Ichabod Crane appearance and a talent for making enemies.

rival, the new Liberal leader Mackenzie King, sneered that Meighen's wife Isabel had the appearance of a "dairy maid," although Isabel Meighen had exactly the buxom, fair-haired sort of beauty King most admired, and King's condescending attitude was secretly shared by influential Ottawa journalist Madge Macbeth.

In 1924, under the pseudonym "Gilbert Knox," Macbeth published *The Land of Afternoon*, a witty, scandalous *roman-à-clef* about the sleazier side of Ottawa politics. *The Land of Afternoon* was a deadly accurate portrait of Ottawa "society" and its crowd of snobs, sirens, parvenus, lechers, hangers-on and string-pullers. It dealt frankly with two of the dirtier political games, seduction and blackmail, and most sensational of all, the characters were clearly recognizable.

The Land of Afternoon's two idealistic innocents from the prairie town of Pinto Plains, Marjorie and Raymond Dilling, were obviously Isabel and Arthur Meighen from Portage la Prairie, and Macbeth's portrait of the cerebral Dilling captures Meighen perfectly:

"He abandoned himself to reading almost as a man abandons himself to physical debauch, and Marjorie, furtively watching him, could scarcely believe that the stranger occupying that frail, familiar shell was, in reality, her husband. There was about him a suggestion of emotional pleasure, an expression of ecstasy, as when a man gazes deep into his beloved's eyes.

"'Ah,' he would murmur, 'three thousand, six hundred and forty-two – annually! Seventy-nine thousand less than . . . well, well!'

"His cheeks would flush, his breathing would thicken, his forehead would gleam with a crown of moisture, and he would lose his temper shockingly if the children spoke to him or played noisily in the room.

"Long afterward, a rural wag observed that Prohibition touched few persons less than Raymond Dilling, who could get drunk on Blue Books and Trade Journals any day of the year!"

In contrast to her egghead husband, Marjorie Dilling is a pretty, feather-brained little titmouse who hasn't a clue about the "right" people to know or "the Thing" to do. Her first social encounter with the formidable Lady Denby [Lady Borden] shows Ottawa at its most painfully pretentious:

"'Have you any children?'" Marjorie asks.

"'No,' said Lady Denby, implying by her tone that the propagation of the species was, in her opinion, a degraded and vulgar performance.

"Marjorie tried other topics; church work, conundrums, Sir Eric's health and gastronomic peculiarities. She offered her favourite recipes, and patterns for crocheted lace, interrupted, thank Heaven, by the entrance of the snow-covered children and the consequent confusion that they caused.

"In her domestic activities she was perfectly at ease, hanging damp garments on radiators to dry, wiping tear stains from ruddy cheeks, and even arranging a juvenile tea party in a corner of the room.

"She chattered happily all the while, never for a moment realizing that in the Upper Social Circles, the last task in the world a woman should undertake cheerfully is the care of her children; that even allowing them to stay in the same room and breathe the rarified air with which the exalted adults have finished is a confession of eccentricity, if not *bourgeoisisme*. She had no idea that there were mothers, outside of books – or possibly New York – who not only considered their children a nuisance, but were ashamed to be surprised in any act of maternal solicitude.

"As it was, Lady Denby sipped tea and nibbled toast as though vast distances separated her from the rest of them, distances that she had no wish to bridge. Marjorie came to the conclusion that she was not only deaf but suffering from the frailities of extreme age, her contradictory appearance nothwithstanding.

"She was amazed to learn that opening her own door was, in future, quite out of the question. If she could not, or would not, engage the permanent services of a domestic, she must, at least, have someone on Wednesday afternoons to admit her callers. Furthermore, she must be relieved – relieved was Lady Denby's word – of all bother (also Lady Denby's) with the children.

"Again, without in the least having said so, Lady Denby managed to convey the fact that she considered Marjorie a very pretty woman, and that it would be wise, in view of her husband's position, to make the most of her good looks. In the Capital, she observed, much weight was attached to one's appearance, and Marjorie would find herself repaid for dressing a little more – another interesting word of Lady Denby's – 'definitely.' The word was puzzling. Marjorie made all her own and the children's clothes, her husband's shirts, his pyjamas and summer underwear, and she was humbly proud of her accomplishment. She had no doubt as to her ability to make more 'definite' clothes, could she but understand exactly what Lady Denby meant."

One of those ruddy, snow-covered children was Maxwell Meighen, a rambunctious little boy who definitely did not get along with Lady Borden. "She hated kids," he says. "She was severe and stiff. She'd give you a cookie, then warn you not to get crumbs on the floor." Max Meighen vividly recalls having to "pass stuff" on his mother's dreaded "afternoons": "Sometimes we'd have as many as seven hundred people tramping through in one afternoon, all the MPs and their wives, they'd bring all their relatives and stuff sandwiches in their pockets. In winter when the streets were never ploughed it looked like the retreat from Moscow."

Isabel Meighen did make all her own clothes – she bought one good dress a year – and she *was* intimidated by Lady Borden, but the portrait of

Isabel Meighen, her life would have been happier if her husband had been more popular.

"Marjorie Dilling" doesn't do her justice. Isabel Meighen was more than pretty; she was strikingly beautiful, with a voluptuous figure, dark blue eyes, porcelain skin and masses of curly fair hair. She loved to dance, and danced well, but her opportunities to cut a social swath were severely limited by the demands of her three small children, her husband's anti-social personality – Arthur Meighen would leave his own parties to go to bed with a book – and no money.

Arthur Meighen was a struggling country lawyer when he was elected Conservative MP for Portage la Prairie in 1908. Country lawyers made a frugal living and his parliamentary stipend was quickly absorbed by his family: his oldest son, Ted, was three and Max an infant; the third child, Lillian, arrived in 1910. Isabel was only twenty-five when she first arrived in Ottawa, and with her squalling babies and trousseau of handmade clothes she must have felt right off the farm.

She was. Isabel Cox was born in Granby, Quebec, but raised on a farm near Birtle, Manitoba. Her father, Charles Cox, died when she was four and her mother moved west to live with a sister; she later married the town postmaster, W.H. Wood. Isabel was teaching at a one-room school by the time she was seventeen, riding the two miles each way on horseback. This independent young teacher wasn't about to moulder away on a prairie homestead without seeing something of the world, and in the summer of 1902, when she was nineteen, Isabel went to Winnipeg to see the fair.

She met Arthur Meighen by accident in a hotel lobby. Isabel was visiting friends, Arthur was waiting for a client. He must have stood out in the crowd, a tall, very thin, pale young man in a sober, shabby suit with a reserved, rather arrogant manner. The client was late, Arthur was impatient; reluctantly, he allowed himself to be introduced to Miss Cox by one of her friends.

Isabel must have found Mr. Meighen more formidable than she later found Lady Borden. He was nine years older than Isabel, handsome, silent and superior. Isabel's main conversational gambit was futile; Mr. Meighen had no interest in the fair and not the slightest intention of going. She must have been astonished when, just as she was leaving, he invited her to go to the theatre; the name of the play was appropriate: *Still Waters Run Deep*. Isabel accepted.

Isabel Cox and Arthur Meighen were married in Birtle two years later, on June 1, 1904. They made an odd, but complementary couple. Isabel's sense of humour and friendly ways made it easier for Arthur to come out of his shell, and he brought to her life an intellectual dimension it would have otherwise lacked. Isabel was a capable, highly organized woman used to doing a farm girl's chores; Arthur didn't have the sense to come in out of the rain. Like Annie Thompson, "Nan," as the family called her, had to dress her husband every morning to make sure his socks matched and he didn't wear bedroom slippers to the House of Commons. Arthur was so absent-minded he once forgot to pick up baby Ted from the sitter's; Isabel came home late to find an empty crib and Arthur sound asleep in bed. She had to keep track of all his appointments: if she didn't remind him, Arthur would miss dinner with the king. They had no common interests. Isabel went dancing with friends, and she even disciplined the children. When Ted and Max got out of control, which was most of the time, she whacked their legs with the rubber belt from an old washing machine, with effective results.

Arthur had no interests apart from his books and politics. He seems an odd choice to represent a farming community, but western Canada was full of misfits and eccentrics, and Meighen soon found a unique place in the community. He was the "smart boy," and prairie farmers always sent their smart boys to Ottawa to enhance their image and get them out of the way.

Isabel went to Ottawa too. She was the first prime minister's wife from western Canada, a place populated, in the Upper Canadian mind, with peasants in sheepskin coats, yet Isabel, accustomed to the space and sunlight of the prairies, must have found Ottawa dark, cramped and dull. Her life would have been happier had her husband been more popular. Arthur's vice wasn't drink, or women, although in *The Land of Afternoon* Raymond Dilling had an affair with his secretary, it was ideology.

When Arthur Meighen believed in something, no amount of charity, common sense or political expediency would make him compromise. He was out of sympathy with an industrialized, radicalized post-war Canada where bootlegging was a mainstay of the economy, and he had inherited a wartime government that had no further reason to exist. The Liberals who had deserted Laurier drifted back to the Liberal Party, and Meighen's administration gradually unravelled. On December 6, 1921 Meighen's government went down to crushing defeat at the hands of the Liberals under Mackenzie King.

King, however, turned out to be more unpopular than Meighen, and four years later, on October 29, 1925, the Conservatives won 116 seats to only 101 for the Liberals. But the balance of power was held by a third party, the Progressives, a farmers' reform party that came out of nowhere to take 24 seats. Meighen stubbornly refused to court the Progressives, even though many came from Manitoba, and they sided with King, who clung to power for months, often by a single vote. In June 1926 King threw in the towel and asked the governor-general, Lord Byng, for permission to call another election. Byng refused. King resigned in a huff, and Byng called on Arthur Meighen to form a government.

Meighen's triumph lasted three days. An obscure rule demanded that newly appointed Cabinet ministers resign their seats and seek re-election; in the meantime the government was an administration in name only, and

Meighen himself could not sit in the House of Commons. With no support from Liberals or Progressives, the Conservatives suffered a humiliating defeat in the House, and a resounding defeat in the next election. Meighen resigned the leadership in 1926; seventeen years later he made one last, unsuccessful bid for election.

Isabel Meighen left political life at an age when many wives entered it. She was probably glad to see the end of Ottawa. She took little interest in politics, and she must have borne much of the burden of her husband's bitterness towards Mackenzie King. Meighen made no secret of his loathing for the "most contemptible charlatan ever to darken the annals of Canadian politics," and according to Bruce Hutchison, his physical revulsion for the "windy dumpling" made Meighen nauseous. The feeling was mutual. King hated Meighen, and gloated over his defeat.

In *The Land of Afternoon* the Dillings return gratefully to Pinto Plains, but in real life the Meighens moved to Toronto where Arthur became vice-president of Canadian Securities. He was appointed to the Senate by his successor, R.B. Bennett, and enjoyed a second political career in the Upper House. His business prospered, as did his family: Ted became a lawyer in Montreal – Ted's son Michael is also a Conservative senator – Max joined the investment company and Lillian married a Toronto businessman. By the time Arthur Meighen died in 1960, his family was firmly established as part of Canada's social and financial elite.

Isabel lived in her own apartment on Avenue Road after Arthur's death. She travelled widely until she was nearly ninety, and continued to knit and sew for her family. She died in September 1985 at the age of 102.

CHAPTER 9

Other Men's Wives: Mrs. King and Mrs. Patteson

$\mathcal{W}$ILLIAM LYON MACKENZIE KING did not have a wife. He considered this a very serious handicap, and until his death, still single, at seventy-five, King pursued many eligible women, and some highly ineligible, with intentions that were honourable, and dishonourable. He was engaged only once, at twenty-three, to a German-born nurse, Mathilde Grossert; King broke it off after a tempestuous row with his parents. Two years later, Rex, as he liked his women friends to call him, fell in love with Lord Minto's teenage daughter, Lady Ruby, and, on the rebound, had a passionate affair with Marjorie Herridge, the forty-two-year-old wife of the minister of St. Andrew's Presbyterian church in Ottawa. Rex courted any number of American heiresses, several rich widows and a divorcée, Julia, Princess Cantacuzene, daughter of former American President Ulysses S. Grant. He cast amorous glances towards Princess Patricia, beautiful daughter of the Duke of Connaught, and at the age of fifty-two pinched the thigh of Lady Byng's lady-in-waiting, an indiscretion that confirmed Lady Byng's opinion that the prime minister was a toad.

King had countless opportunities to make a good marriage. He was energetic, ambitious and, as a young man, not unattractive. Zoé Laurier and other influential Liberals thrust hundreds of willing young women in his direction; he rejected them all, including the heiress to the Salada Tea fortune. As the years passed King's confirmed bachelorhood convinced the public that he was either asexual or homosexual; King himself declared that he would marry for love or not at all. It seemed political folly. How could a prime minister manage without a wife?

Very well, as it turned out. King's twenty-two years in power, starting in 1921 when he was only forty-six, proved that a wife was by no means essential, and could even be a handicap, especially when the prime minister had a mother and a mistress.

King introduced his mother to Ottawa society as soon as he arrived in

William Lyon Mackenzie King, his heterosexuality was sometimes out of control.

1900 as deputy minister of labour. As an eligible, if inconspicuous, civil servant, King was invited everywhere, and his dinner companions were bemused when, at a lull in the conversation, Mr. King suddenly produced a photograph from his pocket exclaiming, "Have you ever seen a sweeter, more beautiful expression? She has the face of a young girl, don't you think?" Peering at a snapshot of a withered, aged woman with a mane of unruly white hair, the guests politely agreed that yes, she did have a spiritual, almost fairy-like quality. Surely she couldn't be Mr. King's mother? As Mother's photo was passed reverently around the table, Mr.

King took the opportunity to impart the information that Mother was really a very significant person, the thirteenth and last child of the famous rebel, William Lyon Mackenzie, and that he, her eldest son, had dedicated his life to carrying on Grandfather's great reform tradition. By the time Mother's picture was returned to his pocket, King had accomplished three important things: he had directed attention to himself, he had created the impression that he was a man of consequence, and he had made an indelible impression on the guests, who left whispering: "Who *was* that fat man with the weird mother? Oh yes, *Mr. King*."

King also displayed numerous photos of Mother in his shabby suite in the Roxborough apartments, artfully arranging them in silver frames on tables near the lamps, so when he invited friends in for sweets after the theatre everyone's gaze was immediately drawn to Mother, who, with luck, led the conversation to King's favourite topic, himself. As the years passed Mother's pictures increased in number and size, culminating in a large oil portrait before which a lamp perpetually burned, and a marble bust, whose cold, white lips King kissed in moments of triumph. Mother was King's icon, his Madonna and Medusa, the White Goddess who guided him to the Holy Grail of political power.

Few people in Ottawa ever actually met Isabel King. She died in 1917, when King was still young and obscure, and until the last year of her life she lived in Kitchener or Toronto, visiting Willie only at Kingsmere, his summer cottage in the Gatineau Hills north of Ottawa, where she saw almost no one except Willie's neighbour, Mrs. Herridge. King used his mother as a "gooseberry" to cover his moonlight trysts with Marjorie, and Mrs. Herridge must have been grateful that Mrs. King seemed oblivious to the nature of her son's "friendship."

In the medical parlance of the time Isabel King suffered from "nerves," a catch-all term used to describe every form of emotional or psychiatric disorder that did not require the patient to be committed to a lunatic asylum. ("Brain fever" seems to have been a more serious disorder, often resulting in death; it tended to be associated with men, although men also suffered from "nerves," and may have been a code word for syphilis. Until the invention of miracle drugs in the mid-twentieth century, disease was as powerful a taboo as sex: tuberculosis and cancer were rarely named, and if the disease was sex-related, forget it.)

"Nerves," like neurosis today, was a fashionable ailment among women, a sign of "sensitivity" until, as in the case of Isabella Macdonald, the nerves ran amok and caused everyone anguish and inconvenience. Freud did not begin publishing his psychiatric studies until late in the nineteenth century and his work was not known in North America for another twenty years – King was reading Freud, with much benefit, in 1920 – so for Isabel King, like her Macdonald namesake, there was little analysis of what might be causing her "nerves," and certainly no cure. The asylum was literally a "looney bin," a forbidding stone warehouse reserved for those whose behaviour was too violent or obscene to be tolerated in the community, as well as for the senile, the retarded and other harmless handicapped whose families refused to care for them. Committal to the asylum was a virtual death sentence: inmates – "patient" is a misleading word – were locked, virtually naked, in dark, cold cells, poorly fed, beaten, abused and left to rot, or kill themselves, in conditions of unspeakable squalor. Having a relative in the asylum was an appalling social stigma, not only because madness was believed to be the wages of sin, possession by the devil or proof of "bad blood," but because it meant that the family had failed in its responsibility to care for one of its own.

The neurotic and psychotic were generally looked after, like everyone else, at home. Rest was the only prescription for nerves, and Isabel King seems to have spent much of her time in bed resting her "weak heart," as her illness was euphemistically described. She suffered from depression, bursting into tears over the most unimportant incidents, interrupted by periods of manic activity and fits of uncontrollable laughter. She once caused a scandal in church by laughing loudly during the sermon, and when she did the same thing at an Ottawa dinner party, King, writhing with mortification, decided that Mother on pasteboard was safer than Mother in person.

Isabel King had reason to be hysterical. Her husband, John, a handsome man whose stupidity was exceeded only by his pomposity, was an utter failure, a pathetic Micawber who lived on expectations that were never sufficient to keep the Kings out of debt. John King made a half-hearted attempt to practise law, but he found that toadying to the powerful Toronto Liberals who still had some loyalty to the Mackenzie name was a better way of getting on, and the King family spent their time doing what Isabel, with some shame, called "wirepulling." Perhaps to escape responsibility, or because she was cast in the role of Mackenzie's impoverished daughter, Isabel King developed a fantasy that she was a young girl; she fancied white lace dresses with ribbons and bows and wore her hair loose down her back like a child of twelve. With her white curls and ghostly gowns she was a spooky, macabre figure: neighbourhood children called her the Queen of the Fairies. Her manner was playful, flirtatious and sexually provocative; she was constantly demanding hugs and kisses and assurances that she was the prettiest girl in the world. Her seductive behaviour was directed largely at her children, especially her eldest son, Willie, and it was motivated by powerful incestuous impulses – Willie developed the habit of lying beside Mother in bed, with his arms around her, kissing her while she chattered or cried.

Apparently unable to accept the fact that Mother's behaviour was abnormal, the family coped by indulging her: the madwoman in the attic became the focal point of the household, the wonky cog around which the King family neurotically revolved. The two girls, Bella and Jennie, did all the housework, brushed Mother's hair and dressed her up in pretty clothes; the boys, Willie and Max, jumped to satisfy her every whim. Because Mother's whims were childish and unpredictable, and Father was improvident, the family lived in a state of severe emotional stress.

Isabel King, daughter of the famous rebel, John King who traded on his father-in-law's name and their eldest son Willie, about 1908.

Willie ran away to university at seventeen and never lived at home again. But Mother pursued him. Willie had hardly installed himself in residence at the University of Toronto before Mother invited herself to share his room for a weekend; the university said no. King fled to Chicago, then to Harvard; Mother immediately made plans to visit him. King's brief, unhappy engagement to Mathilde seems to have been a desperate attempt once and for all to keep Mother out of his bed.

"My dear Billy," Mother wrote tearfully from her own bed the morning after she received the traumatic news of his engagement. "For hours I have been lying awaking thinking of you. I have never crossed you in your life and do not intend to do so now but I think there are many many things to think about before you take this step." Pointing out Willie's financial obligation to his family, Mother went on:

"I am getting old now Willie, and disappointment wearies and the heart grows sick. Sometimes when I hear you talk so much about what you would like to do for those that suffer I think charity begins at home and as you do so shall be done to you. I am not grasping for myself but I do feel for your sisters & I know you who have got such a big heart will not forsake me.

"I have waited till the dawn would break to write to you and I trust an answer will come that will relieve my mind. I am very wearied but that is nothing new for Mother. It is only one more lesson not to put your trust in anything under the sun. Goodbye. May every blessing attend you is the loving wish of your Mother."

You will not forsake me. The note, scribbled in quavery pencil on smudged paper, made King's choice clear: his mother or his wife. King characteristically compromised: he reneged on his promise of marriage to Mathilde, but, unknown to Mother, he continued to correspond with Mathilde and visited her regularly, even after she married someone else, for the rest of his life.

King had no real intention of marrying Mathilde. Like Mother, Willie was a split personality: he could write impassioned love letters while feeling "in a dull, cold mood." His "private" or emotional life had nothing to do with his "public" intellectual life: in the midst of his agony and ecstasy over Mathilde, King aced his Harvard exams.

"I miss your morning kiss and the loving little talks we used to have in the summer," Mother wrote to twenty-one-year-old Willie in 1896. "I have missed you very much and this last week I have had a cold & I think that makes me feel particularly lonely without you. Possibly your mentioning 'What Are the Waves Saying' made me fancy I saw you throw yourself on the sofa when you were tired and say 'Now Mother, sing for me.' All I know is that I feel very lonely without you.''

What does a son make of a letter like this? Understandably, Willie developed very confused ideas about love. Mother used the world ''love'' indiscriminately, ambiguously and always in relation to herself: *Do you love me?* was her incessant, querulous demand and of course no one ever loved her enough. Isabel King evaluated her children's behaviour exclusively in terms of their love for her, and they tried to outdo each other to prove which one was ''best.'' Willie almost always won, but he grew up believing that love was expressed by manipulation, punishment and control.

King's repudiation of Mathilde was characteristic of all his courtships: a period of wild, hysterical infatuation followed by a confession of love, then a sudden, violent revulsion. ''I am insensibly in love with Kitty Riordan,'' nineteen-year-old Willie confessed to his diary in the summer of 1895. ''I admired her every action, word and thought. I could see my purity and goodness in her character, a beautiful innocence of heart and mind.'' During the Labour Day weekend at the Riordan's Muskoka cottage, King brought things to a head: ''I knew it was not right for me to allow myself to become thus enraptured with this girl of 17 and felt that she could not but resent it. I tried hard within the last week to free myself and not to appear as I felt. It has made me feel miserable. I could not bear her indifference, which I felt to be perfectly just and right, and resolved to free myself by telling her all. Which I did. I was glad to see the relief which it brought to us both. I told her I could not help my becoming fascinated but also said that I was desirous only that this should result in a life's friendship and nothing more. We both felt better and older friends from that moment.''

The next day King ignored Kitty and paid exaggerated attention to other girls. ''Kitty tried to appear indifferent and offended because I had not read to her,'' King smugly reported, ''but I did not mind in the least.'' Kitty got her own back: ''Kitty has been very unpleasant all day,'' King wrote on August 30. ''I do not like such an exhibition of *feigned unconcernedness* in such a young girl. I am sorry her character is not without some of the less noble attributes which I deemed at first were wanting.'' It was all over by September 4, when King took Kitty out in the canoe: ''I did not enjoy the paddle at all. I have found that she is not the sincere &

beautiful character I thought but rather one who would sell herself to society and who will ever be purse proud, if she is able to. I regret ever having spent so much time with her.''

The manipulativeness of King's behaviour towards Kitty is chilling. He courts her and wins her confidence with a dishonest confession, then insults and rejects her. ''Love'' meant fear and loathing; King didn't know what love was, never having experienced it. He certainly knew what sex was. He seems to have dealt with Mother's sexual aggressiveness the only way he probably could, by denying it: Mother would always be ''pure'' and ''good,'' sex would always be bad. King would never be able to love the kind of woman he wanted to, a woman like Mother, but it didn't stop him loving women who were not pure and good. King was by no means asexual; in fact his heterosexuality was sometimes out of control: ''It was very hard for me to stay in,'' he wrote one night at university, ''I felt I must go out & stroll around. Alas I have much to conquer as yet. Oh I wish I could overcome sin in some of its more terrible forms.'' ''Stroll'' meant to King what ''cruise'' means today: from the age of eighteen until he was in his forties, and possibly after, King regularly cruised the streets at night looking for sex. Women had to be bought, but they were cheap and plentiful. Sex with prostitutes allowed King to play out the forbidden act of making love to his mother, whom he knew wasn't ''pure,'' and he must have been relieved to find that a relationship with a woman could be brief, straightforward and devoid of social complications. ''Got into another trap, cost me $1'' he confesses at twenty-two, but his repeated, compulsive ''sins'' only added to his burden of guilt. ''I now feel terribly sorry & disgusted at my action. I fought hard against temptation. I cannot bear to think of it – Why am I so weak? Why cannot I keep where I strive so hard to be? I will try harder the next time.''

Sin added an irresistible thrill to sexual intercourse, but he derived no lasting pleasure from sex, in fact it filled him with disgust, and he was haunted by fears of venereal disease. King seems to have viewed prostitutes, as he did prospective wives, as a source of relief for his anxieties, and until he finally fell in love ''working girls'' were King's most intimate female companions.

He soon discovered that prostitutes were just that, factory girls, shop assistants, seamstresses, the young, pretty, pitifully underpaid daughters of the working poor who didn't mind turning a trick or two to put clothes on their backs and food in their stomachs. They weren't that different from King himself: he had to hustle his intellectual wares to wealthy patrons like John D. Rockefeller, the American financier for whom he worked as a labour consultant between 1913 and 1917, and for ten minutes in a dark alley Willie King's $1 would buy as much as Rockefeller's millions. King made friends with some of the girls, on the excuse of trying to turn them to a path of virtue, but really because he was lonely and curious, and he got to know some of the quite well, at least until the girls realized that Mr. King had neither money in his pocket nor marriage on his mind.

Prostitutes introduced King to the invisible world of the poor, the vast underworld of ghettos and tenements, squalid cellars and fetid factories which respectable young men of his class never encountered. King realized that Canada's wealth came from sweated labour, and that the dirtiest, most degrading work was done by women. Looking for sex, Willie King discovered his mission in life and the salvation of the Liberal Party: he would champion the poor and lead the fight for social justice.

King's grandiose ambitions always far exceeded his performance, but he was more sensitive to women's financial problems and political demands than most of his contemporaries were, and he launched his career by exposing the exploitation of women in Toronto's garment trade. As a politician King was able to relate easily to women from all walks of life; he had an enormous circle of women friends, married and single, rich and humble, and kept up a regular correspondence with hundreds more; one of his oldest friends, the wealthy English Liberal Violet Markham, sent poor Rex large sums of money for years, and was stunned to find on his death that he was worth a fortune.

King was first elected to the House of Commons in 1908 as Liberal MP for North York. Sanctimonious and puritanical on the surface, King was dismissed as an intellectual whose political career would not last long, and he went down to defeat with the Laurier government in 1911. However, Laurier found him a job working for the Liberal Party, and King stuck to Laurier faithfully: Arthur Meighen dismissed Rex as another lap dog in Laurier's *ménagerie*. During the war, King was one of very few Ontario Liberals to support Laurier in opposing conscription, and he was beaten again in the election of 1917, but when a wave of pacifist sentiment and socialist ideology swept through Canada after the war, King emerged as the leading spokesman for modern liberalism as well as the champion of Quebec, although he spoke not a word of French. King was sensitive to the working class, but only with the intention of keeping the workers hard at work, a capitalist philosophy that appealed to Toronto millionaires like Sir William Mulock, Laurier's old benefactor, who threw his support behind King after Laurier died in 1919.

At the Liberal leadership convention that August, King, still an eligible bachelor of forty-four, successfully wooed the several hundred women delegates with his boyish charm and passionate idealism, a combination perfected nearly fifty years later by a slightly older Liberal bachelor, Pierre Elliott Trudeau. He encouraged the formation of a women's wing of the Liberal Party and later appointed one of its organizers, Cairine Wilson, Canada's first woman senator. The prospect of women in the House of Commons made King profoundly nervous, as it did everyone else, but as prime minister he did his best to entice the first woman MP, Agnes Macphail, into the Liberal fold, apparently offering her every Cabinet post but his own, all of which Agnes scorned.

King's secret with women was that, far from being a celibate recluse, he was part of a sophisticated love triangle that would have stood the country on its ear had anyone guessed the truth: for thirty years King was the accepted lover of another man's wife, Joan Patteson.

Joan Patteson met King soon after she moved into the Roxborough apartments in 1918. Joan and Godfroy Patteson occupied the adjoining suite, and Joan's relationship with Rex probably began with a polite "good morning" and a casual chat over the garbage. A Conservative, Joan was at first leery of King's reputation as a political radical, but perhaps because she was a little lost and at loose ends she soon invited the lonely bachelor in for tea, then Sunday dinner and an evening playing records on the gramophone.

Joan was forty-nine, five years older than King, a matron with a grown son overseas, and she must have felt herself well past the age for romance. However, it was hard not to feel sorry for King, who didn't seem to have a friend in the world. His mother had died of cancer a few months before, and no doubt King showed Joan the little silver box with Mother's wedding ring and a lock of her hair, and her shawl on the chair where she always sat, and her room, untouched since the day she died. Joan was sentimental and she too had suffered: her young daughter Rose had died twelve years before and now her nest was empty.

Not for long. Rex began spending more and more time at the Patteson apartment. He too was at loose ends, ekeing out a meagre living working

•

for the Liberal Party; he loved to talk and he found in Mrs. Patteson a sympathetic listener. Joan's life was uneventful. Godfroy was a manager with Molson's Bank; the Pattesons had little money and no prominent friends. They must have been impressed by all the famous people Rex knew, his tête-à-têtes with Laurier, his friendship with the Rockefellers, his inside gossip about Ottawa personalities, his cross of St. Michael and St. George that Joan affectionately straightened when he attended a banquet for the Prince of Wales. Rex was the most interesting friend the Pattesons had ever had, and by the time Rex became famous himself he was a fixture at the Patteson dinner table.

"It is apparent to me that I am sitting up too late in these visits to the Pattesons," King wrote in his diary in the spring of 1920. "It is so delightful to have the time free & quiet and I am very fond of Mrs. Patteson, but I realize it is not in the interests of my work, and perhaps it is better for us to see less of each other."

King's seduction of Mrs. Patteson followed the same pattern as his seduction of Mrs. Herridge: late nights reading aloud to each other while Godfroy yawned in his chair, long spiritual discussions ending in bursts of tears, confidential confessions, the exchange of books with *billets-doux* tucked inside, and, to raise the erotic temperature, frank talk of King's desperate need "to find a woman to share my life." King proceeded with extreme caution. His affair with Marjorie had ended ignominiously one night when Dr. Herridge threw him out the door, and he treated Godfroy Patteson with grave courtesy although privately he considered Godfroy "a very stupid man."

Was Godfroy too stupid to see what was going on? Or did he care? Godfroy's attitude to the *ménage-à-trois* in which he suddenly found himself remains a mystery. Godfroy seems to have been much like John King, a lazy opportunist who saw in his wife's influential friend Rex a very advantageous opportunity for wirepulling, and the Patteson's social status certainly went up as King's political fortunes rose. Godfroy was always friendly to King; he may have guessed that King was not a sexual threat, or believed rumours that he was "queer," or maybe he left Rex alone with his wife because they both bored him to death.

By the summer of 1920 Rex and Joan were passionately in love, and predictably, love threw King into a panic. The crisis came during an emotional Labour Day weekend when Joan and Godfroy were King's guests at Kingsmere; King could bear the agony no longer, and the next day he made one of his confessions to Joan: "These storms of passion, for that is what they are, are madness and wrong. They 'rock the mind' and must cease. We both have strength enough to see that, and we will help each other to what is best for each, hard as the struggle may be – and it is hard in this lonely solitary life."

Having once again repudiated love for friendship, Rex could be expected to end the friendship. He didn't. During the next two weeks King worked out an intimate partnership with Joan that would last for the rest of his life. How King managed to break his cycle of attraction/ revulsion is not known because Joan left no record and key pages have been cut out of King's diary, but on September 15, after much prayer by the boat-house, King writes: "Joan and I pledged our lives to united effort and service today. God grant we may be given strength to endure." Rex spends the next evening with Joan and Godfroy as usual, reading aloud Wordsworth's "Ode to Duty" and Matthew Arnold's "The Happy Warrior."

King's relationship with Mrs. Patteson became, to all intents and purposes, a marriage. Rex dropped in to see Joan at all hours of the day and night and they often talked until the early hours of the morning; he came regularly for lunch and dinner and afterwards they read aloud or listened to records on the gramophone. He telephoned several times a day, usually first thing in the morning and before he went to bed; he bought her expensive jewellery in honour of their private anniversaries and had it engraved with both their initials. They exchanged flowers, personal gifts and cards on birthdays and holidays, and every Easter Rex took Joan to New York City to see *Parsifal* at the Metropolitan Opera. In April 1923 they spent a week together on the beach at Montauk, New Jersey, travelling incognito in the prime minister's private railway car. The next year Joan bought them twin Irish terriers, Pat and Derry, and soon the prime minister and Mrs. Patteson walking their dogs became a familiar sight along the Rideau Canal.

Joan and Godfroy spent their summer holidays at Kingsmere in "Moorside," the cottage once owned by Marjorie Herridge. Joan redecorated the cottage and planted the flower-beds, chose King's menus, directed the servants and greeted his guests. She was sometimes mistaken for a hired housekeeper and rudely snubbed; King too was ungrateful – no sooner had Joan fixed up Moorside than King decided he wanted it for himself. Joan was furious, but the Pattesons settled for a small cottage in the woods. It was with Joan's advice, and Godfroy's copies of *Country Life*, that King gradually transformed Moorside into a woodland version of Woburn Abbey. With its English gardens, bird baths and artificial "ruins" constructed from bits and pieces of demolished Ottawa buildings, Rex's estate at Kingsmere became a private Shangri-la where he and Joan could indulge in long, confidential talks and moonlit walks in the woods. Joan Patteson was King's "country wife."

King had politics to distract him from the tensions of this threesome, and Godfroy, who was frequently ill, may have had whiskey: entries in King's diary depict Godfroy as an ineffectual wastrel, but then King's malice is understandable. For Joan the strain was terrible. "She was quite sad when I met her first," King reports in May 1921. "She spoke of her fondness for me, and of having to give me up. Too, she feels that a great struggle has been come thro' successfully – she said she felt as if she had nursed me thro' a great illness for wh. she had been partly responsible – How true. She spoke of the anxiety she had suffered for months. Her sorrow & tears were a reaction now that the struggle was over – dear little soul – she would have been an ideal wife – if only we could have met years ago. Her tender simple loving nature is what mine needs & craves."

Did Joan realize that Rex had chosen her to play Mother? "She has filled the place of my mother in my heart," King said happily. King certainly found erotic pleasure in playing the interloper in the marriage bed, but apart from being married to other men, Joan Patteson and Isabel King could hardly have been more different.

Joan Patteson was not old enough to be King's mother, nor was she a neurotic invalid. She was strong and healthy, a woman with sensitivity, tolerance and generosity of spirit whose love for King was great enough to overcome almost insuperable obstacles. Joan did not "mother" King; she was his soul mate, his friend and companion and lover, certainly in an emotional if not physical sense, although Joan was sexually mature and their phsyical relationship may have included various kinds of erotic contact. Their relationship was one between equals; King had more respect for Joan than he had for anyone else. He asked her advice and he confided in her his secret fears, desires and dreams.

During their long confidential talks Joan realized that Rex was haunted by Mother's ghost. Mother spoke to him in his dreams, saying "I am alive!" He made a cult of her portrait, her wedding ring and hair, and believed that her spirit resided in the yellow boat-house at Kingsmere where she had spent her last summer. He often prayed to Mother at the boat-house, explaining: "She was more like God than any being." King's "visions" of Mother didn't fade with time, rather they increased in intensity, and Mother's image became more surreal, more powerful. "I see that Mother's love, my love for Mother, controls me absolutely," King confessed in 1921, nearly four years after her death. For Willie, Mother wasn't dead at all.

The illness Joan nursed King through was serious. Isabel King always worried that Willie had inherited her "sensitivity," and for all his adult life King suffered from a chronic fear that he might go mad. Sometimes he came very close: "Neither your letter nor your actions are those of a sane man," Mathilde Grossert wrote angrily in 1898, having received one too many gibbering letters from her suitor. Joan seems to have come to the same conclusion. Although King was always tightly controlled in public, in private his emotions and imagination, always keyed to a feverish pitch, occasionally ran wild. Like Mother, King suffered from bouts of paralyzing depression that left him weeping in bed for days and weeks; paranoid fantasies made him prey to irrational fears and violent hatreds; extreme anxiety gave him a compulsive need to manipulate and control. King also liked to play at being a child: "It is a love of a child for his nurse," he wrote after his passion for Mathilde had burned itself out. "She is more to me like a mother than a sweetheart."

Much of King's fear of madness came from his "secret vice," masturbation. Masturbation was one of the most potent taboos of King's generation: it was believed to produce homosexuality, sterility, impotence, blindness, hairy hands and insanity, although, like most taboos, it was almost universally practised, with no apparent ill effects. One of the reasons doctors urged King to marry was his addiction to this "unhealthy" habit, but King's diary records that his heroic attempts to subdue his "passions" rarely succeeded, and masturbation may have saved King's sanity.

King was worried enough about his mental health to see a psychiatrist, Dr. Adolph Meyer, but Dr. Meyer just gave him a pep talk on married love, seeing King's problems as the consequence of celibacy, not the other way around. However, after buying a copy of Freud's *Interpretation of Dreams*, King began to record his dreams or "visions" as he called them. He interpreted them himself, in the most banal and ludicrous way, and never grasped Freud's concept of the subconscious. But simply by recording his dreams, and reading them on paper, King was able to come face to face with Mother.

"I had a most distinct vision of dear mother later in the morning while still asleep," he wrote on January 5, 1935. "I saw her first in a room in which there were others, a rather dark & crowded room. I gave her a garment, a pretty little gown I had secured for her while abroad. I saw her get up and go out of the dark room along an open way. She had put on the garment but it was still open above the waist behind. I went later to see where she was. It was past or through a sort of ladies' dressing room in another building, or another part of the same one. I looked into the room where she was lying on a bed, her head on a pillow, she had on the garment I had given her. Her hair was the most celestial silvery quality I have ever seen, her features most celestially pure and refined, very delicate, her eyes clear & limpid & sparkling. No celestial being was ever more lovely.

"Notwithstanding there were others in the room, women, I walked down the step and round the foot of the bed where she lay and took her in my arms. She seemed very frail, so spiritual was she, but she put her lips to mine as I lifted her up & kissed me in a manner that seemed to be breath seemed to come from her to me. It could not have been a more affectionate or firm embrace. I seemed to be in my underclothing as I came near her side but not to feel embarrassment, with the little group of other women beyond who were also resting, feeling they were admiring my love for my mother & understanding it."

King interpreted this vision as a "celestial manifestation" and it brought him intense joy. Mother often appeared to Willie in the ten years between 1925 and 1935. She was usually wearing a loose garment or night-dress and embraced him, or joined him in bed. King's visions occurred in the morning, when he often woke with "inflamed passions," and it's fair to assume that they were wet dreams or erotic fantasies.

What really happened between Mother and Willie? Was King, at sixty, having incestuous fantasies about a woman dead nearly twenty years? Or was he playing out, in the safety of a sleeplike trance, a sexual trauma that had actually occurred?

The depth of King's psychic distress and its crippling side effects imply more than a state of arrested development. A series of snapshots of Willie and Mother taken at Kingsmere when Willie was about thirty show them cuddling on the grass like honeymooners; Mother's pose is sensual, lan-

Mother and Willie cuddling at Kingsmere.

guorous, Willie is beaming like a bridegroom. Rex was never photographed like that with any other woman.

King leaves other clues besides his erotic "celestial manifestations." He always wrote about sex in terms of fire—his passions were "inflamed," he was "on fire"—and the image of the "open fire" recurs repeatedly in his accounts of his passionate pursuit of Marjorie Herridge and Joan Patteson. In Mother's portrait, she is seated in front of an open fire, and the light from the flames, together with the light from the lamp King placed in front of the painting, makes her appear to glow with an inner radiance as if she too were "on fire." Mother is also wearing a white dress much like a night-gown.

King had recurring dreams about being caught in a public place with his pants down; he also had a fetish about nurses, dominant women in white, who could remove his clothes and examine him while he lay helpless in bed. King did spend a good deal of time in bed with Mother, certainly during the last year of Mother's life when she lived with Willie in the Roxborough apartments.

King's macabre account of his year with Mother is as grotesque as anything in literature. Isabel King was dying from cancer of the bowel; she was in terrible pain and so heavily drugged that she often had no idea who she was. She should have been in a hospital or nursing home, but she and Willie would have none of it; instead he bought Mother a white enamel hospital bed and hired a nurse. Willie played physician-in-chief; he fired the doctor who said Mother's illness was terminal, and hired one who said she would live. They shared Willie's cramped suite more like husband and wife than mother and son; Mother rarely let Willie out of her sight and when he did go out she suffered heart palpitations and shortness of breath; she clung to him, her arms around his neck, repeating over and over how much she loved him; she wouldn't go to sleep until he lay down next to her in bed. Willie called her "darling" and "sweetheart" and on Mother's seventy-fourth birthday he arranged a private little party. "When I told her it was about 4 in the afternoon when she was born 74 years ago, I began to give her a kiss for the years that had gone by since then, and so I kissed her 74 times, and at the end thanked God for her and her mother. I gave her a few more kisses for the years to come."

King was now the dominant partner in this dance of death and he took almost sadistic pleasure in Mother's suffering: he dismissed her illness as a cold or catarrh and tried to persuade the doctor to reduce her pain-killers; he went to heroic lengths to prolong her life when Mother repeatedly said that she wanted to die; he forced her to get out of bed, and carried her around in his arms, long after she found the pain intolerable; he even administered her enemas. Mother died peacefully on December 18, 1917 when Willie was away.

Joan Patteson wasn't Rex's nurse or mother, she was his psychiatrist. Joan listened, realized that King needed help, and expected it from her. What could she do? She did the most inspired thing she could have done under the circumstances—she encouraged King to confront Mother's ghost by raising Mother from the dead.

Seances were all the rage in the 1920s. Usually they were just parlour games, people giggling around a ouija board in a dark room while a "spirit" rapped out answers to personal questions. But some people took the spirits very seriously: Sir Arthur Conan Doyle, author of the Sherlock Holmes mysteries, firmly believed that he had spoken to his dead son Raymond in the Great Beyond. Most seances were conducted by professional mediums, usually women, who claimed to have unusual psychic powers or a "spirit guide," and a few of them boasted that they could "materialize" the spirit.

Through his dreams and fantasies King had already developed a very close rapport with the spirit world: all of his family was dead except Jennie. Willie, always liking to be the centre of attention, arranged their spirits around himself in a kind of angelic chorus of perpetual praise. Mother, Father, Little Bell and Max spoke to Willie in his dreams. He asked them for advice and prayed to them in times of crisis, but to be able actually to *see* Mother and hear her voice!

King began to consult mediums shortly after he and Joan pledged themselves to a life together and Joan was an integral, even essential part of King's spiritualist adventures. King describes a "quite wonderful" seance in 1932, "mother, Isabel [his sister], Max, grandfather all appearing & talking much with Joan." The medium at this seance was Etta Wreidt, a dowdy old lady from Detroit who used a "talking trumpet": the spirits spoke through a trumpet placed in the centre of the table. The ability to hear Mother's voice pleased King immensely, and he never doubted for a moment that it was Mother speaking.

The medium Etta Wreidt, photographed at Kingsmere with Godfroy and Joan Pattison and an unhappy Mackenzie King. The Pattison's dogs, Pat and Derry, were always in the picture.

Spiritualism was a fraud as well as a fad. Most of the mediums had worked in theatre or vaudeville and they all had a gimmick. Some concocted "spirits" out of photographs covered with gauze or cotton wool, others used fans, or electric shocks, some had trick tables, or "ectoplasm" made out of bread dough, but most relied on a wide range of voices and a fabulous cast of characters: if all else failed they could conjure up St. Luke or Napoleon, and they did. For a Presbyterian like King, who truly believed in life after death, the mystery of a seance – the round table in a dark room, hands joined in a circle – created an irresistible illusion that he was Orpheus in the Underworld.

Soon Orpheus and his Euridyce decided to dispense with mediums altogether. "Joan and I had started to see if we could get results from placing our hands on the small table," King wrote the next year. "It has spelt out the word 'Godfroy' & was underway with other words when we had to stop . . . later we got quite a number of messages." The tapping table oocupied Rex and Joan for many happy hours during the next few years. They were able to pose questions to King's whole pantheon of dead friends and relatives and to get answers that were universally reassuring. "Mother sends love," was one of the most frequent, but Grandfather, Sir Wilfrid, King George V and a celestial cast of thousands were always there with friendly encouragement. The questions were trivial and the spirits' answers equally banal; the whole exercise must have been unbearably tedious, except that it gave Rex and Joan the chance to spend time alone together in a dark room holding hands.

Of course there were no spirits and the table did not tap on its own. What was going on?

Spiritualism was a very modern form of interactive theatre: the audience – in this case King and Joan – created the characters and played the role of both actors and playwright. A good medium was a director; she set the stage, gathered the cast and, like a smart psychologist, she encouraged her actors/audience to ask, and answer, all their own questions – the "spirit" was simply a projection of King's own persona, and because it was himself, it was utterly convincing.

Professional mediums worked for money: using funerals, obituaries and personal contacts, they exploited wealthy people who had recently been bereaved; through these people they were introduced to a wide circle of friends of the same class. One of these friends was always an accomplice, someone who, usually unwittingly, assisted in the manipulation of the scene or provided inside information about the members of the circle. Armed with this knowledge, it was a simple matter for the medium to dazzle the circle with spiritual "revelations"; once their trust had been gained, the audience provided everything the "spirits" needed to know – if not, the spirits suddenly fell silent, or disappeared, to everyone's dismay.

Joan was a superb medium, but she wasn't in it for money, and she genuinely shared King's faith in the spirit world. She knew King's heart, and she seems to have understood that spiritualism allowed King to project his fantasies on a big screen, in public, and by sharing them in this way, become less frightened and obsessed by them. As long as the table was tapping Mother was under control: King could summon and dismiss her at will and tell her what to say. He incorporated Mother, an increasingly distant and harmless image, into a personal Parsifal myth in which he, the King of Peace, was destined to save the world. Unlike Hitler, with whom King felt a deep personal bond, King did not attempt to impose his megalomaniacal fantasy on the rest of the world and was always puzzled and disappointed that the world paid no attention to him.

King's obsessions, visions, fantasies and table-talk with the Great Beyond did not interfere with his ability to run the country efficiently for twenty-two years, in fact they may have helped, and King's "double life" was so deeply buried that during his lifetime he was believed to have no imagination at all. As a politician King was secretive, scheming and excessively cautious; he was proud not of what he accomplished, but of what he prevented. He did not offer inspiration or particularly progressive leadership, but he wasn't a reactionary and he kept Canada from falling apart, a very considerable accomplishment.

King finally retired in 1948, and Joan was with him when he died on the evening of July 22, 1950. He had been gradually sinking for a long time, the victim, ironically, of a diseased heart. In the afternoon King felt a sudden violent chill and sent for Joan. Joan's account of King's death in a letter to Violet Markham are her only surviving words about this man to whom she gave thirty years of her life:

"He wanted me and Camille [the chauffeur] came down to get me – that was after 5 o'clock – and the doctor got out [from Ottawa] at 7 o'clock & gave him morphine. The two hours were the worst I ever went thro'. I did not think he could endure the pain much longer & the terrible effort to get breath – nor could he have the Doctor said. So the morphine gave him relief & he became unconscious & never spoke again. He was so

195
•

sweet & kept praying that God would let him live to finish his work, thanked me for what I had done, but I don't think he realized it was the very final attack – At 9:42 Saturday night it was over and we were alone.''

Godfroy had gone up to King's room to say goodbye but Joan wrote that ''he broke down & could not stay longer.'' Although King often secretly wished for Godfroy's death, it probably would have destroyed his delicate relationship with Joan by raising the spectre of marriage. Godfroy too was essential to King's psychic equilibrium.

Joan, like Euridyce, disappeared. Historians who crossed the Styx into the murky world of King's diary were so spooked to find Mrs. Patteson that they expurgated her relationship with King from the original transcript; when not referred to as ''Mrs. Patteson'' she appears only as ''J'' or ''. . . .'' Joan also seems to have destroyed her own letters and notes from Rex, and her letters to him, if any, have vanished. Like Mother, Joan Patteson is a ghost, a casualty of the public prudery she and Rex secretly and successfully defied.

CHAPTER 10

Grandes Dames Agnes Macphail and Jeanne St. Laurent

$\mathcal{O}$ N A MARCH AFTERNOON in 1922, a young woman in a plain blue wool dress attempted to make her way through the noisy crowd of MPs gathered in front of the Commons chamber. The crush was so great and the echo in the stone foyer so loud that she had difficulty making her "Excuse me, please!" heard over the din, and although she knew some of the men by sight, and had been introduced to one or two, none of them paid the slightest attention to her. Craning her neck, she spotted the door to the Opposition benches and, with the judicious use of an elbow, had almost reached it when she felt a hand on her arm.

"Excuse me, miss," a man's voice said quietly. "This is the members' lobby."

"Yes, I know."

"Are you looking for someone?"

"No, thank you."

"May I direct you to the spectators' gallery?"

The young women's cheeks burned. She glared at the man, then abruptly pulled her arm away and strode through the door to the Commons chamber.

"You can't go in there, miss!" But it was too late, Agnes Campbell Macphail was in, and she remained in for nineteen years, the first woman elected to Canada's House of Commons and, for fifteen years, the only woman.

For twenty-seven years, from 1921 until 1948, Canada was governed by two bachelor prime ministers, Mackenzie King and R.B. Bennett. Since the first two decades of this period overlapped with Agnes Macphail's term in the House of Commons, and since Agnes was more popular than either King or Bennett, she was Canada's *de facto* "first lady," a term she loathed. A sharp-tongued radical feminist whose views on the equality of women were decades ahead of her time, Agnes Macphail cast an iron mold for the women who succeeded her in parliament, and made the role of

Agnes Macphail, MP, arrives on Parliament Hill. "Everything I wore was wrong . . ."

prime minister's wife politically irrelevant. Agnes was a rose in no man's lapel. "To have part of life can never be enough," she told women. "One must have all."

A bouquet of roses was sitting on Agnes's desk when she took her seat that March day. She was touched by this gallant little gesture of welcome from a bachelor colleague, and humiliated later to discover that the roses were the price he had paid for betting she would lose the election. "These ironical roses were emblematic of my reception to a House hitherto sacred to men," she said later. "I was intensely unhappy. Some of the members resented my intrusion. Others jeered at me. Everything I said

199
•

was wrong, everything I wore was wrong, everything I did was wrong, to hear comments about them. The men did not want me in Parliament and the women had not put me there. Men and women were both mad because they did not know anything about me. I had entered as an Independent and everybody was critical.''

It didn't help that Agnes represented the United Farmers of Ontario, an agrarian party dedicated to cleaning up government corruption, or that she came from South East Grey, a back-of-beyond rural riding near Lake Huron, or that she was a spinster schoolteacher of thirty-one with horn-rimmed glasses and sturdy brown Oxford shoes, but the real problem was that Agnes was a woman.

"When I walked into the lobby men sprang to their feet," she said. "I asked them to sit down as I'd come to walk around. I didn't want them doing me favours. I was right. I found that I couldn't do my job without being ballyhooed like the bearded lady. People in the gallery pointed me out and said 'Right there, that's her!' ''

Agnes hated the patronizing platitudes that greeted the arrival of the first "lady" member of the House. Typical was this welcome from C.H. Dickie of Nanaimo: "As regards the lady member who represents South East Grey, I hope she will find political life pleasant and will exercise a refining influence on our assembly. I may say that a great many of us in the West did not at one time view with pleasure the granting of the franchise to women . . . we thought, perhaps in an old-fashioned way, that it might detract from their charm if they entered the field of politics. We believed that the sex for whom we have so much admiration and love were not temperamentally fitted to cope with the intricacies and intrigue of public life and at that time we would rather have seen these engaged in an occupation less open to unpleasant influences."

"I'm not a lady, I'm an MP," Agnes retorted. "This old fashioned chivalry is all hollow. It means nothing except that men think women inferior. I'm no gulf stream in the cold ocean of political life."

This was the first federal election in which women had voted and "the boys" in the House, as Agnes always called them, had no idea what to make of a lady in their locker room, especially one who did not act like a lady. In 1922 a lady was expected to wear silk dresses and high heels and mince about clinging to her husband's arm. Agnes did not mince. She refused to wear a hat in the Commons, claiming that hats impeded her ability to think, and when she rose to make her maiden speech on March

29, 1922, two hundred and forty-four men were astonished to hear a deep, resonant voice that carried to all parts of the cavernous chamber. "What women really want today is perfect equality with men," Agnes told them calmly. "I think women just want to be individuals, no more and no less."

With her sensible shoes and dark tailored dresses Miss Macphail was often sneered at as "mannish," yet it didn't take the bachelors in the boys' club long to realize that Miss Macphail was an emotional, sensual and attractive young woman. She wasn't pretty in a conventional sense, but she wasn't homely either, and during the long hours of debate men's eyes could not help but be drawn to the solitary figure on the backbench with her pale skin and rosy cheeks, her luxuriant long black hair, and, behind the horn-rimmed glasses, a pair of laughing, intelligent dark eyes.

Agnes: "I want for myself what I want for other women – absolute equality."

201

Men fell in love with Agnes Macphail. She was honest, easy going, and she enjoyed a good argument; back home she had gravitated to the parlour, where the men discussed issues, and avoided the kitchen, where the women gossiped. Men had brought Agnes into politics, run her campaign and voted for her. She had rejected several suitors, managing to stay friends with all of them, and soon had a circle of admirers in the House, including a French-Canadian for whose sake she tried, and failed, to speak French. She grew accustomed to intimate teas *à deux* in a corner of the parliamentary restaurant, and mash notes delivered to her desk in the middle of debate. "You have very nice ankles, Agnes," R.B. Bennett said *sotto voce* one day as he walked in front of her. She didn't really, but Agnes

Bachelor R.B. Bennett: "You have very nice ankles, Agnes."

and "Bonfire" Bennett carried on a public flirtation that caused Ottawa's tongues to wag.

Mackenzie King, "the fat man full of words" as Agnes dismissed poor Rex, courted her obsequiously for what Agnes believed to be purely political ends. A story went around Ottawa that King had tiptoed up to Agnes's sixth-floor office late one night only to beat a quick retreat when he found her already entertaining one of his Cabinet colleagues. The story may be true: Liberal MP "Chubby" Power used to pursue Agnes through the halls too drunk, unfortunately, to be anything more than a bore.

In her forties Agnes had a serious relationship with one of her closest political allies, Alberta MP Robert Gardiner. Gardiner apparently proposed and was rejected; he was defeated soon after. He refused to see Agnes again and died unmarried, a bitter recluse. Agnes remained single by choice: marriage would have cost her her job. The idea of married women working outside the home was anathema to the majority of Canadians, and Agnes would have been expected to parrot her husband's political opinions. If she didn't quit as MP, she would likely have been defeated.

Agnes regretted not having children, but at the emotional centre of her political feminism lay a deep revulsion against domestic slavery. She had grown up on a poor farm in a hard-scrabble area of Ontario where a woman's fate was back-breaking labour. Her mother had made herself a martyr to her misery; Etta Macphail was so compulsive about housekeeping she was known in the neighbourhood as "killing clean." Agnes hated housework and everything it implied about a woman's menial status.

Young women moved from their father's house, where they minded children and did chores, to their husband's house, where they minded children and did chores. "A woman's place is in the home" was such an unquestioned cliché of Canadian life that Agnes was being almost blasphemous when she said: "I do not want to be the angel of any home. I want for myself what I want for other women – absolute equality. After that is secured men and women can take turns at being angels."

However much pride a housewife took in her work, the fact remained that she had no income. Canada was still a relatively poor, agricultural country of eleven million people, and very few women inherited money or property of their own. Except for what she might make sewing or selling eggs, a wife was dependent on whatever her husband gave her or bought for her, and that was often nothing. She kept her "mad money" in a tea cannister or an old jar; her husband did the banking. Her house or farm was in her husband's name. She had no right to it or to the income from its sale and no right to financial support if he deserted her. She had no pension and no savings; if her husband died first, as he usually did, she moved in with a married son or daughter where she minded children and did chores until she died.

Agnes was born free. It never occurred to her that her freedom should be curtailed because she was female, and when it was, she rebelled. She had a terrible temper, which got her into trouble, but her rebellion was fueled less by rage than by a thirst for life, adventure, experience, wisdom, *all*. "In my very early teens I saw that men did a job in the world outside their home and women did not," she said. "At fourteen I turned it around in my mind this way: a woman has children – the boys do things and the girls marry and have other children – and I asked myself: 'Does this thing never end in a woman being a person and making a contribution in addition to, or in place of, having children?' " When inevitably asked why she never married, Agnes replied: "The *person* could not be subjected." When women were constitutionally recognized as "persons" in Canada in 1929, Agnes had already been a member of parliament for seven years.

Agnes respected the work women did in the home – she had done plenty of it as a girl – and because she respected women's work she fought against the dependency and humiliation inherent in the housewife's status. "I believe the preservation of the home in the future lies almost entirely in the hands of the men," she said in 1925. "If they are willing to give women economic freedom in that home, if they are willing to live by the standard they wish the women to live by, the home will be preserved. If the preservation of the home means the enslavement of women, economically or morally, then we had better break it."

Prophetically, Agnes was speaking on a bill to liberalize divorce: men could divorce their wives for adultery, but women had to prove their husbands also guilty of incest, bigamy, rape, sodomy or bestiality. For women the social stigma of divorce was more punitive than an abusive marriage, and understandably the divorce rate was negligible. Divorce was a dirty word; when the Prince of Wales wanted to marry Mrs. Simpson in 1936, the worst thing anyone could say about her was that she was a "divorcée." Agnes wasn't afraid to get her hands dirty, and by forcing men to discuss rape and sexual perversion with a woman, in public, she began the process of confrontation that would eventually drag the secret of domestic violence out of the basement. It was a brave thing to do: in

1925 contraception was whispered about in respectable female circles, but contraception implied marriage, safe sex and family planning – Agnes was talking about unwilling, ugly, sinful sex.

Gregarious and good-humoured by nature, a politican by conviction, Agnes learned to live with winks, sniggers, sexist jokes and the occasional smear – the Conservatives tried to link her with a homosexual convict she had befriended – but men soon learned that Agnes could give as good as she got. "Don't you wish you were a man?" yelled one heckler. "Don't you?" Agnes replied. When a man repeatedly interrupted her speech by shouting "Aw, get a husband!" Agnes made him stand up, looked him scornfully up and down and asked the crowd in mock despair: "How could I be sure that someone I married might not turn out like this?" Agnes's speeches were always pithy and provocative and her scathing wit could bring crowds to their feet. "I am what I am and I tell them what I think," Agnes said. She was good copy; on the social pages Amaryllis's snooty sisters sniped at Miss Macphail's appearance, but on the front pages Miss Macphail's opinions made news.

Agnes was no flapper – short shirts and cocktails would have scandalized her strait-laced Scotch constituents – but she was very much a part of the rebellious, almost anarchistic mood of the "roaring twenties" when women cut their hair, burned their corsets and smoked in public. Flying was all the rage and movies, radio and the gramophone were replacing vaudeville as mass entertainment. Everyone who could afford a cheap Model T drove a car, and like all major cities Ottawa had an electric railway. The magnificent Peace Tower at the entrance to the new Centre Block on Parliament Hill now dominated the Ottawa skyline, and to the east the Chateau Laurier hotel and imposing Union Station gave the capital a more imperial appearance, although the saws in the lumber mills still screeched and the stench of the E.B. Eddy pulp and paper factory hung over the city like a pall. The workers' shacks to the west of Parliament Hill had been wiped out in a fire in 1900, and many of the moldering old mansions on Wellington St. were demolished to make way for five- and six-storey public buildings with elevators, electric light and telephones. Sparks St. and Rideau St. had developed into busy shopping districts, and the ready-to-wear department store was replacing the dressmaker and sewing machine.

As Canada became industrialized, the exodus of farmers from the land worried Agnes. She saw it as a loss of independence, a betrayal of Canada's homesteading tradition, and her worst fears were confirmed when she visited striking coal miners in Cape Breton in 1925. She encountered scenes of starvation and destitution that sickened her, yet when she reported the suffering of the miners' families to the House of Commons, her pleas for assistance were brushed aside on the grounds that the strike was led by communists. Canada had no organized welfare system, no unemployment insurance and no old-age pension; Agnes Macphail was determined to make sure we got them.

Attempts to discredit Agnes as a socialist and a troublemaker only enhanced her reputation, and by 1930, when she turned forty, Agnes was a celebrity. Women students at the University of Toronto voted Agnes Macphail the woman they most wanted to be; Mary Pickford finished second. She was Canada's foremost advocate of prison reform and women's rights, not an odd combination in Agnes's mind, and a passionate peace activist: Agnes got into the most trouble when she proposed banning cadet training in schools. She had been one of the first women delegates to the League of Nations; she had attended international women's conferences in Washington and Prague, and she had hobnobbed with the controversial British MP Lady Astor. Agnes had won four consecutive elections, more than could be said for Prime Minister Mackenzie King, who had just been defeated, and she had survived the disintegration of the United Farmers Party. Agnes was an Independent. Agnes was Agnes, and Agnes had bloomed.

She wore a pince-nez perched on her nose, and when not in use the delicate gold-rimmed spectacles hung by a black velvet ribbon from her bosom. Her thick greying hair, beautifully finger waved, was arranged in a chignon that accented her high cheek-bones; she wore dark red lipstick and pencilled her eyebrows. Her school-marm Oxfords had long since vanished in favour of fashionable pumps; her clothes were elegant, expensive and distinctive. She like to wear black, and her favourite costume was a long cape that she swirled around her to make a dramatic exit. Like her evangelist compatriot, Aimee Semple Macpherson, Agnes Macphail was a charismatic performer: only her message was different.

Was anybody listening? In her invincible innocence Agnes had assumed that the world was full of women like her, but where were they? Women had the vote; why weren't they rushing into politics? The money was good – Agnes made more than $4,000 a year in the Depression – and her life was full of excitement, good friends and challenging work. Agnes had jumped off the deep end and found the water fine, but when she came up for air the other girls were still huddled in their clothes on the shore.

Agnes frightened women even more than she frightened men. She frightened men because she was a woman in a man's world; she frightened women because she was alone.

The Spinster is perhaps the most powerful mythic figure to emerge in the twentieth century. Earlier goddess images, even scary ones, were associated with sex, fertility and salvation – Medusa's head was nothing more than a woman's genitals – and their power derived from procreation. Queen Victoria was the Great Mother of the British Empire, and even Willie King's mother served him as a symbol of eternal life. In the sixteenth century Elizabeth I of England, a freshly minted Protestant, substituted herself, the Virgin Queen, for the Virgin Mary; the doctrine of Immaculate Conception still linked virginity magically to motherhood and the Virgin herself was an object of veneration.

The Spinster appeared with contraception. Many cultures historically practised infanticide, and women had always found ways to terminate a pregnancy, but celibacy had been the only sure way of preventing it; the invention of the synthetic rubber diaphragm gave women a simple, safe, secret and highly effective method of birth control. The moral and psychological ramifications of contraception are still violently debated, but the sexual implications were apparent immediately: if a woman could have sex without children she didn't need a husband.

The technological revolution that produced the diaphragm had already produced the typewriter and the telephone, and it was quickly discovered that women were more adept than men at operating these tricky appliances. These were respectable white-collar jobs – secretaries wore starched white blouses – not the filthy factory work women had been used to. Middle-class women went to work during the First World War, when it was patriotic, and they took pride in their new skills. Nursing was now a decent vocation, thanks to the war, and for women with a high-school or university education there was teaching, social work or, for the dedicated few, medicine. Wages were low and hours were long, but single women who had been stuck at home found that by pooling their resources they could live on their own. They were no longer some man's sister or daughter, and they had money in their purses.

As long as she had been at home, invisible and dependent, the unmarried woman had been a harmless object of pity and a scapegoat for the

family's problems, "poor Aunt Aggie" who was too peculiar or too ugly
to catch a man. Now that she was, quite literally, out of the closet, the
spinster became a sexual threat: if she was doing "men's work," then she
must be "mannish," lesbian, frigid, sterile, unfeminine, unattractive and
unmarriageable.

The Spinster – the word itself hisses misogyny – is one of the most
lethal stereotypes women have ever encountered. The Old Maid was ridiculed, vilified and socially ostracized; she was segregated in the workplace
and deliberately impoverished. She was forced to wear ugly, "mannish "
clothes to work and to behave in a prudish manner; if she didn't she was
fired. The Spinster was a working girl, but she was working for The Boss,
and the boss made sure that doing a man's work didn't mean enjoying a
man's privileges, including extra-martial sex: once identified as an "old
maid" a woman was a sexual pariah and her chances for marriage were
virtually nil. The Spinster stereotype deprived her of sexual freedom by
depriving her of sex.

Most spinsters worked because they had to: sixty thousand young men
did not come back from Flanders' fields, thousands more came back crippled in body and spirit, and for every one of those men there was a woman
who had to get on with her life. For women like Agnes who *wanted* to
work, making the choice between spinsterhood and marriage required
extreme self-denial.

Work was a choice most women were not prepared to make. The
Spinster stereotype cut to the quick of a woman's sexuality; at least in
marriage she had that. Women may have admired Agnes Macphail, they
may have envied her, they may have even wanted to be her, but politics
was still men's work and Agnes Macphail was an old maid.

Agnes enjoyed the admiration of women, resented their envy and was
deeply hurt by their hostility. Believing that all people are born equal,
Agnes could not understand how women could accept inferiority without
doing something about it, yet she found women not only believed themselves to be inferior, they were satisfied to stay that way. Single women
found it impossible to emulate Agnes's achievement: they didn't have the
education, the money, the social status, the confidence or, to be blunt, the
male support to win a nomination; married women interpreted Agnes's
message as a rebuke: they were second-class sell-outs. Their tempers
weren't improved by the suspicion that it was true.

"If women are exclusively interested in private life and not in a place in the world, then they are not worthy of the franchise," Agnes said. "I am fed up with auxiliaries. Join with the men. Be adults together." Agnes staunchly resisted efforts to segregate women in politics – women in the basement serving coffee and pie – but she also resisted tokenism. At a political meeting where women were demanding a seat on every committee, Agnes flung her cape around her and stomped off claiming that she was "sick and tired of this woman business. if I didn't get anything by merit, I didn't want it." It was 1933, affirmative action had not yet been invented, and Agnes *was* sick and tired of timid, lazy women who wheedled and whined for favours from men. Her flash of temper was used by men to show that Agnes wasn't a feminist, and their malice damaged her reputation unfairly. Agnes spoke ceaselessly in favour of equal rights for women, equal pay, financial support for deserted wives, divorce, day care, income-tax deductions for working wives – all issues that are being bitterly argued about sixty years later – and she spoke alone. She was probably the first woman in Canada to suggest that a husband take his wife's name, and in the bleakest days of the Depression she was the only person to speak out about the desperate plight of unemployed single women. Agnes was so far ahead of her time that few women understood what she meant: while white-glove feminists were fussing about Senate appointments, Agnes was worrying about systemic sexism in education and prejudice against women in the professions. Women who were frightened by freedom, or who thought it a reward for good behaviour, had a hard time getting Agnes's point: women were already equal, if they would only act that way.

More worldly women knew the cost of revolution: women who play men's games get killed. Bake a pie or be burned at the stake? It was safer in the kitchen. Agnes burned. She became isolated. Her intellectual independence made her enemies and cost her alliances; she had no powerful political machine to protect her, and she could accept a Cabinet post only if she sold out to the Liberals. She turned down a Senate seat – she quipped that she was too young to be laid out on mortuary slab – and after 1933 she affiliated herself with the new left-wing Co-operative Commonwealth Federation, the party closest to her social-democratic views, but she found the CCF as patriarchal as the other parties, and the more sexist socialists tagged Agnes as a Red and home-wrecker.

The poverty and unemployment of the Depression made it impossible to talk about working wives, equal pay or day care, and after the outbreak of the Spanish Civil War in 1936 Agnes's advocacy of peace rang hollow even in her own ears. Her beautiful clothes were now a terrible embarrassment: dancing in the ballroom of the Chateau Laurier with millionaire Prime Minister R.B. Bennett, Agnes Macphail was a *grande dame*, a woman of wealth and refinement light years away from the people of South East Grey, and Bennett was the most hated man in Canada. He lost the election to Mackenzie King in 1935, but Agnes won her seat – for the last time. She was joined in the House of Commons by the second woman MP, Louise Black, widow of the former Conservative Speaker, George Black, a madman from the Yukon who shot rabbits out the window of the Speaker's chambers. Mrs. Black represented everything Agnes abominated – a dutiful wife who won her seat on her husband's popularity – and Mrs. Black, not Agnes, was the coming trend.

Agnes lost her seat to a Liberal on March 26, 1940, two days after her fiftieth birthday. It was a hard blow. She felt tired and looked older than her years; she had been rejected by her "ain folk," the Scotch of Grey county, and she was unemployed. "I told the people the truth at all times and they say the truth will make you free," she quipped, "well it certainly set me free!" Agnes received no reward, not even a pension, for her years of dedicated service in the House: Mackenzie King was glad to see the end of troublesome Miss Macphail.

Agnes did not have all, she had almost nothing. She had lost her family – the Commons – and her constituency. She had spent her income generously, not only on herself, but on her friends, her relatives, her protégés and her former supporters, and now she was broke. She scrabbled desperately at several different jobs until she was elected to the Ontario legislature in 1943. Provincial politics was a terrible come-down, but it was here that Agnes stopped being an Independent and formally joined the CCF. "I have become more radical," she said in 1948. "I realize too that there is nothing so powerful as an idea whose day has arrived. Timing is the thing!"

Agnes saw several of her ideas arrive: the family allowance, which gave mothers the first money of their own most of them had ever seen, old-age pensions, which Agnes considered pitifully inadequate, and the first attempts at equal-pay legislation. Yet she was disappointed that no more married women were working in 1951 than there had been in 1931, and there was still only one woman in the House of Commons. The old suffragettes were dying and no young women were taking their place. Why? Had it all been a waste? A mistake? Why did educated women gather a shawl of ignorance about them? Why did they fritter away their time in empty tasks? Could they not see that their children's welfare depended on the law, education, health, business, and unless they addressed these things there wasn't much point in baking pies? Agnes had a relentlessly logical mind – a man's mind she must have been told – and no fear. Fearlessness was her shield in the political wars – journalists compared her to the Saxon warrior-queen Boadicea – and defeat left her unprotected.

At sixty Agnes was prematurely old. She had undergone a hysterectomy when she was in her forties, a drastic cure for agonizing menstrual periods, and she had become crippled by arthritis. In 1945 a cerebral thrombosis nearly ended her career; she hung on until she lost her seat in the 1951 Ontario election. A few months later a second thrombosis left her partly paralyzed, restless and cantankerous; her appearance was so changed that her friends didn't recognize her. She had become, in fact, the ugly old maid. In 1945 Robert Gardiner had left her $7,000 in his will, enough to enable her to buy a house, but now, unemployed and burdened with medical bills, Agnes felt so fearful that she agreed to accept a Senate seat, if one were offered. It wasn't: the new Liberal prime minister, Louis St. Laurent, had no compassion for crotchety old Miss Macphail. On February 11, 1954 Agnes suffered a heart attack; she died two days later in Toronto and was buried in a howling blizzard in the family plot in Priceville, Ontario.

A bronze bust of Agnes Macphail was placed in the main corridor of the House of Commons, but her achievements were virtually forgotten and her ideas dismissed; it would take another generation before Canadian women began to act on Agnes's simple advice: "A woman's place is any place she wants to be."

On a grey, icy day at the end of November 1948 a black Buick drove up to the Roxborough apartments on Ottawa's Laurier Ave. West. A uniformed chauffeur got out and opened the back door for a short, stout old lady in a black persian lamb coat. The old lady hurried inside, her arms full of parcels, while François, the chauffeur, unloaded boxes from the trunk. After he had carried the boxes up to the prime minister's suite and stowed the jars of homemade jam beneath the prime minister's bed, François drove the Buick back to Quebec City.

Jeanne St. Laurent had arrived in Ottawa. She didn't intend to stay long. "My home is in Quebec City," she said, and she meant it. Jeanne was the boss of the St. Laurent household, and she resented the demands of public life as an intrusion on her privacy and a diminution of her authority. Nobody told Jeanne St. Laurent what to do, not even Louis.

Louis St. Laurent succeeded Mackenzie King as Liberal prime minister in 1948 after serving as justice minister since 1941. He was sixty-six, an upright, gentlemanly French-Canadian lawyer motivated by a stern sense of public duty. Jeanne was sixty-two. They had been married forty years and had raised five children; now there were seventeen grandchildren. St. Laurent was at an age when most men retire, and Ottawa in 1948 was not an attractive or welcoming place for a *Québécoise grandmaman* who spoke English with a heavy French accent that revealed her rural roots in the Beauce region of eastern Quebec. As a girl Jeanne Renault had been sent to the Ursuline convent in Halifax to learn English and social graces, but after her marriage to Louis in 1908 she lived exclusively in the francophone world of Quebec City, and although Louis, whose mother was Irish, was perfectly bilingual, Jeanne was always shy speaking English. Ottawa was a bustling, modern city after the Second World War, but it remained a bastion of Anglo-Protestant superiority: in public Jeanne spoke English because no one else spoke French.

Although she was a passionate Liberal and by no means *indépendentiste*, Jeanne was not the slightest bit interested in the social claptrap of post-colonial Ottawa. She preferred the company of her grandchildren: the children were a lot more fun. Ottawa was in the doldrums – Mackenzie King had bored everyone to death. There hadn't been a prime minister's wife for nearly thirty years, and no one knew what to do with one; Jeanne wasn't about to step into Lady Borden's pointed little shoes, and no one could remember Isabel Meighen. At Rideau Hall the influence of the governor-general had waned since the appointment of the writer, John Buchan, Lord Tweedsmuir, a crotchety Scot who hid in his room writing books until he fell on his head in the bathtub and died. Débutantes were old-fashioned, the Dufferins' toboggan slide was rotting and skating parties had been supplanted by bring-your-own-bottle jitterbug dances. Girls were wearing short skirts and bobbysox. It was no time for Grandmaman Jeanne to be a style-setter, and Ottawa was full of serious young men carrying the troubles of the world in their briefcases.

Bored by social rituals of politics – "Oh Louis," Jeanne sighed when yet another banquet loomed up, "do we *have* to go?" – Jeanne was given no political role to play, as Agnes Macdonald had been John's dragon at the gate and Zoé Laurier had doled out patronage as Wilfrid's powerful "minister of charitable affairs." Louis St. Laurent was a corporation lawyer and he ran Canada from a House of Commons boardroom with a sharp eye on the bottom line; he had no woman in his Cabinet and the idea of a woman in any corporate boardroom was preposterous. Jeanne had no bigger role in his job as prime minister than she had in his law practice, where her main function had been to run a perfect household and keep the children quiet when he was at home. Jeanne by no means disliked politics. She was a keen backroom conspirator who adored gossip, read newspapers avidly, gave freely of her advice and expressed violent opinions about Louis's opponents, particularly Quebec's abominable Maurice Duplessis and his Union Nationale, but whenever Jeanne was in full flight Louis frowned, clenched his teeth and growled "*Jeanne!*"

Jeanne was denied a public presence. She was old and, like Zoé Laurier, she was dismissed as a simple *bonne femme* by newspaper reporters who never rode in her limousine, met François, visited the St. Laurent mansion on Quebec City's Grande Allée or had the sophistication to see that Jeanne's clothes came from Fifth Avenue, New York. In private, in French, Jeanne was ebullient, strong-minded, *formidable*, while Louis was charming, charismatic, "God" to his children, who adored him, yet the public saw only rare staged glimpses of "Uncle Louis," as he was later tagged, and none of Jeanne. The only son in a poor, farm family of girls, Louis developed a puritanical sense of duty and extreme, almost self-destructive modesty. He shunned the press; the idea that the public might be interested in his hobbies, his children, his wife, was utterly distasteful to him: he would be judged by what he did, not by who he was. Jeanne was his wife, and she remained at home where she did what other women of her age and class did – she played bridge.

Jeanne also played poker, for money, late at night. Card parties had been Zoé Laurier's secret life, and they were the main pastime of Canadian wives until the 1960s, when other games became more exciting. Card parties were also one the few ways marriageable young people could meet – Louis did not dance – under proper adult surveillance, and at the turn of the century twenty-year-old Jeanne Renault wooed Louis St. Laurent over cards, holding her hand like a fan in front of her face and gazing over the top with limpid, sparkling eyes. Louis was smitten – he would always say that Jeanne was the most beautiful woman in the world – but he was a hard catch. He was poor and struggling to establish himself in his law practice: he had turned down a Rhodes scholarship to go to work to repay his sisters for his education. Jeanne spent a great deal of time visiting her own sister in Quebec City, but weeks and months went by between her chance meetings with Louis, and he never ventured any farther than walking her home.

This would not do. Jeanne had her heart set on handsome black-eyed M. St. Laurent. She had first seen Louis in 1905 at his Laval University graduation ceremony where he won all the prizes. Jeanne paid no attention to the prizes, but when Louis walked across the stage to receive his degree from the governor-general, Lord Grey, the sleeve of his gown caught on Lady Grey's chair and Louis nearly tumbled into her lap. "That's the man I will marry," Jeanne said to her companion, Marius Barbeau.

Louis needed her, Jeanne could see that. He was shy, clumsy – at a party to honour his seventy-fifth birthday Louis leaned over the cake to blow out the candles and stood up with icing all over his suit – and oblivious to practical things. Jeanne was thoroughly practical: she wanted a good husband who could give her a comfortable home.

Jeanne Renault was wealthy by the standards of rural Quebec. Her father, Pierre-Ferdinand Renault, was the leading merchant of the Beauce and Jeanne, the seventh of twelve children, was raised to expect the best. The Renaults always had servants – Jeanne never did housework in her life – and the girls were educated to improve themselves. Louis was poor, but he was a professional and had better prospects than a farmer or a merchant. Jeanne wasn't about to let Louis get away.

In the summer of 1907, Marius Barbeau brought Louis to a bazaar in Beauceville. Jeanne was busy, but she bluntly suggested to Louis that he go to her home and introduce himself to her mother. He did, and the couple began corresponding after Louis returned to Quebec City. Louis's letters caught the eye of Papa Renault, who insisted that he write on postcards. Louis obliged, and when winter came Jeanne had a whole box full of postcards.

Jeanne was now twenty-one and papa had had enough of this hanky-panky. He took the train to Quebec City and accosted the young lawyer in his office: What were M. St. Laurent's intentions? Stunned, Louis mumbled um, yes, um, he was contemplating marriage, um. That did it. Jeanne and Louis became engaged and they were married in Beauceville on May 19, 1908.

Jeanne and Louis St. Laurent on their wedding day.

Marriage brought them both good fortune: Jeanne had a brilliant, devoted husband and Louis suddenly found himself living in relative luxury. Jeanne's wealth enabled them to rent an eight-room apartment on Rue St.-Jean complete with a maid, and the Renault connections in Quebec helped establish Louis's reputation. Louis's legal practice prospered and when their first daughter, Marthe, was born the following March, Jeanne's happiness was complete.

Over the next thirty years Jeanne built a private world that essentially excluded the world outside. Her home on the Grande Allée was her castle, her nest, her *domain*. She rarely left it except to shop with François – neither Jeanne nor Louis ever drove – and she ran it with meticulous attention to detail. Louis came home every day for lunch and the meal, a full-course formal dinner, was served by a maid in uniform precisely a twelve: "Exactness is the *politesse* of kings," Jeanne like to say. A king could have come for dinner any day and felt perfectly at home, and years later, when the Queen Mother came for dinner in Ottawa, she and Jeanne hit it off famously.

215

Every meal was a gourmet feast, even if Jeanne and Louis were eating alone with the children. "I never ate a hotdog until after the Second World War," recalls her youngest daughter, Madeleine. "I'd never seen one." Jeanne had a cook and every morning she would direct the preparation of the daily menu. She adored sweets, and it showed; she became very fat. She also developed high blood pressure but it didn't interfere with her passion for food: after dinner she often treated herself to a rich custard of maple syrup, cream, sugar and butter. Louis, who was always trim, remonstrated with her, but Jeanne was never self-conscious about her weight. Fat was fine with her. She made her own pickles and jam, an annual ritual her granddaughter Jean Riley recalls as "almost a religious occasion."

Madeleine describes the St. Laurent house as "une chambre mortuelle" – a funeral parlour – full of dark furniture, Oriental rugs and porcelain vases. Jeanne kept the house immaculate. She kept the five children immaculate too, and supervised their friendships to make sure that they didn't take up with unsuitable people. "Everything had to be perfect," says Jean, who remembers *grandmaman* as a bossy, rather intimidating woman who certainly ruled the roost. "She liked to do everything well and she cared a lot about style, details of the table setting, what kind of gloves you wore. She cared about clothes, she really *cared*."

Louis also led a highly regimented life: off to the office at 8 a.m., dinner at noon then home for supper at 6 p.m. After the children were in bed he worked in his study for several hours, then he and Jeanne had a game of cards or dominos before bed. Apart from Louis's work and their small social circle they had no outside interests; their one indulgence was fishing at their summer home on the Île d'Orléans. With his impeccable dark suit and neat little mustache Louis St. Laurent was the quintessential corporate lawyer: disciplined, discreet and Liberal. Even at home the St. Laurents' behaviour was highly stylized. "It was a very dignified family," says Madeleine. "I never saw my parents in a passionate embrace. They never kissed in front of the children. There were certain things we could not discuss with them – they didn't want to know. They ignored those things they didn't want to know."

For the children, Jeanne's rituals made home a secure haven where they were always sure of lots to eat and *maman*'s undivided attention. "I loved it," remembers the second daughter, Thérèse. "Our house was *the* place to be. The five of us did everything together, we enjoyed each other's company. Our friends complained that we didn't find anybody interesting apart from ourselves." The St. Laurent universe revolved around Louis – "He was the kingpin," says Madeleine – even when he was absent. "He was the kind of man you'd do anything for," remembers Jean Riley. "Of course, *grandmaman* set you up to think he was God." Jeanne was by no means servile: Louis and the children learned to respect her temper. "She

Jeanne with her first three children.

was her own person," says Madeleine. "Nobody pushed her around. She was perfectly happy."

The bell-jar of Jeanne's *bourgeois* heaven shattered on December 4, 1941. Prime Minister King telephoned to summon Louis to Ottawa. Jeanne had heard rumours: Louis would be asked to be minister of justice. She was furious. Louis was nearly sixty and had never run for public office in his life. But Canada was at war and Louis had a profound sense of duty. He went to Ottawa; two days later the Japanese bombed Pearl Harbor. Louis was sworn in as justice minister and elected to the House of Commons in Laurier's old riding of Quebec East.

Jeanne found it hard to pick up the pieces. Her children had grown up. The oldest had families of their own. Madeleine was in the army. Now Louis was gone, their money was going – Louis's income shrank from $50,000 to $15,000 – and the two housemaids had to be let go. For the first time in her life Jeanne was alone. She dug in: the house on the Grande Allée was her bunker and she would die there before she surrendered.

It would be a fight. In 1950 the young men with trouble in their briefcases who ran post-war Ottawa had another house in mind for Madame St. Laurent, a cold, inhospitable stone mansion on the banks of the Ottawa River. It was Jeanne's fate to be the first reluctant tenant of the rogue white elephant of Canadian public housing, the prime minister's official residence at 24 Sussex Drive.

Gorffwysfa or "place of peace," as the house was originally called, was built in 1868 by wealthy Ottawa miller Joseph Currier as a wedding gift for his third wife, Hannah. Designed in a Gothic-Revival style to complement the new parliament buildings to the west, *Gorffwysfa* was one of the most modern and beautifully finished houses in Canada. "The mantle-pieces are of marble," wrote the Ottawa *Citizen*, "the woodwork is of the best possible material and quality; the floors being walnut, butternut and pine, the boards about three inches wide; the stairs are oak, and the doors and windows ash, butternut and walnut. The building is heated with hot air and furnished with hot and cold water baths. The plastering is done in the best style of the art, with rich cornicing and ornamental work in every room. The dimensions of the building are 82 × 40 feet and the cost will probably exceed $15,000."

After Hannah's death in 1901 the house was sold to Senator W.C. Edwards for $30,000. Edwards's nephew Gordon eventually inherited the house and was living there quietly in 1943 when he received notice that his home would be expropriated by the Government of Canada. The only reason the government offered was the possibility that the area would become commercialized. This was ridiculous. Sussex was the classiest street in Ottawa–Rideau Hall was just around the corner–and Edwards certainly had no intention of turning his family home into a hotel. Infuriated, Edwards fought the expropriation in court: he demanded $261,190 for the property, the government offered $125,000. After three years of bitter wrangling the Exchequer Court awarded Edwards $140,000 for the house and grounds.

Gordon Edwards lived on at 24 Sussex Drive until his death in November 1946: it turned out that the government had no idea what to do with the property. His heirs stripped the house of its priceless antiques and Impressionist art, leaving only an out-dated stone shell that was badly in need of repair. No suitable tenant could be found for 24 Sussex and the government did not bother to maintain it; water pipes burst, windows were smashed and the grounds were overrun with weeds. By 1950 *Gorffwysfa* was uninhabitable.

It hadn't escaped the notice of *Gorffwysfa*'s embarrassed owners, the Department of Public Works, that Prime Minister St. Laurent did not have a suitable residence in Ottawa. Since 1941 he had rented rooms in the Roxborough apartments, commuting to Quebec City on the weekends, but the Roxborough had become something of a fleabag since the days when Willie King courted Mrs. Patteson. The building was antiquated, the suites cramped–Louis's refrigerator was in his closet–and the furnishings filthy; the St. Laurent's apartment was no place for a prime minister to entertain. Jeanne spent very little time in Ottawa and she adamantly refused to sell their home in Quebec City. It had been their home for thirty-five years, and they were too old now to cast themselves adrift. Louis could not afford a second house in Ottawa, and he was perfectly content at the Roxborough, a home-away-from-home for most of the Liberal Cabinet where the nation's business could be comfortably carried on over dinner and drinks.

Nobody bothered to inform Louis or Jeanne St. Laurent that 24 Sussex had been designated as the prime minister's official residence, and nobody thought to consult them about the extensive renovations.

The house was completely gutted: the carved staircases, fireplaces and wood panelling were ripped out, turrets and wings were torn off and others added, walls were knocked down, the front portico and gingerbread trim were removed and the Gothic details of the exterior flattened into a forbidding grey façade. Inside the house was a barrenland of grey wallboard, grey drapes and grey broadloom – the ultimate in good taste in Canada's Mushroom Period – with one pink silk sofa and Empire chairs upholstered in red velvet. The furnishings were purchased by the Department of Public Works and chosen by a committee of interior decorators from Eaton's, Simpson's and Morgan's: if 24 Sussex looked like a hotel on the outside, it looked like a department store on the inside. The renovation cost $287,250 and the furnishings – the house came completely equipped with silver, china, crystal and linen – amounted to $105,000. Adding the $140,000 paid to Gordon Edwards, plus extras, the total cost came to $557,319.

Jeanne and Louis were aghast when they were unexpectedly presented with this monster home. They hadn't asked for it and they didn't want it; Louis finally agreed to move in only on condition that they pay rent. "I'm not going to live in here!" Jeanne cried when she walked through the front door. "I cannot live with that wallpaper!" The hall had been papered with giant chrysanthemums. "I think the stores gave things they couldn't sell," sighed Thérèse. The chrysanthemums left and Jeanne stayed.

She was terribly lonely. She knew almost no one in Ottawa and found it difficult at her age to make new friends. Louis worked day and night; Jeanne watched television, chain smoked and talked to her children on the phone. She trained the staff, something she was expert at, and, as always, spent a good deal of time in the kitchen.

Jeanne established 24 Sussex as a family home. She felt no desire or obligation to hold open house or to entertain anyone except the necessary poohbahs, most of whom left her unimpressed, although she was very fond of the queen. She went to the coronation in 1953 by ship – she refused to fly – and stayed home when Louis went around the world in 1954. Jeanne liked to travel by car with François, her maid and a daughter or two – her three daughters were always being summoned to her side – in the stately style of a Chinese empress. She accompanied Louis on his election campaigns, sitting dutifully on the platform during the interminable speeches and coughing discreetly when she became bored. "I've spoken too long," Louis quipped once. "My wife is coughing." Jeanne made no secret of her resistance: "If my husband is elected I won't sleep very much," she told a reporter on one election night, "If he is defeated I will

Jeanne and Louis with their three daughters Madeleine, Marthe and Thérèse.

sleep very well. Then I will go back home." Louis won by a massive majority.

Jeanne may have been wiser than Louis: they were too old for this job. By 1957 Louis was seventy-five and he looked sick and frail. The government was old too – twenty-two consecutive years in power – and arrogant, St. Laurent was faced with a younger and very aggressive Conservative opponent, John Diefenbaker, and during a rowdy debate over the government's construction of a trans-Canada gas pipeline, St. Laurent seemed to lack the strength of will to control his caucus or salvage his legislation. Day after day he sat slumped in his seat while Diefenbaker tore him apart, and during the 1957 election campaign in June he appeared trembling and distracted. Diefenbaker and the Conservatives won a stunning upset victory.

Louis was devastated. Jeanne was delighted: she was going home! She was out of 24 Sussex in a flash. Stowing her evening gowns in the attic on the Grand Allée, she said triumphantly to Madeleine: "I'll never wear these again!"

Louis resigned as Liberal leader and sank into a deep depression; his face was so ashen, his legs so shaky that it appeared he would not have long to live, yet back home he slowly regained his strength and his spirits. Jeanne never left home again: she died on the Grand Allée on November 13, 1966, just three weeks after her eightieth birthday. Louis died on July 25, 1973, at the age of ninety-one.

CHAPTER 11

The

Three

Mrs.

Diefenbakers

*J*OHN DIEFENBAKER was the most romantic man young Olive Freeman had ever met. It was the autumn of 1917 in Saskatoon, and
John was just back from the war, wounded in action it was whispered,
although the exact nature of John's injury and how it was received
remained mysterious. Olive looked closely for a scar or a limp but could
see nothing and John never spoke of it, not even to her brother Hal. Olive
was too polite to ask, in case it was one of those things girls were not
supposed to know about, and admired John for his bravery. She was a little
in awe of him. He was twenty-two, very tall and rather stand-offish, at
least by Saskatchewan standards, and he had an unnerving way of staring
at her. When she played the piano in church she could feel John's brilliant
blue eyes boring right through her back. John always walked her home
after her Sunday-school class and Hal teased her about her *beau*, but it
seemed to Olive that John was just being nice to Hal's kid sister.

One Sunday on the way home John suddenly turned to her with his
disconcerting hawk's stare and said: "Will you marry me?" Olive burst
out laughing. She took it as one of his dry jokes and it wasn't until she
saw the flush rising in his neck that Olive realized John was perfectly
serious. "But I'm only fifteen!" she blurted.

Fifty years later Olive will share a more public humiliation with John
Diefenbaker, but for the moment his acute embarrassment put a serious
crimp in their romance. Olive Freeman was the great love of John's life –
he had known that as soon as he met her – and he had approached her with
the same directness he approached the great goal in his life: to be prime
minister. John would not allow the fact that he barely knew this girl to
stand in the way of his happiness any more than he would later allow five
consecutive election defeats to stand in the way of his becoming prime
minister of Canada.

Olive mentioned John's proposal to no one – she was already a model of discretion – and John retreated in confusion. He was a law student. Imagine proposing to a girl who wasn't even of legal age! John buried himself in his books. Olive went back to school. Two years later the Freemans left Saskatoon and Olive went on to study at McMaster University in Hamilton, Ontario. She and John lost touch.

Almost ten years later, in the summer of 1928, they met by chance on the train. Olive was teaching school in rural Ontario, spending her summers in Huntsville where she made a little extra money as the postmistress

*The great love of John
Diefenbaker's life,
Olive Freeman.*

at a summer resort; John was practising law in Prince Albert, Saskatche-wan, and making a name for himself in the court-room. They were both single, and John was still in love. Olive had grown up to be a lovely young woman, slim, graceful, her brown eyes and milky skin set off by dark hair bobbed in the latest style. Her skimpy summer dress showed off her legs, but Olive was still a good Baptist. She wore little make-up – she didn't need to – and she was as self-possessed as ever. John, spiffy in a light grey gabardine suit with matching vest, was now very much the young man about town, even if the town was wild and woolly Prince Albert; he was successful, well-to-do and very pleased with himself.

John decided to try again, and he wrote to Olive in Huntsville. The letter went astray, and Olive never received it. Weeks passed and John waited in vain for a reply. A year later, on June 29, 1929, John married his Saskatchewan sweetheart, Edna Mae Brower.

Edna was twenty-nine, a lively redhead who adored parties, clothes and fast cars. John had a fast car, a new Buick, and he drove fast, rocketing down the gravel roads so recklessly that he somtimes spun off into the ditch. He drank too, although not as much as his friends, and played poker with the boys far into the night. Apart from hunting and fishing, which John loved, there wasn't must else for him to do in Prince Albert. He was too uncoordinated for hockey or curling – like Louis St. Laurent, Diefen-baker couldn't even dance – he hated swimming and couldn't sing a note. John Diefenbaker did like sex, however, and like Hollywood movie star Clara Bow, Edna Brower had "It."

She wasn't pretty, her eyes were set too close together under heavy brows and her front teeth were crooked, but she had a good figure and loads of personality. She blew every cent she earned on clothes and she liked to strut her stuff: it wasn't hard to turn heads in rural Saskatchewan and Edna quickly turned John's. She was engaged to a car dealer when they met, but John didn't let that stand in his way, and he pursued Edna with the relentless concentration that he brought to the practice of criminal law.

Edna wasn't an easy catch. She was in no hurry to settle down. Like Olive Freeman, Edna was a schoolteacher, but there the resemblance ended. Olive was serious, scholarly; Edna was a chatterbox who could barely spell. Olive was mature beyond her years; Edna was flighty and flirtatious. Olive had a stern sense of moral duty; Edna was the spoiled youngest daughter

*John and Edna Bower,
now Mrs. Diefenbaker,
at the time of their
wedding, 1929.*

of a doting mother. Edna had no intellectual or ideological interests what-
soever; John had almost nothing else.

They made an odd couple, the boop-boop-a-doop little farm girl and
the shy, gawky young lawyer, yet in many ways they complemented each
other. Edna's warmth and friendliness helped bring John out of his shell;
John's political ambitions gave Edna an outlet for her social energies. Edna
knew that she was marrying a politician: John had already run for parliament twice, and lost.

The man who had beaten John was, of all people, Mackenzie King. In
1925 the prime minister had been parachuted into Prince Albert after he
lost his seat in North York; Prince Albert was safe Liberal territory and

Diefenbaker put up nothing but a token Conservative resistance. The next year, however, John came within a thousand votes of defeating King, and faint stirrings of life were detected in the Saskatchewan Conservative Party.

Edna took to politics like a duck to water. She loved meeting people – John hated it – and Edna soon became John's campaign organizer, advance scout, publicity agent and chauffeur. John was too shy to drive into a strange town alone; Edna would go ahead, drop into the general store or Chinese café, strike up a conversation, find a few friendly faces and track down someone who would introduce John around when he arrived. She never forgot a face or a name and she briefed John meticulously before he rode into town: ''Mrs. McDougall is a Baptist, she knows your mother, her son George was killed in the war, ask which regiment he was with, she is anxious about her pension. Then we'll drop in on Bert Hall, that's Hall's Pharmacy on Main St., I bought some aspirins there and he seemed friendly. Freddy Beamish runs the gas station, he has a daughter with diabetes, her name is Jean, be sure you ask after her, we'll have him fill the tank before we leave . . .''

When Edna returned with John in tow a few days later, even diehard Liberals were curious to meet the Conservative candidate with the funny-sounding name and nice wife. As John shook hands up and down Main St. Edna stuck to his side like glue, prompting him with names and tidbits of information as people were introduced. Everyone was impressed that this man they had never met before knew so much about their personal lives, and as the crowd warmed up, so did John. Diefenbaker loved an audience, whether it was in court or on a street corner, and before long his eyes were twinkling and he was laughing uproariously at his own jokes. John's jokes were funny – his wit was his most beloved, and feared, characteristic – and by the time John and Edna left town, Bert Hall would be ''Royal Albert'' Hall for the rest of his life.

Mainstreeting in rural Saskatchewan in the Depression was hot, dusty and disappointing work. John's political fortunes were slow to improve: between 1929 and 1940 he ran in three elections and lost them all; he became leader of the Conservative Party in Saskatchewan in 1936 largely because nobody else would take the job. John's German name was used to brand him a ''foreigner,'' although his father had come from Ontario, and his buck teeth and fiercely kinky hair made him a rather frightening public figure. R.B. Bennett's autocratic and ineffective performance as prime minister between 1930 and 1935 destroyed Conservative hopes federally, and a Conservative government elected in Saskatchewan in 1929 was so discredited by its ties with the Ku Klux Klan that it failed to elect a single member in 1934.

In spite of his political misfortunes, John and Edna seemed to be blissfully happy. They hugged and held hands in public; John phoned Edna several times a day and she breezed in and out of his office. Their little bungalow was spotlessly clean and beautifully furnished; Edna even had a maid, a local girl who slept in the basement. The Depression left them financially unscathed – crime did not blow away with the topsoil – and Edna always had the best of everything Prince Albert could offer. Edna's mother moved into town and Edna was always running over to see her in the car, or dashing downtown for groceries and gossip. Prince Albert was dazzled by Edna's trousseau, and if some people complained that Edna seemed a little ''fast,'' motherhood would soon settle her down.

Edna turned a small bedroom into a nursery and waited. John was sexually vigorous. He once told a male friend that he was ready for sex any time, any place; however, he limited his performance to the marriage bed, and always on Sunday, a small rebellion perhaps against his Baptist upbringing, or because the maid was out. Possibly John made up in enthusiasm what he lacked in experience, or suffered from some sexual difficulty he was unwilling to admit, but Edna confided that she came to dread these ''Sunday sessions.'' She said that John used a condom because he did not want children, but this is hard to believe; John got along famously with other people's children and could easily have supported a family of his own.

Whatever the problem, Edna did not become pregnant. Without babies to look after or housework to do – Edna didn't even sew – Edna was soon bored out of her mind.

Prince Albert was a northern boom town gone bust where crime and politics were the major industries; it boasted a federal penitentiary, a provincial jail and an imposing court-house, all courtesy of successive Liberal governments, but it was something of a backwater for a restless young woman like Edna. John was too busy with his thriving law practice to pay attention to his wife's distress; he was in his office by 8 a.m. and frequently brought work home with him. John fell into bed, exhausted, just as Edna was ready for a movie or a game of bridge. Political campaigns were short and sporadic, and the rest of the time John lived for his work. Edna had bought a dinner service of expensive china in anticipation of entertaining

John's important friends; now she discovered that John had no important friends. Prince Albert "society" was Liberal to its toes, and the upstart Diefenbakers were emphatically excluded. They could have built their own social circle, but dinner parties were John's idea of hell. John was a loner. All the things Edna enjoyed, parties, cards, dances, weddings, John avoided like the plague. Edna's china stayed in the cupboard; John listened to the radio, she listened to the clock tick.

Edna went to dances with other couples; John went to bed. John was up by 5 a.m., Edna liked to sleep in. During the day she tried to fill the empty hours. She plucked her eyebrows and painted her nails; she went to the hairdresser, talked on the phone, clipped recipes out of the *Ladies' Home Journal*, worried about her weight and brooded. She had her share of grievances. One was John's younger brother, Elmer. Slow-moving, good-natured and unemployed, Elmer drifted around northern Saskatchewan as John's unofficial, self-appointed political agent. Quite deaf and, as they say in Saskatchewan, a few bales light of a load, Elmer was a non-stop talker who had nothing to say. He drove Edna up the wall. When Elmer arrived at their door one day, suitcase in hand, Edna walked out; she stayed with her mother until Elmer left.

"Poor Elmer," as Edna called him, was nothing compared to John's mother, Mary Bannerman Diefenbaker. "She was a nasty, cranky, head-strong, powerful old woman," says a family friend, Hugh Arscott, "and she could be very demanding." Mary Bannerman was cut from the same rough Highland tweed as Helen Shaw Macdonald, and like Helen, Mary was intensely ambitious for her eldest son, John. A big, buxom woman with a square jaw and forbidding expression, Mary terrorized her meek, bookish husband, William, and ruled her two boys with a rod of iron. Elmer never got up the nerve to marry, and Mary lost no time establishing her authority over Edna: in John's life, Mother came first.

In the first volume of his memoirs, *One Canada*, John describes his mother as "canny and 'a wee bit fey.'" That is putting it kindly. Mary Diefenbaker was vulgar, selfish and manipulative. John, like everyone else, was afraid of her. "Dief was immature in many ways," says Tom Van Dusen, a journalist who worked for Diefenbaker after he became prime minister. "Everything he did was to please his mother, and he could never please her. Mrs. D. was a great lowering cloud on the horizon."

John tried to put as much distance as possible between himself and his mother–he may have gone into politics simply to get out of Saskatchewan,

John, Edna and Mary Diefenbaker, a nasty, cranky, headstrong, powerful old woman.

a feat he finally accomplished at the age of forty-five – but his mother was always as close as the telephone. She expected John to call her or write to her every day and he did. The penalty for disobedience was worse: his mother had heart palpitations and John, guilt-stricken, rushed to her bedside. "She always threw heart attacks whenever Edna and John had some special occasion to celebrate togehter," says John's good friend Emmett Hall. "Christmas was pretty grim for Edna." One Christmas Edna apparently stormed out of the Diefenbakers' house saying she had had enough of "that bitch," and took the train home alone. Edna made her resentment of his mother clear to John, who resented it, but old Mrs. Diefenbaker seems to have had no inkling of Edna's feelings towards her: Mary's letters to John express nothing but gratitude and affection towards Edna, who sent her cards and gifts on special occasions and called her on the phone when John was too busy.

Like Isabel King, Mary Diefenbaker was a professional invalid, although no one could accuse her of "sensitivity." She lived to be nearly ninety, and for the last forty years of her life she complained of rheumatism, arthritis, pains in her legs, bowel obstructions and heart palpitations. Her doctors' bills cost John a fortune, but the cause of Mary Diefenbaker's troubles was perfectly obvious: she was neurotic and obese. She rarely left her gloomy frame bungalow in Saskatoon and demanded to be waited on hand and foot:

"My new maid is going to set me wild," she wrote to John in Ottawa in February 1941. "Her name is Gwen Jones. what she don't know will fill a book. she is a big strong girl. red headed and not a bit good looking she lives about 17 miles from Langham. but unfortunately she never did any house work. just helped her father to work the farm she can't cook. can't even cook meat. has no idea in the world how house work should be done. Oh what a week I put in I never worked so hard in my life. but no use I could not teach her anything. After she made my bed yesterday I asked her if she saw anything wrong with it. she said it is very untidy. now what can you do with a girl like that? she goes this week. by spring there will be no maids to be had. so we will all have to work."

Mary Diefenbaker was virtually illiterate, and her response to John's performance in parliament reveals that she was also ignorant and bigoted:

"You sure give those babies the right kind of dope. They dont seem to be able to answer questions do they? It was sure a good speech you give them. and the press wrote you up in great shape I was just proud of you once more. you seem to have away of putting things so different from most speakers you sure hit the nail on the head every time more power to you. The war dont look so good, day after day I look for a change. It is long in comming but I am sure it will come sooner or later. but canada must do a lot more than she is going now. Those frenchmen in quebec should have a bomb or two to wake them up."

Like Mackenzie King, John concealed his mother's deficiencies by mythologizing her: by the time Diefenbaker became prime minister he had inflated this cranky old witch into a heroic Highland matriarch who had brilliantly guided her son's feet up the ladder to success. In fact, young John's interest in politics was stimulated by his father, Will, a Liberal schoolteacher who took a keen interest in history and literature and introduced John to Shakespeare, Gibbon, Macaulay and biographies of the great British statesmen. As a result, John came to see politics as a theatre in which Great Men made speeches that changed the fate of the world, and as a politician John always saw himself as the hero of his own epic. Mary Diefenbaker was interested in politics only because John was a candidate. In the heat of the 1940 federal election campaign, she wrote him an encouraging letter from Victoria:

"It wont be long now will it? I feel it in my bones that you are going to make the grade this time. and dont you dare disappointe me or I dont know what I will do to you.

"We heard your speach over the air our radio is old and not so good but Elmer and I heard it all. your Dad did not get it all. it was very good and your voice was quite natural you did not speak down in your throte the way you did the last time I heard you. another thing I liked about it was you were not so rough and abusive as you are sometimes. How ever I hope you give the Devils Hell on the platform. So you see I liked your speach and was very proud of you."

After several pages about her various stomach complaints, Mary closes: "Now John if you do not make it Keep you chin up dont let yourself go. you must be very tired and I know your nerves are all on end. Just hang on to yourself and thum your nose at them. I know you will do what I want and will come off all right. lots of love and the best of wishes. when it is all over I want a long letter tell me all about it. love and Kiss from Mother."

John did make it – he was elected to the House of Commons as Conservative MP for Saskatoon Lake Centre – but for Edna, John's triumph came too late.

Three years earlier Edna had developed insomnia. She had always been tense, high-strung, a little "eccentric" people said. Edna may have been getting back at old Mrs. Diefenbaker: if she was sick, wouldn't John rush home to her? The answer was no. It never occurred to John, as it never occurs to most husbands, that he might be contributing to his wife's nervousness. John could be as domineering as his mother: he had a habit of begging out of social engagements at the last moment, humiliating Edna, who stayed home or went alone, and insulting his hosts. Edna was certainly getting back at John: insomnia gave her an excuse to move into the spare bedroom and sleep alone.

The doctor prescribed sleeping pills. Edna slept, but she woke up so dizzy and groggy that she could barely get out of bed before John came home for lunch. She became obsessed with her weight and dieted compulsively. She took laxatives by the handful; she may have been bulimic, eating then vomiting, and she likely took the popular diet pills advertised in the magazines. She hennaed her fading hair and began using rouge and mascara; Edna's youth was all she had, and she was growing old.

There were rumours that Edna was an alcoholic and that she had spent time in the mental hospital at Battleford. Both are possible. Edna may have turned to liquor as a narcotic. She had plenty of male friends; it would have been easy for her to tip the hotel keeper or the bartender at the Legion hall to slip her a bottle. Alvin Hamilton, later a protégé of John in Ottawa, recalls John buying Edna a bottle from the blind pig in the parliamentary press gallery. After Edna's death John stopped drinking entirely; he claimed that liquor impaired his judgment, but he may have had more painful associations. Edna, like most women alcoholics, would have been adept at hiding her drinking; Betty Ford, the attractive wife of former American President Gerald Ford, lived a busy life in the glare of public scrutiny while secretly addicted to both alcohol and prescription drugs.

Edna may have been helped by a psychiatrist, or perhaps John's election victory prompted her to make a supreme effort. She splurged on a new wardrobe and on May 13, 1940 hopped on the train with John for a new life in Ottawa. Edna certainly made a hit with the first young man she met on the train, James Sinclair. Sinclair was eating breakfast alone in the dining car when "a vivacious attractive redhead" sat down across the table from him. She immediately introduced herself as Edna Diefenbaker. "My husband will be of great assistance to you in Ottawa because he is going to be prime minister," Edna announced. "I don't think so," Sinclair replied, "because I'm a Liberal MP." They both had a big laugh. "I was absolutely charmed by Edna," Sinclair recalled. "We went to the parlour car and talked. I was very attracted to her personality. I remember she had deep dark red hair and great blue eyes. We were sitting side by side talking when John came in. We got quite a relationship going. Four or five times a day she would remind John he was going to be prime minister." Meeting Edna persuaded Sinclair that he should return to Vancouver and marry his redhaired fiancée, Kathleen; he did, and in March 1971 the fourth daughter of that marriage, Margaret, married Prime Minister Pierre Elliott Trudeau.

Edna soon learned to mainstreet on the train: it was a two-day trip and she had a captive audience. In the morning after breakfast she would make her way to the parlour car where she would strike up a conversation and get to know people; when John emerged Edna would be able to introduce him to everyone as "the next prime minister." Everyone thought it was a joke but John. John's mother was by no means confident. She cautioned him about jumping into the upcoming leadership race: "You should think it over very carefully. There is no doubt about you having the abality to fill the position. you know the jealously there is in this world and you must think about your health. not having had experience and the responsibility will be so great and enother thing. the ones that has been there for years will be wild and might not work with you as they should." John didn't run.

"I have never been happier with John than I am here in Ottawa with him," Edna wrote home. "I am making new wonderful friends of all political and religious persuasions. I am again so happy with my Donny Boy." Edna threw herself into John's career: she sat in the gallery listening attentively to his speeches, clipped newspapers for every mention of his name, read and answered his personal mail and cooked turkey dinners for the grateful press. John made a favourable impression in the Commons and Edna was popular with everyone: she was well dressed but not pretentious, proud of John, yet friendly, an easy-going, enthusiastic country girl from Saskatchewan.

Only a few people noticed the anxiety under Edna's cheery veneer. She talked too much and she blew John's horn too loudly. "She got to be a bit much," says one old reporter. "She was too pushy, too anxious. She was pushing John all the time, 'Why don't you write something about my husband?' Reporters write what's there. We don't need to be told what to write. It put people off. John knew exactly what he was doing. He had an agenda, a program, he could handle himself. If a guy's wife is pushing him all the time, you begin to wonder what's wrong with him."

Ottawa wasn't Main St. Saskatchewan. Once John found his audience in the House of Commons, he didn't need Edna to be his drummer any more. John had his important friends now, colleagues, acolytes, secretaries, people like himself who lived in an ideological world of legislation and debate; Edna couldn't pretend to understand half of what they were talking about, and, what's more, nobody cared.

What was Edna to do? There was plenty to keep her busy, if she wanted. She could have run a soldiers' canteen, worked for the Red Cross, assisted refugees, sold Victory bonds or, if she felt like being completely frivolous, gone skiing. Edna did none of these things. She was completely dependent on John, who did none of these things either, and her dependency produced paralyzing insecurity. Edna was not alone: in 1941 the wife of James Gardiner, the Liberal minister of agriculture, drowned herself in the Rideau Canal.

It is tempting to blame John for Edna's isolation and depression; Diefenbaker was a self-centred man with a single-track mind. "He was like a train," says a former aide. "If Edna couldn't keep up, she would go overboard." Yet he was also a uxorious husband who welcomed Edna's contribution to his career, consulted her on important decisions and in public praised her to the skies. Perhaps this was the problem; Edna was sucked into the vortex of John's personality. John was an exhausting man to live with – his nerves were always all on end – and he was desperately insecure. How does any wife deal with a fifty-year-old man who has an emotional age of four?

John demanded constant reassurance. He called Edna four and five times a day not for advice as much as for confirmation of his own opinions. He threw temper tantrums over trivia and flew into wild rages at real or imagined political enemies. It was Edna's job to calm him down. John's caustic tongue and prickly personality – he got those from his mother – made him a popular MP but an explosive companion; Edna never knew if John was going to come home joking or hysterical. John required a special diet – he had suffered from a bleeding ulcer in his youth and much of his stomach had been removed – and he needed help getting dressed because he was colour blind.

In the early years of her marriage Edna probably found John's emotional dependency flattering: John was going to be a Great Man and she would be his helpmate. Yet John was taking much more from his marriage than he was giving. It never occurred to him to do something Edna wanted to do, just to please her, and it certainly never crossed his mind to sacrifice his own interests to hers. If Edna thought that John would stop being a spoiled brat once he was elected, she was disappointed, John never grew up.

He tried. In the spring of 1944 he was offered a trip to Australia. He found the temptation almost irresistible – John would go anywhere, anytime with anybody – but it meant that he would be away from his parents' golden wedding anniversary on May 2. John wrote to his mother explaining the dilemma, and she replied on April 19:

"Well John I dont know what to say about it. you will have to deside for yourself. I dont want you to consider us at all we are all right so if that is on your mind for get it. The only thing that troubled me was the danger of the trip. and you all told me there was no danger. and strange to say you got me to believe it. just for get about the 50th anniversary. let it ride the same as the other 49. for that does not worry me at all. of course it would have been nice if the whole family could have been here we could have gone to the Bessborough for dinner but that cannot be so let us forget it. I dont want you to fly here. Now boy do what you think is best. Lots of love from us both to you and Edna."

John did not go to Australia, and he did not go to his parents' anniversary. He phoned and sent flowers instead. That evening Mary Diefenbaker sat down and wrote John a long letter:

"I was sorry I did not do better on the phone. I took asparin all morning trying to keep cool so as I could talk to you. but just before you called the Roses arrived and it knocked me out. Fifty Roses when all I wanted was sons. I never was so disappointed in all my life even after getting Edna's letter saying she wished you folks could be here but that Politcks seemed to have upset everything. I never thought that politicks would keep you from coming home to our golden wedding as you told me it was the one reason why you did not take the trip to Australia. I told you then to forget about it. But when you didnt go I did think you would be here today. but politics comes first. I did not know you loved them that much. Well John I have shed a lot of tears today. and I heard your Dad crying too. but he is not like me he dont say anything and I just rave. Well the *Big* day will soon be over and I am thankful for that I have not eaten a thing since morning. got some dinner for Will but could not choke anything down myself. There are very few live to see their fiftieth anniversary I am not saying this to make you feel bad. but I just cant understand it. Now John write and tell me why. love."

John never again defied his mother. Edna gave up. She was forty-six, a difficult age for any woman, especially a childless woman facing menopause. Her hair started to fall out, the result of stress and years of harsh dyes, and she wore bizarre turbans to hide her baldness. She felt so ugly and shabby she became convinced that she embarrassed John, and perhaps she did. By the spring of 1945 Edna no longer pretended to be cheerful; she felt inadequate, inferior and deeply depressed.

Edna knew that she was ill, but she had no idea why, and became panicky in her efforts to find a cure. In April or May 1945, just as the war was ending, Edna went to Toronto to consult a psychiatrist, Dr. Goldwin Howland. Dr. Howland was concerned. "I feel she is an extreme case of an obsession," he later wrote to John. "It is a big obsession including her home and your family and I think, yourself. The obsessions in these three quarters are greater than her judgment and these cases are always very difficult."

Howland did not elaborate on the nature of Edna's obsession. He apparently recommended electric-shock treatments, and Edna entered the Homewood sanitorium in Guelph, Ontario. Electric shock was the new "miracle cure" for mental illness in the 1940s: electrodes were attached to the patient's scalp and a series of powerful shocks were administered in an effort to correct the brain's own malfunctioning electrical system.

Edna's psychological distress is revealed in a pathetic, frightened letter she wrote to John shortly after she arrived at Homewood:

"Really John you must come to see the situation. Dr. MacKinnon has no interest in me whatever he wont see me. now John this is just a place for people who can afford to keep their relatives out of mental hosipatals.

"They are practically all mental here Dear or have no home. They give shock for those who can afford it & can take it but apparently they don't want you cured here.

"There is no routine at all. Oh God if I only could explain it to you Dear. John you couldnt get well here seeing what I see I thought it would only be nervous patients–but it is everything on my floor they are on their own & will be here for years–there isn't a hostess to arrange our day or walk with us. No body sleeps & every body is on pills.

"You must come. I'll never improve here talk about throwing your money away for no purpose you must get up at 7:30 & then stay alone as the living room is filled with people who seem to look normal but in reality they are not.

"I can see why Dr. MacKinnon doesn't want you here for a month he is a liar & no heart. Thinks he is quite the big shot what all did you tel him he told me you had explained my case & won't let me give him my history told be frankly he didn't believe me now John you know I want my feelings back & I liked my life.

"My hair has practically gone dead & is coming out completely apparently they have never had a case like this before.

"If you dont come – Im going to leave I'll try home Ottawa or any place but there is nothing conducive to health here they are really tough John – How I wish I knew if it was drugs or breakdown no one here has had the head or vacancy I have had so I wonder if its too many drugs for years. I could battle the hair get a wig if necessary. Well John do something Im not committed and you know Im sane.

"Please please come otherwise I'll write mother & she will come I know. There must be someone who can tell why this stony feeling is here my skin is dead also my head & they must have run into like cases somewhere – Im not hysterical nor panicky Im reasoning it out & if you were here you would understand it just means years if you leave me dear its just

Edna, nearing the end of her life suffering the ravages of mental illness and soon to succumb to leukemia.

a money making place John – you must investigate your speech was fine dear Im hungry for news no one here talks my language Dear. I think an apt with a nurse would be better & not much more . . . my place is in Ottawa with you my brain is so clear its just something has gone wrong with my nervous system its either drugs or the breakdown Id like so much to see another physycrast as he would which is wrong with me as for drugs they are giving me new ones that make me sleep longer & I know they are stronger well that isnt a cure is it? They give me pheno Barb after meals & I throw it down the toilet as I have turned to stone as I dont need them at all . . .

"Please tell me you will come soon otherwise Ill go clean crazy & disgrace you Dear & so far Ive been normal through it all Ive been alone in my room now for hours & you never expected that & if you are upstairs you are confined to barred rooms & John you wouldn't let them do that when my mind is clear its all emotions & nerves & fear from my hair which is wrong & you know it.

"Come come soon & try & find out if I can have shock & get well. All My Love Edna."

John did not rush to Homewood. For all his egocentricity he was not a stupid man and he must have realized, even if he refused to admit it, that Edna's chances of recovery were better without him. John concealed Edna's whereabouts and the nature of her illness, but it was an act of kindness as much as guilt: the social stigma of madness would have damaged Edna's reputation even more than his career. John wrote to Edna frequently, hired a private nurse and kept in constant touch with Dr. Howland.

Edna remained at Homewood for nearly a year. Until February 1946 her treatment appears to have consisted of rest, sedation and psychotherapy. "It is one of the hardest cases I have had, causing me great anxiety as to whether this was going to be a permanent case or not," Howland wrote to John in July 1945. "I think we may expect from time to time relapses but she will finally get well. It will depend on you more than anyone else whether she remains well or not. She is a very fine woman indeed and her ideals are the best and she is completely wrapped up in your interests but it would be better if she had more interests of her own. She dislikes housekeeping which is, unfortunately, part of her life's work.

"Between now and the time the House opens in Ottawa perhaps it would be possible for you and your wife to take a holiday together for two or three weeks. I do not feel certain whether starting her directly at work at home is quite the wisest thing after such a serious illness. I almost think she would sooner go to Ottawa. She was tremendously interested in your saying you might start practice in partnership in Vancouver. She said 'it is the wish of my life and perhaps my husband is becoming tired of sitting on the Opposition side of the House.'

"During her whole time here I do not think she has said a single thing against you, which is very unusual for a wife. But she is terribly afraid you will be disappointed when you see her, so for Heaven's sake when you do come be delighted with her condition."

Edna's inability to express even normal anger towards John indicates that she was very far from cured, and her treatment seems to have been designed to make her a properly functioning wife, precisely the role she had repudiated. Did John really suggest to her that he would leave politics? The idea was as absurd as Howland's suggestion that a summer vacation was all Edna needed. Howland's evasiveness suggests that Edna's doctors wanted no trouble from a famous criminal lawyer and high-profile MP.

"I note she is now going to take electric shock treatments, so that she is getting her own way," Howland wrote to John on February 27, 1946. "I personally feel that the main hope is in shock treatment."

Edna had a series of electric-shock treatments and was discharged from Homewood on March 26, 1946. She returned to Prince Albert, where everyone assumed that she had been staying with John in Ottawa, and outwardly she was her usual talkative, happy-go-lucky self. However, Edna was too insecure to spend much time in Ottawa, and she and John lived most of the year apart. They had never had much in common except anxiety, and now Edna had no formal role in John's life. John could do nothing for Edna except feel guilty.

"Try & write a little oftener," Edna wrote from Prince Albert. "I get so blue when I don't get mail. All for now Dear. Good Luck God bless you, Always Edna."

John wrote and phoned, as he did to his mother; Edna kept his scrapbook of newspaper clippings and praised his speeches on the radio. She wrote him little notes full of local news and comments on the political scene and promised to come to Ottawa, but illness or an accident always intervened. Edna remained obsessed with her appearance – "I look a mess but will come anyway," she lied – and distraught about her health.

"Today my throat has been terrible," she wrote one Sunday after

John phoned. "I get very discouraged when it is like this as I am desperately afraid it is something serious because if it was poisin it should be gone now.

"I felt pretty good all week but this day has surely taken the pep out of me. Just pray for me Dear I want to get well & be with you this is no life for either of us.

"I hope I feel better tomorrow & Ill write you a better letter but Im sick tonight. I love you John & want to be with you always. Write often, All My Love, Edna."

Edna did not get well. Alone in Prince Albert during the dark, freezing winter months she became suicidally depressed:

"Im lonesome for you & dont let myself think of how happy I was in Ottawa with you when I was well," she wrote early in 1947. "If only this pain in my throat & head leaves me I will never ask for another thing. I see how busy they are in Ottawa with gay parties & all & I dont envy them all I want is my health.

"How was the dance at Government House? beautiful women & dresses I suppose. Oh well such is life – Good Night Dear be as good as you can to me it may not be for long."

Edna's repressed rancour towards John surfaces obliquely in a note she wrote him in February 1947: "I wrote a blue letter this afternoon & I'm sorry but I guess you will never realize how badly I was hurt last August it just wont heal no matter what I do I wake up out of a sound sleep with it on my mind and a pain in my heart I hope you never suffer like this.

"If I were well enough to go some place & get away from worry & too much responsibility but Ottawa isnt the place I have such an inferioty complex over myself & with everyone down there looking their best I just cant face it. Its pretty awful here I never go anywhere and naturally you get introspective with no outside interest you hated P.A. & longed to get east so you cant wonder Ive not been on a train for six months.

"All for now forgive me if I am blue Im ill & nothing in my life but lonliness & see nothing much ahead. Love, Edna."

Edna was now whipsawing John emotionally exactly the way his mother did, and Edna's letters to John are strikingly similar to Mary Diefenbaker's. In her efforts to win John's love, Edna seems to have unconsciously transformed herself into the rival she hated.

John did not rush to Edna's bedside. He did not quit politics or move to Vancouver; his now infrequent, impersonal letters were dictated to a typist and addressed: "My Dear Edna."

Did Edna realize that death was close? Her mental illness may have had hidden roots in the cancer that killed her four years later. In the autumn of 1950 Edna was feeling so low that she went to the doctor; he diagnosed advanced leukemia. Edna said nothing: John was going off to Australia and she didn't want him to cancel out. She wrote John newsy, happy letters and decorated their new bungalow in Prince Albert. "I love it," she wrote. "I hope you do."

When John came home for Christmas Edna was dying. John was stunned. He moved her to a hospital in Saskatoon and lived with Elmer and his mother for the last month of Edna's life, visiting her faithfully every day. Edna suffered terribly, but in front of visitors she was always in good spirits and more concerned with John's health than her own. Edna died in John's arms on the morning of February 7, 1951 and was buried next to John's father in the Diefenbaker family plot overlooking the Saskatchewan River.

"At the cemetary poor old Victor, the coloured C.N.R. Red Cap, broke down and sobbed," Elmer wrote to his uncle Ed. "He loved to carry the bags of John and Edna and sent beautiful roses to Edna while she was in the hospital. At the same time the C.N.R. passenger train stopped when it came alongside the cemetery, while the engineer, fireman and conductor stood at a silent salute while the coffin was lowered–Those are magnificent gestures! Those are things that the railway men do for John."

For John, Elmer?

Olive Freeman and John Diefenbaker had never completely lost contact. In 1944 Olive was teaching in Owen Sound, Ontario, when John came through on a speaking tour. She debated long and hard whether to go to his meeting. It had been years since she had seen him, he had promised to write and hadn't, he was married, yet he was an old family friend and she was proud of his success. Olive went, late, and huddled in the shadows at the back of the hall, "I was in full flight," John said later, "and then I spotted this little face at the back. I talked for ten minutes and I had no idea of what I was saying."

They talked briefly after John's speech. Life had been hard for Olive. In Huntsville she had met Harry Palmer, a lawyer and cellist with the Toronto Symphony who was playing with a summer dance band; they married in 1933 and the following year their daughter, Carolyn, was born. Two years later Harry Palmer died suddenly of kidney disease, leaving Olive a single mother with a pre-schooler to raise. At least she had a job to return to, but women teachers were notoriously underpaid, and Olive had to fall back on her Baptist frugality to make ends meet. "My mother was thrifty," Carolyn recalls. "She would get the last drop of milk out of a bottle. We didn't just eat an apple, we ate the core."

Hardship made Olive resourceful. She taught English to Polish airmen to make a little extra money, and every summer she took Carolyn up to Algonquin Park where they shared a cottage with friends. Olive trekked all their food in by canoe, chopped wood, fished, cleaned the fish and fired up the wood stove to cook the meals. "My mother would tackle *anything*," says Carolyn. "She was very handy. She could wallpaper, paint, tile a floor, do carpentry. One year she rented a cement mixer, put in a sidewalk and built a garage." Carolyn's gift of a peg-board for her mother's tools was one of Olive's most treasured Christmas presents.

Olive raised Carolyn to be self-sufficient and she never felt sorry for herself. She made the best of her independence; she had to: in the 1940s being a widow was socially more deadly than being a spinster. Olive chanelled her energy and talents into her work; she developed a skill at student counselling, at that time a new and suspicious frill in the school curriculum, and by the time John Diefenbaker looked her up again in 1951, Olive Palmer was in Toronto as assistant director of guidance for Ontario.

John may have seen her picture in the newspaper, or perhaps Olive's brother Hal, now a professor of French at McMaster, told his old friend where she was. Both John and Olive were coy about the beginning of their secret courtship, possibly because it began quite soon after Edna died. John seems to have discarded most of Olive's letters to him, as he apparently destroyed almost all his correspondence with Edna, and they both liked to dash off undated notes, so the exact time and circumstances of their reunion are unknown – even Carolyn was kept in the dark. They likely met at Christmas 1951 when John passed through Toronto on his way to Saskatoon. His first dated letter to "My dear Ollie" was written in Saskatoon on January 6, 1952:

"I am at mother's today but will be leaving for P.A. on the freight tonight – it takes *only* seven hours to travel 91 miles! Mother has been confined to her bed and seriously ill since the New Year but is sitting up today.

"I have a heavy agenda for today – one radio speech to be broadcast over six provincial radio stations on Tuesday evening – and another for the 16th annual meeting of the Vancouver Board of Trade for Friday next."

John's preoccupations – his mother and himself – had not changed. Yet

Edna's death had shaken and frightened him, and he would make an effort with Olive not to be so selfish. Olive was the only woman, apart from his mother, who could make John feel like a fool, and he respected her for it. John could neglect and exploit women, but he was not contemptuous or condescending, and even during his most difficult years with Edna, he never blamed her. John was lost without Edna, and his mother, now eighty, was failing. Olive would replace them both.

"Wonderful visit – and memories too," John wrote Olive in an undated note that may have been scribbled on his arrival in Saskatoon. "Hope you are as happy as I am."

She was. At fifty Olive must have felt as if she had won the Irish sweepstakes: John was no longer the gauche young man she had laughed at, but a witty and charismatic personality who filled her life with energy, excitement and love. Olive was soon calling John "my darling" and writing him long, chatty letters. Olive never took John as seriously as he took himself and she liked to take little jibes at some of his political friends: "The company you keep!" she wrote when John told her of his plans to meet a famous Toronto preacher. "It would be a curious experience to spend time with the Templetons if they're the roaring type of evangelists I imagine." Olive was religious, but she did not roar, and she did not approve of John roaring either.

John spent every weekend he could in Toronto. He checked into the Royal York Hotel, phoned Olive and waited for her by a side door; Olive zipped up in her little grey Austin, John jumped in and they spent the day on the town or visiting John's friends. On rare occasions Olive would invite John to her house in Willowdale, but in 1952 it was almost impossible for a single woman to entertain a man at home alone without causing gossip, and Olive, with the morals of Ontario's youth in her care, could not risk a whiff of scandal. Neither could John. They dared a weekend together at the Couchiching conference in Orillia, where John made a speech, and another at the United Nations in New York, but their behaviour was so circumspect that a few weeks before their marriage one of John's closest friends dismissed their friendship as nothing special.

John wrote to Ollie almost daily just to chat about his daily routine and legal work: "I enjoyed myself in the Court. One forgets everything else when engaged on a good case. If I practised law I could make an income – but what fun I would miss in Parliament!" For all his court-room histrionics John was a laxy, indifferent lawyer; he took plum cases for high fees and left all the dog work to his resentful junior partners. Olive was more than his intellectual equal. John had skimmed through university on veterans' dispensations – his war wound appears to have been a hernia – while Olive had studied Greek and English literature, taught French and had a good knowledge of classical music. It was Olive who supplied John with the quotations from Homer and Pericles that gave his speeches their impressive intellectual depth, and when John became prime minister he made a brave, if futile, attempt to speak French.

John was often down in the dumps: "I am a kind of woe-begone person today – with a lonely complex from looking at the dark side of things," he wrote, "Away with such nonsense!" Olive was also emotionally on edge:

"My darling," John wrote to her one Monday after leaving Toronto, "it is unusual for me to write you so soon after seeing you but there's a reason. I don't like to see you saddened or disturbed – and this is to take you in my arms (figuratively) and wipe away the tears. All of us have the days of everything being all wrong – all we need then is just a little bit of consideration. I should have been doing so this morning – and by the time you receive this you will be removed from the need of a word. Anyway, you were just Ollie of 35 years ago for a few minutes this morning."

The strain of their clandestine weekend courtship was compounded by John's uncertain political future. His riding of Saskatoon Lake Centre had been eliminated through redistribution. Where would he run? Or would he run at all? The Conservatives still languished in Opposition, and in 1948 John had lost his bid for the leadership to a Toronto Tory, George Drew. Diefenbaker's prairie populist ideas were anathema to the reactionary Drew, and John's quiet disappearance from the political scene would have been welcomed by the Conservative establishment.

John quixotically decided to contest the Liberal stronghold of Prince Albert where he had lost twice before. "I am a long-faced, dour, melancholy person every time I think of getting into the P.A. fight," he wrote to Ollie at the start of the election campaign in May 1953, "but being in I must just get out and work. There is quite a lot of encouraging support but it couldn't bring a win at this time. I have to take 3000 votes from each of the other parties – what a menacing picture! However faint heart never won an election either. I miss you so much my darling – and the campaign won't be over for at least 2½ months. When I come east I must see you if only for a short hour. Lovingly, John."

John's letters to Ollie during the campaign provide a fascinating glimpse of the apprehensive and sometimes discouraged candidate hiding behind John's confident public mask. "Well, I am now starting out to the country – the beginning of a 2½ month pilgrimage," he wrote a day or two later. "It's a horrid thing to view at this distance but whether in or out I will not fail to do my best. It is a frightening picture – and more so than it was even two weeks ago. Heartaches and worry – but fight! Well I must *away*!"

It was John's first campaign in twenty years without Edna, and he missed her. He brought his secretary, Bunny Pound, from Ottawa to organize his headquarters and he travelled the dusty country roads with Elmer. "Tonight I will speak at Wild Rose (50 including the gopher population)," he wrote to Ollie. "It's terrific, the battle, and the personal attacks are terrific but I think I am making headway. The canvassers report in general about 40% for me – that is not enough but it is a more encouraging prospect than when I started. The CCF are very strong though and tonight the *Holy* Man from Weyburn (Premier Douglas) – 'Wholly Unreliable' Elmer says – will speak here. He will tear me to pieces it has been announced in advance."

Tommy Douglas was more than John's match on the public platform and by the last day of the campaign John was nervous. "It has been a terrifically gruelling siege – everything but swords and shotguns," he wrote to Ollie. "Never have I undergone more abuse without replying in kind. Possibly I made a mistake in following that course but that was the strategy I mapped out to begin with. I cannot even hope a prophesy. What will be the outcome? I am neither hopeful nor hopeless. It is tough. I don't think we have lost ground during the last week – but haven't gained too much either.

"I am frankly unable to say what I think. Will this be the last letter anyone will receive on House of Commons stationary? Drew can't win (that is certain). I doubt our total will exceed 82 – I am low as compared to other estimates. Since May 23 I have spoken at 65 meetings. Is it all to be ineffective? Monday will tell. If I win I shall be rewarded, if not, I shall not reveal my depression.

"Well my darling – your letters have been a source of deep strength to me. Next week I will go fishing – and (if elected) I will be down to see you soon."

Ollie phoned John on Sunday morning. "I must have sounded dopey," he wrote her later in the day, "for I had just awakened after a four hour sleep. I was very tired – and incoherent – but it was a real joy to hear from you.

"It's over now except for the people. I should have a chance but whether I can win is another question. The campaign against me has been sustained and vitriolic. I am hopeful that it was overdone and overplayed . . . I will phone as soon as a trend becomes apparent. If only it turns out as we hope for it would be a great victory. It seems like an eternity since I suddenly realized on University Avenue on May 16th how foolish I was to choose Prince Albert.

"The press men are arriving here – already five are here and more to come. I hope it doesn't turn out to be a Roman Holiday with myself as the lion food.

"The 'probs' for tomorrow are fair weather – the vote can be a record breaker – certainly never has the electorate been more aroused pro or con.

"Yesterday was my last letter to you I thought – will this be the last on H of C stationary? I am hopeful that it will not. Lovingly, John."

Like a man condemned to the gallows, John kept scribbling distraught little notes to Ollie. "This the fateful day!" he wrote on Monday morning. "I am not doing any work – just standing around in the committee room. The Liberals have a large car force at the polls. So have the CCF. We have 75 cars. I had only 6 hours sleep last night – got up at seven o'clock. Why? I don't know. Well eight hours from now the polls will close. ??? I am still hopeful."

The Liberals swept the country, but John Diefenbaker won the seat he would hold for the rest of his life as "The Man from Prince Albert." "I *am* using H of C stationary again!" he wrote gleefully to Ollie on Tuesday morning. "*And* very happy at the unbelievable result. Myriads of messages came to me today. Well that's over – I mean the campaign . . . but it is going to be hard for me to get away. I have to speak to several organizations *and* be made the Chief of the Cree Indians (16 tribes) on August 22. Can't you see me smoking the Pipe of Peace after it has been sucked by about 25 other chiefs and headmen before I start. They tell me I *dare* not wipe it off before using.

"The captains and the kings depart – all is quiet in my office – but the Liberal High Command is astounded. Certainly I will never have a more satisfying victory – for from the time we drove up University Avenue on

May 15th [16th] the hopelessness of everything stayed with me – but Elmer never gave up his spirit of unbounded optimism. He put up with a lot of my inanities!

"Ollie I am afraid that Drew has had it. This 'politics' is a ruthless pursuit. The papers are in full howl. Time will tell . . . Affectionately, John. (In very formal circles also to be known as M.P. Prince Albert)."

At the height of the campaign Olive passed a more arduous test – she visited John's mother in Saskatoon. Mary Diefenbaker had known of John's new romance for some time and approved; perhaps she missed having Edna around. Mary lay in wait for Olive with a large photo of Edna on the table beside her. "That is John's first wife," she said to Olive. "No matter what you do, you'll never be a patch on her!" Olive dealt with the old bitch as Edna had, by attempting to placate her, until John finally put his mother in the hospital where she could infuriate the medical staff. After John's victory in 1957 a new nurse complained: "That crazy old lady at the end of the hall thinks she's the prime minister's mother!"

John and Olive were quietly married in Toronto on December 8, 1953. They were in Mexico on their honeymoon before the news hit the press: it was the last real privacy Olive Diefenbaker would be allowed to enjoy.

Three years later John was elected leader of the Conservative Party, and in June 1957, following one of the most exciting election campaigns in Canadian history, he finally became prime minister at the age of sixty-two. Olive embarked on her fourth career. "The whole direction of my life is that I am John's wife," she said. Olive had been a good mother, a popular teacher and a successful bureaucrat: now she would be the best prime minister's wife Canada had ever seen, and she was.

It was not an auspicious time for a fifty-five-year-old grandmother to provide a role model for baby boomers rockin' to Elvis Presley, but Olive was never intimidated by the young. "I recall walking down the Sparks St. mall in Ottawa one day last summer," she told a meeting of guidance counsellors a few years later. "This is a great hippie hangout. It was hot, airless. The hippies were the dirtiest, the hairiest, the most unprepossessing crowd. I was inclined to shy away from them, but we saw that it was too late. They all got to their feet, bowed deeply and said 'Good morning, sir and madam.' My husband said, 'Good morning, gentlemen,' and we went on our way."

Olive was cool. She had natural dignity and an almost regal *presence*. When President John F. Kennedy brought his glamorous wife to Ottawa

Olive with Jackie Kennedy: who's best dressed?

in 1961, Jackie Kennedy knocked everybody out with her short skirts and pillbox hats. Olive stuck to traditional styles, but when one looks at their photographs thirty years later, it is Olive who appears better dressed; Jackie looks skinny and scared.

It was an ugly era for women's fashion, and sleeveless dresses with narrow, mid-calf skirts did nothing for aging women with sagging arms and puffy ankles. The hats were hideous. Olive loved hats. Hats were her one great extravagance. Olive had hundreds of hats. She had so many hats that she built a whole closet for them in her dressing-room. Olive seldom wore the same hat twice. She shared John's sense of theatre: hats were her trademark, her way of catching peoples' attention; John always wore a splendid black Homburg. Like the queen, Olive never wore hats that concealed her face, and she had better taste than the queen. She had better taste in clothes too. Olive liked simple, elegant dresses in rich fabrics and solid colours; she limited her jewellery to an antique amethyst necklace and a triple strand of pearls. She never looked chintzy and she photographed beautifully.

Olive was the first PM's wife to go public. It was her choice, and John's. The Diefenbakers shared a conviction that government belonged to the people, and as the peoples' elected representatives they had an obligation to serve their constituents. Olive opened up 24 Sussex Drive to the press and members of parliament; she hosted garden parties and invited diplomats in for tea. Everyone was thrilled. No one could remember the last time Ottawa had a "hostess with the mostest," and Olive had just the right combination of ease and good manners. Olive's ancestors went back to the Mayflower: she wasn't intimidated by Old Ottawa any more than by hippies.

Guests discovered to their dismay that the Diefenbakers' parties could be very, very dry. One scorching summer afternoon John and Olive hosted a reception for members of the press gallery and their wives; a cheerful sweaty crowd turned up anticipating gin and tonic, but Olive served tea. Hot tea. The reporters thought at first that it was a joke, then several stomped off in a fury; it is said that this *faux pas* marked the end of Diefenbaker's honeymoon with the press. "Olive made a lousy cup of tea," grumbles one old newsman.

Olive was rigorous. "My mother believed there was a right and a wrong, and you don't mess around with the wrong," says Carolyn. Booze was wrong, although Olive could be persuaded to drink an occasional glass of sherry, and she loathed snobbery. "If anyone put on airs, watch out!" Carolyn laughs. "She hated phoney accents." Olive rarely lost her temper, but she had a stare that could turn an offender to a pillar of salt. There were a number of Conservative wives Olive simply could not stand, and others she criticized for not pulling their weight. Like Agnes Macdonald, Olive was very judgmental about people, and her judgment was not always sound: she tended to criticize people loyal to John, and to be friendly towards his mortal enemies. Some people complained that Olive isolated John socially from his colleagues – Olive did not play bridge – but it seems more likely that John, with his puritanical habits and lone-wolf personality, preferred to spend his spare time with Olive.

Olive was right: being John's wife was a full-time, twenty-four-hour-a-day job. John insisted that Olive join him for breakfast at 7:30 a.m. although, like Edna, Olive preferred to sleep late. Olive spent her mornings answering letters by hand – she had no office and no secretary, although her mail often ran to fifty or more letters a day – and organizing a daily schedule that would fell an ox. Olive awakened the sleeping monster, Society, and she became its slave. Even John objected that two teas in one afternoon were two too many, but Olive's sense of duty made it hard for her to say no, and in five tumultuous years she set a record for attending teas, bazaars, bake sales and charity socials that no subsequent PM's wife has dared to emulate.

Olive was constantly photographed. This was John's idea. John was constantly photographed. Diefenbaker's infatuation with the media far surpassed a politician's normal desire to get his image or his message across. John did nothing and went nowhere without first alerting all the newspapers and radio stations, and he was one of the first politicians in North America to make effective use of television. Olive was dragged, willy-nilly, out of domestic obscurity into the full glare of the public spotlight. She flatly refused to make speeches, but she was interviewed and reported on *ad nauseam*.

Amaryllis's sob sisters drew in their claws for Olive: she got sympathetic, even sycophantic press. No one ever found a run in Olive's stocking or a frown on her face; she was invariably kind, gracious and serene. Olive's public image was so saintly that she developed a reputation as a smarmy goody-goody. Better a bore than a bitch, Olive must have thought. "There's nothing cosy about her," the Toronto *Star*'s Lotta Dempsey astutely observed. "It is not difficult for bovine women to be tranquil. Olive's calm is born of intelligence, awareness, discipline and self-sacrifice. She does not suffer fools gladly."

Olive was blessed with a poker face. "I hear people say I sit through everything without a flicker of emotion," she told Dempsey. "But Ottawa is a goldfish bowl. John knows he can trust me to indicate nothing, to say nothing." As the daughter of a small-town clergyman, she was accustomed to enduring intense scrutiny of her dress and deportment, and her years in the school system had taught her how to protect herself in a competitive and critical crowd. Because Olive said nothing substantial, it was assumed that she had nothing substantial to say, and because the questions she was asked were trivial, her answers were banal.

Olive was the perfect wife. It was a role she found honourable. John and Olive both had a passionate commitment to equality and justice, and if Olive, by helping John be a better prime minister, could assist in a process of reform, her life would be meaningful. Olive shared John's goals and she could be as emotionally partisan as he, although her chief function was to calm him down. "Olive was like a blue lagoon," says Tom Van Dusen. "She was totally calm. Dief would blow his top and Olive would be sitting there doing her needlepoint. 'Now, John,' she'd say. That made him even madder, but after a while the storm would blow itself out and he'd be okay."

John demanded that Olive be with him constantly. At night she sat beside him knitting while he watched wrestling or hockey on television and worked up a speech. "Poor John is perched on the bed, his hair standing up in a cockatoo ruffle, sorting out material for a speech on defense tomorrow," she wrote to John's mother in 1979. "It's a hectic life, I want to tell you." She even went hunting with him, sitting in the car with her sewing while John went galumphing off across some farmer's field after a goose. Diefenbaker loved making speeches—his campaign rallies had the evangelistic quality of tent revivals—and Olive was the first PM's wife to become a fixture on the public platform, ankles demurely crossed, bouquet in gloved hand, eyes glued to the back of John's head. Her gaze was more apprehensive than adoring: nobody knew exactly what John was going to say, not even John. He seldom spoke from a text, preferring to play off the day's headlines or hecklers in the audience, and on a good day he could have his audience rolling in the aisles although reporters were hard pressed to make sense of what he had said. John always finished a speech soaked with sweat and Olive was anxious that he get into dry clothes as soon as possible. "We have to get John out of here!" Olive cried to his aide Greg Guthrie one night when John was mobbed at the Civic Auditorium in Winnipeg. Guthrie, a former artillery officer, charged through the crowd, hoisted John in the air and, using him like a battering ram, bulled his way to the door. Dief was still shaking hands.

Olive may have been able to calm John's temper, but she was helpless to control his megalomania. John was now the Great Man of his boyhood dreams, and he was determined to cut a heroic figure on the world stage. Olive had not had time to unpack after their victory in 1957 before John spirited her off to London to see the queen. It was a rough flight, and during one bout of turbulence Olive cracked her head against the ceiling of the aircraft, crushing two vertebrae in her neck. It was a portentous beginning.

The paint was barely dry in the dining room at 24 Sussex Drive when the queen arrived in October to open John's first session of parliament; in

February 1958 John called a snap election, dragging Olive through two frenetic national campaigns in less than a year. Olive campaigned on crutches: her knees were badly swollen and she was in such pain that she slept only four hours a night. John's landslide victory in 1958 spurred him on: an endless succession of prime ministers and foreign dignitaries arrived on Olive's doorstep to have their photographs taken with Prime Minister Diefenbaker. In October 1958 John and Olive took off on a two-month world tour of fourteen countries; the following March they were back in London for a Commonwealth conference, and in June the queen turned up again with President Dwight D. Eisenhower to open the St. Lawrence Seaway.

Excited as a kid in a candy store, John shared Olive's reluctance to reject an invitation. "Tomorrow (Friday) night Olive and I are going to a *Big Sassiety* (father's word) *Ball*," he wrote to his mother on January 31, 1958, "Saturday night to the Gov't Dinner to Churchill's son-in-law

Olive with John and that "great lowering cloud" Mary Diefenbaker.

(Sandys) and Sunday night we will go to the Governor-General's dinner party. On Saturday night thereafter we go to Toronto on the night train for the Toronto Board of Trade dinner on Monday night (there will be 1200 at that dinner) and I haven't a word yet on my speech which will be broadcasted later over CBC. Who got me into this job anyway? (You will answer me won't you by saying 'You yourself.'")

John drafted all his own speeches, with Olive's help, and they didn't come easily. He frittered away hours fussing over a few trite remarks to a dentists' convention when a junior staff member could have done the job in half the time. John had no sense of priority, and absolutely no comprehension of the hard, relentless labour involved in running a country. He spent most of his five years in office shaking hands, cutting ribbons, making speeches and dashing around the world collecting honorary degrees. John was determined to have more honorary degrees than Louis St. Laurent, who had twenty-two.

"Yesterday I went to Kingston where I received another Honorary LL.D. from Queen's University," he wrote to his mother on October 21, 1960. "In the morning I met with the Prime Minister of Malaya. This evening I go to Montreal to speak to the Navy League and tomorrow evening have to speak at a dinner meeting of the Conservative Party – tomorrow afternoon we will have about 300 of the delegates to tea at 24 Sussex. There is no rest from this, for next week will be heavier than ever."

Lack of sleep and anxiety over lost time made John hysterical, and before long rumours started that he was mentally ill. In fact he was only too well aware of his predicament. Writing to his mother as he was about to leave for a Kinsmen convention in Hamilton, John said regretfully: "Tomorrow there is an important debate in the House on unemployment and naturally there will be criticism at my absence." It never crossed his mind to turn down the Kinsmen.

John's official engagements for June 6, 1958 reveal how little time he spent on affairs of state:

"8:30 a.m. – Place a wreath on Sir John A. Macdonald's monument.

9:00 a.m. – Dental appointment

9:30 a.m. – CABINET – Room 375 House of Commons

10:00 a.m. – Mr. J.J. Cahill, Premier of New South Wales, Australia.

11:00 a.m. – House of Commons

11:30 a.m. – Students (250 grade 7 and 8) from Brampton

12:00 – Cabinet resumes

12:00 – Delegation representing the Canadian Hospital Association and the Catholic Hospital Association.

1:45 p.m. – To have picture taken with Page boys of House of Commons – entrance to the Chamber.

2:30 p.m. – House of Commons

3:00 p.m. – Leslie Saunders [writer]

4:00 p.m. – National Film Board to take pictures of the Prime Minister.''

John spent more time schmoozing than he did in Cabinet or the House of Commons. No wonder that his government quickly fell apart. After nearly a quarter-century in Opposition, the Conservatives were insecure about exercising power; the Cabinet was new, inexperienced and in some cases incompetent. The ministers formed cabals and conspiracies and fought among themselves; John was usually so oblivious about what was happening that he learned of his ministers' quarrels in the press. He was also getting very deaf, and relied on Olive to whisper in his ear what people were saying. It did not make Olive popular in the party. ''She could nail people to the mast,'' says Tom Van Dusen. ''A little barb, and somebody would fall to the ground.''

As John's power crumbled he became defensive, some said paranoid, and Olive became more and more protective. His enemies were hers, and she was a formidable opponent, but Olive had no power to stop the drift into chaos; she had no place in John's office, where his loyal female secretaries ruled the roost, no place in the Cabinet room, and no place in the party backrooms, where her presence was resented.

Olive, like John, was a loner. She had hundreds of acquaintances and millions of admirers, but no allies and very few close friends. Few people ever saw Olive with her guard down. One was Peggy Green, a Diefenbaker campaign worker in Saskatchewan: ''She'd call and say 'I'd love to come over and sit and talk with you and put my feet up.' I don't think anybody really realized that she wore herself right down and she needed to be very open and honest with someone and just relax and enjoy getting into a *home* other than a hotel.''

Olive loved to put her feet up and take off her girdle. When she couldn't stand politics any more she went to see Carolyn. Carolyn and her schoolteacher husband, Don Weir, were rolling stones, five kids in all, and Olive could be guaranteed a day or two of anonymity in some unpredictable corner of the world. When the Weirs were moving out of their house in Scarborough, Ontario, Olive turned up, put on an old shirt and a pair of Don's pants, and heaved all their cast-off junk into a pickup truck. When the truck was full Olive drove to the dump and heaved all the junk out again. "There was my mother, the prime minister's wife, standing in the back of the truck in her mink jacket and Don's enormous pants, throwing all this stuff into the dump," says Carolyn. "She was having a wonderful time." On the way back Olive and Carolyn stopped at the grocery store. "Aren't you Mrs. Diefenbaker?" the clerk asked, squinting at Olive. "No," Olive smiled, "although a lot of people say I look like her."

When the Weirs were teaching at a Canadian military base in Metz, France, Olive flew to Luxembourg under an assumed name. Carolyn met her at the airport in the Weirs' ancient Volkswagen and drove her surreptitiously to the base. Olive was perfectly happy to camp out on an air mattress in the Weirs' living-room until the commander discovered that the prime minister's wife was on *his* base. Carolyn only heard Olive's side of the phone conversation: "No, I do not want a Mercedes. No, I am not staying at headquarters. No, I don't want a dinner. No, we are going to the market tomorrow." And that was that.

Olive's freedom came more quickly than she perhaps expected. The Diefenbaker government was paralyzed by dissension and everything it did was unpopular. In the 1962 election the Conservative majority slipped to sixteen; the next year the government was defeated in the House, and on election night, April 8, 1963, the Diefenbaker government fell to the Liberals.

Like Wilfrid Laurier before him, John refused to quit, and, like Laurier, he was betrayed by his most trusted colleagues. Laurier, however, did not suffer Diefenbaker's humiliation of being repudiated by the party he had three times led to victory. For four traumatic years John carried on as leader of the Conservative Opposition in the face of cruel and devastating criticism from within his own party; he was said to be insane, or dying from Parkinson's disease, and after he failed to win the election in 1965, the party demanded a leadership convention. Still John refused to quit. In September 1967 he ran for his own job, and lost.

Olive was angry, upset and very bitter about how the party had treated "her John," but in public her *sang froid* never failed her. Confronting his enemies Casear-like in the full glare of the television lights, John trembled violently and his eyes watered, but Olive never lost her composure. Only years later did she discuss this "deeply hurtful experience" in a note to John's young protégé, Sean O'Sullivan: "I can meet the world with my head held high, but I will never get over the hurt, and I don't want anyone offering 'soporifics.' Therefore, I won't talk about it."

"Olive was very distressed," recalls Greg Guthrie. "She felt deeply for the Chief, but when I drove back to the hotel with them after the convention, John started to sing in a quavery falsetto 'When you come to the end of a perfect day.' Olive laughed."

Perhaps Olive laughed because she would never have to sit on another folding chair, shake another hand or stand in a receiving line until her feet were killing her. Olive was sixty-five, exhausted and ill.

Olive had high blood pressure, an irregular heartbeat and difficulty catching her breath; political rallies frightened her because she found it hard to breathe in the crush of people. She had forced herself to attend hundreds of rallies, and in the last desperate days of John's leadership the crowds become hostile and violent: after one meeting Olive gave a heckler a karate chop in the gut in order to get to her car. Olive took pride in her endurance; she never showed fear, pain or fatigue, although she was often so tired that she suffered from the "blind staggers."

In contrast to Edna and Mary Diefenbaker, Olive did not call attention to her health, and her illnesses were real. In January 1959, at the height of the Ottawa social whirl, she went into hospital to have a lump removed from her breast; it was not malignant, but it gave Olive a scare. She was not as stoic as she appeared. "Old age is *Hell*!" she wrote in a note to John. "Aren't we a couple of old crocks!"

Olive's heart was wearing out. By 1970 John found it hard to understand why Olive couldn't keep up with him any more: he was charging around the country having a wonderful time playing the Elder Statesman. "What I can't do is to be in constant attendance, standing in crowds by the hour," Olive wrote him from hospital. "You see, I'll be *fine* and will do all that is necessary. I'm not a power-house like you!!! But I'll get by."

"He expected more of her than was humanly possible for her to give," says Peggy Green. "I wonder if there weren't some fun things she might have liked to do." If there were, Olive never let on. Being the PM's wife was a whole lot more fun than teaching guidance in Toronto, and Olive wasn't one to look a gift horse in the mouth. She enjoyed having a chef at 24 Sussex – cooking wasn't her idea of fun – she liked hobnobbing with royalty and she was glad of a chance to see the world. Not many grand-mothers packed all the excitement Olive did into their lives, and she never spoke a word critical of John or politics during her ten years in the public eye. One thing could be said for life with John: it was never dull.

Olive stopped travelling with John, but she still packed his suitcase and left him a note when he had to leave before she was awake:

"Sweetie,

"You have a clean shirt for every day. Please always use one. I would send the suit you wear to be cleaned at once. Then wear it and save your good one. It looks *nice* on you.

"Have a good time.

"Miss me – but not too much and *call often*. I'll miss you – too much. Olive.

"Have some prunes every night – without fail. And wear your thing to bed and *put it on* first thing every morning. By order, your e.l.w. 'ever loving wife.'"

John's "thing" was a truss for his hernia, and he was still on a strict diet: he may have been the only grown man in Canada to eat Red River Cereal for breakfast. Olive was still giving him instructions on how to dress: "Wear white shirt marked X with new suit for opening and new black-and-white tie. You will look really sharp!!"

John left Olive little notes in exchange:

"Ollie – 5 a.m.

"You are a darling – what a sweet note you left for me. I will be back tomorrow evening and in the meantime will be missing you. John."

John now allowed Olive to sleep in:

"7:50 a.m.

"My darling, I went in to say 'good-bye' – you were sleeping. You looked so serene and beautiful. To my Love, John."

John was nearly eighty, but he still wasn't ready to quit. He kept his seat as MP for Prince Albert, and when he wasn't on the road he was in his office at the House of Commons. As her heart failed Olive spent more and more time in hospital. One of her last notes to John was written in a quavery hand on her personalized notepaper, "A Note from Olive Diefenbaker":

"Sunday, early

"Darling,

"Who but you should have the first note from Olive Diefenbaker – in her finest early-morning Spencerian Hand. To say the least: You're *wonderful*–and so kind and good.

"It has been dreadful to come [to the hospital] and come and come so often. I hope with all my heart that this is the last time and thank you with all my heart for all you have done in the midst of all the other things that had to be done regardless.

"You can see I'm pen-tied, I'm just as tongue-tied but there is so much I would say if I could but I'll stop for every minute I expect to hear a certain rubber print in the doorway. So just thanks for everything. Love. Ollie."

Olive knew that she was dying, and she and John planned their funerals. They would be buried together in Ottawa's Beechwood cemetery; Olive's funeral would be simple, John's, as befitting an Elder Statesman, all pomp and ceremony. Olive arranged to leave her mink coat, few pieces of jewellery and some photographs to Carolyn; otherwise, she possessed very little. John had given her a grand piano in 1962, and Olive practised religiously during the Cuban missile crisis when the world hovered on the brink of nuclear war; perhaps it was bad memories, but she left the piano behind at 24 Sussex Drive. Puritan to the end, Olive Evangeline Freeman Palmer Diefenbaker prepared to leave life as frugally as she had entered it.

On December 20, 1976 Olive came home from the hospital for Christmas. "Dress up the house," she told her housekeeper, Cora. Olive dressed up too: she arrived in John's new Oldsmobile wearing a pink linen dress embroidered with rosebuds. A bedroom had been fixed up for her on the main floor, but Olive wandered about the house, as if seeing it for the last time. Three days before Christmas she was sitting in the library when John called from his office, in a flap as usual. Olive calmed him down, then asked to speak to his colleague, Robert Coates. "John keeps phoning me," she said quietly. "I am not well enough to handle it. Could you do something to stop him?" Coates promised to try.

Olive joined Cora in the kitchen for lunch. She was laughing at one of Cora's stories when she felt faint; Cora jumped up to catch her as she slumped forward. Olive was dead. Her funeral was more to John's sentimental taste than her own, and Olive was buried in Beachwood cemetery on Christmas Eve.

She did not rest there for long. John changed the funeral plans he and Olive had worked out so painstakingly: he would not be buried in Beechwood after all, but on the grounds of the Diefenbaker Centre, the museum he was building in Saskatoon for his monumental collection of memorabilia, and Olive would be buried beside him. John lived less than three more years, a lonely, pathetic shadow of a man. "Where's Olive?" he had demanded once when she became lost in a crowd. "If I lose her, I'll lose everything."

John Diefenbaker died on August 16, 1979 and the next day Olive's casket was quietly disinterred and taken to the funeral train that would carry John's body west to Saskatoon; Olive's body was waiting by their open grave on the banks of the Saskatchewan River when the mourners arrived for John's service. Olive and John Diefenbaker were laid to rest together on a windswept bluff, directly across the river from William, Mary, Elmer and Edna.

Olive's gravestone bears no epitaph. Perhaps the best is provided by Lotta Dempsey: "She was a lady, she was a *lady*, in the best sense of that old-fashioned word."

CHAPTER 12

Moody Maryon

*M*ARYON PEARSON sits in her chair with the watchful stillness of a coiled cobra. As the minutes pass, her hooded eyes betray not a flicker of expression, her manicured hands remain motionless on the arms of her chair and her pale, puffy face is an inscrutable mask. When she speaks, her slow drawl reveals nothing, and her smile is a knife drawn across flesh.

Facing Maryon in front of the fireplace at 24 Sussex Drive in the spring of 1965, interviewer Donna Soble writhes with anxiety, her whole body urging the prime minister's wife to *say something*. Finally a wide, thin gash spreads across Maryon's face and her tongue flickers out.

"You must know the old phrase, 'Behind every successful man . . . ,'" she says.

"Oh yes!" cries Soble, "There stands a . . . "

"A *surprised* woman," drawls Maryon. The gash spreads from ear to ear, and a glint of laughter brightens her eyes. Maryon has delivered another stinger with perfect timing.

"Life is a comedy to those who think and a tragedy to those who feel," Maryon Moody wrote on the fly-page of her diary when she was twenty. Maryon thought. Bright, witty and easily bored, Maryon was a character out of an English novel by Nancy Mitford or Evelyn Waugh, authors of the smart "society" satires she read avidly all her life. She affected a world-weary, aristocratic air peculiar for a doctor's daughter from Winnipeg, and smoked her cigarettes in a long holder she waved like a sceptre. She could be a snob, contemptuous of people who were not well-bred, and not, like herself, white, Anglo-Saxon Protestants. "You'll be one of them within six months!" she chided her nephew, Christopher Young, when he married a Roman Catholic, and she thought it "so odd" when his sister Sheila married a man who was half-Jewish. Maryon was reflecting the prejudice of the time: anti-semitism was an accepted fact of

Canadian life, particularly in Ottawa, and Maryon later came to like and admire the Jews she met in the civil service. Maryon was critical of people on so many grounds she could hardly be accused of racism.

"A lot of people thought Maryon was a bitch," comments one retired mandarin. "She played a tough game." Her tongue was caustic and her language salty; she liked a Bloody Mary for lunch and a stiff gin or two before dinner, and she could help a friend demolish a bottle of scotch. By the genteel standards of her time, Maryon drank, and rumours that she was an alcoholic were widely believed, certainly by Olive Diefenbaker, to whom Maryon, with her cocktails and swear words, must have seemed the last word in licentiousness.

"He was one of the most entertaining men I have ever known," Maryon said wistfully of her husband, Mike Pearson, shortly after he died in 1972. It was the highest compliment Maryon could pay anyone. Maryon only asked, no, she *demanded* to be amused. Her favourite word was "tiresome," a word she used to describe everything that wasn't "amusing," and during her twenty years in politics, tiresome was a word Maryon used frequently.

"I married Mike for better or for worse, not for lunch," she snapped at a reporter who questioned her about her apparent unhappiness in public

Maryon in her Garbo glasses, "She could cut you off at the knees."

life. Maryon hated campaigning, and unlike Olive, she didn't put on a smiling face about it. Maryon rarely put on a smiling face about anything, and she developed deep furrows between her eyes that gave her a perpetual frown. She wore sunglasses on the platform to shield her eyes from the television lights – she suffered from a mild case of glaucoma – and everyone assumed that Maryon, like Garbo, wanted to be alone.

"Is there anything anyone would like to bring up?" the chairman inquired at one political meeting. "Yes," Maryon said *sotto voce*, "the last four cups of coffee and six doughnuts." In Edmonton she was asked, "How does it feel to be back in the west?" "Not very good," she retorted, and when a Toronto reporter asked if she was enjoying herself, Maryon answered in one word: "No."

"If Olive Diefenbaker was a creamy unguent that soothed and lubricated political life in the capital, Maryon Pearson was a splash of astringent right in the eye," wrote journalist Susan Riley in *Political Wives*. Maryon's brusqueness frightened reporters, who decided euphemistically that Mrs. Pearson was "a very private person," a cliché that would clang after every subsequent wife however extroverted her personality. Maryon was left alone, in the way a fierce and yappy little dog is avoided, and her view of politics as a farce was treated as an indecent secret.

Politics in the early 1960s was often a farce, a national Punch and Judy show starring a cast of characters so bizarre that in retrospect they seem hardly credible. Flailing at each other at centre stage were John Diefenbaker and Lester B. Pearson, who used the nickname "Mike" partly because he lisped, and whose bow-ties and rumpled suits made him appear on television like an amiable clown. Maryon always referred to Diefenbaker as "that awful man," and in the House of Commons Mike Pearson was no match for Dief's rapier wit and Perry Mason court-room style.

Pearson was a national hero when he took over the Liberal leadership from Louis St. Laurent in 1958. As minister for external affairs in the St. Laurent government, he had been awarded the Nobel Prize in 1957 for his efforts in diffusing an international crisis over the Suez Canal and establishing a United Nations peacekeeping force in the Middle East. However, his leadership did not begin auspiciously. The Liberals were in disarray after suffering a surprising defeat in the June 1957 election, yet Pearson, over the vehement objections of Maryon and his executive assistant, Mary MacDonald, moved a motion in the House calling on the Diefenbaker government to resign and hand power back to the Liberals. It was an idiotic thing to do, and Diefenbaker laughed the Liberals into oblivion: he called a snap election and won the largest majority in Canadian history.

"They were very lonely years," recalls Mary MacDonald of Mike's years in Opposition. "You could feel the hatred in the crowds, or even worse, nobody cared."

Pearson never quite recovered from his initial blunder in the House. He had spent his entire career in the quiet corridors of diplomacy, first as a member of the department of external affairs for twenty years, then as minister since 1948, and he was never at ease in the public eye. However, when Soviet nuclear weapons were discovered in Cuba in October 1962, Diefenbaker hesitated about accepting nuclear warheads for American missiles stationed in Canada, and Pearson was able to capitalize on his enormous reputation as an international power broker to advocate Canada's acceptance of the weapons as part of our commitment to the NATO alliance.

The crisis over nuclear arms caused the disorganized Diefenbaker government to collapse, and the Liberals squeaked in with a minority government in 1963. Pearson's five tempestuous years as prime minister were marked by scandal, bitter Cabinet resignations, brutal infighting and vitriolic criticism from Diefenbaker, who relished his role as Opposition critic, but the government managed to pass both medicare legislation and the Canada Pension Plan, as well as to introduce a new Canadian flag, the "Pearson pennant," as Diefenbaker called it, and to celebrate the happiest year in Canadian history, the 1967 centennial anniversary.

Maryon was sixty-one when Mike became prime minister in 1963. Like Jeanne St. Laurent, she was too old to learn new tricks. Her two children, Geoffrey and Patricia, were married and the Pearsons had eight grandchildren, although Patricia says, "My mother was not a 'children person.' " Maryon's idea of a good time was a new novel or an afternoon of bridge, it wasn't sitting on a metal folding chair in a cold curling rink somewhere in Mike's riding of Algoma East listening to three hours of mind-numbing political rhetoric.

"Who was that bag of wind who introduced you tonight, Mike?" she asked after one meeting.

"He's one of the hardest party workers in northern Ontario," Mike replied.

"No wonder we're in trouble," she said.

The biggest windbag of all, unfortunately, was Mike himself. Witty and charming in private conversation, Mike was a bore on the public platform, a nervous, righteous parson's son unable to establish a rapport with his audience. "How did I do?" he anxiously asked Maryon one night. "You missed several opportunities to sit down," she retorted. After Mike began to incorporate Maryon's one-liners into his speeches he started to get some laughs.

"Maryon and Mike's marriage was not made in heaven, but neither was it a hell, as some have suggested," historian John English wrote in *Shadow of Heaven*, the first volume of his biography of Lester Pearson. Mike not only took Maryon's jabs in good form, he found her as entertaining as she found him. Others, unfortunately, did not. Maryon's barbs could be cruel and insulting, particularly when she "took a scunner" to someone she thought was putting on the dog, and Mike never intervened to prevent her being rude. For all his smiling, affable manner, few people got close to Mike Pearson, and those who did found he could be cold and unscrupulous. Maryon would sacrifice a friendship for a clever quip; she sacrificed some of Mike's friends too, and so did he: Pearson's rift with his friend and finance minister, Walter Gordon, left deep scars.

Maryon was a middle child, a "courteous, cautious and careful" little girl sandwiched between her self-possessed older sister, Grace, and her talented younger brother, Herbert. The Moody children were born only a year apart – Maryon on December 13, 1901 – and they formed a squabbling little triumvirate within an extremely disciplined and restrictive household. The Moodys were Methodists: no liquor, no smoking, no dancing, no cards. Dr. Arthur Moody was rarely home and Maryon's mother Elizabeth, a former superintendent of nurses at the Winnipeg General Hospital, ruled her family much as she had the nurses, with a rod of iron.

Maryon soon learned to subvert the rules. She and Herbert smoked on the roof of the Moody's big house and sampled the bottles of homemade wine their father kept hidden at the back of a closet, filling the bottles with water to hide their crime. By the time Maryon was twenty, she had developed a passion for everything forbidden: liquor, cigarettes, dancing, cards and sex.

"My mother loved men and the company of men," Patricia says. "She always had lots of *beaux*." With her square face and irregular features, Maryon Moody was not beautiful, but she was an audacious flirt, and in the tradition of Émilie Lavergne she developed a *risqué* style and talent to amuse that men found very attractive. Soon after she entered Victoria College at the University of Toronto in 1920, Maryon attracted a coterie of suitors, among them Ken Kirkwood.

Ken Kirkwood was exactly the sort of nice Methodist boy nice Methodist parents want to marry their daughters, and in the summer of 1922 Ken accompanied Maryon, Grace and Mrs. Moody to England. If Ken anticipated that a shipboard romance would sweep Maryon off her feet, Maryon's dark eye was roving elsewhere: "Met Mr. Wittle the ass't purser – *very* nice officer," she confided to her diary on June 13. The next night she wrote: "Morning passed quickly reading Ken's collection of poetry etc. Went out after dinner – met Mr. Wittle & talked to him with Ken for awhile. Came in & read and walked around the deck again at 10 o'clock – seeing the elusive Wittle on our way to bed about 11 p.m. He mentioned the prospect of a bridge party in his cabin in the near future. Hope it comes off. He is very good looking and funny and interesting to talk to."

Maryon spent the next two days on the top deck reading Tennyson's erotic poem "Maud" and getting "a weatherbeaten countenance" in the hopes of encountering the elusive Wittle. On June 16 she writes: "At night was the much looked forward to *Concert*. It was a cross between a joke and a bore. Went out afterwards and talked to Mr. Wittle for awhile – walked around the deck a bit and went to bed reluctantly. There was a marvellous sky – clear and starry with the reflection of the sunken sun in the west."

The next afternoon "Grace & Ken & I slept and read on top deck until 3 o'clock when Mr. Whittle took us down & showed us the huge engine room the secret workings of whose mighty wheels and cylinders thoroughly inspired us! Had tea. After dinner we played bridge till about 9:30. Then we went out to inspect the festive scene on deck. Many little coloured lights were strung along the ceilings & they had the curtains up along one side of the ship. They brought the victrola out and proceeded to trip the light fantastic – as the stony hearted Captain wouldn't allow the officers to dance only about 4 couples indulged. We were not willing to become spectacles to the staring multitude. We went down to the 2nd class dining saloon and played and sang Mr. Whittle's songs & regaled ourselves with chocolates. We also danced a bit down there. We came up and walked around a bit – talked to D.W.W. for awhile & then we turned in."

Maryon and D.W.W. had progressed to a first-name basis, and possibly to stolen kisses behind the lifeboats. "Last day on board!" Maryon laments on June 19. "Alack and well-a-day! Would that we had another week – I've loved it on board – but that's the worst of all good things. They end! Went to church this morning. Ken didn't come. Felt very rotten (sore throat and other troubles) after lunch so slept all afternoon. Saw D.W.W. and told him I couldn't see him that night as I was going right to bed. He gave me another piece of poetry – which I tore up. But he is nice & I like him. Packed all our clothes, put on my suit and went up to the lounge to talk to Ken. I told him all about it at last and he was wonderful. Nothing like a good friend in time of need! Went to bed safely about 10:30.''

Poor Ken, the classic chump. Maryon seems to have come close to losing her virginity, and she will soon shed her religion, and Ken, like an old pair of socks. At twenty, Maryon's sweet-and-sour personality, with its peculiar combination of recklessness and inhibition, is clearly defined; she is a conventional, naive young woman who craves adventure, and her expectations relate entirely to men. Maryon was as wealthy as Émilie Barthe, but she was no Madame de Staël either. For Maryon, men, unfortunately, only came with marriage, and like Cinderella, Maryon lived with the sound of the clock striking twelve. She writes of Paris:

''We went to the 'Opera National' the most beautiful opera house in the world perhaps. It is a gorgeous place & *huge* – all red velvet & gilt – marble and huge glistening chandeliers out on the promenade where all the lovely gowns gather between acts! We saw *Thais* which was more wonderful than I could have imagined. It was *magnificent – gorgeous* – the music – the singing – the acting – all perfect. I was thrilled all 'thru. As we came out and were coming down the steps who should leap forth hat off and hand outstretched but Ed Weaver! Gus Nanton was with him and they asked [us] out to dance – it was then nearly 12 – but early in Paris they assured us. Grace told Miss Hind [their chaperone] we wouldn't be in till later on and off we went! We got a taxi and drove up Rue de Montmartre where all the gay Parisien cafes and cabarets are. We went to Pigalle – there was a wonderful orchestra which played *all* the time (til 5 am) never stopping but changing the dances of course . . . There were lots of people all very full of pep (and spirits!) It was wonderful. We danced nearly all the time. Ev and I had a marvellous time – most exciting. We stayed till about 2 am & then loaded with trophies we reluctantly left and came home to bed. It was an amazingly wonderful night altogether.''

After a three-month ''grand tour'' of England and Paris, the Moodys sailed for Canada on September 14. ''Got a wonderful long letter from Ken on board – all about Venice,'' Maryon writes in her diary. ''We *will* miss him on this trip.'' Not for long. ''After dinner tonight we danced on the deck," Maryon writes the next night. "I danced all evening with a 3rd year Harvard man–very nice–looks a bit Spanish. His name is Mr. C. Chapman."

Maryon's mother was willing to turn a blind eye to her religious scruples in the interest of marrying her daughters off, and she was willing to run the risk of Maryon's rebellion in exchange for a prize catch. The pool of eligible young men in Winnipeg was small. The Moodys were part of Winnipeg's tight little social elite, a generation of Ontario Protestants who had gone west with the railroad and had made their fortunes in the boom years before the First World War. Maryon wasn't as rich as Gus Nanton, whose father was a financier, but she lived in high style in a big house in suburban River Heights and knew only the "right" people. Although Dr. Moody had a large practice among Jews, immigrants and French-speaking Roman Catholics, these people were beyond the pale socially, and in spite of her father's urging, Maryon never learned to speak French with any fluency and always maintained a fastidious attitude towards the unwashed.

Maryon never seriously challenged the comfort, security and idleness of her life. She loved reading, and in England she had been thrilled by the Impressionist paintings of J.W.W. Turner, but unlike her friend Marian Hilliard, who went into medicine, Maryon shied away from scholarly discipline or unorthodox behaviour. Rather than freeing her, her experience at Victoria College, Toronto, made her more timid.

"I am proud of you and of the work," she wrote wistfully to Ken on hearing of his appointment to teach at a missionary college in Turkey. "As I have said to you before–women can't accomplish these things themselves but they can help in a humble way and be just as eager and ambitious about them. It's no use pretending I *like* being a woman–and admire her sweet humble helpfulness–I *don't*–I have always thought my great misfortune for being born on the 13th was being born a girl–but–Oh well, one *does* resign oneself, since one must."

Maryon was just twenty-one and about to enter her final year of university. Not only had she already given up, she hadn't even tried. She wasn't going to *attempt* to challenge her crippling role in life. Maryon's letter reveals the sexual anxiety experienced by generations of women students facing the spectre of Old Maid: she had to choose between being a "man" and being a girl. It was no contest. Her repressed sexuality is expressed more graphically in her next letter:

"Wouldn't it be glorious to be *natural*! But as Herr Teufelsdrockh asserts in *Sartor Resartus* – each person's self becomes his *clothes* – and it is a civilization of clothes that rules the world. One is apt to agree with him if one actually sits down and contemplates the world – the church, the streetcar, the college, the stores, law courts – naked! I suppose the trouble is that man won't recognize that he is also an animal and he tries to disguise the fact from himself – as far as possible – life is just one sham after another."

Maryon's cynical, negative pose is already in place. She will go through life as a satirist, a woman of the world who will always see the skull beneath the skin.

"We have Leslie [sic] Pearson for our History group," Maryon wrote to Ken three weeks later. "Just came back from 3 yrs in Oxford – I think he must be interesting."

Mike Pearson – Maryon rarely called him Lester – was Maryon's history professor at Victoria College. He was just four years older, a war veteran, a good athlete and, in spite of his small size, a big man on campus. Like Maryon, Mike was an indifferent scholar – his passion was baseball – an uncomfortable Christian and a coddled child of the Methodist establishment. They shared a view of life as a cocktail party – Maryon spent more time at sorority meetings, tea dances and bridge parties than she did studying – and they made each other laugh. Marriages have been built on less. On March 13, 1924 Maryon wrote to Ken Kirkwood:

"But the most wonderful thing on earth has happened to me at last – and I really can't believe it *is* me yet – but it must be because I feel his very heavy signet ring on my finger – Can you keep a secret Ken? I think you are safe enough being so far away – but don't tell a soul because we aren't telling the public till after term. I am engaged! There – even when I write it down I can't believe it – but it's true – and we love each other more than anything else in the world – Today is the 1st week anniversary of our engagement so you see no wonder it's still strange to me – And I've only known him really at all well – a little over a month. I am engaged to Lester Bowles Pearson – but I call him Mike (unromantic name isn't it?) . . . We really have reversed the order of things though and fell rather precipitately in love before we had been *friends* very long – now we are busy getting to know one another. It's rather a fascinating passtime! . . . Oh I just *can't* believe that I am actually going to be married – *I* who always thought myself immune – and meant to have a career! Isn't life strange and interesting and *wonderful*."

This girlish gush to Ken, the rejected suitor, reveals an exceptional lack of empathy with other peoples' feelings, or an unconscious desire to protect herself by causing others pain. To marry Mike, Maryon jilted another student, Art Ross: "He will get over it I suppose in time because he is young," she writes cavalierly to Ken. "I tried hard always to be fair to him but I know I wasn't always – but flesh is weak – and he did care so much. He was awfully manly about it – and only said he would be there if ever I did want to see him – but not to see him out of pity. Oh – it was heartbreaking and I truly felt like a *worm*. He is only 22 Ken – do you think it will be all for the best for him in the end? It seems terrible to go thru life inflicting wounds on people."

Maryon loved the role of heart-breaker: perhaps it allowed her to express her anger at not being a man. While love appealed to her, domesticity did not: "You know what I have always thought about marriage," she wrote to Ken in May 1924, "that it seems to be a 'settling down' of two young people both perhaps with good minds and full of intelligence, into a sort of humdrum rut of meals – economy – and eventually family! Well – it has never appealed to me – as such – and I have always dreaded the idea. But Mike seems to feel exactly the same way – we don't want to settle and stay set, as it were, with the whole wide world to see and so many things to do. I want to do something myself – besides keeping house for him. It will be wonderful to be together and to do and think together but I do want to do some mental work myself – and I shall try to get some book reviewing for magazines or for the newspaper to do – Also we don't want to stay in Toronto all our lives – and I think shall take the odd chance in foreign climes. He is full of brains and could get university work almost anywhere. He is going to write a bit too. I should love him to get into the diplomatic service some day – and be Ambassador somewhere – after all why not dream? . . . I think we are both full of Ambition and we both believe in one another so thoroughly – I am quite sure he will do something big in the world some day!"

Maryon was dead right about Mike's career, and dead wrong about her own. "Maryon never worked a day in her life!" scoffs her brother, Herbert. Her plans to write, to study, to work all mysteriously evaporated, although she was forced to spend a year at home before her marriage. Maryon quit a job in a bookstore after a week or two and complained about her brief stint in a library as "musty for a life's work – librarians so often become mummy like." On the other hand she hated sewing and embroidery, only tolerated cooking – "I refuse to have recipes occupy more

Maryon and Mike on their wedding day, August 22, 1925.

space in my mind than literature and the Greater things of Life'' – and was bored by gentility. ''I seem to have lost touch with some things in this life at home,'' she wrote Ken sadly from Winnipeg six months before her marriage. ''It is so different from College life – so much more teaing (big, dull social ones – not dear cosy little tête-à-têtes where one converses – at these one only simpers) & sewing & oh various disturbances.''

In Winnipeg, Maryon fell into the social machine that ground restless young bluestockings into wives. Her mother planned the wedding. It would not be Maryon's wedding, but a double wedding with Grace and her fiancé, Norman Young, and it would not take place, as Maryon wished, in the fall of 1924 but on August 22, 1925. Maryon would just as soon have eloped, but Mike turned out to be a cautious careerist: marrying a student in his first year teaching would create a scandal, and Mike was so apprehensive about his position at the university that Maryon could not even return to Victoria College as a graduate student.

"If Mike had married a flibbertigibbet then there would have been two of them," Herbert Moody says acidly. Mike's career owed much to Maryon's vicarious ambition: he was a failure on his own. "There is something curiously loose-jointed and sloppy about his mental make-up which is reflected in his physical bearing," observed Mike's wealthy and powerful Liberal patron, Vincent Massey. Massey, a friend of the Pearson family, had secured Mike his position at the University of Toronto, as well as his scholarship to Oxford, but Mike spent more time coaching the varsity athletic teams than he did doing research, and Massey, who went to Washington as Canada's first ambassador in 1927, appears to have used his influence to get Mike out of the university and into External Affairs. Pearson charmed the undersecretary, O.D. Skelton, and on August 10, 1928 he was appointed first secretary at an annual salary of $3,450.

Maryon became an "Ottawa wife" and she helped to set the pattern that remains in place today. In the 1930s the Canadian civil service was small, male, English-speaking, Protestant and Oxbridge. Mike's colleagues were exactly like himself – clergymen's sons who had been educated at Oxford or Cambridge, usually on a scholarship, and had returned to Canada to raise the intellectual tone of public life. Many of them acquired English manners and an English accent, along with the snobbery that betrays a true colonial and an attitude of contempt for everyone not exactly like themselves. It was a familiar milieu to Maryon, and she adapted to it by becoming a modern version of her mother.

Maryon absorbed herself entirely in Mike's career. In the closed, secretive world of the Ottawa mandarins, as Pearson and his colleagues liked to think of themselves, the wives were expected to combine the social skills of a geisha with the morals of a missionary. Maryon's life revolved around entertaining, and being entertained, either at cocktail parties, which she liked, tea, lunch, dinner or afternoon bridge. The ritual required the exchange of innumerable calling cards, and an obsessive interest in the diplomatic pecking order so each rival could be treated with appropriate deference or disdain.

Maryon must have been good at her job because Mike's star rose steadily, although he was less experienced than his colleagues. In 1935

Pearson was posted to London where Vincent Massey was high commissioner, and Maryon could indulge her interest in art. "The pictures were very marvellous but we haven't seen nearly enough of them yet," she wrote of her first visit to Britain's National Gallery. "We are going back for a whole day again." Her response to art was emotional and discriminating: when she spoke about painting her eyes brightened and her voice became excited. "Saw two or three rooms full of Turners!" she wrote of a visit to the Tate Gallery. Vincent Massey was the patron of Canadian artist David Milne, and Maryon was able to buy several beautiful Milnes for $25 each; they are now worth thousands.

Maryon delighted in the theatre and the flesh-pots of Mayfair. Some of Mike's colleagues thought her vulgar, but her wit and forthrightness made her more truly cosmopolitan than they were, and as Canada timidly stepped on to the world stage, the Pearsons were the right people in the right place. When war broke out in September 1939, Mike insisted that Maryon return to Canada with the children; she did, but in a towering rage at missing the action. In 1942 Mike was transferred to Washington. Maryon was unimpressed – she complained to the press that wartime Washington was too crowded – but three years later she, at least, achieved her goal: Mike became ambassador to the United States.

These decades in Maryon's life remain shrouded in silence. Mandarins abhor publicity, and Maryon was secretive. Her Washington diary for 1944 is just a skimpy listing of times for cocktails and hairdressers, Spanish lessons and war work, which she hated.

"I sometimes feel I never really knew Mum," Patricia says. "We were not that close. She was always busy."

Mike and Maryon moved in a fast crowd, a crowd that included aristocrats, movie stars and spies, and they had very little time for their children. Geoffrey and Patsy were consigned to the care of nannies, and, at the age of twelve, sent away to boarding-schools hundreds of miles from mum and dad. They saw their parents on vacations, and communicated by correspondence. "There was no praise," Patsy remembers of her mother, "in letters, yes, but not to your face. She was a very, very critical person. I felt constrained at home. I was always backing away from her. She could cut you off at the knees."

Patsy, a gentle girl, remembers her mother as cranky, bossy, moody, argumentative, opinionated, negative and frustrated: "She never lost her temper, but she was angry a lot of the time. I was intimidated by my mother."

Maryon was still dancing on the deck with the elusive Whittle. She became, in her own mind, a character in a novel, a novel she never wrote. It was her one great regret. As Mike's younger colleague, Charles Ritchie, reveals in his own diary, *The Siren Years*, it was a romantic, adventurous era and the diplomatic world allowed privileged access to all levels of society from the *haute* to *la boue*. Maryon was a sharp observer of people: "*The King is quite an ordinary man with an almost bald head*," she wrote in 1922 on seeing King George V in London. "Queen Mother very cosy & like a little pussy cat," she decided in 1967. "All against the 'Blackamoors' i.e. Africans – Had good giggles with her." Prince Rainier of Monaco also impressed her: "He is *fun*. He said they are having a dinner in Montreal tomorrow of 200 people & bringing over a Casino band and dancing girls! Wish we could go to *that*." She found Princess Grace of Monaco "simple and charming," but Britain's Princess Margaret did not fare so well: "I see by the paper her colour will be orange this year," Maryon wrote to a friend. "I hope her disposition will not be as lemon as usual."

Maryon may have had a personal reason for her public silence: she had a very close friendship with a very public man, Graham Towers, governor of the Bank of Canada. Graham Towers was four years older than Maryon, tall, handsome, clever and rich, the sexiest man in Ottawa, and Towers and his wife Mollie were the Pearsons' closest friends. People who saw Graham and Maryon at parties observed that they had a special bond: "Oh, she was fond of him," recalls Roland Michener, whom Pearson appointed governor-general in 1967. "When they were together, you could tell they were good buddies alright." Michener does not suggest any impropriety. Unlike Mike, who nursed a single drink and liked to go to bed early, Maryon and Graham Towers shared a love for late-night parties and risqué jokes, and Towers had a reputation as a womanizer.

"He liked to screw," one of his friends says bluntly. The very model of a dour and bloodless banker during the working week, Towers apparently enjoyed a secret life of seduction. "Lie down, I want to talk to you," was his opening gambit to one attractive woman journalist. Sexual politics is part of the game, as Wilfrid Laurier ably demonstrated, and Towers, famous for his bawdy stories, apparently went well beyond flirtation.

Maryon and Graham were not clandestine about their relationship. They flew to Toronto together for weekend parties with mutual friends; Graham frequently drove Maryon down to his summer home at Murray Bay when Mike was away or too busy to go. "Drove to M. Bay in am w.

Graham," Maryon wrote on June 22, 1967, and on September 29, "Graham's 70th birthday!" Mike's birthday and her own are unremarked.

Maryon's affection for Graham created scandalous rumours in Ottawa that swirl around to this day, yet it did not damage Mike's career or create a rift between the Pearsons and the Towers, who continued to be a foursome. It might have been an "arrangement," or a matter of business; Towers was Maryon's financial adviser, and she was a whiz at investing Mike's money. Maryon kept all the accounts, gave Mike a frugal allowance, bought all Mike's clothes except his bow-ties, bought and drove their car and purchased an apartment block with the money from his Nobel Prize. Graham Towers enriched Maryon's life; he did not destroy her marriage or diminish her love for Mike, yet, as one mutual acquaintance puts it, "I can't see them *not* getting into bed together."

Mike and Maryon Pearson "moved in rather different circles in Ottawa," says Roland Michener. "One good reason for this is that he was fully occupied, and she had little time with him when he was in full swing." Pearson liked to cultivate an image as an easy-going good ol' boy, but as John English reveals in *Shadow of Heaven*, he was an ambitious workaholic who left his wife alone for weeks and months on end and, like John Thompson, communicated with his children largely by letter. Mike was fifty-one when he decided to jump into politics in 1948, and for Maryon the transition was hard, especially since Pearson was parachuted into the remote and sparsely populated Ontario riding of Algoma East.

"Most of her life people came to her," says Mary MacDonald, "but if you're the wife of the MP, you go to the people." Maryon was shy and stiff with strangers, and the Indians, loggers, miners, fishermen, railroaders and bush rats of Espanola and Manitoulin Island weren't exactly Maryon's crowd, but she was a trooper. She put up with being billeted in strangers' homes because the local hotel was deemed unfit for ladies; she attempted to make small talk with the women about cookies and children; she did without her pre-dinner drinks and she didn't smoke. No wonder she got edgy. Campaigning in the 1950s was primitive, especially along the north shore of Lake Huron. Mike, Maryon and Mary travelled by car, alone, driving through the bush from one tiny whistle-stop to the next, often late at night in the fog. "There was one night when the three of us were not speaking," Mary admits. However, she and Maryon hit it off: "I didn't want her job and she didn't want mine. You didn't argue with your boss's wife, you worked your way around it." Meetings were held in church basements and curling rinks and some communities were so small that only three or four people would be in the audience; when Maryon finally fell into bed, she often found herself in a home with no running water and an outdoor toilet, yet she was supposed to look, and act, immaculate.

Mike put Maryon through seven election campaigns, the last four coast-to-coast as well as in Algoma. ''We've lost everything, you've even won your seat,'' Maryon lamented when Diefenbaker swept the country in 1958. However, she didn't lament when the Liberals won in 1963 and Maryon finally got a crack at 24 Sussex Drive. Maryon and Olive Diefenbaker were always polite to each other – Maryon sent Olive a book when she was in hospital and they exchanged cordial notes–but Maryon couldn't stand Olive's smiley face and Olive found Maryon ''morose.'' When Maryon redecorated 24 Sussex, starting a renovation war that shows no sign of ceasefire, Olive wrote to her friend Marie Bendas: ''Some say the results are hideous. For example – our pale pink sofa has been upholstered in a very bold blue chintz, the small chairs in vivid yellow. The blue dining room which we thought distinguished she has done in an all-over gold and white paper which to us makes it look like a watered-down shoe-box. The pictures are very modern and very garish.'' As for Maryon, she found Olive's blue dining-room ''ghastly'' and the living-room ''so stiff and grey and *unlived in*, with far too many little chairs arranged in far too many little groups so that it looked like a public meeting.''

Maryon began the tradition of hanging Canadian art at 24 Sussex Drive, borrowing from the National Gallery or from the painters themselves, and she had acquired a substantial art collection of her own. Her taste was eclectic and avant-garde: she admired Joe Plaskett, William Kurelek and Jean-Paul Riopelle as well as Emily Carr and Pegi Nicol. Maryon did some painting herself while Mike was in Opposition. ''I don't have any talent,'' she told an interviewer, ''but I would like to do it again. You have to have somewhere you can set up your easel and make a lot of mess and leave it, and you also have to have time. I did realistic work–portraits, still life, things like that. Nothing really imaginative.''

She did do one imaginative and controversial thing, she started a collection of Canadian folk art and antiques which she displayed in her basement ''Canadiana Room.'' Today, Maryon's armoires and weather-vanes would be admired as works of art, in 1965 they were dismissed as worthless junk. When she left 24 Sussex in 1968 her collection was dispersed,

Maryon and Mike cutting a rug in Algoma East. She loved to dance.

although some pieces made their way upstairs, and her art collection, donated to External Affairs, has been hidden away at their guest house, 7 Rideau Gate.

Maryon did not become a public patron of the arts. She was too intellectual to be an ornament, too conformist to be an intellectual, and she hid her ambivalence behind a crusty face. In 1965 she sent a photo of herself in a Hallowe'en mask to her friend Issy Chester: "If only I could always wear my mask I wouldn't have to be told to Smile all the time."

Maryon loved dressing up, and the social whirl of the centennial year was exactly to her taste. "She was *crazy* about clothes," Patricia remembers. "Appearance was important, who wore what, the way people looked. 'Why don't you get your hair cut?' she'd say when you walked in the door." Maryon didn't care for hats, they tended to look like a leafy vegetable growing out of her head, but she permed her hair and spent hours at the dressmaker. Her taste was fussy, and she fancied lace that made her look stout and overdressed. Her sporadic 1967 diary reveals her self-consciousness about her appearance:

"June 19: 5:30. Meet Queen at Uplands. She looked gorgeous in pink & white with yellow silk coat. I looked dull & governessy in navy blue." The next day she observed: "Queen in blue coat & lovely blue & white straw hat," and on July 1, "Queen looking *divine* in blue garter ribbon, tiara and embroidered white top with blue garter skirt." Maryon loved jewels too, and when French President Charles de Gaulle abruptly cancelled his visit to Ottawa, Maryon wistfully wrote in her diary: "No bijoux for Norah [Michener] and me!"

In Montreal, de Gaulle had shouted "Vive le Quebec libre!" at a mass rally. Interpreting this as a call for Quebec independence, Pearson sent him a note of reproach; offended, de Gaulle stormed off home, taking his gifts with him. The diplomatic crisis created a crisis in the kitchen at Rideau Hall, where the Micheners' temperamental chef, Zonda, had created a spectacular banquet. The Micheners, as usual, rose to the occasion:

"Each of the one hundred and twenty guests was notified by telephone that the party was off," Peter Stursberg related in his biography of Michener, *The Last Viceroy*. "The meat course had not been started but the fish was being cooked and it was distributed to the household staff and they had Arctic char that day as only Zonda could prepare it. All was not lost: Mike and Maryon Pearson and Roland and Norah Michener ate the de Gaulle dinner, the full seven courses, in the privacy of the dining room at Rideau Hall . . . They toasted each other in the champagne specially selected for the French president. It was a cheerful dinner party . . ."

Roland Michener smiles when he recalls that night. "We laughed at de Gaulle," he says. "Maryon enjoyed it thoroughly."

Maryon and Norah had a long but prickly friendship. Mike and Mich, as their husbands called each other, had known each other from Oxford days, and Norah, a dainty blond from Vancouver, was just as smart and ambitious as Maryon. Norah had returned to university after her children were grown to earn a PH.D. in philosophy; she was also a gourmet cook who spoke flawless French and a stickler for status and protocol. Michener,

a Conservative, was made Speaker of the House of Commons by Diefenbaker in 1957, and Norah became a fixture in the gallery scribbling little
notes of advice to her husband in the chair. "Madame Speaker," as she
came to be known, also distributed a handbook on etiquette to the wives
of senators and MPs, alerting them to the niceties of calling cards, the
correct wearing of gloves and other archaic mysteries of Ottawa behaviour.
Much of it had to do with the proper way to curtsy to the governor-
general. At a garden party: "When you are presented you offer your hand,
curtsy and say 'Good afternoon, Your Excellency,' " and after dinner at
Rideau Hall, "His hostess will rise and leave the dining room first, turning
at the door to make a full curtsy to His Ex. before going out. Every lady
in the room will follow suit."

Like hell, said Maryon, and when Mike appointed Mich governor-
general in 1967, Maryon announced: "I'm damned if I'm going to curtsy
to Norah Michener!" She didn't, and after considerable tearing of hair the
curtsy was abolished.

Maryon had more than her share of trouble with the visiting dignitaries who made pit stops in Canada during 1967. Her account of feeding
United States President Lyndon Johnson is worthy of *Apocalypse Now*:

"May 25, 1967:

"9:30 [am] Told Johnson here for a small dinner.

"10 – Told Johnson here for *lunch* at H[arrington] Lake. "MacDonald
flew into action, organized kitchen, supplies, box lunches for Press etc etc.
I went up to lake at 10:30. Found hordes of people. Security all over the
house looking for bugs. 12 men putting up flagpole for a U.S. flag – I
organized dining room for 6 – Johnson, Butterworth, Rostow, Martin,
Ritchie, Pearson – 6 officials on porch – including Geoff.

"Picnic tables for Press up on hill behind house – helicopter flying over
constantly – security men in 2 boats on lake. Mike arrived about 1 pm.,
Johnson & Co. arrived 1:25 in helicopter – another arrived with press. Blew
leaves all over grounds.

"Said how do you do to Johnson. He as ponderous as ever. They all
had drinks but not him. Lunch served at 2 pm. I had tray in my room.
Menu: tomato consomme, sweetbreads & mushrooms, green salad, straw-
berries & sponge cake. Johnson had 2 large helpings of sweetbreads. M. &
Johnson talked alone after lunch for 1/2 hour. He (LBJ) then addressed
assembled company but said nothing much. I said goodbye & he held my

hand & gazed into my eyes saying thank you but no apology for short notice. He had no idea what it all involved.

"Press made *much* of the menu. They never heard of sweetbreads I guess. Spent next three days at lake – recovering."

Maryon's obvious dislike for Johnson was political as well as personal: she opposed the war in Vietnam. She had strong political opinions and they were more radical than Mike's: she disagreed with his decision to allow nuclear arms on Canadian soil – she was forced to quit the anti-war Voice of Women as a result of his about-face – and she lobbied hard to have more women appointed to the Cabinet and senior boards. Maryon admired the one woman in the Liberal Cabinet, Judy LaMarsh, a big, brassy, temperamental young woman who dressed like Klondike Kate and swore like a sailor. LaMarsh was the best Cabinet minister Mike had: she brought in the Canada Pension Plan, organized medicare and master-minded the dazzling centennial celebrations. The Honourable Judy also radicalized the image of women in politics: she made it okay to be tough. When Judy blew into town, Norah Michener's white gloves and calling cards were gone with the wind.

Maryon enjoyed a good fight. "I love getting all the inside stuff from the Hill," she told a reporter, "and in his job Mike is pretty well plugged in." She watched a lot of television – she liked the controversial CBC show, *This Hour Has Seven Days* – and she was a secret political junkie. On September 9, 1967 she spent the entire day watching the Conservative leadership convention on television: "Dief badly beaten but got all the news coverage & sat to the end. It took an incredibly long time (9 hours!) for so many votes . . . Dief gave his emotional swan song – all the newsmen *so* sorry for him – but not us."

Maryon gave her all in 1967, and after nearly twenty years in politics she had had enough. "Very tired. My God, we're old aren't we?" Maryon wrote in May 1967 before the rush of the centennial celebrations had even started. After six frantic months of state banquets, receptions and cross-Canada tours, Maryon wrote: "Home for dinner – delicious meat loaf!" Trinidad and Tobago had just been lunched, as had the Dutch, Norwegians, Ghanians and almost everyone else. Lunches generally bored Maryon, but she was fascinated by the Africans – black people were still rare in Canada – and she was even more interested in the gifts they brought, which she listed in detail, noting sadly that the poorest countries gave the best presents.

Mike was seventy, and on December 13, 1967 he gave Maryon a birthday present: he would retire in the spring. In April 1968 he was succeeded as Liberal leader by Pierre Elliott Trudeau. Mike was ill, and he died of cancer just after Christmas 1972. Maryon was lost. "The void he left in my life is such that I simply can't believe he is gone," she wrote to Issy Chester. In 1975 Mary MacDonald took Maryon to China; she enjoyed it but Maryon was not an intrepid traveller. Flying and foreign food upset her timetable and her stomach: her single memory of a trip to Moscow was a breakfast of caviar, cold meat, eggs, sardines and sweet orange juice that she found "very strange." She seemed to spend most of her time packing and unpacking, and in 1968 she bailed out of a trip through Africa because of the heat and indigestion.

Maryon lived alone in Rockcliffe until 1979 when she entered a nursing home in Toronto. The following year she fell and broke her back, and when she came out of the anesthetic after the operation, her mind was gone. She fell again and broke her hip, then was transferred to Queen Elizabeth Hospital in Toronto where she lived on, unknowing and unmoving, until she died at eighty-eight on December 26, 1989.

Everyone who mattered in Liberal Ottawa, starting with Governor-General Jeanne Sauvé, turned out for Maryon's memorial service in St. Bartholomew's Church on January 23, 1990. It was a light-hearted event, as if a tell-tale trace of cigarette smoke could be sniffed wafting over the mourners, and Maryon's hearty laugh could be heard from the crypt. Maryon had a black sense of humour. Not long before he died, Mike acquired a glass eye after an operation for cancer, and Maryon, annoyed that the cartoonists depicted him as "a frightfully dishevelled old creature," became more vigilant about his appearance.

"You can't go out like *that*!" Maryon barked one night when Mike came down in his best suit.

"Oh, for heaven's sakes Maryon!" Mike said, "There's nothing wrong with this suit!"

"Mike," Maryon replied impatiently, "you've got your eye in upside down."

CHAPTER 13

. . . .

The
Multiple
Lives
of
Maggie T.

$\mathcal{M}$ARGARET SINCLAIR exploded into the Canadian consciousness on the evening of March 4, 1971 when she secretly married the prime minister, Pierre Elliott Trudeau. The wedding took place at 5:30 p.m. in a small Roman Catholic church in North Vancouver, and news of the marriage was not released to the press until the Trudeaus were leaving their private family reception. The press photographs of Mrs. Trudeau showed a radiantly beautiful young bride with dark, curly hair and a dazzling smile. Her wedding dress was unusual, a long white caftan with a hood that made her look like a Greek naiad or a Christmas angel, whatever turned you on, and underneath she more than likely wore a sexy lace garter-belt, although nobody but Pierre would have guessed at the time.

When Margaret and Pierre arrived in Ottawa after a three-day skiing honeymoon she was already an international celebrity – United States President Richard Nixon had awakened them at 6:30 a.m. the morning after the wedding to offer his congratulations – and a woman of engrossing mystery. Margaret had been seen only once or twice with Pierre and dismissed as just another of his casual dates. All that was generally known about her was that she was twenty-two, had grown up in Vancouver and her father had some connection with the Liberal Party.

Margaret arrived in Ottawa dressed in a flared coat with white fur trim and a matching white fur hat like a star in the movie *Dr. Zhivago*. She looked sixteen, sweet, naive and nervous, a young doe caught in the glare of the television lights, and she spoke, when she spoke at all, in a girlish whisper. Pierre too was shy, radiant, a blushing bridegroom at the age of fifty-one. As they sped away in their black limousine, only grouches were rude enough to wonder why such a sophisticated prime minister was marrying a woman young enough to be his daughter.

The limousine took them to Pierre's castle, 24 Sussex Drive, a house Margaret later described as a "great squat toad." She had been there often

*Was she wearing a
sexy lace garter-belt?*

enough, as Pierre's secret "country mistress," but this time she was arriving by the front door, and Margaret felt a chill she tried to shrug off: "The weekend we married six feet of snow fell, laying a great cold hand over the city. Driving down the street from the airport was like finding our way down a tunnel. The snow had piled up on the pavements in towering mountains of ice, soon to turn into great filthy piles of gritty slush. But the day we came home to 24 Sussex Drive there had been a fresh fall and an air of stillness and magic lay over the scene – the immense white garden, the big windows lit up cheerfully to welcome us. In the back of the car I hugged Pierre."

Margaret did not emerge from her ice palace until the snow melted in May, when she accompanied Pierre on a state visit to the Soviet Union. One hundred reporters were on the trip, all of them dewy-eyed about Margaret, but Pierre declared his wife off limits to the media; Margaret would give no interviews and no one was to approach her. This embargo was both infuriating and peculiar; it was now known that Margaret had a degree in English and sociology from Simon Fraser University in British Columbia, she had associated with, even lived with, student radicals, she was a self-declared hippie, and her father, James Sinclair, had been a Cabinet minister in the government of Louis St. Laurent. Why was Pierre Trudeau treating his intelligent, interesting wife as if she were an infant, an idiot or a deaf mute?

Margaret, all trembling, blushing charm, played her role like a pro. Nobody had bothered to brief her about what to expect as the prime minister's wife and she had to wing it all the way; Margaret was exceptionally good at winging it, but it was exhausting, and she bitterly resented official protocol that put Pierre in the lead car with the Soviet leaders, and herself in the second car "surrounded by ambassadresses and their incessant 'quack, quack, quack' of small talk." Being pregnant didn't help.

Pierre treated his child bride's pregnancy the way cardinals elect a pope; Margaret was sequestered in her big stone house while an anxious nation waited for the tell-tale puff of smoke that signalled the arrival of a Trudeau heir. In the meantime Trudeau set about refocusing the spotlight where he thought it belonged: on himself.

Pierre, the aging *enfant terrible* of Canadian politics, had bounded on to the national stage in 1965, one of "three wise men" from Quebec recruited by the Liberals to exorcise the demon of separatism. A millionaire law professor with a reputation for political radicalism and open contempt for his prime minister, Mike Pearson, Trudeau joined the Liberal Party only weeks before he was elected in the safe Montreal riding of Mount Royal. No one like Trudeau had been seen in Ottawa since Wilfrid Laurier, and Trudeau affected Laurier's manner of indolence and insouciance, while beavering furiously behind the scenes to build his power base as minister of justice.

Trudeau shared Laurier's flare for costume. One day Pierre would appear on the Hill in a flowing cape and floppy hat, a Spanish conquistador, the next day in sandals, with socks, an itinerant scholar, the day after that in a black leather coat, a spy from the Czechoslovakian secret police. He always wore a fresh rose in his lapel, or, in his Spanish mode, clenched between his teeth, and, like Laurier, he provoked rumours of scandalous liaisons with both sexes. While Laurier played the Romantic Poet, Trudeau played the Swinging Bachelor, carefully concealing his rigorous Jesuit asceticism beneath a sly, sensual mask.

Physically, Trudeau resembled the Russian dancer Rudolf Nureyev, a small, muscular man with high cheek-bones and slightly slanted eyes who always seemed poised for combat. He held a brown belt in judo, he was an expert swimmer and skier, and he loved to show off: at one royal reception he twirled a saucy pirouette behind the queen's back. In the twilight of the Age of Aquarius, Trudeau's *Afternoon of a Faun* performance was irresistible; he was elected Liberal leader in the spring of 1968 and in June was swept into power on a wave of Trudeaumania orchestrated by Liberal girls in miniskirts who screamed and danced along his path like ecstatic Bacchantes. Trudeau was too far past thirty to be trustworthy – he "forgot" his age, claiming to be forty-six, not forty-eight – but he was younger than his dour Conservative opponent, Robert Stanfield, who couldn't even catch a football, and like forty-six-year-old bachelor Mackenzie King in 1921, Trudeau became associated with youth, progress, justice and – the magic word of the Sixties – freedom.

Margaret saw right through him. They met, appropriately, at a Club Med resort in Tahiti during Christmas 1967. Margaret, a teenage Lorelei, was sitting on a raft in the lagoon. "There was a man skiing in the bay; I followed his progress idly, more than a little impressed by the ease of his performance. When he later came over to my raft we started a 'What are you doing here?' and 'What do you study?' conversation that soon, casually, led to student rebellion, and Plato and revolution – I wasn't particularly impressed. He was shy, almost too shy, and when he asked me politely if I would like to go deep sea fishing with him, I didn't bother to show up – Pierre struck me as very old and very square – a nice-looking middle-aged man with funny old-fashioned shorts and a stripy T-shirt."

Margaret went off with her current heart-throb, Yves Lewis, "a beautiful, almost god-like man, with silvery hair bleached to the colour of sunshine, with eyes as green as the water he skied on." Margaret was infatuated: "Yves changed me and he also made a mark on my soul," she wrote later in *Beyond Reason*. "He became a symbol for me, a romatic fantasy I was never to quite shake free of." But as far as Yves was concerned, Margaret was boring and *bourgeois*.

"I found her eyes extraordinarily beautiful," Pierre later said of his fatal encounter with Margaret. Her periwinkle blue eyes enchanted him, and so did her hip chatter about revolution. To Pierre revolution meant the French Revolution, but to Margaret revolution had nothing to do with politics; it had everything to do with drugs and sex, and at nineteen she thought she was "quite something." Pierre, like so many men of his generation, suddenly realized that a beautiful young woman could be "free": sexually available, thanks to the pill, without the inhibiting complication of marriage. While square old Pierre had been decorously dating, fearful of entanglement, a whole generation of Lolitas had come of age and promiscuous sex was, in the lingo of the time, groovy, man.

His dilemma was: how could he make himself sexier than Yves Lewis? The old man's answer was obvious: power. Pierre had gone to Tahiti undecided about contesting the Liberal leadership; he went home determined to win. No doubt Trudeau reached this decision on intellectual and political grounds – he was deeply committed to a federalist view of Canada – but he was the underdog: young, inexperienced and single. Charisma, not competence, won Trudeau the leadership, and Margaret would always have a symbiotic association with Pierre's political success. Margaret went to the convention with her parents, who were supporting another candidate, John Turner, and, caught up in the hysteria, envious of the groupies around Pierre, Margaret succumbed to Trudeaumania. Pierre spotted her in a hallway, broke through the chanting crowd and kissed her on both cheeks. Margaret didn't see him again for eighteen months.

"I had forgotten her for a year or two," Pierre later confessed. "But I always remembered her eyes." For Prime Minister Trudeau, now the disco-dancing Mick Jagger of international politics, Margaret Sinclair was just another photo opportunity, a decorative date to be seen with on a slow Saturday night in Vancouver. Margaret hadn't given Pierre a second thought; she was obsessed with Yves Lewis. She had trailed after him to Berkeley, California, but Yves, still in his beach-bum phase, told this uptight chick to get loose; Margaret loosened up in Morocco, wandering around stoned in her "magic sandals" and shacking up in hippie communes. Vancouver was never very far away: her father sent her money and she stole off for weekends at tourist hotels. After seven months, sick, frightened and fed up with the filth and degradation of drugs and ubiquitous sex, Margaret came home "a weird, vegetarian, mystical flower child." Yves was now involved in some underground revolutionary movement; he told this flakey chick to get lost.

When Pierre called, Margaret's first thought was: I've got nothing to wear! The mystical flower child went shopping for clothes. Clothes were Margaret's passion. As the fourth child in a thrifty Scottish family of five girls, Margie always resented having to wear washed-out hand-me-downs from her older sisters, so she learned to sew and got herself a Saturday job in the fashion department of The Bay. She became obsessively self-conscious about her appearance: Was she too fat, too skinny, too small? Were her breasts droopy, her feet big, her teeth crooked? Margie was smaller than her sisters, and in the boisterous, competitive Sinclair family it was hard for her to make her presence felt. "My father used to complain jokingly that even our dog Sally was a bitch," she said later. Her father didn't help: "And this is number four!" he'd introduce her to guests. "No!" she wanted to scream, "I'm *Margaret*!"

The Sinclair sisters' identity crisis resolved itself so that Heather was the oldest, Betsy the baby, Janet the introvert, Lin the dreamer: Margie was the cutest. A curly-haired *coquette* at the age of four, Margie quickly learned that "being cute and pretty helped an awful lot, and I could quite easily fool my teachers with a smile and a few clever words." She dealt with boys the same way: "I always had a boyfriend, and I would have died if I didn't. My sisters said I was boy-crazy, and I'm sure it was true. I was a prude and a terrible flirt."

Margie's macrobiotic Moroccan phase was an identity she was wearing like a dress she had already discovered was out of fashion. Whoosh! Off came the granny glasses and Indian cotton shirt, on went a little French dress in handstitched white gabardine. Her long frizzy hair was pulled back in a sleek chignon and at 7 p.m. on August 9, 1969 Margie presented herself to the prime minister looking like a Barbie doll. It was Trudeau who looked a little weird in a bright yellow ascot, and in the back of the car on the way up Grouse Mountain Margaret wondered if he might be a bit of a creep. The horde of photographers waiting at the Grouse's Nest restaurant broke the ice: Pierre and Margaret agreed that they preferred simple meals in unpretentious places. Nervous, anxious to please, and charmed by Pierre's old-fashioned gallantry, Margaret soon let her hair down: "That first date set the pace of our relationship. It was never really to change. I talked, chattered, explained, expounded; he asked me questions.''

Margaret babbled on about Yves, drugs, mysticism, Morocco and, in a refrain that would become terribly familiar, her own unhappiness. As Pierre listened, Margaret was impressed by his calm, rational responses; he frightened her a little, but he took her seriously. He suggested that she become a writer, or a sociologist. Why didn't she move east? "Aha," Margaret thought, "Now he's invited me to go and live with him in Ottawa." At the end of the evening Pierre dropped her off with a peck on the cheek and a polite: "If you come to Ottawa, let me know. I'd love to have you come for dinner.''

"At that instant," Margaret wrote later, "I decided that I wanted this man for myself.''

Pierre never knew what hit him. His relationships with women had always been controlled and categorized; he had never encountered an aggressive child of the counter-culture with an agenda of her own. "One day I'd dream of being a movie star, the next day I was going to be a great writer,'' Margaret says of her youthful fantasies. "Most of all, I dreamed of being a rich, celebrated, beautiful, totally happy woman with an extremely famous husband and many beautiful children.''

Margaret landed in Ottawa in a matter of weeks, fixed up with a junior job in the civil service and a swish Rockcliffe address. She had barely set foot in Pierre's shabby bachelor pad before her imagination was busy redecorating the prime minister's residence, and after a spoonful of his tasteless food she saw herself in the kitchen preparing delicious little snacks. Margaret instantly perceived what other women had missed: Pierre needed a mother.

Pierre had lived with his mother until he moved to Ottawa at the age of forty-six, and now Grace Elliott Trudeau was bedridden and dying in Montreal. Unlike Isabel Grace Mackenzie King, she did not move in with her son – Trudeau's highest compliment for his mother was that she did not disturb him – and for the first time in his life Pierre was alone. Shy, almost reclusive, and sensitive, Grace Trudeau had encouraged Pierre's intellectual and creative pursuits, yet maintained her dark, old-fashioned house in Outremont as a safe refuge to which he could always return. Politics had pushed Pierre out of the nest, and now, at fifty, an age when his friends had families of their own, he was in danger of becoming everybody's bachelor uncle, a balding, slightly pathetic figure with soup stains on his trousers. Like Margaret's hippie clothes, Pierre's old costumes no longer fit; he was a lost boy.

With her high cheek-bones and brilliant blue eyes, Margaret bore a striking resemblance to Grace Trudeau and to Pierre himself – Maggie and Pierre looked so much alike actress Linda Griffiths played them both perfectly in a one-woman show – and for two emotionally immature people the narcissism of gazing at their own image must have been irresistible: it was only after she married Pierre that Margaret became obsessed with finding herself, frustrated perhaps by constantly looking in a mirror.

"My wife helped me to understand new values, what interests young people today," Pierre told an interviewer in 1975. "I was able to listen to her and understand what their worries were, what their aspirations and ideals were." As Richard Gwyn writes in *The Northern Magus*: "Insatiably curious intellectually, and quite without a sense of the ridiculous, Trudeau questioned her intently about troubled youth, Consciousness Three, peace, love, freedom, identity, organic baking and everything else in the Whole Earth Catalogue." At one stage Margaret convinced Trudeau that the

Maggie and Pierre bore a physical resemblance to one-another.

293

whole Cabinet should take a course in transcendental meditation; Pierre practised yoga, but the Cabinet balked.

Most of Margaret's philosophy came from popular songs. Pierre never listened to popular music – he was too old, too fastidious and too franco-phone – and possibly familiar Beatles lines like "Give peace a chance" or "Love is all you need" struck him as both profound and original, although even the Beatles had given up on the Maharishi. Pierre had been too immersed in Quebec politics to pick up the rhetoric of the New Left, which Margaret knew by heart, and while he had travelled around the world, he had never camped out on the beige broadloom of West Vancouver. Margaret's West Coast culture was as exotic to him as Shangri-La, and gazing into Margaret's blue eyes, square Pierre fell for it all.

That much of Margaret's mysticism came from marijuana seems to have escaped Pierre. He knew that she smoked pot, she talked about it all the time, but Pierre did not smoke at all, and if he ever tried a joint his only "high" would have been a sore throat. Pierre disapproved of her smoking – it was politically explosive as well as personally repugnant – and Margaret, anxious to please, learned to conceal the extent of her dope habit. Did Pierre not realize that this free, flakey flower child was frequently stoned out of her tree?

Pierre was embarrassed to be seen with a flower child at official functins and he persuaded Margaret that she would be bored by old fogies. Another woman would have felt insulted, but Margaret fell happily into the role of "country mistress," the simple peasant girl who was too naive to function in Ottawa society, and she played it perfectly: the one time Pierre took Margaret to a ball she burst into tears because everyone stared at her. Intensely secretive by nature, Trudeau loved the clandestine and shocking nature of his *affaire* with Margaret, and so did she. Hiding like two giggling children at 24 Sussex or the prime minister's summer residence at Harrington Lake, they could play out their most intimate fantasies far from the world's prying eyes, and when it came right down to it, Margaret and Pierre had a terrific time in bed: for all the harsh things she later said, Margaret always praised Pierre's sexual energy, and her own.

"She touched me," Pierre said to explain why he fell in love with Margaret. Uninhibited and earthy – she had adopted the counter-culture's profanity too – Margaret touched Pierre's repressed psyche, the sensual, irrational, impulsive aspects of his personality he had severely disciplined and denied since he was a child. Pierre attempted to deny Margaret too:

for ten months they fought, fucked, split up, made up, dated others –
Barbra Streisand made Margaret scream with jealousy – cried, courted and
finally, at Harrington Lake, Pierre said, "Well, Margaret, perhaps we
should talk about getting married?"

"In a second I was on my feet flinging my arms around him," Margaret said. "I leaped from the rock I was perched on into the lake where I
swam around and around in circles like a frenzied dolphin."

She was too excited to hear what Pierre said next: Margaret must
promise to be faithful, give up drugs and stop being flighty. She must, in
other words, stop being all those irrational, erotic things that had made
Pierre fall in love with her. It seemed, at the time, easy enough to do, and
Margaret would have promised anything. Margaret made no demands of
Pierre, and he offered no concessions.

"I believe that marriage is a regressive institution," Trudeau said in
1975, four years into his own marriage. "One recreates the dependency
relationship *vis-à-vis* one's parents, one's father if one is a girl, one's mother
if a boy. It was a good thing I did not marry sooner because I was very
domineering and doubtless would have wanted to remake my wife – which
is to say, destroy her personality."

That Trudeau could speak these self-satisfied words, in the past tense,
at a time when he knew that both Margaret and his marriage were deeply
troubled, indicates that although he loved his wife, he was unconsciously
acting out the Pygmalion role he so abhorred.

Pierre locked Margaret away in a big stone house the way his father
had locked his mother away in a big brick house; that, in Pierre's experience, was what a man did with a wife. And the wife stayed there: she bore
children, went to mass, served tea to friends. Charlie Trudeau, Pierre's
tough, street-smart father, was seldom home, and Pierre followed suit: he
warned Margaret that he was "extremely solitary by nature."

Charlie Trudeau died in 1935 when Pierre was only fifteen, leaving his
wife and three children a fortune estimated between three and five million
dollars. Handsome, swarthy, a hard drinker and a fast talker, Charlie was
a character right out of a gangster movie, a gambler and a hustler who
punched out anybody who crossed him. Charlie got his start in business
running a chain of service stations; he sold out to Imperial Oil for more
than a million dollars, then speculated in apartment houses, mining stocks
and pro baseball. Aggressive and athletic, Charlie Trudeau insisted that his
shy, intellectual eldest son play sports – Charlie was a sometime boxing

promoter – and taught Pierre to affect a lippy, dead-end kid contempt for "les snobs."

Pierre was in awe of his father, and terrified. "Charlie could be brutal," recalled a family friend. "For his family, his vivacity had a dark side. When he was in a rage, or got roaring drunk, it was hard to stand up to him." Pierre himself spoke of the beatings he received from his father. "Actually I didn't like him very much," he said to one friend. "You never knew what to expect."

Was Grace Trudeau also beaten by her abusive husband? And did her teenage son devote himself to body-building, not, as commonly believed, to please his father, but to defend his mother? Pierre was always extremely protective of his mother, and his fear of marriage may have been rooted in traumatic memories of his father's violence towards her. Margaret's vulnerability and her resemblance to his mother would have aroused Pierre's desire to shelter her, and Margaret's professed interest in mysticism would have led him to believe that, like his mother, Margaret would spend her days in prayer. The catch was, of course, that Pierre was no longer the son; he was now cast as Charlie Trudeau.

Margaret gave birth to a healthy son on Christmas Day, 1971. Justin Trudeau was the first baby born to a prime minister's wife in more than one hundred years – Mary Macdonald had been the only previous one – and Margaret, the child bride, re-emerged as Margaret, Madonna. It appeared that the playboy prime minister had found a paragon of domestic docility, and that a characteristically banal Canadian Camelot was emerging on the Rideau Canal. Trudeau himself adopted an entirely new and unpleasant persona: he was now Papa, a scowling, puritan, tight-fisted disciplinarian who treated the public like recalcitrant children, and by the election of 1972 he was intensely unpopular.

In the middle of the campaign, cynical reporters were dumbfounded when Margaret suddenly jumped on the press bus. "Hi!" she said brightly, "I hear you have fun back here." This was the first opportunity any of them had had to exchange a word with the prime minister's wife, and not only did the Madonna speak, she launched into a long, rambling rap. "I'm free," she said. "I'm not public property, I'm not my husband's property either. We're on different trips. The way he is running the country has nothing to do with me." And as for being "first lady," Margaret shrugged: "I abdicate. Anybody who wants it can take it." Was she happy being a mother? "Oh, I'm just Old Mother Earth," she laughed.

Margaret's garrulous behaviour was disconcerting, and her words caught the attention of a Toronto psychiatrist, Mary McEwan, who perceived a deep resentment of politics and dissatisfaction with both her marriage and the role she was playing. "Her description of herself as Old Mother Earth is alarming," McEwan later told *Chatelaine*. "Anyone who visualizes herself as Old Mother Earth in her twenties is having problems." McEwan also noticed that Margaret loved an audience: "She has very little desire to be a private person. A person who wants to be inconspicuous, conforms."

Margaret's little gig in the spotlight was just a flip of the mermaid's tail before she submerged again, but eight months later, pregnant with her second child, she reappeared in her Earth Mother costume, talking serenely about growing organic vegetables and making her own baby food, praising life with Pierre as a bucolic idyll free of the boring constraints of conventional society. Her manner and appearance conformed so perfectly to the Arcadian fantasy that it seemed, however, unrealistic in light of Pierre's personality, perfectly credible. Only the Trudeaus' small circle of friends knew that it was really Margaret who was boring – her single topic of conversation was herself – and nobody but Margaret knew that in November 1972 she had hidden a note in her drawer: "I am so lonely. I should be happy. I am married to a man who loves me and I have a wonderful baby. But I am terribly unhappy."

"I have to have a fantasy in my life; I can't long survive without one," Margaret wrote in *Beyond Reason* and her fantasies came close to schizophrenia: "It wasn't long before my childhood habit to be secretive, to split myself into separate isolated parts, each carefully locked away from the other, began again with a vengeance," she said of becoming the prime minister's wife. "I became two different people."

She became, in fact, several different people, a chameleon whose personality was dissociated and unpredictable. Margaret acted out her fantasies, and as soon as one psychodrama bored her, she invented another; her Earth Mother incarnation was followed by a phase as Perfect Wife, during which she sat at Norah Michener's feet studying the fine points of protocol, invited other wives to tea and redecorated the house in expensive West Van style. In 1974, bored by playing dolls and jealous of Pierre's power trip, Margaret reinvented herself as Politician: hair neatly bobbed, dressed in matronly skirts, she accompanied Pierre everywhere during the summer election campaign, still breast feeding her five-month-old son, Sasha, her second child born on Christmas Day.

By now Pierre had been written off as an arrogant snob, a Marie Antoinette who greeted a group of demonstrators on Parliament Hill with: "Eat shit." He had mismanaged the economy and indulged a passion for technocracy that was both inefficient and ruinously expensive. His insistence on making Canada bilingual, while popular in Quebec, created controversy and antagonism in other parts of the country, and he seemed indifferent to the problems of minorities, women and the poor.

Apprehensive that Pierre would lose the election, Margaret thought, "if I fought the election by his side, demonstrating . . . how happy we were together and what a devoted family man he was, Pierre would have a better chance."

Thousands of people flocked out to see her, and when Margaret stood on a platform beside her embarrassed husband speaking tremulously about how Pierre was "a beautiful guy who taught me a lot about loving," the laughing audience took her to their hearts. Margaret seemed so innocent, so honest, the old Philosopher King must be a sweetie after all.

Margaret knew she was a hit – she predicted the Liberal majority more accurately than Trudeau's advisers did – and by the end of the campaign she was dreaming of running in the next election in her father's old North Vancouver seat. But the morning after the election, Margaret crashed:

"I sat having my breakfast on the porch of the freedom room watching the white sailing boats in the sparkling bay. I waited for a phone call of thanks, of praise, of something, from someone. I waited, and I waited. It was absurd of me – everyone was exhausted, why should they have thought of me? But something in me broke that day. I felt that I had been used."

Margaret was no longer in love with Pierre, and had not been for a long time. As with her earlier multiple selves, she had believed her passionate country mistress fantasy only as long as it was unfulfilled: once she married her extremely famous dream husband, Margaret woke up, as she did the morning after the election, alienated and depressed. No wonder she was unhappy: she had fallen in love with a figment of her imagination, a chimera, like Yves Lewis, and she had married her father.

James Sinclair was forty when Margaret was born on September 10, 1948, and he was fifteen years older than her mother. He was handsome, domineering, intimidating, a hard-working, puritanical Scottish immi-

"Pierre is a beautiful guy."

grant who had worked his way up, first to the Cabinet of Louis St. Laurent where he served for seven years, then to the presidency of a large cement company. Margaret recalled her childhood as "curiously barren": her father disapproved of almost everything that mattered to girls – boys, rock music, clothes – and Margaret found herself competing fiercely with her sisters for his affection. "There hadn't been much laughter at home," she says in *Beyond Reason*, "nor touching nor demonstrative love; and certainly no praise."

Margaret caught her father's attention by acting out: "Dad and I fought, about the boys, about the rock music, later about politics, values and money." Margaret was so rebellious that she moved out of the house when she was sixteen, and she never went back for more than a pit stop.

Although the Liberals won a 140-seat majority with Margaret's assistance, the victory left her crushed. "Something in me broke that day."

Her anger paid off: when her father forbade her to go to the University of California at Berkeley, Margaret threw such a tantrum that he bought her a car to drive to Simon Fraser in nearby Burnaby. After she moved out, he gave her such a generous living allowance that other students knew she was rich; he took her to Tahiti that fateful Christmas—Margaret was vacationing *en famille* with her parents and two sisters—and her trip to Morocco was his graduation present.

The more trouble Margaret made, the more her father attempted to placate her. She was, as she said later about herself, "a spoiled bitch." Margaret learned that she could manipulate a much older man because he loved her, and that she could depend on his financial support no matter how much she angered him. Margaret was always too busy being free to get a job, and her freedom was financed by Dad.

In her husband's house Margaret apparently behaved much as she had in her father's house; she fought bitterly with the cooks and the steward, sulked when she didn't get her way, ran up enormous bills and quarrelled with Pierre over money. As was true of Laurier, Pierre's domestic habits were monastic, and since he associated his wealth with his frightening father, he was notoriously parsimonious. Pierre gave Margaret half his salary; it was never enough. While Margaret despised materialism in the Establishment, she demanded luxury for herself.

In the summer of 1974, Margaret ran away to Paris to find Yves Lewis. She pretended that it was just another of her "freedom trips," a week away by herself, and Pierre had gone fishing with Justin. Yves was not at the address she had cherished for five years, and Margaret moved on to Crete, where she camped out on the beach and passed the days in "a romantic reverie, a soothing daydream of almost adolescent romance," probably fueled by a good stash of hash. She was incommunicado for two weeks.

Pierre was worried, but he had always told Margaret: "Do what you want, be yourself." Margaret, who had always defined herself in terms of other people's expectations, had no idea who she was or what she wanted, and Pierre, by way of advice, was always offering her another challenge – "Why don't you read Plato?" – that intensified her anxiety. His job also provided rich material for her day-dreams.

Although Margaret depicted her life at 24 Sussex as a suffocating grind of official chores, it was anything but. She had blissful summers at Harrington Lake and exotic Caribbean vacations; she met hundreds of celebrities, including Prince Charles, with whom she felt a strong rapport, and Cuban President Fidel Castro, whom she adored. Trudeau was a fringe member of the international Jet Set, a bizarre crowd of rich publicity-seekers whose sole function in life was to be themselves, and through Pierre's network of famous friends the ordinary girl from Vancouver, as Margaret liked to think of herself, entered America's dangerous *demimonde*.

One reason Trudeau guarded his privacy with the ferocity of a pit bull was that he didn't want to be photographed partying with people whose pictures appeared in *People* and *Playboy*, but Margaret didn't mind. Stars like Elizabeth Taylor had been an influential part of her childhood: "I remember getting mad at my sister Janet because whenever we played paper dolls she always got to have Elizabeth Taylor and I had to play with

Debbie Reynolds. I wanted to play the femme fatale, but I always had to be the goody-goody.'' Soon after returning from Crete in a "high and edgy state," Margaret sat next to a "high-powered American" at a New York dinner party:

"I fell in love. It was sudden, it was fantastic. I became like someone possessed. We danced all evening. I cried all night. When we got back to Ottawa the next day I raced upstairs to our private refrigerator and drank off the half bottle of vodka I found there. Pierre, who caught me at it, was appalled. 'Have you been unfaithful to me in Paris?' he kept on asking. 'Have you? Have you?'''

The screaming escalated. Margaret became more and more violent and distraught. She flew out of control, and, in a frenzy of rage, tore the words, "la raison devant la passion" off the personalized quilt artist Joyce Wieland had made for Trudeau. Pierre was cold as ice. "You're sick," he said.

The man was apparently US Senator Edward Kennedy, but it doesn't matter since the *affaire* seems to have happened entirely in Margaret's mind. Now she was "frightened, lonely and very mad." Another husband might have sat her down and said, "Okay, lets talk about it." Another husband might have wept and stormed until their anger blew itself out. Pierre advised Margaret to see a psychiatrist.

Reluctantly, Margaret checked into the Royal Victoria Hospital in Montreal. Like Edna Diefenbaker, she felt she didn't belong there. Margaret flushed her tranquillizers down the toilet and secretly brewed herbal tea from marijuana. After a week she confronted reporters gathered on the grounds, telling them: "Please go away, I am suffering from severe emotional stress." Then she called her security guard, checked out and went home with a new personality.

Margaret as Ophelia appeared a few days later on CTV's "Canada A.M." in a long, sympathetic interview with Carole Taylor. Gaunt, timid and sad, Margaret sat on the grass at 24 Sussex and talked about her life in Elsinore. It was a disturbing performance. While Margaret spoke in her soft little voice of how constant surveillance and the stress of public expectations had led to her depression, her manner remained eerily composed. No skipping about with rosemary sprigs: Margaret sat absolutely still. She wore an expensive silk shirt and her hair was brushed into a smooth helmet. Ophelia was on TV, acting a role.

Margaret concealed her marital problems and minimized the seriousness of her illness: who wouldn't sympathize with a young mother trying to find herself? She received bouquets of flowers and letters praising her honesty. She called off her "*affaire*" with the high-powered American and took up photography. Early in 1975 she became pregnant again, and when Michel was born in October she seemed happy, healthy and perfectly reconciled to her public role. Only the wistful expression on Pierre's face and Margaret's strained smile revealed that their bruised marriage had not healed; Margaret and Pierre retreated into separate solitudes, and as Pierre became cold and distant, Margaret seems to have relied on prescription drugs and marijuana to control her anger and lift her out of depression.

Her career in photography was short-lived, although she studied hard with professional teachers who praised her ability. For several months Margaret schlepped around Ottawa in jeans and a headscarf draped with cameras like a donkey, yet she seemed more concerned with her image as Career Woman—she told a reporter that some day she expected to support Pierre – than with building a creative reputation. She failed to follow through on assignments, and infuriated the *paparrazi* by using her privileged status to muscle in on celebrities for exclusive shots. As she grew bored with photography, she took an interest in day care – her nannies ran a small nursery in the basement of 24 Sussex – environmental causes and emotionally disturbed children.

When she jumped to her feet at a state banquet in Venezuela to sing a song to the president's wife, it seemed that Margaret had flipped out again, but she had really just jumped back into the spotlight. Back in Ottawa, she phoned in to a radio hotline show when she heard callers criticizing her and coined the phrase that made her immortal: "I'm more than just a rose in my husband's lapel!" Public opinion was hotly divided about Margaret. Was she honest, creative, spontaneous? Or was she egocentric, selfish, a pain in the neck? Margaret summoned journalists to 24 Sussex Drive to expound on her philosophy of life. "I live right now," she told *Saturday Night*'s Sandra Gwyn. "I don't care very much about yesterday. The only thing that exists is here. What happened yesterday didn't really exist. Any memory I may have of it is a distorted view at best and why rely on that now?" Gwyn decided that Margaret was "a bit of a bore." Ottawa reporter Judy Morrison encountered a distracted, dishevelled Cleopatra lounging in bed chain-smoking, periodically spraying the room with lilac air freshener to kill the smell: "When Pierre came home from the office he came up to me not to kiss me but to sniff me," Margaret said later.

On the night of March 4, 1977, her sixth wedding anniversary, Margaret Trudeau was seen at a secret Rolling Stones recording session in a Toronto nightclub. She was alone. When the *paparazzi* discovered that Margaret was staying at the same hotel as the Stones they jumped to the logical conclusion: Margaret had run off with a Stone. In fact, the Stones were embarrassed to find Margaret the Groupie among their entourage. Lead guitarist Keith Richards was facing trial in Toronto for possession of heroin, and all the band needed to party it up was the prime minister's wife with a couple of joints and a Mountie.

The Stones didn't know, and neither did anyone else, that Pierre and Margaret had agreed to a ninety-day trial separation and Margaret was, more or less, free. The Stones did know that she was being shadowed by a plain-clothes policeman, and they treated her with exquisite politeness. Whatever sex & drugs & rock & roll went down after their concerts, and it went down, went down, publicly at least, without Margaret, who had the sense to absent herself. She apparently spent most of the weekend playing with Richards' young son and, as she often did, writing letters to Yves, letters she never sent.

The youngest and most beautiful of the PM's wives, Margaret, as Pierre had predicted, was the first to split. Even after their separation became official in May, the Trudeaus played down its seriousness, saying that Margaret was simply pursuing a career in New York, and for two years Margaret continued to spend almost half her time in Ottawa, living in a suite of rooms on the top floor of 24 Sussex where she played the role of Mrs. Rochester, the madwoman in the attic in *Jane Eyre*.

It was a bizarre relationship. Margaret would join Pierre's guests for drinks before dinner, then retreat to her attic while they went out on the town, and she visited with Pierre while he dressed for a date, giggling while his new mistress cooled her heels downstairs. However, it enabled Margaret to stay close to her three children—Michel was not yet two when she left, Justin only five—and although she was attacked in the media for abandoning her children, she apparently spent more time with them than she had during her marriage.

Margaret also lived at 24 Sussex because she had nowhere else to go. She had no job, no income, no apartment and no divorce: Margaret and Pierre did not divorce until 1984. Pierre gave Margaret room and board in Ottawa but he called her bluff: Okay, if you want to be free, be *free*.

''Freedom's just another word for nothin' left to lose,'' the song says, and it's a line Margaret came to know by heart, the hard way. Whatever fantasy she may have had about the Stones, it didn't work out, and Margaret went to New York, where she had a photo assignment from *People* magazine. Margaret's appeal to *People* was her network of contacts among the reclusive *haute monde*, royals like Prince Charles who shunned the tabloid press, but now that Margaret was no longer the prime minister's wife, access to these people instantly vanished, and so did Margaret's assignments. *People* was much more interested in Margaret herself, and Margaret obligingly babbled: "If I don't feel like wearing a bra, I don't wear one. I'd never let my nipples show at a state function, though – I'd be frightened the old men would have heart attacks."

Margaret's nipples were not in a class with Elizabeth Taylor's, and at the age of thirty Margie Sinclair was trying to reassure herself that she was still the "cutest" in a league where she couldn't compete. Skinny and so knock-kneed that she usually wore jeans or long skirts to hide her legs, Margaret dissected her body as a coroner would conduct an autopsy, examining each part in turn until she finally decided that her cute little bum was the source of her sex appeal. Why not make the most of it? Margaret would become a Movie Star.

She made two terrible movies – neither was ever released – and discovered how tough it could be to work for a living. Over Christmas 1978, Margaret and Pierre apparently came close to a reconciliation: Pierre promised to leave politics, naively believing that when Margaret told *People* magazine, "I've had enough of being public property," she actually meant it, but his domestic scenario, an isolated house in the Laurentians, filled Margaret with dread. "I liked star status," she confessed later, "not as a wife but in my own right."

Margaret was no longer a wife, and she wasn't a star, but she could enjoy star status by hanging out at a Manhattan disco, Studio 54, and if she got her picture in the tabloids often enough she would be famous. She was photographed with all the Beautiful People, Andy Warhol, Liza Minelli, Truman Capote, although Margaret was so naive she didn't realize that some of her boyfriends were gay, and she forgot that fame lasts fifteen minutes.

Pictures of Margaret partying half-naked – one photo showed her bare crotch – enraged Liberals, who interpreted her behaviour as a deliberate attack on Pierre, even an attempt to bring down the government. The feeling was mutual: Margaret apparently told friends that Pierre had given her a black eye, but others claimed she had come back from New York with the shiner. Margaret was mad as hell, but for all her indiscretions she never openly criticized Pierre, and her exhibitionism won him widespread sympathy as the cuckolded husband. It was not a role to Trudeau's taste, but he played it with grace and dignity, possibly realizing, as Margaret as yet did not, that her fury was directed at herself.

Margaret was almost suicidally self-destructive. She had cast away everything she loved, and observing Margaret's "love affair with that faceless horde of interviewers and photographers who exploited and tormented her," Philip Marchand commented in *Chatelaine*: "It was a relationship in which the media magnified and devoured her. In return, she was like a woman who discovers the masochistic pleasures of giving herself, without restraints or limits, to a lover who despises her."

Margaret found a lot of lovers to despise her. In London she was trashed by a rock singer, a "lean, rich, muscular, sexy cowboy, a romantic wounded rebel, a medieval cavalier," who abused her and took her money; she had a brief fling – it started in the back seat of a Daimler – with movie star Jack Nicholson, until Angelica Huston turned up, and Margaret got the gate: "I felt instantly crushed. I felt a fool. I had almost managed to convince myself that eventually I could work my way into his heart. That I was so wrong was one more blow, reinforcing Pierre's bitter words about people using me, and how I would never find happiness with another man, that I was too immature, too narcissistic to have a true relationship with anyone. He had said it, and now I was tempted to agree. I was doomed."

In the showbiz salons of Belgravia and Manhattan the ordinary girl from West Vancouver was out-classed: "I couldn't prevent myself from feeling relatively deprived – some part of me has always wanted to be super-rich, to own twenty-nine pairs of shoes and drive a Bentley. So I started to resent Pierre, his money and his meanness, the way he seemed to have taken the children. I grew increasingly hostile and paranoid and a huge rage built up inside me. My physical health was rapidly deteriorating. I was troubled by headaches and an ulcer, and it got so bad there was almost nothing I could eat without pain. In my misery I began to convince myself Pierre had pushed me out, that he wanted me gone, dead."

In a pathetic cheesecake photo in *Maclean's* magazine, Margaret looked like a Holocaust victim. She was emaciated, her face skeletal, her hair a tangled rats' nest. Her lips were drawn back from her teeth in a death mask, and the dark smudges around her eyes betrayed the real cause of her distress: cocaine.

In 1979 cocaine was still a taboo word in Canada, and not once in all the heated public debate about Margaret's outrageous behaviour was it ever suggested that she was a drug addict. "There were many times when I would have liked to blame all my mistakes on cocaine," she wrote sadly in *Consequences*. "I can't, in all truth, do that. But it had a terrible, negative effect on my life – I found it made me boastful, obnoxious and argumentative. What was so seductive about it, after I had been on it for a while, was its secretive side compared to marijuana, which makes the room reek. But it was its insidious accessibility that was to be my downfall. I had no difficulty getting it, no matter where I was."

Margaret had been initiated to morphine and tranquillizers in hospital, and in New York cocaine was passed around after dinner with the brandy: Studio 54 resembled a chemical laboratory. Margaret was heavily into drugs before she left Pierre, and after, to freeze the pain, she mixed herself a lethal cocktail: "With the coke I took Valium, coke to get me up, Valium to bring me down again. Only Valium did more than than bring me down. It made me low and depressed – far lower and more depressed than I had ever been naturally – so that I actually *needed* the cocaine to become exuberant and euphoric once more."

She supported her habit, and herself, by living off the land, and, in a penultimate act of self-immolation, by writing, or, more accurately, talking a book. For her scandalous memoirs, Margaret was paid an advance of $50,000 by Britain's Paddington Press; it was a fortune for a woman who never had a cent of her own, and Margaret blew it in an orgy of clothes, champagne, caviar and cocaine. After all, the book would be a best seller, a movie, and Paddington predicted that her royalties would run into the millions. Over a period of months, Margaret talked to British writer Caroline Moorehead, a woman she pays tribute to as "my disciplinarian, my lie detector," and the interview sessions unwittingly became a form of psychotherapy. Margaret was terrified of psychiatrists and lied to them shamelessly, but a book would be *hers*, like a baby, and the part of Margaret's identity that always remained secure was the conviction that she was a good mother. Moorehead knew nothing about Margaret or Canada – the book is full of absurd errors – but her probing questions forced Margaret to analyze her actions and emotions. *Beyond Reason* is self-serving and full of fantasies, but by the end Margaret *knew* they were fantasies, and her book rings true as a self-portrait of an anguished, intelligent woman struggling towards maturity.

Beyond Reason was published in April 1979 at the height of the Canadian election campaign, and Liberals predicted that it would destroy Trudeau's chances for re-election. In fact, Margaret's portrait of Pierre as Bluebeard jibed perfectly with the image Trudeau had presented to the Canadian public since his marriage: he apparently treated his wife exactly the way he treated everybody else, with cold contempt, so what else was new? *Beyond Reason* only reinforced the public's negative feeling, but it blew the lid off 24 Sussex Drive, making the prime minister's private life as much public property as his political life, and it shattered the plastic image of the Barbie/Madonna/Earth Mother prime minister's wife. Margaret, it turned out, had repeatedly screamed to Pierre, "Fuck you! Fuck you! Fuck *you*!" in front of a crowd of Japanese dignitaries in Tokyo. The incident had so shocked reporters that they covered it up, but in *Beyond Reason* Margaret blew their cover herself. "It wasn't easy to live that one down," she admitted. "The trouble was I needed direction, not freedom. My outbursts were cries for attention." After one "truly sleazy evening" in New York, Margaret woke up in a litter of empty glasses, cold, desolate and alone: "Looking out the window as dawn came up, all I could see were the garbage cans in the basement area eleven floors below me. I covered sheets of paper with a desperate scrawl: 'Help me, please.'"

Her public anger was a release, and a relief; a lot of wives would like to tell their husbands to "fuck you" from time to time, but feel guilty, and don't. But why was Margaret so angry that she literally threw herself over walls?

"The last time I saw Ryan I had to climb over his back wall because he wouldn't let me in the front door," Margaret told *Playgirl* reporter Celeste Fremon in a humiliating account of her brief affair with Hollywood star Ryan O'Neal. "See these big bruises on my arms? I got so *angry* at Ryan, I wanted to beat him up. But when I hit him, all I did was just bruise *myself*."

Fremon met Margaret in Los Angeles, expecting to interview her about *Beyond Reason*. Fremon encountered a wild-eyed Ancient Mariner in red ankle-strap shoes who plucked her by the sleeve and began compulsively to tell the story of her own voyage on the slimy sea of drugs and despair. Like Coleridge's Wedding Guest, Fremon listened in fascination and horror, her tape recorder running all the time.

Margaret was high, and in the throes of another fantasy: "I'd *like* to remarry very much," she said, laughing. "I've scared most of the men in this town half to death since I've been here. They just *run* when they see me coming. They take one look and think, 'Un oh, this lady's desperate to find herself a *home*!'"

Margaret was desperate, and, she knew, very close to hitting bottom. All her fantasies had turned to ashes. Yves Lewis had committed suicide the year before, and on the night of May 22, 1979 Pierre Trudeau lost the election. Margaret spent election night in New York kicking up her heels at Studio 54. Photos of her grinning from ear to ear angered the Liberals, who liked to think that the disaster was all Margaret's fault, but a few days later, sick in bed with the flu, Margaret told Celeste Fremon a different story: "I cried, cried, cried when I realized that Pierre had been defeated. All I could think was, 'Oh, I've lost my nursery.'"

Margaret had lost her home, the attic at 24 Sussex Drive, and she was no longer the prime minister's wife: "I felt so angry and depressed, I've never danced so hard. Just to go out and *smile* and *dance*! In my pink pedal pushers and m' dancing shoes."

She was free at last, and she was nobody. She fell into despair, obsessed with violence, death and the smell of blood. Only now was she able to blurt out to Fremon the terrible secret she had been hiding from so long:

"This is a story that Pierre has asked me never to tell, but since he's no longer my husband, we're going to get it straight. In my first year of university, I was dating the captain of the football team, and one day we just went a little too far, and I got pregnant. I was seventeen and didn't know what to do. I couldn't go to my mother, I couldn't go anywhere. So my hairdresser gave me a slip of paper with the name of a doctor who had become an alcoholic and lost his practice. The doctor didn't even give me a Valium. He just took the knife and *ground* that baby out of me. So I went home. I went to bed and didn't tell anybody. I told no one. The next night I was working at the Hudson's Bay Company and I was losing a lot of blood. I was kind of hurting, but I was being brave. So on my break I went down and ordered a pound of jelly beans. And while she handed me the jelly beans, I felt, PLOP, I felt the baby come out, because that's the kind of abortion I'd had, where you just have the cramps until the fetus drops out. So I went up and flushed it in the toilet of the Hudson's Bay Company bathroom. And from then on I knew something about life. I don't know what it is that I learned, but I learned something very, very important. Very important."

Margaret went through her abortion completely on her own, and her secret left her with a crippling burden of guilt. For a girl raised in a Calvinist ethic, a girl who got pregnant was a whore, and Trudeau's own puritanism probably reinforced her feeling of inferiority. Margaret's teen-age pregnancy makes sense of her compulsive promiscuity, her ambivalent attitude towards men and her need to display herself, a scarlet woman, in the public eye. It also explains her secretiveness, her fear of power – she was too scared even to talk to her mother – and her intense dislike of women she considered "goody-goody." Margaret was a beautiful woman who feared that she was ugly. She was always trying to please, and when that didn't work she pretended she was someone else, an innocent virgin who had her whole life to live over again, differently, but she always ended up with the captain of the football team feeling used, degraded and hurt.

Playgirl published the interview in September 1979. Margaret's confessions created a wave of scandal and disgust across Canada, but Margaret was okay, she had nothing left to lose. "I don't want to die," she told Fremon at the end of the interview. "I don't want to be alone anymore with my pain. I don't want to die alone. I want to be helped. I don't want to have to hide, hide my pain. I don't want to lie anymore. I want it straight, and I want it clear, and I want to understand that this is life, and it ain't easy. I want to live. Perhaps in defeat – in de feet, in de head – in defeat one learns how to win. Perhaps when you hit the bottom, that's when you're given grace."

Margaret was given grace, and strength, as well as her sense of humour. "I have to really clean up my life and take care of myself," she said. And she did. She returned to Ottawa, now just another single mother, and with a $60,000 payment from Paddington Press, she bought a modest brick house and arranged to share custody of the boys with Pierre. She got off cocaine, apparently with the aid of lithium and Tofranil, drugs prescribed by a psychiatrist to make her eat and sleep until she turned into a vegetable, then she flushed them down the toilet too: "It was the hardest thing I have ever done. I sweated constantly; I threw up; I had diarrhea; I shook, first with cold, then with heat. I felt dizzy, weak, paranoid. And then one morning I woke up feeling better."

Things went better for Pierre too. He had decided to retire as Liberal leader when in December 1979 the Conservative government was suddenly defeated in the House. Pierre stayed on, and in February 1980 won a stunning election victory. "Welcome to the eighties," he grinned. The next four years were the most productive of Trudeau's political career: he won a resounding vote of confidence for federalism in Quebec, and he patriated the Canadian constitution. In June 1984 Trudeau retired and divorced Margaret.

Paddington Press went bankrupt, owing Margaret more than $250,000 in back royalties. She got a job as a hostess on a television morning show, and in 1984 she married Ottawa real estate dealer Fried Kemper. She gave birth to another son, Kyle, and, at forty, to a daughter, Alicia. Margaret the Mad Housewife was just Margaret the Housewife after all, a middle-aged mother of five content to cook, ski and play bridge.

In the spring of 1990 an Ottawa newspaper published an old photograph of a cute little curly-haired girl tiptoeing through the tulips on Parliament Hill. Who was it? Who else? Margaret Sinclair Trudeau Kemper posed for the same shot again wearing a little white dress and smiling nervously at the camera. It was just another flip of the mermaid's tail. Peace, Margaret.

CHAPTER 14

The

Education

of

Ms. McTeer

$\mathcal{S}$OME WOMEN BECOME FAMOUS because they change their names, Maureen McTeer became famous because she didn't. Maureen is a feminist, and she was a militant, twenty-one-year-old feminist when she married Joe Clark, the Conservative member of parliament for Rocky Mountain, Alberta, on June 30, 1973. It was becoming fashionable, even *de rigeur* for young married women to retain their names if they had a career, and Maureen intended to practise law. She didn't want to be known as the "wife of" an MP at law school: "I felt it was something private. If the professors didn't like the Progressive Conservatives, it would have aroused great hostility towards my marks, which were already bad enough."

Ms. McTeer would have studied law in total obscurity except that in the spring of 1976, when she was in her third year, her husband Mr. Clark decided to contest the leadership of the Conservative Party. Joe Clark was thirty-six and looked ten years younger, an amiable, gawky stringbean from the west with a weak chin and a baritone voice that seemed to big for his body. He had been elected for the first time in 1972 and was still virtually unknown outside the party, but he represented the reform ideology of the retiring leader, Robert Stanfield, and had developed a network of powerful friends within the party's hierarchy. Joe was everybody's second choice, and to the nation's astonishment he was elected Conservative leader in June 1976, beating out Claude Wagner, Brian Mulroney and the first woman to contest the leadership of a national party, Flora Macdonald.

Clark was such a dark horse that he was laughingly dubbed "Joe Who?" by the press. The epithet did not sit well with Maureen, a passionate Progressive Conservative who took her politics, like her feminism, straight-up. "All this 'Joe Who?' nonsense arose because the press had not done their work," she says. "One national reporter said to me, 'I have to interview your husband. Where was he born?' I thought, 'This is a leadership convention. If little ol' me, with no pretense at political smarts here, knows that we had a good chance, where are all these great political strategists who are supposed to be telling you what's happening, why it's happening, and they don't even know where he's from!' They don't know who I am. 'So you're Mrs. Clark?' 'Well, no, my name's Maureen McTeer.' Aha! Because they had nothing else to write about that became the issue.''

And a huge issue it was. Conservatives, large and small-C, sat up in shock and cried: ''First Margaret, now a libber!'' Typical was the response in Maureen's own family: ''I come from a very traditional family, Roman Catholic. My father was a dreadful chauvinist. He could *never* understand why I didn't change my name. It was beyond him. Years later, when he was dying, he sent me a birthday card, 'Mrs. Joe Clark.' ''

Joe Who?

"Is Maureen Clark a Bitch?" shrilled a Canadian men's magazine, quoting Quebec Premier René Lévesque describing Maureen as "a very attractive, bitchy woman in an elegant sort of way." Ms. McTeer inadvertently raised the spectre of the Spinster, and now the castrating bitch had sneaked into the very centre of power! In the collective subconscious, Ms. McTeer was immediately identified with contraception, abortion, divorce and all the other threatening implications of a self-sufficient, independent woman, and this woman *had a man*. Joe Clark took the brunt of the hysteria and paranoia about his wife's separate identity: Who was boss! Who wore the pants in the family? Couldn't this guy even get his wife's *respect*?

"That there could be an equal partnership in marriage was never even part of the possibility of discussion," Maureen sighs. "To have a strong woman you need a *very* strong man."

The idea of equal partnership came as a surprise to the Conservative Party. Joe Clark had been elected leader, not Joe Clark/Maureen McTeer, and although she had worked hard on his campaign – Joe said he couldn't have won without her – there had been no assumption that Maureen would be sharing equally his political responsibilities. Was this going to be a dual leadership? And if so, what were Maureen's qualifications? She had been a prominent Young Conservative and had worked hard in the party's backrooms for ten years – she and Joe met when she became his constituency assistant in 1972 – but she was still only twenty-four and had never held public office.

Alarm over Maureen's role was compounded by her physical presence. She was a big, broad-shouldered young woman with a square jaw, piercing blue eyes and a way of crossing her arms across her chest as if to say, "Okay, so what?" Joe, on the other hand, was self-effacing, easy going and cursed with a nervous laugh that made him sound like a nerd. "Clark looked uncomfortable with his own body," Jeffrey Simpson observed in his book on the Clark era, *Discipline of Power*. "He carried himself awkwardly, his arms pendulating in unnaturally long swings. When he ran, which was seldom, he looked like a wounded heron . . . Clark's hands were always busy in uncommon gesticulations, as if they were uncertain of their proper role at the end of his arms. Clark had long, bony fingers and his most instinctive mannerism – thrusting his left hand forward with fingers outstretched but slightly crooked – made the hand look like a chicken's foot scratching aimlessly at the air." Uncoordinated and unathletic, Joe suffered from coming from cowboy country, where men were men and smelled like horses, and because Joe did not live up to the stereotype of the Bud Man, his manhood was suspect: a newspaper cartoon depicted a butch Maureen riding Joe like a broken nag. Maureen, not Joe, appeared to be the dominant personality; she radiated confidence and determination and she didn't take any "crap" from the press.

"Next to the Canadian Bar Association, the media are the most *reactionary* people I have ever met!" she says. There were as many Bud Men in the press corps as in the Conservative Party, and their *machismo* was insulted when Maureen took part in Joe's press conferences, corrected his French and used the word "we" when discussing party policy. Never before had a leader's wife acted as a partner, an executive assistant or a spokesperson, and Maureen's personal opinions favouring access to contraception and abortion were controversial. Maureen smashed through the wall that had traditionally barred wives from expressing political opinions or taking an active role in making policy. There was blood everywhere, and most of it was Joe's.

Joe became The Wimp, the hapless, hag-ridden, hare-brained Dagwood Bumstead of the daily Ottawa comic strip. Joe was too raw, too straight, too nice a guy to know how to deal with assassination by ridicule, and the more hurt and helpless he appeared, the more vulnerable he became. "It was a horrendous time," Maureen recalls. "Joe could do nothing right. There was an entrenched view of leadership that was defined by Pierre Trudeau." Maureen had played hockey as a girl and her first instinct was to bodycheck Joe's enemies into the boards.

"I am an aggressive defender of those whom I love," she says stubbornly. It wasn't just that Maureen didn't suffer fools, she had to smarten them up. She lacked Agnes Macphail's sharp wit and the easy camaraderie that enabled Agnes to deal with "the boys"; Ms. McTeer came on like a cross between Florence Nightingale and Germaine Greer, and the more she intervened "to take the heat from Joe," the more wimpish he seemed.

As Joe's popularity plummeted, the Conservative Party put heavy pressure on Maureen: "They said, 'We're going to lose the next election if you don't change your name." She started calling herself Maureen McTeer Clark. Nobody could get it right. "Finally I said to my husband, 'Who am I here? This is ridiculous.' He said, 'Maureen, can you just call yourself one thing and leave it at that? I don't want to talk about this issue any more. Let's just be consistent.' So after a year I said, 'Forget it, come on,

Joe, I'm going to use my name, you can use your name, I know I'm married to you.' He said, 'Fine, let's just get rid of the issue.' We never did, did we?''

If Pierre Trudeau was Joe's *bête noir*, Margaret Trudeau was Maureen's. Margaret had made her marriage fair game for the media, and by giving birth to two sons on Christmas Day, had set an impossible standard for her successor. Maureen's first child was due on Hallowe'en. ''I said to my doctor, I will hold on until November 1, or I will have her early because I can see the press, the press will say: 'Two angels and a witch.' It will be seen as one more example of our incompetence. My doctor thought I had taken leave of my senses. Is this woman nuts? But that was the level of criticism we were forced to bear.''

Catherine Clark was born on November 6, 1976. It had been a hard pregnancy, and between morning sickness and Joe's leadership campaign, Maureen flunked third year law. She was humiliated – she had never failed at anything in her life before – and determined not to give up. ''I want that piece of paper!'' she told Bonnie Buxton from *Chatelaine* magazine. ''It's like stopping building a house when you're almost through. There's a certain respectability to a degree, an assumption that you must have something on the ball because after all you're a lawyer, which is baloney. I've gotten over being angry, I've gotten over being disappointed and upset, and now I've just steeled myself to the boredom of another year at law school.''

Maureen was no scholar. She didn't go to university for intellectual discipline, or to blow her mind, she went for the ''piece of paper,'' her ticket to respectability, and she scrabbled through law by cramming and borrowing other students' notes. She disliked law; she wanted to take a job with a cable-television station, but Joe, who had twice failed to graduate from law school, persuaded her that a law degree was a wise investment. Ms. McTeer was basically trying to please her husband.

Joe was thirteen years older, Maureen's mentor as well as her husband, and while he verbally endorsed the idea of an equal partnership, he really expected his stressed-out student wife, the mother of his colicky infant daughter, to take up Olive Diefenbaker's immaculate mantle as the gracious *châtelaine* of Stornoway, the official residence of the leader of the Opposition.

''I suffered from shell shock for the first two weeks,'' Maureen says of her move to Stornoway. No wonder, Stornoway was a vast, empty barn

*Moving into
Stornoway, spying
something unpleasant?*

of a house, the ugly stepsister of 24 Sussex Drive and the victim of decades
of neglect. No politician wanted to be Opposition leader any longer than
he could help, so Stornoway was treated as a temporary camp site on the
way to power; if it looked too comfortable, people would assume that you
intended to stay there. Stornoway had been purchased by a trust company
in 1950, the same year as 24 Sussex, for considerably less money, and it
had not been gutted. It had also not been furnished.

The Clarks had enough furniture to fill a couple of upstairs rooms. That was it, and when it came to money, they didn't have a bean. Maureen was on the spot; Margaret Trudeau was spending a fortune sprucing up 24 Sussex, Maureen's budget was $15,000 and she had no time to fuss about interior design. Was Stornoway going to be another sign of incompetence?

Maureen, as usual, was aggressive: "I'm not into chintz. I like clean lines. I like very definitive statements in colour or art and that's how we decided to proceed." She hired a friend, architect Cecelia Humphreys, to take charge. Humphreys was even more aggressive. The walls of Stornoway's main rooms were painted dark shades of brown and hunter green, the hardwood floors were left bare, comfortable furniture was scrounged from government warehouses and the Art Bank provided a wealth of contemporary Canadian paintings. Humphrey's modern eclecticism shocked Old Ottawa – "Their sofa is navy blue *corduroy*, my dear!" – but Maureen was pleased, although the brown walls "were considered one more example of *my* eccentricity."

Stornoway came with no staff. For large parties Maureen was forced to rely on her family and the generosity of the Conservative matriarchy who catered and served and loaned her extra table-cloths, cutlery and glassware. She ran out of liquor and ice at her first reception for the press – shades of Olive! – but a friend ran off for more, and she shocked the establishment by serving *crudités* – "*Raw* veggies, my dear!" – to people who had lived for generations on crustless white-bread sandwiches. Maureen attempted to make a virtue out of necessity: "Because of the squeeze financially I think we're going to depend on a lot of informal things, buffet dinners, say, or a skating party where everyone comes in and there's a great big pot of baked beans and French bread . . ."

Beans! And over at Rideau Hall Lily Schreyer, the wife of the governor-general, was serving cabbage rolls and perogies! Things were getting out of hand. In the bitter Ottawa winters the Clarks kept their thermostat at a frigid sixty-two degrees and wore woolly sweaters to keep warm; they drove a beat-up Volvo and gasp! they bought their clothes on sale!

"I bought a number of things for the convention at one quarter of the original price," Maureen blithely told *Chatelaine*. "I like permanent press things – just spin 'em around in the dryer."

It was the Drip-Dry Decade, a black hole for fashion, but Mo and Joe, as they called themselves in those days, looked as though they shopped at a discount store. They didn't care, in fact they stated proudly that they were out to "deglamorize" the myth of political leader – they were just "ordinary Joes" doing a tough job. The Clarks established an image that was directly opposite to the Philosopher King and his Ophelia: Mo and Joe were Country & Western and a little bit corny.

Maureen deeply resented being cast as "hicks from the country," but it was true. When Joe took off on his first international tour he demonstrated so much innocence abroad that he looked like Elmer Fudd chasing the pesky wabbit, in this case his own lost luggage, and Maureen had never been anywhere except Joe's home town of High River, Alberta. The twang in her voice betrayed her Irish origins in the Ottawa valley; she had

"Mo," wife of the Leader of the Opposition.

grown up on a small farm in Cumberland Township, just thirty kilometres east of Ottawa, the second of the six children of John and Bea McTeer.

The McTeers raised horses, kept a garden and earned extra money at a variety of small government jobs. They lived simply and the kids were expected to pitch in. Maureen learned to do chores and cook for a crowd, neither of which she particularly relished, and until she went to a convent school in Ottawa at the age of thirteen, she attended a local country school.

"At first we weren't allowed to go to the school. It was a French school, and the argument was we'd hold the other kids back. My father made a deal with the trustees: if we did not come first in the class he would voluntarily withdraw us from the school. But we didn't know that. We wondered why he was so demanding in terms of academic work. He used to say 'You'll thank me,' and we did. He was eccentric for his time. I carry on my father's tradition."

Maureen had the good fortune to grow up bilingual, and the unusual opportunity to grow up like a boy: "Because we were five girls until my brother came along, my father raised us in a unisex fashion, as if we were boys. We were the best football players. We were incredible hockey players. It wasn't until I was twelve when I really came to grips with the fact that I would not play in the National Hockey League no matter how good I was."

John McTeer was a hockey player who hadn't quite made it to the NHL; Maureen was determined to make it on her own ice, and her style was pure Rocket Richard: control the puck and skate like hell. Her father inadvertently offered her an arena where she could compete: politics, John McTeer was a True Blue Tory in a True Grit riding, but he never gave up hope, and by the time Maureen was twelve she was tagging along with him to political rallies. John McTeer never won an election, but politics gave his ambitious daughter an identity – she was John's girl, Maureen McTeer – and a glimpse of a wider world beyond the horse barns and hockey rinks of Cumberland Township.

"By the time I was eighteen I had very defined views of where I was at and where I was going," she says. "I would just go *nuts* if I had to do nothing with my life." A debating scholarship took her to the University of Ottawa and she paid her way by doing research for the Conservative Party. Maureen was four years younger than Margaret Sinclair, and she would never have dreamed of wandering barefoot around Morocco smoking hash; hippies were scarce in the Young Conservatives, and that was okay with Maureen. She wore her hair short in a curly permanent, avoided student radicals and made a name for herself as smart, competitive and serious. She shunned the all-night, wine-soaked consciousness-raising sessions of the early women's movement – "All that awful outpouring of *feelings*" – and cheered for Conservative leader Robert Stanfield, a decent, dull manufacturer of male underwear. Like Joe, Maureen grew up in the claustrophobic cocoon of Conservative ideology, a world view whose essential rightness she never questioned.

"When I was eighteen I knew everything there was to know," she laughs. "Now I'm thirty-eight and I figure I know nothing. I was *very young* when Joe became leader. You can do anything when you're young. You're never even going to die when you're young. I had boundless energy, but I had no context in which to put it. You look back on your life and you say, 'Could I have done this?' You walk into a room and you think, 'How could I have been so cocky at age twenty-three to be assuming I could do this?' As Catherine says, 'Where do you get *off*?' If it had been ten years later I would have been a lot more cautious. I would probably have been more traumatized. When you're twenty-three you just *assume* the world's your oyster."

And for six months it was. Just when things seemed bleakest for Mo and Joe, the Trudeau marriage fell apart; Margaret cavorted around the world in a series of celebrity-sex scandals, Pierre sank into a blue funk of anger and misery. During the 1979 election campaign, Margaret's book *Beyond Reason* stirred up anxieties about the prime minister's personality which Trudeau's contemptuous behaviour did not dispel, and the Philosopher King suddenly seemed a tired, old man.

Joe Clark was twenty years younger, honest and eager, and in a Liberal environment that looked like a scene from the soft-porn movie *Caligula*, his grass-roots style was reassuring. After three years in the public eye, Maureen had attracted support from career women who admired her outspokenness and independence, and reassured the old guard that she wasn't a lesbian. Compared to Margaret Trudeau, Ms. McTeer seemed sensible, responsible and not so scary after all.

Maureen campaigned hard, mainstreeting and making speeches on her own but always, relentlessly, promoting Joe. She astutely used the phrase "*When* Joe is elected," never "*If* Joe is elected," making it seem that a Clark victory was already in the bag, and she made efficient use of her time, hitting shopping malls and coffee parties literally on the run. While

Joe huddled with his advisers trying to decide whether or not to wear his galoshes, Maureen had her boots on and was half way down the street.

On May 22, 1979 the Conservatives squeaked into power with 136 seats to 114 for the Liberals, but it was a minority government and the NDP, which traditionally supported the Liberals, held the balance of power. Joe Clark became prime minister on June 4, the day before his fortieth birthday; Maureen was only twenty-seven. A prescient tribute to her importance in the campaign was paid by the New York *Times* correspondent Andrew Malcolm: "She seems so decisive, so effective and so genuine when glad-handing that someone suggested the Conservatives would have gotten a majority in Parliament had she been the candidate, instead of the minority won by her husband, whose image is not so decisive, not so effective and not so genuine."

In Ottawa people whispered that Maureen had married ineffectual Joe Clark as the quickest way of acquiring power for herself, and she was constantly compared to Rosalynn Carter, "Mrs. President," the powerful wife of ineffectual United States President Jimmy Carter. The image of the Machiavellian Ms. McTeer is absurd, but Maureen never made any secret of her ambition, and, like Jeanne St. Laurent, another country girl, she had married "up." Marriage was still almost the only way women could improve their status; women MPs were scarce and suspect, and Maureen would have had to wait ten or twenty years for even a nomination. "I remember sitting in the family room at 24 Sussex, looking out at that exquisite view of the Ottawa River and feeling totally exhilarated that we had done it," she said.

If Maureen had any illusions that she would be an equal-partner prime minister, forget it. She was frozen out: "I never had an office in Joe's office and I didn't want one. Every time you'd walk in, it was like you had leprosy. 'Oh God, here comes The Wife.' Anything you say, or disagree with, 'Ugh,' even though as far as I'm concerned half the time I give much better advice than the people who've got the big title and the big pay." Neither Joe nor his staff offered Maureen any clear role to play, nor any protection from the inevitable curiosity of the press and the jealousy of his rivals. "If you're a wife, you have nowhere to go," she shrugs, looking back. "My assumptions that people would be happy to have an intelligent, active, educated, opinionated *person* were obviously naive."

Maureen found herself rammed into the traditional role she had been fighting to be free of all her life: "When you are with the 'Minister,' you are 'The Wife.' You are always 'The Wife.' It makes no difference on God's earth who you are, you are always 'The Wife.' They say it with a purpose. It is delegitimizing in terms of decision-making and policy. You can never be part of that. 'Wife' is a pejorative title these days, and always has been as far as I'm concerned, and 'Wife' is someone who is always trying to cause problems, right? For people in political office, their titles mean a lot to them, their access to the 'Minister' means a lot to them, and a spouse can be nothing but a major threat.''

Maureen was shocked to discover that the most intense hostility came from women: "I am a feminist, and throughout my life I have done everything possible to promote women, but I have no illusions that the people who have caused me the most heartache and grief are women.'' She suffered from gratuitous and unprovoked insults by older wives who saw her as a sexual threat, and fierce criticism from fast-track women who envied her proximity to power. In fact there was no proximity. "We don't discuss Cabinet or caucus or things I have no right to know," she says of her personal relationship with Joe. "And I don't want to know.'' Joe did not ask his wife's advice about particular policies, although Maureen volunteered her opinions on issues she cared strongly about. "We have a very strict rule that we don't impose extraneous things on our time to ourselves,'' she says. "We have a private life, we have a public life. Otherwise politics becomes your only focus.''

Maureen rarely saw Joe, and she did what most lonely wives do, she redecorated the house. This was a tactical error. Margaret Trudeau had invested six years of her lonely life, and much of her substantial, fragile ego decorating 24 Sussex to her own taste, and Margaret was still very much on the scene. Although she and Pierre no longer shared a marriage, they shared three sons, and Margaret continued to take a deep personal interest in Pierre's domestic arrangements at Stornoway. While Maureen went out of her way to be tactful and kind about Margaret, Margaret did not reciprocate. "Maureen is simply not my sort of woman," Margaret revealed in her second book, *Consequences*. "Bouncy, worthy, humourless and now riding high. Intelligent. Very cold.''

Margaret was upset about losing one of the last contacts with her marriage, and she left 24 Sussex with anguish that soon turned to anger: "Within days I started hearing of the pillage, the rape, of 24 Sussex. All that was beautiful, all that I had chosen with such loving care, was now ripped out and replaced with all that was most mediocre. The full-length yellow silk curtains were chopped in two, to dangle aimlessly in mid-air. [In the dining room] my Fortuny covering was ripped off and replaced with beige paper, while above it the elaborate ceiling, which I had taken such pains to leave very plain, stood out in gaudy gold . . . Maureen removed the neutral carpet that I had chosen for the ground floor and replaced it in the hall with huge patches of the most suburban black and white linoleum . . . and she decided to turn what had been our formal and charming library into a sort of emperor's anteroom where courtiers visiting the Prime Minister could drink coffee out of A&W coffee mugs from an ever-bubbling cafeteria machine. I could no longer decide whether I was more depressed by what I had inherited [Stornoway] or by what Maureen McTeer was vandalizing of my past.''

The Battle of the Draperies, as it became known, was unfortunately the most memorable event of Maureen's brief stay at 24 Sussex Drive. In December 1979, only weeks into his first session of parliament, Joe Clark's government was suddenly defeated in the House of Commons and the country was plunged into another election. Maureen and Joe were optimistic: Trudeau appeared to be finished as Liberal leader and they felt certain of a massive Conservative victory on February 18, 1980.

A more sophisticated Maureen McTeer hit the shopping malls this time. She was slimmer, and she wore her straight, shoulder-length hair swept back off her face. She had invested in some power suits to enhance her image as a career woman, although she wasn't. She had not yet been called to the bar, and her last bar-admission exam was the Friday before election day.

''I have other things I want to do with my life than fight an election campaign,'' she snapped at one reporter. Maureen wasn't responsible for the unexpected fall of Joe's government, and she was under very heavy pressure to pass her exams. If she postponed even one, she would have to rewrite them all, yet she couldn't bear to let Joe down by staying home to study. Maureen didn't blame Joe for the government's defeat, she blamed the Liberals, and she threw herself fiercely into the campaign.

Law books under her arm, Maureen criss-crossed the country, trying to study in airplanes and between speeches. She didn't attend one class of the bar-admission course. She rarely got more than three hours of sleep a night, migraine headaches incapacitated her for hours and as the campaign faltered she grew so tense that her hands were clenched into tight little fists. There was nothing Maureen could do to save the Conservatives:

Clark's indecisiveness had alienated his own party members, and Pierre Trudeau was reborn as good, old Single Dad. Maureen arrived in Toronto the day before her last exam "absolutely beside myself." Convinced that she was going to fail, she called a classmate who coached her for six hours, then she went out to one of the last rallies of the campaign:

"On the way out of the arena, a man said 'Maureen.' I turned around to shake his hand and he grabbed the fleshy part of my arm and tore all the ligaments. I have never known worse pain. I was so heartbroken that someone would want to hurt me, who didn't even know me, I was just overwhelmingly in grief. Of course it was my writing arm. We flew back to Ottawa and the next day I went to the exam. I wrote three hours in the morning, two hours in the afternoon, then I went home, showered, changed and said hello to my child." She attended two political rallies in the evening, then threw a party for her own campaign workers: "That ended about midnight, and the next day I had to go to Montreal. The woman who was babysitting Catherine was very, very pregnant and in the middle of the night she goes into labour. Four in the morning she comes to my door to tell me she's going to have her baby. So I become the father, 'Arrghhhh!' So call out to the Mounties, 'Get us a car!' There's no car to be found anywhere. One of the guards finds a rickety old police car, puts the two of us in it and we go down to Civic Hospital, drop her off and call her husband who's on the campaign plane with Joe. That was my sleep. The next day it was obvious to us that there was no way on God's earth we were going to win. On Monday, the defeat. On Tuesday, I really do believe my brain stopped. Mentally, I short-circuited, my brain was completely unable to absorb any more stimuli or information. After the 1980 election I was 'non compus mentus' for about a year. I graduated from my bar-admission course and I don't remember it, I don't even remember going.

She said of the defeat later: "Nothing, other than a death, will ever hurt me again in that way, as deeply, as completely." She continued her daily routine, moved back to Stornoway, took a holiday in Hawaii, but she was literally "out" of her mind. She remembers almost nothing of 1980. "That's how my body and mind allowed me to heal. The stresses are so great that if your body doesn't stop or your brain doesn't turn down, you'd go crazy."

Law offices did not line up to hire the wife of the former Conservative prime minister and she was in no shape to practise law, but by the end of

The year following the 1980 election was a blank for McTeer. Although she was called to the bar she didn't remember the achievement.

the year she slowly came out of her daze. She began to work on a book about the official houses where she had lived, 24 Sussex Drive, Stornoway and the prime minister's summer home at Harrington Lake. She found writing hard but absorbing and when her glossy picture book, *Residences: Homes of Canada's Leaders*, was published in 1982, Maureen McTeer finally emerged, elegantly dressed, as a person in her own right.

For Maureen McTeer Clark, the worst was yet to come. In January 1983, only sixty-six percent of the delegates to the annual Conservative Party convention endorsed Joe Clark's leadership. Joe felt that it was a vote of non-confidence and agreed to a leadership convention in June, hoping to increase his support. Instead, his support evaporated to his rival,

Brian Mulroney, who was waiting anxiously in the wings. Mulroney had impressed Conservatives as a shallow opportunist with more blarney than brains in 1976, and he was determined to redeem his humiliation by building a powerful network of support within the rank and file of the Conservative Party. The political trend was towards the right-wing neo-conservative ideology of US President Ronald Reagan, with which Mulroney felt comfortable, and away from the populist social activism of Joe Clark. In 1983 Mulroney appeared to have everything Clark did not: money, smarts, sex appeal and a granite jaw. He also had a lovely wife, Mila, who was even younger than Maureen, close connections with big business and roots in Quebec, where the party was traditionally weak.

Mulroney did not have a seat in the House of Commons, and while he apparently supported Joe Clark in public, Joe and Maureen were aware that Mulroney's supporters were working behind the scenes to oust Joe from the leadership: "There were constant plots," Maureen said. "It's a little like cancer–you're never sure where it's coming at you from. I wish I was tough. Joe is made of steel. He would get up every morning and go to the office to find out which yahoo was trying to undermine him. I just can't put up with it. I just can't stand it any longer."

She rode horseback and went for long walks. "My mother and I used to have this little game that after a meeting she'd drive into a secluded area and roll the windows down and say, 'Now, *scream*! Get it out! Shout it! Here are the arrows, kill them!' I don't get angry, I get hurt by things. I am an exceedingly sensitive person, sensitive to a fault. I am very sensitive to people's feelings, sensitive to criticism, unjustified criticism. I am a stoic when I make a mistake. I expect I will be corrected, but I find there's a lot of skullduggery, personality assassination, innuendo, negative kinds of comment about my commitment to my family, to my religion. I find those things very difficult."

She broke down in tears during one speech when a young female student asked her, for the millionth time, why she kept her own name; the press ridiculed "Ms. McTear" for showing feminine weakness. Maureen developed a much thicker skin.

Both Joe and Maureen had spent virtually all their lives within the Conservative Party–politics *was* their life–and the growing realization that the party was about to repudiate them was shattering. Old friends deserted Joe for rival candidates, people they trusted were friendly to their faces while ridiculing them behind their backs. Maureen tried to cope with the humiliation by distancing herself. "I kept saying, 'No, this has nothing to do with us as people. We are here, and you could have two sticks here and it would still be the same.' You have to have a context that allows you to say, 'Yes, it is emotionally, personally and professionally devastating,' but you have to step aside and say 'You're healthy, your family still loves and supports you, your own integrity, your own sense of self and principles cannot be touched, your inner self cannot be touched by this external set of events.' It is not always easy, but it is very important. I am a very spiritual person. I have a strong sense of faith, and fate, and I feel that has saved me from a kind of emotional wasteland because I am too sensitive to all these things. It has not been easy. I am a very strong person, but I am not a tough person. I am not used to the guerilla warfare and street-fighting where so much takes place these days."

What does a wife wear to her husband's assassination? Maureen wore a long, shimmering purple gown and paced the stage of the Winnipeg Convention Centre just as Hecuba had paced the walls of Troy while her husband Hector was slain below, spitting venom on her enemies: "You yahoos," I thought, "If you think you are hurting Joe and me with this, you're not. I'm thirty-one. I'm a lawyer. I've written a book. The world is my oyster. Joe and I can do anything. We've got our act together. It's not us that's in trouble, you're the ones who are in trouble." She blinked back tears during the singing of O Canada after Brian Mulroney was elected leader, but her fists were clenched and her head was high.

Joe did not quit politics. He was re-elected when the Conservatives won again in 1984, and was rewarded for his loyalty with the plum Ministry of External Affairs. Maureen considered running herself in 1984, but rejected the idea because she felt that Joe needed her around while they both went through a period of grieving and rebuilding. They also needed to establish themselves in a home of their own and to give Catherine a normal family life outside the public spotlight.

Six years later, in September 1990, Maureen McTeer is the wife of the Rt. Hon. Joe Clark, Canada's minister of external affairs*, and she is also a member of a royal commission studying reproductive technology. The Clarks live in a small, unpretentious house across the Ottawa River from the capital; there's a white Jimmy in the driveway and a homey clutter of family memorabilia in the living-room. This is the Clarks' private space; all of their official entertaining is done in public spaces downtown. They

---

*In 1991 Clark was made minister of constitutional affairs.

shun the "beautiful people" clustered around the prime minister and his wife and cautiously restrict their personal friends to a small, loyal group who won't gossip.

"Those who dislike us are still using things against me in an attempt to bring Joe down," Maureen says. "It's *painfully* obvious, it's very stressful and it's very distressing to our family. I am always getting divorced. For the past seventeen years, every year I have been getting a divorce. Society is so conditioned politically now to judge people exclusively by their personal life. They don't deal with issues any more, just gossip, that is the way we bring people down. My own gardener said, 'Oh, I'm so sorry Ms. McTeer.' What? 'I was just told you were getting divorced.' I said, 'I don't know, am I? Joe's away right now, I'll give him a call.' 'No, no I heard it, it's everywhere!' I said, 'Come on, Louis, give me a break!' This is crazy, the gardener is telling *me* I'm getting divorced!"

Maureen knows where the rumours originate and who spreads them, but there is nothing she or Joe can do. "It's like, 'Are you still beating your wife?' And people want to believe the worst. No one ever says to you, 'I've heard this rumour, is it true?' People will come to dinner at my house and everyone will be tense. I speak to Joe as an equal. I don't say, 'Excuse me, Mr. Minister, would you pour the wine?' I say, 'Get the wine, Joe,' and whoo, whispers! 'You should have seen the way she talked to him last night!' Or Joe says something and I'll say, 'What do you mean? How can you say that?' and 'Ooooo, divorce!' "

Maureen spends a lot of time calming the anxieties of her family, and a lot of time being a mother: "In 1980 Catherine was only three. When we left 24 Sussex her big thing was that the Mounties weren't with us, and she felt very betrayed by them. It was more difficult in 1983. She couldn't understand it, why are we leaving Stornoway? It had really always been her home, the gardener, the yard, the rabbit that kept eating the flowers, this was her world, and all of a sudden we had to move. And people were saying to her, 'Your dad is really stupid, he shouldn't have called that leadership convention.' She wouldn't go to school, she would *not* go to school. One day I went and spent the whole day with her. A little girl came up and said, 'Catherine, I saw a picture of your dad in the newspaper . . .' 'Don't you talk to me about my father!' Catherine says to her. I said, 'Please don't say that, she doesn't mean to . . .' 'I don't want you talking about my father!' She just shouted at her. And the girl opened the picture she had brought with her and said, 'But I just wanted to tell you how handsome he looked.' That remark allowed Catherine to

331
•

begin to go back to normal life. All the things people were saying were not against her.''

When Maureen ran as a Conservative candidate in the 1988 election she sometimes took eleven-year-old Catherine canvassing with her. "We knocked on a door and this woman comes out, angelic as could be, and says, 'Oh, I'd love to meet your daughter.' So Catherine goes up, and she says, 'Catherine, I've always wanted to meet you. I've always wanted to tell you how happy your mother would have been if she had aborted you.' Catherine just looked at her and said, 'You're sick,' but that night at home she cried and cried and cried and we talked about why women have to have abortions and why we personally don't believe in abortion and daddy and mummy love each other and we love you more than anything in the world. She slept like *glued* to me that night. I cancelled all my campaigning the next day, she stayed home from school, it was completely a day off trying to get over this. To her it was just a devastating experience.''

Maureen found being a candidate infinitely worse than being a candidate's wife. "I have never been so badly treated. The assumption that I was a crook, that I was there for no other reason, spending thousands of dollars of my own money, trying to get people involved in the public process, the assumption that I was there exclusively to line my own pocket was absolutely distressing.''

Maureen McTeer had not quite come to terms with the fact that she was still The Wife of the Minister, Joe Clark. She could not practise law – Joe's job placed her in a conflict of interest – and she had worked only two years as a lawyer. She spoke out strongly for equality for women, but she did so as a partisan Conservative, and the Conservative Party of Canada was considered by many feminists to be regressive and reactionary. Maureen, thanks to Joe, had a high public profile, but she had no power base of her own, and no record of solid achievement in the women's movement or anywhere else. For all Maureen's idealism, the voters of Carleton-Gloucester were within their rights to assume that an equally qualified female candidate with lighter political baggage might have been found, and to wonder whether the minister wasn't parachuting his unemployed wife into a high-paying job. Maureen lost to a Liberal.

Why did Maureen want to join the government of Brian Mulroney, the man who caused her so much pain? Did Hecuba team up with Achilles? No. But like Joe, Maureen is a politician, and prepared to make her

Maureen McTeer, the first wife of a prime minister to run as a candidate rather than the candidate's wife.

peace in exchange for power. Rather than blaming the Conservative government for incompetence or corruption, she accuses its critics of being cynics, and emphasizes a personal philosophy that seems to have little relationship to the way the government actually functions: "I am not a Conservative, I am a *Progressive* Conservative," she says defiantly. "I believe we still represent a majority in the party. My brand of political activism is basically anti-establishment. My whole life has been anti-status quo, anti-elite because elites absolutely refuse to take into consideration anyone's interests but their own. The more I see manipulation of power the more adamant I become that only through an enlightened community and enlightened press can we protect democracy." She sees democracy beginning in the family, in the neighbourhood and community, places where women have an important role to play, but she is an individualist, not a collectivist, and has an almost messianic belief in each person's obligation to get politically involved. Maureen is not a radical. "I am a very traditional person," she says: she is loyal to the party, and the leader, whoever he is.

Maureen McTeer's political ideology may be grass roots, but her political lifestyle is high society. She travels around the world with Joe, jets off to New York and Washington for the weekend and hobnobs with world leaders at state banquets. "I treat everyone the same," she says. "I can't *stand* people who put on airs. I treat the gardener like I treat the foreign minister of some country. That's why protocol and I are always at each other's throats. They are there, I tell them, to make people feel *comfortable*, to make people welcome, of course they believe they are there because they are so important the rest of us are supposed to stand in line at attention when they tell us to and in fact they create tensions through their nonsense." She also avoids the "country club set." "They have no titles, but they have status symbols, their cars and their drivers and their name-dropping. I just can't stand that kind of pomposity. You get a lot of that. It comes with the territory."

Maureen takes the attitude that inside every stuffed shirt there is an interesting human being, and she has only been disappointed once. "It was at a state dinner at the governor-general's, and it was a Muslim man who was absolutely beside himself that he had been seated next to a woman. He was apoplectic! We finally agreed to talk. I said to him, diplomatically as I could, and I'm getting better, believe me, 'Look, you're obviously very distraught to have a mere wife beside you. It's your loss. I am not going to change seats. You speak to the man on your left, I will speak to the man on my right. You don't have to talk to me. Please don't feel obligated. Let's act as adults and polite people and *not make a scene.*' "

Maureen hasn't changed, or has she? "I've learned tolerance," she says. "I don't believe any more there is an absolute right and an absolute wrong answer." She believes that she is much stronger and wiser for the failure and frustration she and Joe encountered. "It's natural to say to yourself, 'If I had been on my own,' 'If I had married someone else,' but I don't believe life's that simple. I have given up my professional life because of my marriage. I gave seven years of my life when I was party leader's spouse because there was virtually no option. I think now I have a maturity, an understanding and a knowledge base that is unusual. I am still fairly young, and if I don't die young, I have a continuing contribution to make. If anything my life has made me more conscious of injustice, my social activism is more directed, my political activism is more directed, I have a better opportunity to help people who need help. I have learned how the political system works, how the legal system works, the power system and I think in the long term that means something. My friends look at me and say how lucky I am. Given the options, I think I am."

There is one job for which Maureen McTeer is both experienced and qualified: wife of the prime minister of Canada. Maureen won't discount the possibility, but the opportunity is not likely to come again. "It was Joe's time," she says of 1979, "and we lost it."

Geills Turner: The Last of the Golden Girls

$\mathcal{O}$N HER FIRST DAY on the 1988 election campaign tour Geills* Turner lost her luggage. To be more precise, and Geills is extremely precise, Air Canada lost her luggage. Maureen McTeer would have gritted her teeth and stalked off, stoically prepared to make do with fuzzy teeth and a rumpled suit until it turned up; Joe Clark would have waited until it turned up in Tibet or New Guinea. Geills Turner waits for no man, certainly not a baggage handler. She wanted her luggage, and she wanted it *now*.

Geills Turner has a clear, sharp, penetrating voice, a voice that carries well, especially in airports, and her body language is powerful, especially when she's excited. When Geills is tense and nervous, as she was that night, she also has a very short fuse. In a matter of seconds the airport manager, the RCMP, John Turner's aides and a number of fascinated spectators were swept up into the drama of Mrs. Turner's lost luggage.

Geills was determined to find her bags; she also wanted to know precisely how Air Canada had managed to lose them between Toronto and Montreal, who was responsible, why this person had screwed up and what the hell was Air Canada going to do about it?

Geills refused to be shut up or shooed away, and after a fairly brief delay, her bags were found. Was there a Conservative mole in the baggage room? A disgruntled Grit? Or was it Air Canada just being Air Canada?

Geills was just being Geills, as her husband John says, "her own woman." Well, why not? It worked, and Geills likes things to work, whether they are people, computers or kitchen sinks. "Geills is very much into *process*," says her friend Jean Riley. "She is obsessive about finding out *how* things happen, and why they go wrong. She is oblivious to the fact that people may be watching and judging." Geills likes to do things *right*. "My parents expected us to do well," she says. "Whether it was school or sports or knitting, the attitude was, if you're going to it, do it

---

*In Gaelic it is pronounced "Geels"; everyone calls her "Jill."

well." And she does. "Geills likes to organize things her way because everything she does is done the right way," admits her old friend Sharon Gray.

Her luggage glitch was a signal to Geills that the Liberal election campaign was going to go badly, and it did. Geills campaigned hard, although it was the last thing in the world she would have chosen to do, and she did her job well. If she saw that the ramshackle Red Machine was badly in need of repair, Geills offered her blunt advice about how the glitches might be fixed, but her criticism was shrugged off or bitterly resented. Turner lost the election, and his job. Had he taken Geills's advice, there was no guarantee he would have won, but if he had taken her advice, he wouldn't have been there in the first place.

John Turner was elected Liberal leader on June 16, 1984. It was an easy victory – Turner had been perceived as the heir-apparent to Pierre Trudeau ever since he had run against Trudeau for the leadership in 1968 – yet the decision to run again in 1984 was not an easy one for Turner to make.

"My husband had been out of politics since 1976," Geills says rather testily. "In spite of what people like to say, he focuses on what he's doing, and he was focused full, full, full time on practising law. The idea that he was keeping some sort of political network alive all this time is nonsense. Maybe there were people who in their own minds were keeping it alive. As it turned out, to his *detriment*, he was not up to speed on who were the new people in the party, the fine points of the issues, what backroom fighting was going on, all the dynamics you only notice if you are sitting right there on a day-to-day basis, or if you're a junkie."

Turner quit politics when he was at the top; as minister of finance he had been the second most powerful man in the country, after Trudeau. Ten years younger than Trudeau, taller, handsomer and equally competitive, Turner had always had a cool rapport with the man whose long shadow blighted his career, and after an argument with Trudeau over financial policy, he had retreated to Toronto where his political activity amounted to little more than power lunches at his corner table in Winston's restaurant. As the years passed, Turner's black hair turned white and his waistline thickened, yet Trudeau, ageless as the portrait of Dorian Gray, still danced to his own dialectic on the Ottawa stage.

Geills and John were in Jamaica on February 29, 1984 when Trudeau went walking in an Ottawa blizzard and decided that he would, irrevocably, retire.

"John was faced with the pressure of 'Are you going to run or are you not?' " Geills recalls. "We had decided on this holiday to discuss the problems that might come up if Trudeau were to resign. And we had discussed the fact that if he didn't resign literally in the next five minutes, he'd almost run out of time for any new person to be able to pull it off. He'd left it to the last possible moment of his mandate with a lot of problems. They were twenty-six percent at the polls and everybody *hated* the Liberals! So we were sort of commiserating with whoever was going to have to pick it up, it was almost an impossible task for whoever was going to have this bomb dropped in their lap, and then he resigned!"

A bomb, or a golden egg? Turner was under enormous pressure to run; Geills, as usual, played the devil's advocate: "I think I could see more of the 'realities' than he could. I wasn't all that enthusiastic. He had a lot of people pushing him, a lot of people who were very enthusiastic, so maybe my opinion could be dismissed because I was sort of in a conflict of interest – did I want my life to be totally disrupted? I wasn't going to say 'Over my dead body,' but I was certainly putting up a lot of questions that should have been answered."

It was an agonizing decision for Turner. He was fifty-five years old, financially secure, happy in his work; he had four children in school and university, Geills was looking at a career in computer programming. Why throw it all up? When Turner announced his candidacy on March 16, he was described by his campaign manager as a "complete nervous wreck."

"I think, even in retrospect, that he would have regretted it if he hadn't tried it," Geills reflects. "All the rest of your life you'd say, gee, if only . . . There are a lot of things people regret not having done but time goes by and you've lost the opportunity. So he decided, for better or for worse, that he was going to do it. And he did. His French was rusty, the issues were rusty, the people were rusty, he was rusty, the party had no money, the party was out of gas, there was no organization, it was a mess. He certainly went into it with the expectation of probably losing, but with the idea that he would have four years to build it up to win the next time. So off we went."

John Turner was prime minister of Canada for seventy-nine exhausting, humiliating days. Geills had been right: John was so rusty he looked like the Tin Man. He decided to call a snap election, although he could have waited three or four more months, and on September 4, 1984 the Liberals suffered a crushing defeat at the hands of a rejuvenated Conservative Party. Turner hung on as Liberal leader until his second defeat in 1988, then resigned in the spring of 1990 to return to his law practice in Toronto.

"Success is getting what you want, happiness is wanting what you get," says the motto beside Geills Kilgour's McGill University yearbook photo. Success came quickly and easily to Geills Kilgour in the small, secure world of south Winnipeg. Pretty, blond, athletic, popular, rich and a whiz at school, she was the golden girl that other girls would kill to be, or would cheerfully kill. Geills grew up inside a racial stereotype as a pear ripens in a glass bottle; she didn't know it was there, but everybody else did. "The WASP princess with the patrician manners and the perfect smile," *Chatelaine* magazine described her in 1987, when Geills was forty-nine and going grey. "Geills Turner could be a character in a novel by F. Scott Fitzgerald, that chronicler of the rich, the beautiful and the bored."

Geills was deeply hurt by the story, not only because it contained slanderous remarks – "she can make Imelda Marcos look like Mother Theresa – but because she felt it simply wasn't true. "Anything I've ever read about myself has been totally inaccurate, even my date of birth," she says. Geills was born in Winnipeg on December 23, 1937, not as generally reported, on December 22; she is not a princess or a WASP, her manner is too explosive to be patrician, her smile is toothy, she is striking rather than beautiful, she is not Daisy Buchanan and she is never bored.

"Why do they do things like that?" she asks. The WASP princess stereotype is so powerful that reality is made to conform to it. During a drive for donations to a Toronto food bank, Geills arrived with her groceries in a bag from Town Shoes, a mass-market chain store, taking pains to choose a bag she thought politically neutral: "The next day the story came out that Mrs. Turner had brought her groceries in a Creeds bag. It was not a Creeds bag. Anybody who looked at the bag could see that it was not a Creeds bag. So somebody put a Creeds bag in my hand whether I had a Creeds bag or not. I have been carrying that rap about the Creeds bag ever since." In 1990 Creeds went bankrupt.

Like a Barbie doll, Geills was made to carry a Creeds bag because Creeds was where bored rich WASPs were supposed to shop. She does wear expensive clothes – why not? – but compared to her contemporaries in Toronto, her style is simple, sporty, almost drab. In 1985 *Chatelaine* knocked Geills, "the apotheosis of the overbred, underfed WASP Princess," as "a victim of the little silk dress. Beautiful, but bo-o-oring!" Bored, and boring, Daisy Buchanan and Princess Di: Geills couldn't win.

*"Geills and the
infamous 'not from
Creeds' bag."*

The woman in the glass bottle is probably the most intelligent, even the most intellectual, of all the PM's wives, and the first wife to be over-qualified for the role. "My father said I had a mind like a man," Geills says. "That may have been a chauvinistic comment, but he meant it as a compliment." When Geills entered the University of Manitoba she majored in mathematics and physics; her friends took home economics. It was the 1950s; girls weren't supposed to understand math, and male students were impressed by the blond who could solve difficult problems on the blackboard as easily as she could ace them on the tennis court. Science was "the easy option" for Geills: "I loved it." She switched to McGill in her third year and graduated with a degree in science in 1959.

Geills was an anomaly: a woman in science, and a woman on a career path at a time when universities were supposed to be good places to catch husbands. "I wanted to *be* something," she says. "I never had any limitations put on what I might decide to do. It was never, 'Well, you're a *girl*, you have to limit yourself to this.' " Her father, David Kilgour, president of Great-West Life Assurance Company in Winnipeg, encouraged her to go into business, and she enrolled in a Harvard-Radcliffe graduate program in business administration.

In 1959 Harvard did not allow women into its prestigious MBA program, and Geills found herself segregated with seventy other women taking the same courses as the men but with only a diploma for their efforts. When she hit the streets of Manhattan looking for a job, she also found that the glass ceiling started on the ground floor; some corporations were "not ready" for a woman, and they all paid Radcliffe women half as much as Harvard men: "We weren't militant enough to get upset about it. You'd think it really wasn't fair, but you felt lucky to be in."

Geills got in at IBM, one of two women in an office of forty men, and she was lucky – she worked with the first computer. "I had a lot of fun. I found it challenging. I never felt at all intimidated by men, there was no feeling that my *place* was other than sitting next to them rather than at their feet."

When she transferred to IBM in Montreal, the atmosphere changed. "They paid me *considerably* less money and that was starting to bother me a whole lot. I think they thought, 'This hot shot from New York, we'll fix her.' They gave me *impossible* jobs. Not only were they going to pay me less, they were going to fix me."

The Feminine Mystique had not yet been published, "sexism" had not entered the vocabulary and women's consciousness was at ebb tide; it never crossed Geills's mind that maybe she was being "fixed" because she was a woman. "I was getting fed up with the dynamics in the office. It was very uptight. If I don't respect the guy I'm working for, I'm not a big suck. I might say what I think, which isn't always prudent. I run into people who were at IBM with me and they say, 'Oh, if you had stayed, you would be president of IBM.' Oh, *really*! It amazes me they would come to such a bizarre conclusion, even half in jest."

WASP princesses don't use slang like "suck." To be precise, Geills is a Celt, a Highland Scot descended from generations of Russells, Macdonalds, Kilgours and McCraes – her great-uncle, John McCrae, wrote "In

Flanders Fields'' – and her roots go back to the same stony ground that nurtured the Shaws, the Bannermans, the Macphails and the Sinclairs. Her father was a tough, hard-nosed businessman who worked his way up; he ran Great West Life, but he did not own it, and the Kilgours were never among the idle rich of Winnipeg's agricultural aristocracy. Apart from the descendents of the Selkirk settlers who arrived at Red River in 1812 – Mary Bannerman Diefenbaker was one of them – Winnipeg's aristrocracy goes back to 1882, when the CPR went through, and by the standards of Westmount or Rosedale, their money is very *nouveau* indeed. The Kilgours are a prickly, unconventional family: Geills's brother David was a maverick Conservative MP for ten years until he was expelled from the caucus and joined the Liberals, and Geills judges herself by no one's standards but her own. She is fierce and proud, but not tough, and very touchy, a woman of such explosive energy that she literally leaps into the air when she gets too tense. Geills engages life in mortal combat. It's not that she likes to win, she *has* to win.

Her greatest coup was carrying off Prince Charming, Canada's most eligible bachelor, John Napier ''Chick'' Turner, the blue-eyed hunk with the bedroom smile who made international headlines in 1958 when he danced with Princess Margaret at a party in Vancouver. Today the Turners' living-room contains numerous photographs of Princess Margaret, some very recent with her children, an indication that the friendship runs deeper than a casual date.

Geills met John when she was a student at McGill: ''I was going out with a *much older* man who was a friend of his,'' she grins. ''You realize that my husband is *much older* than I am.'' John is nine years older. Is Geills's remark a joke or a slam? Her words say slam, but her big laugh and ironic tone say joke; like Maryon Pearson, Geills asks a lot of her listeners, and pays the price if they don't get it.

''John was a very suave lawyer about town who had had his 'romance' with Princess Margaret, so he had a very high profile, very *glamorous*. He was *big*. John had just moved into a very glamorous penthouse on McGregor Ave. so we stopped by one night and rang the bell. I thought, 'Is this a good idea?' I wouldn't want someone to ring my apartment doorbell out of the blue. He was there in his shirt-sleeves and he was probably thinking, 'Holy smokes, who are these people dropping in?' So we had a perfectly civilized time.''

Geills was not going to be bowled over by Mr. Big. "When somebody tells me something is good, I inevitably take the position that it can't be all that good. Who the hell does he think he is? We met again at the Ritz and we both bridled and sparred and I left him with some stinger that he didn't forget for a long time."

Soon after Geills returned from New York in 1962, Turner decided to run for the Liberals in the Montreal riding of St. Lawrence – St. George and Geills volunteered to help out. "We did surveys in the riding to find out what impact his presence had in each poll. We got a really good profile of the riding, where he was strong, where his presence would increase the vote, where it wouldn't matter. At the end, we were almost dead on." Turner won an unexpected and impressive victory.

Geills was one of Canada's first scientific pollsters. Her interest in politics was mechanical rather than ideological, *how* to win rather than why to win. "I didn't have any dyed-in-the-wool politics at all," she shrugs. "I thought this looked like an attractive candidate." So did a swarm of lovesick young women who toiled away on Turner's campaign in the hope of a melting glance from ol' Blue Eyes. Geills spent a lot of time with John discussing strategy, and their political sessions surreptitiously turned into quiet dinners together and evenings at the symphony: "We had to keep it very quiet because he had so many women working for him and they all thought they were going to be marrying him. It didn't seem terribly prudent to antagonize this great body of workers."

Geills Kilgour may have been the first woman smart enough to see behind Chick Turner's gregarious jock persona to the sensitive, insecure boy who had been raised by his mother. Phyllis Gregory Turner was a legend in Ottawa, a miner's daughter from Rossland, British Columbia, who made it to the top rungs of the civil service through sheer brains, charm and determination. John's father died when he was two, and he grew up surrounded by Cabinet ministers, mandarins and power brokers. "If John doesn't get to be prime minister he can always be pope," Phyllis liked to say. Political analyst Larry Zolf speculates that, because Turner had no father figure, he adopted the style of the men he met at his dinner table – Turner's clothes are so old-fashioned that Geills says they have a life of their own – and picked up his hip-cat patter from his adolescent friends at Ashbury College. The result, a baffling combination of bank president and hockey player, conceals the fact that Turner is intelligent – he was a Rhodes scholar as well as a track star – philosophical, emotional and religious. John wasn't about to marry a bubblehead, and in Geills he found a strong, independent woman who, like his mother, could de everything.

"It's a family joke," Geills laughs. "John goes to the office and does all that, but everything else is mine. Everything! I've got the whole thing. If it comes to repairing a light switch, cutting the grass, planting trees, organizing, that's me. 'Cause I'm so good at it. But I say, 'I only got to be good at it because I had to do it! I got lots of practice. Why don't you do it?' 'But you're so good at it!' Oh, hell. I'm also the mechanical one. I'm the one who knows how to use an answering machine and a computer and a fax machine and a copy machine, even a complicated telephone. I'm the technician. But I like that. John does the dishes, at least he puts the dishes in the dishwasher. He doesn't mind doing it, some men would."

They were engaged at Christmas 1962, six months after the election, and married the following May. Geills knew that she was marrying a politician, she had helped to invent him, but did she know what she was getting into? "No! *Not at all*! When you're in love, you don't really sit down and analyse what that means. It seemed that my husband had an interesting job." It never crossed Geills's mind to keep her job. She wasn't happy at IBM, and like all women of her generation she had been raised to believe that married women stayed home and had children.

Geills had four children in nine years and settled into the snug, sub-urban routine of Ottawa's Rockcliffe Park. Rockcliffe was much like Cres-centwood where Geills had lived in Winnipeg, a leafy enclave of large stone houses where the right people did the right things, right. With a group of compatible wives, Geills drove car pools, shopped, skiied and threw gourmet dinner parties for Big Jobs. She did it perfectly – even the Turner children are exceptionally bright, handsome and well behaved – cheerfully and apparently effortlessly.

"I did what I had to do," she says now. "I had all the responsibilities of the home. It's not exactly mind-enhancing but it's hard work just to get through the day. John loves to entertain. I am not a social person. I really like being by myself, *a lot*. I could go off and live on an island all by myself for months at a time and love it. I'll entertain because you should, or you owe sixteen people and you have to do it, and I can do it perfectly well, and I can look as if I'm enjoying it, but it's not what I would choose to spend my time doing, if I had my choice. If you spend your whole life doing what you don't like to do, it wears you down."

Geills did not have her choice. Her life was completely programmed, like a computer, by the demands of John's career: "My life was scheduled years ahead, years and years ahead! Not weeks, *years* ahead, years. It was frightening how far ahead! So if someone suddenly said, 'Do you want to go to a movie?' you'd say 'I can't because I'm so tired. This is my one night off and if I don't go to bed early and if I don't iron my dresses, I can't do it.' So your night at home becomes a very precious commodity."

For the first time in her life, Geills discovered that there were limits to what she could achieve, that there were certain things she could not do. She could not say or do anything in public that might contradict government policy or damage her husband's image – she got into hot water for advocating a nuclear-weapons freeze – and she couldn't go to law school: "I applied and was accepted, but I would have had to do it full time and I had a two-year-old and a whole bunch of kids and John was in politics and I knew everyone would suffer very much, so I didn't do it."

During the FLQ crisis in October 1970, when John Turner was minister of justice, Geills suddenly found her house full of soldiers. "There was a poignant picture of my son who was then two on the front page of the *Globe and Mail* playing in the driveway with a guy with a machine gun over his shoulder. That's when you had a sense that this was not funny, this was kind of serious stuff because the paranoia at the time was quite fantastic. There were lots of anachronisms. Soldiers were in the house. Why were they in the house? They were in the house to protect me. But I could get in the car and drive to the grocery store. They should have come to the grocery store too, but they didn't. It was a typical military operation, nobody had really thought it through. There was a lot of theatre involved."

Like Margaret Trudeau, Geills began to feel the suffocating weight of her public role: "When we'd go to the movies together, I'd let John go out first and I'd follow a distance behind because I didn't want to be bothered, I didn't want to be associated with him, so I wouldn't be part of the *package* that was going to be intruded upon."

Geills did not rip the package to pieces, rather she retreated into its depths, distracting intruders with the glittering reflection of her public image. On stage Geills Turner was laughing, exuberant, almost manic – at the 1968 leadership convention Geills, eight months pregnant, bounced up and down like a cheer-leader – so radiant with energy that she seemed to glow in the dark. Geills showed people exactly what they expected to see:

347

the golden girl. Unless they looked closely, they didn't see the muscles tensed like cords in her arms, or the panic in her eyes. "I can do it," she says, "I can do it very well, but I pay a great price. I'm very shy, I'm an introvert, I guess. It goes back to how crowds leave you. Some people get energized by it all, they get buoyed up. I just get exhausted. I have to go to bed. I can do any amount of hard, physical work and feel fine, but crowds leave me whacked out. It's so tiring. It's having to put out all the time. You're smiling away, shaking hands, and that's not how I normally

Eight months pregnant during the 1968 Liberal leadership convention, Geills was so radiant with energy she seemed to glow in the dark.

am. For other people that would be heaven, the spotlights, the warm bodies. For me, it's torture. It leaves you in a very depleted state, and then you have to turn around and do it again this afternoon, and again tomorrow morning and maybe tonight, and people don't realize that, they all want to shake your hand, cameras are hitting you, people want to see what you're wearing, if you're getting mad. I find it very, very hard. If John had to go to a cornroast and we'd been to sixty-five other cornroasts, he wouldn't ask me to go. He knows it's hard on me."

John is buoyed by people. He loved the spotlight, and he didn't mind enjoying it alone. Geills avoided the media like the Black Death. As journalist Susan Riley succinctly puts it, "Being in politics and hating the media is like working in an abattoir and hating the sight of blood. It is exhausting and ultimately self-defeating. Even if your complaints are justified, the media always gets the last word." Geills was unprepared for the shock of public recognition when John was elected leader: "When the results were announced my twelve-year-old son burst into tears, he thought the whole thing was so awful. Then we forced our way through the crowd and he nearly got killed, just for want of air. That was a bad time. He was going to summer camp later that summer and he said 'Maybe I'll make my friends before people know who I am.' Kids are pretty smart, they know people treat you differently when your father is prime minister. The next day I was back in my exercise class. I went into a store next door and all the women came running up to me, 'Oh, you're Mrs. Turner!' I had to turn on my heel and *run*."

The "mystery" of Geills Turner caught the attention of Christopher Newton, director of the Shaw Festival at Niagara-on-the-Lake where Geills is a member of the Board of Governors. "She strikes me as a very alone person," he says. "My mental image of her is of an elegant figure walking down the street away from me, by herself. She often reminds me of a character out of Shaw – fiercely independent but curiously old-fashioned."

The role of golden girl was obsolete by 1984; Geills and John looked like a pair of cut-outs from a 1940s colouring book. Geills was forty-six, her blond hair was turning white, and she was stuck with an image that left her vulnerable to ridicule and abuse – the golden girl has become the "rich bitch." Geills had been too busy doing things she didn't want to do, perfectly, to have the time and the psychic space to develop the confident self-awareness that less gifted women were forced to achieve, and her shiny, brittle shell was maintained by compulsive organization. "Chaos doesn't have a place in our house,'' she firmly told a reporter before the 1984 election.

"Campaign Chaos" was the phrase used by the press to describe the disastrous Turner election campaign, and the Turner jet was dubbed "The Flying Circus." "So much bad organization," Geills sighs, "I don't know how we did as well as we did, as badly as we did. After being on the plane for about five minutes I realized I was either going to have hysterics at the organization, or I was going to have to get off the plane."

Geills is more thunderstorm than blue lagoon; she doesn't knit or do needlepoint, she gets mad. Geills knew a lot more about running a campaign than the people who were running John's, and she told them so; the first batch of advisers was fired, and Campaign Chaos was taken over by the legendary Liberal rainmaker, Keith Davey. Davey decided that Geills should get off the plane. She cheerfully agreed.

"I think he wanted me out of the way. I was strong-minded, had my own opinions. He was probably agreeing with me about the problems but didn't like having it pointed out. So I had my own little tour for about three weeks."

In what *Globe and Mail* reporter Robert Sheppard called "an act of great bravery or political desperation," Geills Turner became the first PM's wife to have a campaign tour all to herself. "Geills was lots of fun, flirtatious," says Sheppard. "It was funny to watch Geills on a stage in Saskatchewan trying to auction off a 'slightly used' set of cookware."

The only member of John's entourage cool enough to accompany testy Mrs. T. was the silver-haired Senator Royce Frith. "We got on this jet in Calgary," Geills recalls, "and I said, 'What's happening today?' and Royce said, 'Well, you're going to have seven speeches.' I said, 'Seven speeches! I don't do speeches! He said, 'You'll be fine.' 'What am I going to say?' 'You'll think of something.' So just put that in your pipe and smoke it. I'd never done any public speaking in my whole life."

She did it, as usual, superbly. Geills barnstormed across Saskatchewan and down the Mackenzie River in the Northwest Territories shaking hands, eating strawberry shortcake and making extemporaneous sock-it-to-'em political speeches. She got on well with native leaders – she and John had taken the kids on long canoe trips in the Arctic – and she loved the north. Geills was such a smash hit – "I'd run her against Maureen McTeer any day," Frith beamed – that plans were made to extend her tour to southern Ontario. Geills bailed out.

"They tell you the more you do the better you are, you're great, you're fine and all that, but nevertheless you get hyper after a while. You're going on raw nerve ends."

If Geills pushes herself too hard she goes, as she says, "out of control." She exercises vigorously every day to relieve her tension, and she disciplines herself to make the best use of her time. She was severely criticized for not being constantly at John's side, but they both knew that she found the stress exhausting, and she hates the role of the "puffy little wife" clinging helplessly to her husband's arm. John might have done better with Geills on his arm; as it was he got into trouble for patting a woman on the bum and he talked like a refugee from a late-night gangster movie. Geills probably saved his seat for him; in the last weeks of the campaign, when it looked as if Turner would lose his own riding of Vancouver Quadra, Geills hit the Vancouver hotline shows and tore through the riding shaking hands door-to-door. It was an impressive vote of confidence from the woman who knew John Turner best, and of the forty seats Turner salvaged from the débâcle, one was his own.

"Politics is very hard on a wife," Geills says. "She doesn't get much credit, she just gets a lot of shit." For Geills, John's six years as leader of the Opposition were a trial by slander, and the most vicious attacks came from within the Liberal Party: "You have sabotage, where you have people in John's office who are Chrétien* people. This was supposed to be part of the 'healing process.' It was *criminal* what these people did. There was a guy in John's office who gave out every nasty quote. Just *fabrication*! Talking about my husband going to the office drunk, never getting to the office until 2 p.m., *absolute total fabrications*. There was a lot of dishonesty for political purposes. Out there is a big, nasty world and people will go to any lengths to get what they want, if it means discrediting the leader, if it means discrediting the leader's wife. I mean people within the party, *especially* within the party. And the press are willing participants in this, the 'unnamed source close to the leader.' They're fed this stuff and they lap it up. How can you fight back? The husband can take the opportunity in a scrum to set the record straight, but what opportunity does a wife have? You get maligned, you get talked about behind your back, you have the most terrible things said about you in print. If you sue, you give them more publicity."

The Turners had sold their Toronto house when John became prime

---

*Jean Chrétien lost the Liberal leadership to Turner in 1984 and won it in 1990.

minister, but Geills never had time to move to 24 Sussex Drive. After the election she had Stornoway redecorated, but neither of the Turners ever really lived there; John was on the road, trying to rebuild the party, and Geills had an apartment in Toronto. Soon rumours circulated that they had separated.

"I've lived apart most of my married life because John spends so much time travelling," Geills says. "Between 1984 and 1988 he was away almost ninety percent of the time, *all* the time, and he wouldn't have contemplated my putting myself through that. Bad enough for him to be putting himself through it. So if I'm sitting alone in a house in Ottawa and my children are in Toronto, what makes the most sense?"

Geills successfully shielded her children from the glare of the public spotlight and she is as protective of them as a mother bear. Geills conceals her maternal role so perfectly that few people realize it dominates her married life; being a good mother is so important that she willingly sacrificed her own ambitions, and, like Annie Thompson a hundred years before, when she was forced to choose between John and her children, she chose her children.

"I'm home with my kids most of the time," she says. "I'm on my own a lot. If I go out with a member of the same sex, I hear that I'm a lesbian, if I go out with a man, I'm having an affair. It makes it pretty hard on people who go to a movie with me. The press don't write anything about a wife unless it's controversial, and if they can't get a handle on it they get into speculating, and they speculate according to their own code of ethics. If they are promiscuous, they will project that image on the wife. They suppose everybody's like they are, in the most diabolical sense."

Geills makes good copy. Her tiffs with sales clerks, secretaries and staff have helped fuel the myth of the Bitch Goddess. Geills is unrepentent. "If someone does something I don't think is appropriate, I will say so. I don't think I'm rude but I'm quite forceful. I've been on the phone having a fairly normal phone call and they'll say, 'Don't shout.' I'm not shouting. People don't like to be criticized, even if they're deserving of the criticism. I'm not about to become a wimp. What do you do? We all go through life not saying what is true because it's going to offend somebody, but we're a nation of wimps anyway."

Geills thinks like an executive: she doesn't cut the grass herself, she hires somebody to do it. Her mind is logical and linear – life is a series of skills to learn, jobs to be done, problems to be solved – and her style is

confrontational. Her idiosyncrasies – she insists on the first row in an air-
plane and Coca-Cola in six-ounce bottles – would be admired as evidence
of genius in the president of IBM, but in a prime minister's wife, eccentricity is evidence of neurosis. Political aides were always telling Geills, "Shhh,
people are watching!" Well, why not? "I've always been a little bit
oblivious," Geills says. "Maybe that's my saving grace. I'm not even
aware of this, I just march along in my own little space talking to myself
and *oblivious* to ninety percent of what's going on. I think that's what
keeps you sane, not being even tuned into that. You go along assuming
that you're just like everybody else."

Guilt isn't Geills's strong suit, and perhaps it is this lack of self-
criticism that gave her the strength to survive six years of shattered dreams,
internecine political warfare and public vilification. Geills likes to win, but
the most impressive thing about her is that she knows how to lose. "It
wasn't devastating at all, not at all," she says casually of John's failure to
win the Liberal leadership in 1968. "On the next Monday I was driving
down Sussex Drive and there was Pierre Trudeau walking down the street
to his office so I picked him up and gave him a ride. I mean, Pierre
wouldn't have been my choice, but the choice was made, and we knew
each other, he and I had always been sort of pals, so life went on."

During the 1988 election campaign, Geills and John both showed
grace under pressure that won the nation's respect, if not the election.
John finally threw off his Superman cape and emerged as Clark Kent,
serious, committed and courageous. Turner took a strong pro-Canada,
anti-free trade stand that hadn't been heard of since 1911, and until the
final days of the campaign turned what could have been a cakewalk for the
Conservatives into a genuine contest. When Turner accused Prime Minister Brian Mulroney of betraying his country by advocating free trade,
Turner earned his place in history, and in a great many Canadian hearts.

"It didn't matter much," Geills says of the defeat. "We worked hard,
and it didn't work. I think I was more saddened by the party. The Canadian people were confused about the free trade issue, the corporations piled
on and frightened people in many cases. If we'd had the support of the
party I think the results could have been different. So it's very hard to be
angry, except at the people who betrayed you, and they're your own
people. It's tough."

Geills always felt that she had a right and a responsibility to express
her political opinions to John. He listened, and he respected her judgment.

Geills has her own opinions. "John would have made a better prime minister than Brian Mulroney."

"He would tell me virtually everything. There's a very big responsibility that goes with that. Sometimes what you don't know doesn't hurt, but you do tend to know everything. I'm quite discreet. I don't talk. I just don't talk, to the point where I'm sure it's very frustrating to people." Geills was intensely interested and very deeply involved in politics, although most people thought her indifferent, and through it all she remained fiercely loyal to her husband.

"I don't know whether that's female somehow, it's more sort of personal. Men can deal with the ideas, not the emotional content of it. If someone who used to support John supports Chrétien, I will judge him harshly. I will say, 'That's the man who destabilized my husband for four years, who had the knife in his back, his hand was on every knife in his back, who cost him untold days, nights of unnecessary pain,' and I don't forgive him for that. John is so strong. He will be pragmatic, 'Well, okay, this is a new deal,' but as far as I'm concerned it's very disloyal. We don't seem to make moral judgments about conduct any more. Anything goes, 'I like you today, tomorrow I'll stab you in the back, just a pragmatic decision, well, sorry about that.'"

Geills is as protective of John as she is of her children. "They are tremendously involved with each other," says a friend, "they care passionately about each other." "My husband is an extraordinary human being," Geills says. "He's spiritual, he's extremely well read, he's got so many facets the press never entertained the idea of learning about. He would have been a much better prime minister than Brian Mulroney."

John Turner rarely looked at his wife at political rallies. Like John Diefenbaker, he was off shaking hands, and Geills realized that it didn't matter a whole lot if she was there or not, so she wasn't. But she was sitting in the front row in a pink suit when John made his farewell speech as Liberal leader on June 21, 1990, and John looked directly at her when he said, "Families can't fight back." Geills smiled and wiped tears from her eyes, and after the speech she found it in her heart to embrace John's successor, Jean Chrétien.

She was fifty-two, her children were grown and she had a life to live. "It's very hard. When you get to my stage, you don't go into an employment agency and say, 'Look, I haven't worked for a hundred years and I need a job.'" She studied photography at Ryerson Polytechnic Institute after the Turners moved to Toronto; her photographs are praised, but she is shy about showing them. Geills has a room of her own, her darkroom, and that is where she spends her time when she needs to be by herself. She reads a great deal, both popular and scientific literature, and supports writers' organizations such as PEN. She is not a socialite. She is not photographed at charity galas wearing gowns that could feed a family of four for a year; she has not adopted a disease. She is interested in the theatre – her impeccable English Country living-room looks like a set from *Brideshead Revisited* – but at heart she's something of a bush rat.

Geills spent the summer of 1990 at her family's cottage on Lake of the Woods pondering how she was going to "accost" her life in the fall. Shoppers in Kenora encountered her husband, the former prime minister of Canada, with the Turners' grocery list and his familiar "Hi! How are ya'?" Geills was back at the cottage, planting trees.

CHAPTER 16

Mila,
The Movie

MONTREAL: a muggy weekday afternoon in July 1972. The Mount Royal Tennis Club is nearly deserted. A good-looking guy in sports clothes sits in the shade, nursing a drink and reading the *New York Times*. A girl in a bikini walks past him towards the pool. He glances up, puts down his paper. His eyes follow the girl. She has long legs, dark hair, a gorgeous tan and a great body. "That's for me," says Brian Mulroney.

Mila Pivnicki is startled to find herself invited for a drink by a stranger she considers an older man. She hesitates. It starts to rain. She accepts. Brian has a big smile and a deep voice. He is thirty-three. Mila is eighteen. She has a big smile, and a cute way of crinkling her nose. Brian invites Mila out for dinner. "I have to babysit at home," she says, "Good," says Brian, "we'll go to your house."

Mila wasn't too crazy about Brian at first. He was a smooth talker, a hotshot lawyer with a reputation as a playboy and he drove a noisy old car that embarrassed her. To overcome her resistance, Brian would telephone, tell her what time he was going to pick her up, and hang up before she had a chance to say no. Another woman would have found this behaviour obnoxious, but Mila was impressed by Brian's determination. She was also impressed by his high-rolling lifestyle and his sense of humour. "Brian made me laugh," she later told his biographer, L. Ian MacDonald.

Mila married Brian at nineteen and had her first child, Caroline, the following year. She dropped out of university a few credits short of her engineering degree. "I was madly in love with Brian," she told Mac-Donald. "I wanted a person who was ambitious, who knew what he wanted, because I knew what I wanted. I knew because of the age difference that he would not wait for me. When I weighed the choice, it was not a difficult decision."

Mila apparently wanted what Jeanne St. Laurent had wanted nearly seventy years before – a successful husband, children, a comfortable home –

and without a second thought she made a choice that had caused Maryon Pearson self-doubt fifty years earlier: Mila would be a rose in her husband's lapel, and proud of it.

It seems a regressive decision for a university student to make in 1973, but Mila admits that she wasn't much of a student. She was also something of a "displaced person": an immigrant and a Serb. She was born in Sarajevo, Yugoslavia, on July 13, 1953 and came to Canada with her parents as a child of five, suffering the trauma of social upheaval that is the

Brian and Mila Mulroney shortly after their marriage.

foundation of the Canadian psyche. Her father, Dr. Dmitrije Pivnicki, had left Yugoslavia earlier to study psychiatry at McGill University, and little Mila was so distressed by his absence that she walked with a psychosomatic limp. In Canada, she was enrolled in a private girls' school, Miss Edgar's and Miss Cramp's, to learn English, French and Canadian customs, a move that isolated her in a crowd of children from wealthy Westmount families. "I know what it's like to have your mother braid your hair even though no one else in your class has braids," she told writer Robert Fulford. "I also know what it's like to be pointed out. It wasn't the best time of my life. I blot out things that aren't too pleasant."

Mila was a big girl – she is over five feet nine inches – fattened on her mother's hearty Yugoslavian cooking. At first the Pivnickis lived over a pizza restaurant in downtown Montreal, but once Dr. Pivnicki joined the staff of the Royal Victoria Hospital and moved up the mountain, Mila began to blend in with the closed, conservative anglophone establishment of Montreal. At home, however, the Pivnickis retained their Serbian traditions – Mila speaks Serbo-Croatian fluently – and an ethic predicated on hard work, self-discipline and achievement.

For Mila, marriage to an older man, a self-made Irish-Canadian whose roots went back to the Quebec mill town of Baie Comeau, offered material success and cultural security. Like Dr. Pivnicki, Brian had overcome isolation, social disadvantage and financial hardship: Brian pulled so hard on his bootstraps his boots turned into Gucci loafers. Psychologically, Mila and Brian came from the same place, and they shared the same values:

"When I got my first cheque I pointed out to her that this was my salary as an MP," Brian once told a dinner party. "She said, 'I have to live on that?' I replied that we both had to."

That sexist joke was right out of the 1950s, and the fact that Brian Mulroney would find it funny in the 1980s is less amazing than the fact that Mila did too. "My husband likes to tease me," she coyly told a reporter in 1984. "I'll sign an autograph and he'll say to me, 'Is that a Chargex card?'"

Mila's shop-til-you-drop spending habits became a staple topic of Brian's dinner-party patter:

"Where's Mila?" asks Brian.

"It's all right sir," a friend replies, "the stores are closed."

"When they hear my wife's in town," Brian sighs, "they stay open."

Brian might as well have said "*the* wife." Not many politicians make their wives the butt of a stand-up comedy routine, but Brian's jokes achieved two political purposes: they directed attention away from his own ostentatious style, and they communicated the message that he could afford Mila's extravagance. "When she wears all her rocks you have to put on sunglasses for fear of damage to the cornea," wrote *Maclean's* columnist Allan Fotheringham about Mila's diamonds. With her brown eyes and olive skin, Mila had a flamboyant gypsy quality and Brian decked her out like a Cartier store: diamond rings, diamond-studded gold bracelet, Piaget gold watch, gold earrings, gold buttons, gold chains and ropes of pearls. Gold teeth would not have been a surprise. Mila's clothes were by Montreal and Paris couturiers, her luggage by Luis Vuitton, her shoes by Charles Jourdan, her hair by Charles of Westmount: Mila flew in from Ottawa to have her heavy bangs trimmed every three weeks. Mila was a trophy wife whose role was to signal her husband's prowess in bed and in the boardroom, and Mila's message was that shopping was as sexy as sex.

"The result is a curiously muted personality, contained and rather predictable," Robert Fulford wrote about Mila in 1987, three years after Brian became prime minister. "Her manner is bright and concerned – yet her answers tend to be vague. She gave me the impression of a carefully edited public persona . . . an actress playing her role without a script, watching for cues from the audience."

In *Political Wives* Susan Riley was rougher: "There is something breathtakingly cynical about the way she allows herself to be used by her husband's political machine. There is nothing wrong with loyalty to a spouse, but everything Mila says, wears and does is calculated to help her husband. It is as if she has subsumed her own personality entirely."

Riley's critique would make Amaryllis envious: "With Mila Mulroney, the nose is the mirror of the soul. In fact, it is amazing how many people have formed an impression of Mila based on her nose, or, to be specific, on the way she crinkles her nose. It has become her trademark, that and the automatic smile, the careless tossing of her chestnut hair, the explosion of noisy delight when she spots someone she knows, however slightly, in a crowd. Mila *works* a crowd, silky and insincere as any political pro, drawing people to her with her long, slender arms for a perfunctory embrace, always keeping one eye on the nearby television cameras . . . She never lets down her guard in public, never gives us a glimpse of what really irritates, amuses or pleases her. She would have us believe that she lives in a world with no rough edges, sudden failings or crude power

"The nose is the mirror of the soul."

grabs, that she and her husband are committed only and always to 'Brian's dream for Canada.' Her speeches are clichés-on-a-string, more platitudinous, if that is possible, than her husband's.''

In one early unguarded moment Mila told a reporter: ''I am a political animal. I love it.'' Fotheringham detected the sharp claws in Mila's soft paws even before Brian became prime minister: ''Down deep she is tougher than Air Canada steak. She has that European inbred earth mother tendency, the instant expert on all her friends' problems, love affairs, clothes and restaurants. One would be unwise to cross her; once betrayed she gives the impression that the boys with the violin cases will be out searching for you.''

"The Mila Factor," as she came to be called, was a key part of Brian's game plan to become prime minister, and it's not surprising that Mila should choose Olive Diefenbaker as her model rather than Margaret Trudeau: Dr. Pivnicki was one of the psychiatrists who treated Margaret during her brief stay at the Royal Victoria Hospital in 1974.

"It's a partnership," Mila liked to say about her relationship with Brian, much as she might speak of a corporation, Mulroney & Mulroney Inc. or, as columnist Claire Hoy put it, Mr. Pomp and Mrs. Circumstance. When she met Brian, his political ambition was fully formed. Like John Diefenbaker, Brian had decided to become prime minister when he was a boy. His decision had nothing to do with any exceptional qualities of character or intellect, nor, as with Diefenbaker, passionate conviction or an interest in public policy; Brian simply wanted to prove that the boy from Baie Comeau could make it to the top, and could make it as Himself.

The acquisitive determination Brian used to win Mila he applied tenfold to his political career. Even as a student at St. Francis Xavier University in New Brunswick his belief in his destiny was so overwhelming that he had no trouble attracting a coterie of loyal cronies who shared his fondness for political shenanigans and late-night bull sessions. In his early twenties, Mulroney was already a skilled debater and a successful political organizer, and later, as a Montreal lawyer famous for his negotiating skills, he built a solid backroom network of ambitious, aggressive young Conservatives who worked out of the bar of the Ritz Carlton Hotel. When Robert Stanfield stepped down as Conservative leader in 1976, Brian and the boys decided to take a kick at the can.

Brian rode into the leadership convention like Lancelot into Camelot – a flashy, mysterious, troublesome stranger. Who was this guy? Mulroney was only thirty-seven and virtually unknown outside Montreal; he had never been elected to public office and his only political experience had been in university. He had never run for a seat in the House of Commons and his grasp of policy was facile. Mila was absent – their second baby was due – and Brian reverted to his bachelor image, the Man from Gladhand.

He had money, and his lavish American-style campaign was an embarrassment to a party cast in the church-basement mold of Diefenbaker and Stanfield, a millionaire who behaved like a rural preacher. With his smilin' Irish eyes, calculated charm and platitudes, Brian, the rich boy from Montreal, was a walking joke. The more people laughed, the angrier he became, and the angrier he became, the more people laughed. "Lyin' Brian" bombed.

His defeat by Joe Clark, a man Mulroney considered a personal insult, was devastating. Brian fell into gloom that lasted until Joe Clark's government was defeated in the House in December 1979. Neither Brian nor Mila have spoken much about these years, but it seems to have been a difficult time for both of them. Brian's life's ambition was apparently terminated at the age of forty; moody and miserable he whiled away the nights drinking with "the boys," leaving Mila alone at home with their two small children. Mila is known to have a temper, and according to some accounts she read the riot act to Brian, or Brian may simply have seen the opportunity presented by Clark's mistakes: he stopped drinking and smoking – cold turkey – and he got to work to present himself as a serious alternative to Clark.

Mulroney had not let the grass grow under his feet. He had entered the corporate world as president of Iron Ore Canada, and without blinking an eye had shut down a company town, Schefferville, much like his own home town of Baie Comeau, a move that made him an instant reputation as a tough manager. Tough managers were respected at the dawn of the Reagan era, and Mulroney's status rose with his income. In 1983 he entered the fray against Joe Clark as the darling of the "cowboy capitalists," aggressive young entrepreneurs who promised to make everybody rich through magical manipulations of the stock market.

"I wouldn't have won the leadership without her," Brian said later of Mila's role in his 1983 campaign. "I mean that in crass, vote-counting terms. There were votes that came to me because of her, lots and lots of them because of her." Mila was more popular with the delegates than her husband was, and on the campaign trail Mila's role was to be Brian's teddy bear: Brian could chill out a room just by walking in the door, but everyone took to warm, cuddly Mila. She was a natural politician.

"She works a room like no one else," wrote Toronto *Star* reporter Catherine Dunphy after following Mila in 1988. "Watch how she and Brian plunge into a crowd after one of his speeches. She hugs, greets, *connects*. It seems natural and unrehearsed, yet inevitably she reaches the door held open by one of the plainclothes Mounties at the same time as her husband. Always she looks delighted to see him. Always there's one more enthusiastic wave to the crowd before she is whisked away, like a rock star. There's no question: she's good at her job."

"She hugs, greets, connects.*"*

Mila's job was to warm up the crowd for Brian and lead the cheering when he appeared. Mila had to *perform*: Mila was Brian's groupie. It was a dumb and degrading role. Why should any wife leap up in ecstasy every time her husband enters the room? Margaret Trudeau would have said "Fuck you!," Maryon Pearson would have lit a cigarette, Maureen McTeer would have gone off to make her own speech; when John Turner ran for the Liberal leadership, Geills went to China on a photo shoot. But Mila was content to be Brian's "biggest asset" – some whispered his only asset – and except when placed on a chair, Mila was never far from the crook of Brian's arm. Her bright button eyes didn't miss a thing.

"If he makes a bad speech, I am the first to tell him," she told Ian MacDonald in 1984. "If there's something that's out of line, I'm the first to tell him." Brian's biggest handicap was an ego the size of the Goodyear blimp that exploded on contact with criticism. His friends described Brian as "thin-skinned," Mila preferred "sensitive"; others would use words such as abusive, vituperative and vulgar. Like John Diefenbaker, Brian flew into rages, and like Olive, Mila took a lot of the heat that could have fried Brian's political hopes to a crisp.

Conservatives warmed to Mila because she wasn't Maureen McTeer. Asked if she was going to remain "Mrs. Mulroney," Mila quipped "What would you expect if your maiden name was Pivnicki?" Mila was a familiar and reassuring icon – homemaker, wife, mother-of-three – as well as an ethnic and a *lady*. Mila was always dressed up – no jeans, *please* – a mannequin whose mascara never ran when she wiped away a sentimental tear and whose lipstick never smudged no matter how many strangers she kissed on the cheek. The American press compared glamorous Mila favourably to Jackie Kennedy, a comparison Brian encouraged.

Mila was thirty-one when the Boy from Baie Comeau stomped on Tin Man Turner to become prime minister of Canada in September 1984. She was older than Margaret Trudeau and Maureen McTeer had been, and a veteran of nearly ten years of brutal political infighting, yet she seemed curiously innocent, as if she had never really understood what the game was all about. When *Chatelaine* magazine chose Mila its Woman of the Year for 1985, it stirred up unexpected feminist fury; Mila discovered that Maureen McTeer had educated a lot of women to expect The Wife to be more than a clothes-horse or a concubine.

Mila quickly discarded her "happy little housewife" image. She would be a "working mother" and the role of prime minister's wife would become a real job. A suite of offices was found for her in the Langevin Block, staffed, decorated and paid for at public expense. Because it is officially part of the prime minister's office, exact budget figures for Mila's office are not available, but the cost probably runs between $100,000 and $500,000 a year, and possibly more. Mila announced that she would be bringing her new baby, Nicholas, to the office with her. She would set a trend: a working mother with on-the-job day care. Mila apparently did not realize that this privilege was not available to millions of other working mothers, and their day care was not provided free by the government. Working women were outraged. Nicholas stayed home.

What would The Working Wife do? An office gave Mila no more political power than Zoé Laurier had as Wilfrid's "minister of charitable affairs," and Mila's office actually relieved her of the onerous chores faced by previous wives: she now had paid staff to answer mail, screen requests for public appearances and make all her travel arrangements. Because of her background, Mila was deluged with pleas to assist eastern European immigrants, but she could not intervene without being accused of favouritism, and her helplessness exposed her irrelevance.

In 1986 Mila decided to "go political." Cautioned to wear her diamonds in Calgary, but not in Saskatoon, she hopped across the prairies reading little homilies to friendly crowds about "Brian's great dream for Canada," a reprise, twelve years later, of Margaret Trudeau's "Pierre is a beautiful guy." But everybody knew what had happened to Maggie and Pierre, and Mila's venture into politics simply exposed her to ridicule: "As we move forward with our program of reform, all Canadians will get richer," she cheerily told an audience in Saskatoon. No politician would make such a silly promise, and when Canadians got poorer instead, Mila took the rap.

"A throwback to old times," said Calgary columnist Tom Keyser, "perky, peppy, preppy and cute as a gnat's knee." It wasn't the image Mila had in mind, yet when she looked at the Conservative front benches, she saw around Brian older women who had made it to the House of Commons on their own, and across the floor, a woman exactly her own age, Liberal MP Sheila Copps, who regarded Mila's wifely pretensions with open scorn. Mila was obsolete.

Mila did what any energetic young socialite would do: she adopted a disease, cystic fibrosis, and became a dedicated and successful fund-raiser. However, charity can be an excuse to have a great party, and Mila's first benefit bash, a $5000-a-ticket hockey gala, earned her the epithet "Evita of the frozen pampas." It was a signal that the rules had subtly changed at 24 Sussex Drive: invitations depended not on who you were, but on how much you were worth, and if access to the PM's social circle could be bought, why not access to his political circle? It was no coincidence that an embarrassing number of Brian's Conservative colleagues became stuck like flies in a mess of scandals involving influence peddling.

Brian and Mila also stuck close to Ronnie and Nancy, United States President Ronald Reagan and his never too thin wife, a signal that the Mulroney style would be California Colonial. It was a mistake: most Canadians regarded Reagan as a dangerous goof, and Nancy was as welcome as moths. In Canada, Americans were associated with Vietnam and acid rain, the Irish with whiskey and the IRA.

Unable to find a role or an identity, Mila recklessly leaped into the Great Redecorating War, and was badly mauled. Stornoway, the Opposition leader's official residence, had been "done" three times in seven years – by Maureen, Margaret, Maureen – when Mila decided to do it again in 1983. She hired Ottawa's trendy Italian designer, Giovanni Mowinckel, and spent $79,000. Mowinckel's hot colours and adventurous chintz-and-check patterns were a hit, and he was soon the designer to *le tout Ottawa*. After the 1984 election, Mila hired Mowinckel to redecorate 24 Sussex Drive for the fourth time in ten years, while over at Stornoway, Geills Turner discovered that the house had been stripped to the bare walls: Mila had apparently moved all the Mowinckel Mediterranean out to Harrington Lake.

The changing of the guard (not to mention the decor) at 24 Sussex Drive in 1984. Mila is in. Geills is out.

Giovanni Mowinckel abruptly left Ottawa in the spring of 1987. He turned up in Italy, leaving behind an appalling mess of angry creditors, unfinished jobs and debts of more than $400,000. Mowinckel had apparently quarrelled with the Mulroneys over unpaid bills, and rumours circulated about Mila's fussy perfectionism. In the bitter aftermath, *Globe and Mail* reporter Stevie Cameron revealed that the Conservative Party had paid over $300,000 for Mila's renovations to 24 Sussex Drive and Harrington Lake, in addition to another $100,000 spent on the houses by the government.

The "loan," as the Conservative Party called it, was legal, but the public found the amount staggering. Brian's jokes about Mila's extravagance came back to haunt her, and the jokes were on Mila. "Ordinary Canadians were appalled and titillated to learn that some of the money was spent on closets large enough to house fifty pairs of prime ministerial Guccis," Susan Riley wrote. "Overnight Miss Goody Two-Shoes became Miss Goody Too-Many-Shoes."

Mila wasn't laughing. Stung by the criticism, Mila slammed the door. She has not given a full media interview since she spoke to Robert Fulford early in 1987. Fulford gives a fascinating glimpse of the almost Oriental rituals that sheltered Mila's life:

"A young woman from the privy council office walked into the first-floor corner office in the Langevin Block with a steel box labelled "PRIME MINISTER OF CANADA." She explained that she was Tris Wilson, that she often travelled with the prime minister's party, and that she was there to record my interview with Mrs. Mulroney. She took some equipment from the box, placed a microphone on top of a pile of decorating magazines resting on an antique pine coffee table, and sat down on the floor with the tape recorder. Bonnie Brownlee, the executive assistant assigned to Mrs. Mulroney, took her place behind another antique pine table. Finally Mrs. Mulroney – a slim, smiling, good-looking woman in a dark grey skirt and sweater – entered. She sat on the sofa beneath a handsome David Craven abstract painting from the Art Bank.

"It was an unusual interview. For one thing, setting it up had been uncommonly difficult. Eighteen months, or about seventeen months longer than normal, had elapsed between *Saturday Night's* first request to see Mrs. Mulroney and our appointment. Her staff had been coy, evasive, and apprehensive. At one point, when an editor had told Bonnie Brownlee that the article was to be written by Elspeth Cameron, Brownlee indicated that she would prefer a male writer. (Cameron eventually tired of waiting and gave up.) Finally, when an interview at last seemed imminent, Brownlee asked that a list of ten or fifteen sample questions be submitted in writing, in advance. That request, unique in my experience, was met. The background staff was also a surprise. Occasionally an uneasy public official will ask that an assistant be present during an interview, but I had never before interviewed anyone in the presence of two helpers. The occasion took on some of the quality of a stage performance and it occurred to me that it might be more appropriately reviewed than reported.''

After all the hocus-pocus and anticipation, Fulford found that Mila had nothing to say. ''She does what she believes the public wants,'' he concluded. Any politician knows that trying to please all of the people all of the time is an impossible task, and Mila finally gave up. After Mulroney's convincing victory in the 1988 election her public appearances became less frequent and more stylized. Her bangs got longer, her make-up thicker, her jewellery chunkier and her police bodyguard heavier. Although her clothes changed with the frequency of a dryer cycle, her face always wore the same blank smile, and, at the age of thirty-six, her giggly, girlish manner was dismissed by one disgusted reporter as ''cutesy-poo.''

Dr. Pivnicki always advised Mila to be self-aware, to keep in touch with her true feelings, yet Mila seemed to define herself exclusively in terms of other people's expectations. Like Margaret Trudeau, Mila was driven by a desire to please, but everything she did caused criticism. No matter how genuine her interest, how earnest and sincere her efforts, she did not strike people as authentic: rather than expressing herself, she was playing to Brian's mirror. Mila was dominated, exploited and depersonalized by her husband's political machine. If she ever stood up and cried, ''I'm not a factor, I'm *Mila*!'' it seems that nobody paid attention.

By the end of 1990, Mila was a myth. Having rapped for years on Mila's bullet-proof glass and found nobody home, Canadians decided to make her up – Fulford's profile was called ''Imagining Mila'' – and to re-create The Wife in their own image. In December 1990 Mila's former chef, François Martin, exhibited a series of colourful paintings depicting Mila as a shrieking harridan in hair curlers, and the satirical magazine *Frank* started running a bitchy correspondence between ''Mila'' and ''Moe'' at the back of every issue:

''Dear Moe, I was watching Joe on television today and it struck me as ironic that for a guy who used to have no chin he now has two. An old

Tory friend of mine used to say that if God had meant Joe to be Prime Minister, He would have given him a chin. Now that he has two, who knows?''

Who knows? At the beginning of 1991, Brian Mulroney was Canada's most unpopular prime minister in fifty years, more unpopular than Britain's Margaret Thatcher, who had just been pushed out of office in a party revolt. He had negotiated a controversial free-trade agreement with the United States that was costing Canadians thousands of jobs; he had rolled the constitutional dice with Quebec over the Meech Lake accord and lost; and many said he had deliberately precipitated a severe economic recession. In January, Canada became embroiled in an ugly war against Iraq that sacrificed Mike Pearson's peacekeeping heritage and did little for Mulroney's popularity, which increased from twelve percent to twenty-two percent, with seventy-one percent of the population disapproving of his conduct and only eight percent undecided. Canada appeared heading for depression, political disintegration and armed insurrection: in one year, Indians had taken up arms at Oka, Quebec, nine members of Mulroney's caucus had broken away to form the pro-separatist Bloc Québécois and the cowboy capitalists had all gone broke.

On the occasions she appeared in public, usually at Conservative events, Mila looked anxious and scared. She was still on stage without a script, and now the audience was howling for blood. Not since Agnes Macdonald had a prime minister's wife faced such political disaster or so much potential violence. Agnes Macdonald feared for her life after the assassination of her husband's Cabinet colleague, D'Arcy McGee, and while no one within the Mulroney government was harmed, Mila was forced to live her life surrounded by secret police. Mila became, once more, the Invisible Lady.

Mila's disappearance from the public stage fueled rumours that she and Brian were separating and on the verge of divorce; in rare photographs Mila looked like the heroine of a tragic European film, while Brian's puffy eyes and bloated face caused speculation that he was once more drinking heavily. In February 1991 the rumours hit the British tabloid *Today*, the Toronto *Sun* and *Frank*. *Today* also hinted at a liaison between Mila and actor Christopher Plummer, based on an innocent appearance they had made together at a literacy benefit.

Mila's office vehemently denied the allegations, and the *Today* story was obviously mischievous, but no other prime minister's wife has had to endure such a cruel public assault on her privacy and dignity. By choosing to play The Wife, Mila lost her power to define herself. A wife's identity is established by her husband, and a prime minister's wife's identity is established by the people who elect him. Mila set no example, fulfilled no expectations, established no lines of communication, and when Brian's dream for Canada turned into a nightmare, there was something inexpressibly sad in Mila's face. It was the face of a little girl in Sarajevo whose father had gone away, a lonely, lost girl wondering what she had done wrong.

Mila didn't abdicate from the role of the prime minister's wife, or repudiate it; she revealed The Wife for what she was, a straw figure carried through the streets to be blessed or stoned, depending on the public mood. Will Mila bury The Wife at last, and drive a stake of holly through her heart?

The Wife

as

Prime

Minister

*I*T MAY BE A VERY short time before a woman becomes prime minister of Canada. Within the orbit of the former British Empire, women have governed Pakistan and India and Margaret Thatcher ruled Britannia for more than a decade. In a Gallup poll taken in October 1990, Audrey McLaughlin, leader of the New Democratic Party, was nearly three times more popular than Prime Minister Mulroney: the poll showed McLaughlin with a forty-three percent approval rating compared to sixteen percent for Mulroney and twenty-five percent for Liberal leader Jean Chrétien. Audrey – she prefers to use her first name rather than Ms. McLaughlin – was also the least known of the three leaders and therefore had the most potential to increase her popularity. She did: in February 1991, after she had spoken out against Canadian involvement in the war against Iraq, McLaughlin's approval rating had grown to more than fifty percent, Mulroney's to twenty-two percent.

The speed of Audrey McLaughlin's political ascent has been astonishing. She was first elected to the House of Commons in July 1987 as MP for the Yukon, and she sailed into the NDP leadership as the front-runner less than three years later, becoming on December 2, 1989 the first woman in Canada to lead a national political party; Audrey topped the popularity polls only ten months into her new job.

Audrey is a socialist and a feminist and feminism is now apparently mainstream, "the No. 1 expression of the new values," according to Environics pollster Michael Adams. Adams defines the new values as "a concern about equality – not only equality of opportunity but equality of condition." Adams's conclusions sound a lot like Agnes Macphail's politics and Agnes's portrait hangs on the wall behind Audrey McLaughlin's desk. Audrey is no Spinster; she is a grandmother, a mother, a divorcée with an interesting past and an attractive woman of fifty-four who has shown that it is possible for women to have *all*.

Audrey McLaughlin addresses the House of Commons for the first time
as leader of the NDP.

McLaughlin is frequently criticized for being passive and indecisive; like Agnes, she may burn, or she may carry out the political revolution she has promised, a quiet revolution in the way decisions are made and carried out, and the new way would be a woman's way: empathetic, organized, collective and non-confrontational. Women have always done business around the kitchen table, and McLaughlin's manner says: "Okay friends, we're all in this together. What are we going to do about it?" She very rarely uses the word "I," except when she says "I want to be prime minister, absolutely."

Audrey has synthesized the image of The Wife, The Other Woman and The Prime Minister. We are not likely to see The Husband trailing around after the prime minister like Prince Philip after the queen, or being chauffeured to his boutique office on Parliament Hill, or choosing wallpaper for 24 Sussex Drive. The idea is absurd. The Wife is absurd. Unless,

375
•

like Margaret Trudeau, she is prepared to abdicate and foment a palace revolt, she has no meaningful public role in a society that no longer views women as the property of men.

Since John Diefenbaker appointed Ellen Fairclough Canada's first woman Cabinet minister in 1957, the symbolic power of The Wife has steadily eroded. Fairclough, a chartered accountant, was as warm and attractive as Olive Diefenbaker, and she didn't have to live with John. Her Liberal successor, Judy LaMarsh, terrorized Mike Pearson, apparently with Maryon's approval. Liberal Sheila Copps, who became deputy leader in March 1991, is more independent and outspoken than either of them. In 1991 only one MP in seven is female, but one of them is Kim Campbell, Conservative minister of justice, Sir John Thompson's old portfolio, and it's hard to believe that Annie wouldn't be pleased. The balance of power between The Wife and the prime minister tilted symbolically after Margaret Trudeau's breakdown in 1974: Margaret filmed a television promotion for the Canadian Mental Health Association, but the CMHA's executive director, Audrey McLaughlin, went on television to discuss the social stigma of mental illness.

Ellen Fairclough, Canada's first woman Cabinet minister.

Our prime ministers' wives have been no more neurotic, irrational, uninformed or incompetent than their husbands; in fact, many would probably have made better prime ministers, an opinion frequently expressed by the public. Almost without exception they have been women of outstanding energy, ability and generosity of spirit. As Maryon Pearson put it, they married for better or for worse, not for lunch, and they married for love. These are romantic marriages, marriages that begin with a whirlwind affair, a secret engagement, cryptic love letters, a mysterious elopement, an obsessive pursuit, and they have brought the wives more than their fair share of loneliness, self-sacrifice, frustration and failure, as well as heady moments of triumph and joy. The wives have performed an impossible task with courage and loyalty, and perhaps their most endearing quality has been their inability to see shortcomings in their husbands that are glaringly obvious to everyone else.

Every generation produces hundreds of politicians, many of them more intelligent, more imaginative and more attractive than the men who have become our prime ministers. What makes a prime minister? Is it luck or timing, aggressiveness, anxiety, instinct? Or has the answer always been standing there, just to one side and slightly behind, wearing a little silk dress and a bemused smile?

CHAPTER ONE:
The Invisible Lady: Isabella Macdonald

The letters quoted are from John A. Macdonald's fragmentary personal correspondence published in *Affectionately Yours* (Macmillan, 1969), edited with an
informative introduction by J.K. Johnson. The original letters are in the Macdonald papers in the National Archives of Canada. My interpretation of Isabella has
drawn on the diagnosis of Dr. James McSherry in "The Medicine of History,"
Queen's Quarterly, vol. 95, no. 3 (Autumn 1988). According to the ninth edition
of the *Encyclopedia Britannica* (1890), "neuralgia" was used to describe everything
from depression and anxiety to sciatica, pleurisy, migraine headaches, nervous
tics, anemia, malaria and "uterine derangements." As well as opium, Isabella may
have received chloral, an early form of chloroform that "may bring on deep
melancholy, weakness of will and an inability to sleep without the drug." Opium
was used for coughs, diabetes and diarrhea, although the doses had to be constantly increased: "If the dose cannot be taken at the usual time, the symptoms
of the disease return with such violence that the remedy is speedily resorted to as
the only means of relief." The opium habit was almost impossible to break: the
only suggested treatments were cocaine and strychnine.

Donald Creighton's classic biography, *John A. Macdonald: The Young Politi-
cian* (Macmillan, 1952), gives a romantic portrait of Isabella and John, but provides vivid detail about Macdonald's life and career at this time. An essay on
Macdonald also appears in volume XII of the *Dictionary of Canadian Biography*
(University of Toronto Press and Les Presses de l'université Laval, 1990). Lena
Newman's illustrated *The John A. Macdonald Album* (1974) has interesting detail
on Macdonald's personal relationships and domestic arrangements, and *John A.
Lived Here* (Frontenac Historic Foundation, 1984) by Margaret Angus describes
his many houses. In Kingston, Bellevue House, a National Historic Park, has
been restored to give an impression of how John and Isabella lived during their
one year there, and their graves are in the nearby Cataraqui cemetery.

CHAPTER TWO:
"That Mole-Catcher of a Wife of His": Agnes Macdonald

Louise Reynolds's *Agnes: The Biography of Lady Macdonald* (Carleton University Press, 1990) provides a thorough and sympathetic overview of Agnes's life, particularly the early years. The quotes from E.M. Biggar, Sir Joseph Pope and *Murray's Magazine* are from this source. The one surviving volume of Agnes's diary is in the National Archives (MG 26 A vol. 559A). Towards the end of her life she asked Macdonald's secretary, Sir Joseph Pope, to send seventeen volumes of her diary to her; they were subsequently lost or destroyed, as was all the correspondence between John and Agnes. Essays on Macdonald, Hewitt Bernard and Thomas D'Arcy McGee are in Volume XII of the *Dictionary of Canadian Biography*. Donald Creighton's *The Young Politician* and *The Old Chieftan* (Macmillan, 1955) deal dramatically with Macdonald's political adventures, and *Sir John A., An Anecdotal Life of John A. Macdonald* (Oxford, 1989), edited by Cynthia M. Smith and Jack McLeod, gives a good portrait of the public Macdonald. For information on childbirth and contraception I have relied on Judith Leavitt's *Brought to Bed* (Oxford University Press 1986) and one of the earliest books on the subject, Marie Stopes's *Contraception* (1923). A vivid, eyewitness account of the Red River rebellion is provided by Major Charles Boulton in *I Fought Riel, a Military Memoir* (Lorimer, 1985), and Pierre Berton tells the exciting story of Macdonald's early railway plans in *The National Dream* (McClelland and Stewart, 1970).

CHAPTER THREE:
Plain Jane Mackenzie

A good portrait of Jane is in Carol McLeod's *Wives of the Canadian Prime Ministers* (Lancelot Press, 1985). Mackenzie's letters to Jane are in the National Archives (MG 26 B vol. 15). Dale Thomson's *Alexander Mackenzie: Clear Grit* (Macmillan, 1960) is the standard biography of Mackenzie, and an essay by Ben Forster is in volume XII of the *Dictionary of Canadian Biography*. Hariot Dufferin's *My Canadian Journal* (1969) provides a fascinating glimpse into the energetic lifestyle of the Dufferin *ménage*, and Sandra Gwyn in *The Private Capital* (McClelland & Stewart, 1984) gives a detailed, if romantic, portrait of the Rideau Hall set.

CHAPTER FOUR:
The Barefoot Baroness: The Return of Agnes Macdonald

Details of Agnes's life between 1873 and 1891 are scarce, although some household-account books are stored with her diary in the National Archives. Agnes had talent as a writer, and always threatened to write her autobiography, but towards the end of her life she became defensive about her privacy and careless about her letters and diaries; nonetheless, her papers may yet be found hidden away in England or Italy. Her account of her journey through the mountains, "By Car and by Cowcatcher," was published in *Murray's Magazine*, London, vol. I, 1887. In the same issue Agnes contributed an essay entitled "Canadian Topics." Here she praised her husband as "the cheery old combatant at the head of Canada's affairs" and gave a gleefully partisan interpretation of the political scene, which suggests that she was more biased than she admitted. Although she wrote more articles for *Murray's*, Agnes was probably criticized for using her position to interfere in politics, and she soon stopped journalism altogether.

Mary Macdonald's letters to her father are in *Affectionately Yours*, edited by J.K. Johnson. I am greatly indebted to Margaret Cohoe of Kingston for her private research on Mary as well as her two papers, "John A. Macdonald – The Family Man" and "John A.'s Daughter and the Faithful Coward," provided by Bellevue House, the Macdonald museum in Kingston. The archives at Queen's University, Kingston, has letters by Agnes, Louisa and Mary, as well as by John A. and Hugh, in the papers of Macdonald's brother-in-law, Dr. James Williamson.

Agnes's massive correspondence with Joseph Pope can be found at the National Archives in the Sir Joseph Pope papers (MG 30 E86 vols. 106–110). Sandra Gwyn's *The Private Capital* has a brief portrait of Agnes.

CHAPTER FIVE:
The Love Affair of Annie and John Thompson

Sir John Thompson was fortunate in his biographer, historian Peter B. Waite of Dalhousie University, Halifax. Waite's *The Man from Halifax* (University of Toronto Press, 1985) is a superbly written, comprehensive account of Thompson's life that deals frankly with his personal life and gives Annie her due as a remarkable woman as well as a major influence on Thompson's career. Waite decoded Thompson's difficult shorthand, and I am grateful to him for decoding some fragments of Annie's diary that had not been published. The voluminous correspondence between John and Annie is in the National Archives (MG 26 D vols. 283, 288–91, 298, 300). Her diary is in vol. 293. I have retained Annie's spelling and punctuation as much as possible, while making the letters grammatical enough to be understood. Scrapbooks and clippings, largely relating to Thompson's death and the public subscription, are in vols. 294–296, 299. They include the account of his death from the *St. James' Gazette*. Ishbel Aberdeen's comments come from her perceptive and entertaining memoir, *The Journal of Lady Aberdeen*, edited by John Saywell and published by The Champlain Society in 1960. A good brief portrait of Sir John Abbott by Carman Miller is in Volume

XII of the *Dictionary of Canadian Biography*. Mary Bethune Abbott apparently left no personal records when she died in 1898: she had eight children and is chiefly famous as the great-grandmother of actor Christopher Plummer.

CHAPTER SIX
The Dutiful Wife: Frances Tupper

Carol McLeod has an essay on Frances in *Wives of the Canadian Prime Ministers*, and Lancelot Press also published a lively short biography of Sir Charles Tupper, *War Horse of Cumberland* (1985), by Vincent Durant. The quote by George Ross and Frances's letters are taken from these sources, as are Tupper's last words. Frances's obituary is from the Montreal *Standard*. The comments by Sir John Thompson come from his letters to Annie (MG 26 vols. 288–290) and the mysterious story of Tupper's relationship with Josephine Bailey is in Peter Waite's *The Man from Halifax*. In the *The Private Capital*, Sandra Gwyn suggests that Tupper had a "flirtation" with Fanny Meredith, the wife of a prominent Ottawa civil servant, and he may have performed an abortion on her. Fanny, like many respectable Ottawa matrons, remained fond of Sir Charles, and he was a close friend of both Fanny and her husband. Ishbel Aberdeen's observation is from *The Journal of Lady Aberdeen*. Tupper's memoirs, *Recollections of Sixty Years in Canada* (published after his death as *The Life and Letters of the Rt. Hon. Sir Charles Tupper, Bart. K.C.M.G.*, edited by E.M. Saunders), gives a detailed, self-serving account of his career for anyone with the stamina to read it.

CHAPTER SEVEN:
The Good Wife and the Other Woman: Zoé Laurier and Émilie Lavergne

Joseph Schull's popular biography, *Laurier* (Macmillan, 1965), is still the standard account of Laurier's life, and more recent biographies in both English and French tend to reflect Schull's idealization of Laurier and repeat his unattributed anecdotes. Schull's research notes are in the National Archives (MG 31 D 5). Almost all of Zoé's letters have disappeared; however, a few notes to a family friend, Louis Gauthier, in the National Archives (MG 27 II H) show her keen interest in local gossip and concern for her friends' financial welfare. Wilfrid's letters to Zoé are in the Laurier papers in the National Archives (MG 26 G 4 vol. 814A–B). Sixteen of these letters were lost or stolen sometime between 1973 and 1984, but archivists who read them claim that they were similar in tone and content to those remaining. The letters are in French, translated by me with the assistance of Lucie Brunet and Robert Chodos.

In *The Private Capital* Sandra Gwyn has a good account of Émilie Lavergne and Zoé Laurier in Ottawa, and I am indebted to Gwyn for the quotes from

Amaryllis, as well as Amaryllis's identity. The existence of Laurier's letters to Émilie Lavergne did not become knnown until 1960, thirty years after Émilie's death, when her nephew Renaud Lavergne showed forty-one letters, in English, to researchers. Portions of the letters are quoted in a student thesis, "Laurier, Citoyen d'Arthabaska," presented to the University of Ottawa in 1961 by Frère Antoine (Maurice Carrier). The thesis also quotes from an unpublished memoir by Renaud Lavergne. In 1963 Renaud gave the letters to historian Marc La Terreur, who presented excerpts from them in a paper to the Canadian Historical Association in 1964 and published a similar article in *Le Magazine Maclean* in January 1966. La Terreur gave the letters to the National Archives, but reclaimed them in 1967, allowing the archives to retain photocopies (Madame Joseph Lavergne papers, MG 27 I i 42). In 1971 the originals were put up for auction by a Montreal antique dealer, Bernard Amtmann. "They are among the most beautiful love letters I have ever read," Amtmann said, valuing the collection at $25,000 to $50,000. The highest bid, however, was $1,500 and the letters remained unsold; shortly after they were purchased by Montreal collector Charles Fisher for $15,000. In 1989 Fisher published the letters in *Dearest Émilie: The Love Letters of Sir Wilfrid Laurier to Madame Émilie Lavergne* (NC Press) with an introduction and interpretive notes, and I have relied on his book as a source. Fisher is convinced that the relationship between Laurier and Émilie was sexual; previous historians believed that it was not. The original letters are currently in Mr. Fisher's bank vault in Bermuda.

The authenticity of the letters has never been questioned, although their history is shrouded in mystery and few experts have had the opportunity to examine them closely. The spidery handwriting certainly appears to be Laurier's, and La Terreur was able to date the letters from internal evidence. The existing letters appear to be a fragment of a much larger correspondence, and in 1967 several letters from this sequence, as well as later letters, turned up in the papers of Mackenzie King. How did they get there? Did King inherit them with Laurier House, or was he given them because of his intimate association with Laurier? Émilie's letters to Laurier were apparently given to her daughter Gabrielle and have now disappeared.

Brief details of the Barthe family are in Armand Lavergne's autobiography, *Trente ans de Vie nationale* (1934). After an erratic career as a Quebec nationalist, Armand became a Conservative member of parliament. He professed to be angered by rumours of his parentage, and quarrelled fiercely with Laurier. While praised for his brilliance, Armand's promise was never fulfilled and he died, unmarried, in 1935. Documents relating to the Barthe family can be found in the Centre de Recherche en Civilization Canadien-Français at the University of Ottawa.

Information about the Laurier's domestic life comes from a memoir by Yvonne Coutu in the Laurier papers (vol. 810) and from *Laurier* (1919), by L.-

O. David: "Sir Wilfrid Laurier," in *Chefs de File* (1934) by Robert Rumilly; *Laurier* (1967), by Raymond Tanghe; *Wilfrid Laurier* (Presses de l'Université Laval, 1986), by Réal Belanger; *The Life and Letters of Sir Wilfrid Laurier* (1921), by O.D. Skelton, as well as Schull's *Laurier*. Zoé's letter to Lady Aberdeen, as well as several notes from Zoé and Wilfrid, are in the Aberdeen papers in the National Archives (MG 27 B5 vol. 3). One letter from Laurier, dated July 5, 1895, refers to a message from Lady Aberdeen transmitted via Madame Lavergne. Lady Aberdeen was notorious for meddling in politics, although this time she was criticizing Laurier's behaviour towards a friend. Ishbel Aberdeen's diary, *The Journal of Lady Aberdeen*, contains frequent references to the Lauriers. Some notes from Lady Minto to Zoé in the Laurier papers indicate that Zoé was also on very friendly terms with Ishbel's successor.

An overview of the period of Laurier's administration is provided in *Canada: 1896-1921* (McClelland and Stewart, 1974), by Robert Craig Brown and Ramsay Cook, and a Liberal perspective is offered in *William Lyon Mackenzie King*, vol. 1, by R. MacGregor Dawson (University of Toronto Press, 1958). King's diary is an excellent source for detail on the conscription crisis of 1917, as well as on Laurier's death.

CHAPTER EIGHT:
City Mouse, Country Mouse: Laura Borden and Isabel Meighen

Carol McLeod's *Wives of the Canadian Prime Ministers* is a helpful source for both Laura Borden and Isabel Meighen. The correspondence between Laura and Sir Robert Borden is in the National Archives (MG 26 H vols. 445-448), as is a note about his domestic arrangements by his housekeeper, Alice Lowe, who also gives the account of Laura's reaction to the fire in the House of Commons. The two volumes of *Robert Laird Borden* by Robert Craig Brown (Macmillan, vol. 1, 1975 and vol. 2, 1980) are the standard authority on Borden's life and political career, although Laura is mentioned only briefly. John English's *Borden, His Life and World* (McGraw-Hill Ryerson 1977) gives an illustrated overview of the years between 1911 and 1920, and *Canada: 1896-1921* by Robert Craig Brown and Ramsay Cook covers the war years with scholarly objectivity. My own novel, *Willie, A Romance* (Lorimer, 1983), depicts Ottawa between 1914 and 1918 from a woman's perspective, and includes portraits of Mackenzie King, Laura Borden and the Duchess of Connaught. Nellie McClung's *In Times Like These*, first published in 1915, offers a superb view of the war and the "woman question" from the eloquent leader of Canada's women's suffrage movement.

Unfortunately Arthur Meighen appears to have destroyed his personal papers and there is almost no documentation of Isabel Meighen's private life apart from some scrapbooks in the keeping of her daughter-in-law, Mrs. T.R. Meighen of Montreal. I am indebted to Maxwell Meighen of Toronto for his recollections of his mother, and to Bruce Hutchison's *Mr. Prime Minister* (1964) for the quotes about Arthur. Roger Graham's three-volume biography, *Arthur Meighen* (1960-65), provides an exhaustive and sympathetic overview of Meighen's life, and Eugene Forsey has written about Meighen in *A Life on the Fringe* (Oxford University Press, 1990). Copies of *The Land of Afternoon* can be found in rare book stores and good libraries: the real identity of "Gilbert Knox" was not revealed until after Madge Macbeth's death, when her papers were donated to the National Archives. The Borden-Meighen period and the constitutional crisis of 1926 is covered, from his own point of view, in Mackenzie King's diary as well in Graham's *Arthur Meighen* and *The King-Byng Affair* (Copp Clark, 1967).

CHAPTER NINE:
Other Men's Wives: Mrs. King and Mrs. Patteson

The most accessible source for Mackenzie King's relationships with women is C.P. Stacey's *A Very Double Life* (Macmillan, 1976). The first volume of King's biography, R. MacGregor Dawson's *William Lyon Mackenzie King*, is excellent on King's early life. King's psychology and sexuality are explored by Joy Esberey in *Knight of the Holy Spirit* (University of Toronto Press, 1980), and Esberey makes the point that King's neuroses were integrated into his political behaviour. King's mental health is also analysed in an unpublished study, "The King of Clubs: A Psychobiography of William Lyon Mackenzie King, 1893-1900," by Lynn McIntyre and Joel Jeffries of the Clarke Institute of Psychiatry in Toronto. Basing their analysis on King's diaries, they discovered "a depressive personality," psychosomatic illness and "a broad array of psychopathology." King's work in social reform "was born of a sublimated desire to be with prostitutes," and his idealization of his mother "is abnormal and partially the result of suppressed hostility towards her." Because of this "unhealthy" love, "King loses the ability to ever love a woman both spiritually and sexually." King's relations with women are also the subject of my two novels, *Willie: A Romance* and *Lily, A Rhapsody in Red* (Lorimer, 1986).

King's voluminous correspondence with his family is in the National Archives (MG 26 J 7); there are remarkably few letters from his mother, who seems to have left the letter writing, as she left everything else, to the rest of the family, on the grounds that she was too sick or tired to deal with it. Unlike Mary Bannerman Diefenbaker, Isabel King was dependent, not domineering: when her youngest daughter, Jennie, gave birth to her fourth child, Mother insisted on going into the hospital with her for a "rest" and occupied the adjoining bed until the baby and Jennie were ready to leave. Jennie found her mother's behaviour impossible, and she was the only one to escape the family's gothic fate: Bella died, unmarried, at forty-two; John King went blind; Max, a doctor, developed tuberculosis and Brights' disease and died in his forties after years of invalidism. Three days after Mother's death on December 18, 1917, Willie dictated to his secretary a single-spaced, ten-page letter to Max giving minute details of Mother's last moments and her funeral, including the size and expense of the flower arrangements and the names of the politicians and newspaper publishers among the mourners. Far from being overcome by grief, King was detached and calm; his letter is chilling in its self-congratulation and the pleasure he takes in how the funeral's "historic interest" will enhance his reputation.

The primary source for King's private life is his own diary, which he kept from 1893 until his death in 1950. Typescripts of the diary are available in the National Archives (MG 26 J Diary) or on microfiche. Unfortunately it is not indexed or annotated, and the whole thing must be read year by year, willy-nilly. King's diary is one of the great documents of democratic politics, part confessional, part history, part hallucination, a social history of Canada as well as one man's search for salvation. However, it cannot be taken at face value; King twisted accounts of events, rationalized his motives and omitted things that he felt would put him in a bad light; it is what the diary unconsciously reveals, or attempts to conceal, that is often most important. Joan Patteson's ubiquitous presence in the diary indicates the depth of their relationship; the diary also contains long references to their spiritualist activities, King's dreams and his megalomaniacal *Parsifal* fantasy that had its roots in his obsession with "purity" and Tennyson's long poem, "The Idylls of the King."

Some of King's papers have not yet been opened to the public, and some may have been destroyed, including his letters from Mrs. Patteson, although notes from her grandchildren survive. Sir Oliver Lodge's *Raymond* is a spiritualist classic, very close to King's own attitude; King occasionally attended seances in Winnipeg at the home of Dr. Glen Hamilton, and Dr. Hamilton's fascinating records and photographs are in the archives of the University of Manitoba, Winnipeg.

King's political career is dealt with by Blair Neatby in the second and third volumes of the biography *William Lyon Mackenzie King* (started by Dawson), *The Lonely Heights* and *The Prism of Unity* (University of Toronto Press 1963 and 1976 respectively), as well as in *The Mackenzie King Record*, by J.W. Pickersgill and D.F. Forster (University of Toronto Press, 1960–1970), which draws heavily on King's diaries from 1939 to 1948. King's relationship with the Rockefellers is investigated by Henry Ferns and Bernard Ostry in *The Age of Mackenzie King* (Lorimer, 1976), and Bruce Hutchison gives a sympathetic popular account of King's career in *The Incredible Canadian* (1952). King published an unreadable book on economics, *Industry and Humanity* (1918), and in 1906 *The Secret of Heroism*, a tribute to his dead friend, Bert Harper, that gave rise to early speculation about King's sexual orientation. *First Person* (Dundurn Press 1988), by Valerie Knowles, is a good account of Canada's first woman senator, Cairine Wilson, a powerful, wealthy and courageous woman who took up the cause of Jewish refugees in the 1930s.

CHAPTER TEN:
Grandes Dames: Agnes Macphail and Jeanne St. Laurent

I have relied on two recent biographies of Agnes Macphail, *Agnes Macphail: Reformer* by Doris Pennington (Simon & Pierre, 1989) and *Agnes Macphail: The Politics of Equality* by Terry Crowley (Lorimer, 1990) as well as an earlier biography, *Ask No Quarter* (1959) by Doris French and Margaret Stewart. Most of Agnes's quotes are taken from Pennington's *Agnes Macphail: Reformer.* Agnes Macphail's papers are in the National Archives (MG 24 C4 III). Historian P.B. Waite has tackled R.B. Bennett's relations with women in "Out of Albert County: In Search of R.B. Bennett," a paper presented to the Canadian Historical Association in 1990. Waite points out the deep affection between Bennett and his younger sister, Mildred, who served as his hostess in Ottawa until her marriage to Marjorie Herridge's oldest son, William, in 1931. The next year, Bennett became infatuated with a younger and very wealthy widow, Hazel Colville. Mrs. Colville apparently ended the relationship two years later, and the only woman close to Bennett when he died in 1947 was his loyal secretary, Alice Millar. Waite suggests that Bennett suffered from phimosis, a tight foreskin, that made erection painful and inhibited his normal sexuality. There is no evidence to suggest that Bennett and Agnes Macphail were romantically involved. Mildred Bennett, whose wedding was the social highlight of the Ottawa season, bore a son in 1932 and died of cancer in 1938. Pierre Berton's *The Great Depression* (McClelland & Stewart, 1990) is a good source for the 1930s from a point of view similar to Macphail's.

Jeanne St. Laurent left almost nothing in the way of letters or other documents. I am grateful to her two daughters, Thérèse Lafferty and Madeleine St. Laurent, and her granddaughter Jean Riley for sharing their recollections with me. Carol McLeod has a good essay on Jeanne in *Wives of the Canadian Prime Ministers*, and Dale Thomson's *Louis St. Laurent* (Macmillan, 1967) provides a basic overview of St. Laurent's life and career. For the description and other information on 24 Sussex Drive I am indebted to Maureen McTeer's *Residences: Homes of Canada's Leaders* (Prentice-Hall 1982).

CHAPTER ELEVEN:
The Three Mrs. Diefenbakers

I had the good fortune to meet John and Olive Diefenbaker on a couple of occasions during 1965 and 1966 when I was a young newspaper reporter and Diefenbaker was leader of the Opposition. I worked for the Winnipeg *Tribune*, a traditionally Conservative paper, and one of us was always sent to the airport to interview the Chief on his short stop-overs between Ottawa and Saskatoon. Dief always had a story – he invented the thirty-second quip – and he treated me with respect and courtesy in spite of the nearly fifty years difference in our ages and my humble status. I was impressed by Olive's serenity, watchfulness and her ability to relate to strangers without being false or superficial.

I am grateful to Olive's daughter, Carolyn Weir, and her husband, Don, for talking to me at length about Olive and John. Diefenbaker mythologized his life, often telling the same story six different ways or making it up altogether. He was notoriously unreliable about dates – in his memoirs he gives the date of Edna's death as 1959, not 1951 – and I have relied on the Weirs' memories to reach a reasonable version of John's various meetings with Olive. Carolyn also confirms John's easy rapport with children: "He was wonderful," she says. "He was as concerned about me as if he had been my father born and bred." The three volumes of Diefenbaker's memoirs, *One Canada* (Macmillan, 1975–1977), offer insight into his personality and his own interpretation of his career.

The definitive source on Edna Diefenbaker is *The Other Mrs. Diefenbaker* by Simma Holt (Doubleday, 1982) and I have drawn my portrait of Edna from Holt's extremely detailed account of Edna's life with John, including the story of her meeting with James Sinclair, the quote from Emmett Hall and the account of Olive's death. *Diefenbaker for the Defence* by Garrett and Kevin Wilson (Lorimer, 1988) is also a good source for stories about Diefenbaker's legal career, military record and Saskatchewan politics. Edna's letters to John are in the Diefenbaker Centre, Saskatoon, as is his correspondence with Mary, William, Elmer and Olive and their medical records. I have retained the spelling and grammar of the original letters. I have also relied on the Centre's oral history project for a great deal of information from Diefenbaker's friends and political supporters, including the material from Hugh Arscott, Peggy Green and Alvin Hamilton. The Diefenbaker Centre is also a treasure trove of photographs, furniture and memorabilia.

For John's period in office, *Renegade in Power* (McClelland & Stewart, 1963) by Peter Newman gives a critical assessment very popular at the time, and Peter Stursberg's oral history, *Diefenbaker, Leadership Gained* (University of Toronto, 1975) and *Diefenbaker*, Leadership Lost (University of Toronto, 1976), reveals the internal disagreements in the government. Sean O'Sullivan provides a mean-spirited glimpse of John's and Olive's last years in his memoir, *Both My Houses* (Key Porter, 1986), as well as Olive's very brief response to John's defeat as party leader. There are a vast number of press clippings about John and Olive; a profile in *Chatelaine* (June 1961) by Christina McCall provided useful detail about Olive's jewellery and the Diefenbakers' domestic life. A video docudrama made about Olive after her death but never broadcast is in the possession of Carolyn Weir. I have relied also on my own memory of Diefenbaker's rallies and television appearances, and on interviews with Tom Van Dusen and Greg Guthrie of Ottawa.

CHAPTER TWELVE:
Moody Maryon

A videotape of Maryon's interview with Donna Soble of CHCH-TV is in the National Film, Television and Sound Archives, Ottawa. While Maryon's responses are generally typical of the platitudes expected of wives at that time, the video shows some of her paintings and the Canadiana Room, as well as Maryon's exceptional self-possession. Susan Riley's essay on Maryon in *Political Wives* (1987) is witty and insightful; Maryon's quips have been repeated so often that they are part of the folklore. John English's *Shadow of Heaven* (Lester & Orpen Dennys, 1989) is the best source on Pearson's life until 1948, although he portrays Maryon as rather gloomy and unhappy. For background on the Moody family I am indebted to Herbert Moody's unpublished family history and a personal interview. I am grateful to Maryon's daughter, Patricia Pearson Hannah, for her memories of her mother, and for lending me four volumes of Maryon's diaries: most useful are those for 1922 and 1967. She also provided photocopies of Maryon's letters to Ken Kirkwood and Issy Chester. Unfortunately Maryon's and Mike's personal correspondence has been lost or destroyed, as has any correspondence between Maryon and Graham Towers, along with Towers's personal papers. Douglas Fullerton's biography, *Graham Towers and His Times* (McClelland & Stewart, 1986), provides some tantalizing comments about Towers. Norah Michener's etiquette handbook is in the Library of Parliament; Peter Stursberg's *The Last Viceroy* (McGraw-Hill-Ryerson, 1989) provides an entertaining view of the Micheners and some anecdotes about Maryon. Sources for Maryon's life between 1930 and 1958 are scarce, and sources for her relationship with Graham Towers prefer to remain anonymous, but Charles Ritchie's *The Siren Years* (Macmillan, 1974) gives a good portrait of their era, as do all the books about the British spies and Pearson's contemporaries, Guy Burgess, Kim Philby and Donald Maclean.

Judy LaMarsh gives an excellent account of her career in *Memoirs of a Bird in a Gilded Cage* (McClelland & Stewart, 1968), which also contains insights into the Pearson government. Olive Diefenbaker's remarks about 24 Sussex are taken from letters supplied to me by Marie Bendas. I am grateful to Mary MacDonald, Sheila Zimmerman and Christopher Young for their personal recollections. Among the press stories about Maryon, Christina McCall Newman's "Mrs. Lester Pearson's New Life in the Limelight," in *Maclean's* (March 1964), is the best. The three volumes of Pearson's own memoirs, *Mike* (University of Toronto Press, 1972-75) give his own chatty but imaginative version of his life. A different perspective is provided in *Gentle Patriot* (1973), Denis Smith's biography of Walter Gordon, and Lawrence Martin reveals Pearson's unhappy relationship with Lyndon Johnson in *The Presidents and the Prime Ministers* (Doubleday, 1982).

CHAPTER THIRTEEN:
The Multiple Lives of Maggie T.

I have relied heavily on Margaret Trudeau's two autobiographies, *Beyond Reason* (Paddington Press, 1979) and *Consequences* (Seal, 1982) and the majority of Margaret's quotes are from these sources. Neither source, however, can be taken completely at face value, and I have used my own memory and judgment in interpreting Margaret's account of her life. There is also an enormous file of press clippings, and a videotape of her "Canada AM" interview is in the National Film, Television and Sound Archives, Ottawa.

We do not yet have Pierre's memoirs, and for the profiles of his parents I have relied on *Trudeau and Our Times*, by Stephen Clarkson and Christina McCall (McClelland & Stewart, 1990), although I disagree with their conclusion that Margaret was a reincarnation of Charlie Trudeau. However, Trudeau does seem to have been unable to deal with Margaret's behaviour until she forced him to confront himself.

For Trudeau's early career, Richard Gwyn's *The Northern Magus* (McClelland & Stewart, 1980), Larry Zolf's *Dance of the Dialectic* (Lorimer, 1973) and Walter Stewart's *Shrug: Trudeau in Power* (New Press, 1971) are essential background. Trudeau's rare comments about Margaret and his marriage are from a BBC interview quoted in Arthur Johnson's *Margaret Trudeau* (Paperjacks, 1977.) Mary McEwan's comments are taken from "Margaret Trudeau's Struggle for Identity," in *Chatelaine* (August 1977). Sandra Gwyn's conversation with Margaret is in "The Sudden Transformation of the Ottawa Wife," *Saturday Night* (June 1976). Philip Marchand's article, "Margaret: Life After Pierre," is in *Chatelaine* (February 1982), and Celeste Fremon's interview is taken from *Playgirl* (September 1979).

CHAPTER FOURTEEN:
The Education of Ms. McTeer

My primary source for this chapter is a lengthy interview with Maureen McTeer on September 28, 1990. Jeffrey Simpson's *Discipline of Power* (Macmillan, 1980) is a good but critical overview of the brief Clark government. Bonnie Buxton's sympathetic profile, "Meet Maureen McTeer," appeared in *Chatelaine* (October 1976). *Chatelaine* also ran a very critical profile by Sean Rossiter, "Will the Real Maureen McTeer Please Stand Up?" (February 1979), which is a good source of information about her family background. By 1984 McTeer was *Chatelaine*'s woman of the year and was profiled by Charlotte Gray in the January issue. Margaret Trudeau's opinion of Maureen's taste is from *Consequences* (Seal, 1982). An extremely negative account of her 1988 election campaign by Robert Mason Lee was published in *Saturday Night* (October 1989). There is also a large file of press clippings that express both positive and negative attitudes towards McTeer.

CHAPTER FIFTEEN:
Geills Turner: The Last of the Golden Girls

My primary source is a lengthy interview with Geills Turner in June 1990. The *Chatelaine* profile, "Will the Real Geills Turner Please Stand up?" by Charlotte Gray, appeared in the May 1987 issue. Geills has given very few interviews and inherited Maryon Pearson's tag as "a very private person." John Turner has not yet published his memoirs, but *Grits* (Macmillan, 1982) by Christina McCall Newman has a good profile, and *Reign of Error* (McGraw-Hill Ryerson, 1988) by Greg Weston gives an inside, if hostile, picture of Turner's brief tenure as prime minister.

CHAPTER SIXTEEN:
Mila, The Movie

Mila Mulroney's executive assistant politely refused my request for an interview after a seven-month delay. Personal inquiries about her schedule and office expenses were not answered and an access to information request filed in October 1990 was unanswered as this book went to press. For the basic information on the meeting between Mila and Brian Mulroney I have relied on L. Ian MacDonald's *Mulroney: The Making of the Prime Minister* (McClelland & Stewart, 1984), which is also the source of Brian's anecdotes about Mila. Robert Fulford's profile, "Imagining Mila," appeared in *Saturday Night* (April 1987). Allan Fotheringham's quote comes from *Maclean's* (September 3, 1984). Susan Riley's profile of Mila in *Political Wives* is revealing and devastating. The Giovanni Mowinckel episode is covered in detail in Stevie Cameron's book *Ottawa Inside Out* (Key Porter, 1989). The passage from the "Dear Moe" letter is from *Frank*, November 19, 1990. The *Today* story is also covered in *Frank*, March 7, 1991. An insider look at the Mulroney administration is provided by Michel Gratton in *"So, What Are the Boys Saying?"* (McGraw-Hill Ryerson, 1987) and *Still the Boss* (Prentice-Hall, 1990), and there is an excellent overview of the government's early years in Claire Hoy's *Friends in High Places* (Key Porter, 1987). Ken Rubin obtained background data for me via the Access to Information Act.

CHAPTER EPILOGUE:
The Wife as Prime Minister

I have interviewed Audrey McLaughlin twice, the first time a year after her election as MP, the second in September 1990. The Environics research was published in the *Globe and Mail* on November 3, 1990. Background on Audrey can be found in a *Chatelaine* profile by Roy MacSkimming (March 1990).

The author wishes to thank the sources of the photographs included in this work for their co-operation during the preparation of this book. Every effort has been made to credit ownership of these photographs accurately, but due to the historical nature of the material provenance has sometimes been obscured by the passage of time. The author and publisher appreciate notification of any corrections to the following list that may be required in subsequent editions of the book.

Sources are listed below following the page number upon which their photographs appear. Due to the large number of photographs from the National Archives of Canada and Canapress Photo Service, abbreviations for these sources have been used as noted below.

12: National Archives of Canada (NAC)/PA134902; 14: NAC/PA121569; 15: NAC/PA121571; 30: NAC/PA25366; 31: NAC/PA26290; 44: NAC/PA33465; 51(left): NAC/PA26525; 51(right): W.J. Topley/NAC/PA26522; 66: NAC/C51986; 72: NAC/PA25745; 82: NAC/PA25511; 83: NAC/C10107; 84: NAC/C10111; 111: NAC/PA25864; 131(top left): NAC/C15558; 131(top right): NAC/PA26528; 131(centre): NAC/PA25390; 131(bottom left): Livernois/NAC/C17964; 131(bottom right): NAC/PA135125; 144: NAC/C1968; 145: NAC/PA25833; 151: NAC/C1964; 159(left): W.J. Topley/NAC/C76323; 159(right): NAC/27948; 164: NAC/C17778; 168: W.J. Topley/NAC/PA26987; 171: W.J. Topley/NAC/PA169229; 177: W.J. Topley/NAC/PA25970; 180: NAC/C46521; 191: NAC/C46560; 193: NAC/C9066; 199: courtesy Doris Pennington; 201: Kelsey Studios/NAC/C6908; 202: Nelson Quarrington, W. Howard Measures Collection/NAC/PA148532; 215: NAC/C09826; 217: NAC/C09835; 221: NAC/C23252; 225: The Right Honourable John G. Diefenbaker Centre; 227: The Right Honourable John G. Diefenbaker Centre/132; 231: The Right Honourable John G. Diefenbaker Centre/133; 239: The Right Honourable John G. Diefenbaker Centre/260; 250: The Right Honourable John G. Diefenbaker Centre/1955XB; 254: The Right Honourable John G. Diefenbaker Centre/1851; 265: Canapress Photo Service (CPS)/Peter Bregg; 274: Gauvin Geutzel & Co., courtesy Patricia Pearson Hannah; 280: UPI/Bettmann Newsphotos; 287: CPS; 293: Brosseau, *Montreal Star*, NAC/PA163903; 299: CPS/Russ Mant; 300: CPS/Fred Chartrand; 315: CPS/Bill

Grimshaw; **319**: CPS/Chuck Mitchell; **321**: CPS/Chuck Mitchell; **328**: CPS/ Drew Gragg; **333**: CPS/Lynn Ball; **342**: Fred Lum, *The Globe and Mail*, Toronto; **348**: Dick Darrell, *Toronto Star*; **354**: CPS/Ryan Remiorz; **359**: John Daggett/ NAC/PA141094; **362**: CPS/Mike Blake; **365**: CPS/Peter Bregg; **368**: CPS/John Major; **375**: CPS/Chuck Mitchell; **376**: Duncan Cameron/NAC/PA129254

INDEX
. . . .

Page numbers in boldface indicate an illustration